# Cisco Networking Academy Progr[...]
# Lab Companion, Volume I

*Jim Lorenz*

**Cisco Press**
**201 West 103$^{rd}$ Street**
**Indianapolis, IN  46290  USA**

# Cisco Networking Academy Program: Lab Companion, Volume I

Jim Lorenz

Copyright © 2000 Cisco Press

Cisco Press logo is a trademark of Cisco Systems, Inc.

Published by:
Cisco Press
210 West 103rd Street
Indianapolis, IN 46290 USA

Printed in the United States of America 1 2 3 4 5 6 7 8 9 0

ISBN: 1-57870-236-4

## Warning and Disclaimer

This book is designed to provide information on Cisco internetworking fundamentals. Every effort has been made to make this book as complete and as accurate as possible, but no warranty or fitness is implied.

The information is provided on an as-is basis. The author, Cisco Press, and Cisco Systems, Inc., shall have neither liability nor responsibility to any person or entity with respect to any loss or damages arising from the information contained in this book or from the use of the programs that may accompany it.

The opinions expressed in this book belong to the author and are not necessarily those of Cisco Systems, Inc.

## Trademark Acknowledgments

All terms mentioned in this book that are known to be trademarks or service marks have been appropriately capitalized. Cisco Press or Cisco Systems, Inc., cannot attest to the accuracy of this information. Use of a term in this book should not be regarded as affecting the validity of any trademark or service mark.

# Feedback Information

At Cisco Press, our goal is to create in-depth technical books of the highest quality and value. Each book is crafted with care and precision, undergoing rigorous development that involves the unique expertise of members from the professional technical community.

Readers' feedback is a natural continuation of this process. If you have any comments regarding how we could improve the quality of this book, or otherwise alter it to better suit your needs, you can contact us at ciscopress@mcp.com. Please make sure to include the book title and ISBN in your message.

We greatly appreciate your assistance.

| | |
|---|---|
| **Publisher** | John Wait |
| **Executive Editor** | Dave Dusthimer |
| **Cisco Systems Program Manager** | Jim LeValley |
| **Managing Editor** | Patrick Kanouse |
| **Senior Editor** | Jennifer Chisholm |
| **Team Coordinator** | Shannon Gross |

# About the Author

**Jim Lorenz** is the Lead Instructor and Coordinator for the Cisco Regional Training Academy at Chandler-Gilbert Community College (CGCC) in Chandler, Arizona. He is a full-time faculty member and was also Lead Instructor for the Microsoft Certified Systems Engineering (MCSE) curriculum. He has 20 years of experience in computers and information systems ranging from programming and database administration to network design and implementation. Jim has taught computer and networking courses for both public and private institutions for more than 15 years.

Jim is a Novell Certified NetWare Engineer (CNE), a Microsoft Certified Trainer (MCT), a Cisco Certified Network Associate (CCNA) and a Cisco Certified Academy Instructor (CCAI). He holds a bachelor's degree in Computer Information Systems from Prescott College.

# Acknowledgements

Brad Niesluchowski has been a great help in putting these labs together and reviewing them for technical accuracy. Brad is a Network Administrator with Higley Unified School District in Arizona and is a graduate of the Chandler-Gilbert Cisco Academy. Ray Moore, Director of Technology for Fountain Hills School District in Arizona, has also been a big help as an author and technical reviewer. Ray is the president of the Phoenix NT Users Special Interest Group and is also a part-time Cisco instructor at Chandler-Gilbert Community College.

I would like to thank Cisco Press Executive Editor Dave Dusthimer, Cisco Networking Academy Editor Vito Amato, and Academy curriculum specialists Kevin Johnston and Dennis Frezzo for their support and guidance.

I would also like to thank the Administration of Chandler-Gilbert Community College for their tremendous support of my efforts and the Cisco Networking Academy Program. Most importantly, I would like to thank my wife, Mary, and my kids, Jessica and Natasha, for their patience and understanding.

# Table of Contents

# Semester 2

# Preface

This manual was developed for use with the Cisco CCNA on-line curriculum and the *Cisco Networking Academy Program: First-Year Companion Guide* textbook for semesters 1 and 2. These labs are based on those in the current Cisco Networking Academy Program (CNAP) with some additional information. Most of the labs are hands-on and will require access to a Cisco Router Lab or a Simulator. Additional paper-based labs, which are practice exercises for complex topics, are included to supplement the on-line curriculum.

All labs and exercises are structured in three parts:
1. **Overview Section**: Includes **Objectives, Background information and a Tools / Preparation section** to help students, instructors and lab assistants prepare for the lab. Includes references to the corresponding chapter(s)in *Cisco Networking Academy Program: First-Year Companion Guide*.
2. **Worksheet Section**: Includes the steps necessary to complete the lab and progress questions.
3. **Answers Section**: Provides the answers to the questions in the labs worksheets.

# Semester 1 Labs

**Cisco Labs - Semester 1 – Networking Fundamentals**
## *LAB 1.1.1 – PC HARDWARE - OVERVIEW*
### *(Estimated time:60 minutes)*

## Objectives:
This lab will focus on your ability to accomplish the following tasks:
- Connect peripheral components (monitor, keyboard, and so on) to the main PC system unit
- Name the typical PC components
- Identify major internal PC components and connections
- Document the configuration of a functioning PC
- Boot a system to a Windows operating system (Windows 95, 98, NT or 2000)
- Use the Control Panel, System icon utility to gather information about the PC configuration

## Background:
This lab will help you become familiar with the basic peripheral components of a PC computer system and their connections, including network attachment. You will also examine the internal PC configuration and identify major components. You will observe the boot process for the Windows operating system and use the Control Panel to find out information about the PC. Knowing the components of a PC is valuable when troubleshooting and is important to your success in the networking field. For some of you, this lab will be a review.

## Tools / Preparation:
Before you begin, the teacher or lab assistant should have a typical desktop Pentium-based PC available with all peripherals such as keyboard, monitor, mouse, speakers or headphones, a network interface card (NIC) and network cable. The system unit cover should be removed, or tools should be provided to remove it. You can work individually or in teams. Before you begin this lab you should read the A+ or PC hardware maintenance training materials. The following resources will be required:

- PC with monitor, keyboard, mouse, and power cords
- Windows operating system (Windows 95, 98, NT or 2000) installed on PC
- Sound card and speakers or headphones
- Network Interface Card and Cat 5 patch cable

## Notes:
_____
_____
_____
_____

# Cisco Labs - Semester 1 – Networking Fundamentals
## *LAB 1.1.1 – PC HARDWARE – WORKSHEET*

### Step 1 – Examine the computer for internal and external components.

**Task:** Examine the computer and peripheral components both front and back.

**Explanation:** The components and configuration of the PC you are working with may vary from the sample answers below.

1. What is the manufacturer and model number of this computer?

| Manufacturer | |
|---|---|
| Model Number | |

2. Remove the PC system unit cover. List at least 8 major internal components inside the system unit (use the procedure in step 3 to find the CPU and amount of RAM).

| Component Name | Manufacturer / Description / Characteristics |
|---|---|
| | |
| | |
| | |
| | |
| | |
| | |
| | |
| | |
| | |
| | |
| | |
| | |
| | |
| | |

3. What are the major external components of the PC, including the peripherals?

| Component Name | Manufacturer / Description / Characteristics |
|---|---|
| | |
| | |
| | |
| | |
| | |
| | |

**Cisco Labs - Semester 1 – Networking Fundamentals**
## *LAB 1.1.1 – PC HARDWARE – WORKSHEET*

### Step 2 - Observe the boot process.

**Task:** Assemble the PC components and attach all peripherals and boot the PC. Observe the boot process.

**Explanation:** The computer should boot to the Windows operating system. If the computer does not boot, contact the lab assistant.

1. Observe the boot process.
   a.   Did the Windows operating system boot OK? _____
   b.   Could you see how much memory there was as the system was booting? _____

### Step 3 – General system information.

**Task:** Click the Start button and select Settings and Control Panel. Click the System icon and then the General tab.

**Explanation:** Here, we are viewing information about the computer using the operating system.

1.
   a.   What is the Central Processing Unit? _____
   b.   How much RAM is installed? _____

# Cisco Labs - Semester 1 – Networking Fundamentals
## *LAB 1.1.1 – PC HARDWARE – ANSWERS*

## Step 1

1. What is the manufacturer and model number of this computer?

| Manufacturer | XYZ Company |
|---|---|
| Model Number | XYZ model |

2. List at least 8 major internal components inside the system unit.

| Component Name | Manufacturer / Description / Characteristics |
|---|---|
| Power Supply | 200 watt |
| Motherboard | XYX |
| CPU type | Pentium II (See step 5) |
| RAM | 64MB (See step 5) |
| Hard Drive | IDE 2GB |
| CD-ROM drive | 24x |
| Floppy Drive | 1.44MB |
| Parallel port | 25-pin EPP |
| Serial port | 9-pin |
| Video Card | XYZ company |
| Sound Card | XYZ company |
| Network Interface Card (NIC) | XYX company |
| Other | |

3. What are the major external components of the PC, including the peripherals?

| Component Name | Manufacturer / Description / Characteristics |
|---|---|
| System unit | Compaq |
| Monitor | Compaq 15" SVGA |
| Keyboard | 101 Key enhanced |
| Mouse | Microsoft |
| Printer | HP XYZ |
| Other | |

## Step 2

1. Observe the boot process.

    a. Did the Windows operating system boot OK? **Yes**
    b. Could you see how much memory there was as the system was booting? **Yes, 64 MB (Megabytes)**

## Step 3

1.
    a. What is the Central Processing Unit? **Pentium II**
    b. How much RAM is installed? **64 MB**

**Cisco Labs - Semester 1 – Networking Fundamentals**
## *LAB 1.1.4 – NIC INSTALLATION - OVERVIEW*
*(Estimated time: 60 minutes)*

## Objective:
- Demonstrate proper installation of a NIC card in a workstation

## Background:
A Network Interface Card (NIC) allows your computer to connect to a local-area network (LAN) and share resources with other computers on the network, such as printers and Internet connections. The type of NIC installed depends on several factors:

1.  LAN Architecture: Ethernet and Token Ring are the two primary LAN architectures in use today, with Ethernet being the most widely used. Ethernet switches are the most common choice for connecting LANs today. They are available in various speeds, including Ethernet (10Mbps), Fast Ethernet (100Mbps) and Gigabit Ethernet (1000Mbps). The NIC should be capable of running at the speed of the switch and in full-duplex mode.

2.  Computer Bus Type: Most NICs you can buy today will go into a PCI slot in the computer's bus. Higher-performance NICs are usually available for use in servers. ISA cards are also available.

3.  Computer Operating System: The NIC and its "driver" must be compatible with the computer operating system. The NIC "driver" is software used to communicate between the NIC and the computer operating system. Operating systems include Windows, Novell, Macintosh and UNIX.

4.  Media Type: The NIC connector should match the network media. Some NICs have more than one connector type. The following table shows some types of cable and connectors.

| Media (Cable) Type | Ethernet LAN Architecture | Connector type |
|---|---|---|
| Unshielded Twisted Pair (UTP) Copper (for example, CAT 5) | 10Base-T, 100Base-TX | RJ45 (modular 8-pin) |
| Coaxial (Thinnet) | 10Base-2 | BNC |
| Coaxial (Thicknet) | 10Base-5 | AUI (DB15-pin) |
| Fiber Optic (multimode) | 10Base-FL, 100Base-FX, 1000Base-SX | ST, SC or MT-RJ |

Network cards (also called network adapters) are relatively easy to install, as long as simple guidelines are followed. After installing the network interface card, you will have access to your LAN or to the Internet.

## Tools / Preparation:
Ensure that a PC is available that can be opened and attached to the network after the NIC is installed. Before beginning this lab, read the *Cisco Networking Academy Program: First-Year Companion Guide*, Chapters 1 and 2. Also review semester 1 on-line Lesson 1. The following is a list of equipment required.

**Cisco Labs - Semester 1 – Networking Fundamentals**
*LAB 1.1.4 – NIC INSTALLATION - OVERVIEW*

1. a computer system running Windows 95 or 98
2. empty PCI or ISA expansion slot
3. PCI or ISA network card (Ethernet adapter)
4. network card driver disk and/or Windows 95 CD
5. network cable
6. toolkit set
7. static mat and wrist strap

## Cisco Labs - Semester 1 – Networking Fundamentals
### *LAB 1.1.4 – NIC INSTALLATION - WORKSHEET*

1.  Turn off your computer and unplug the power cable. Use a static mat and wrist strap to ground yourself.

2.  Remove the dust plate from computer case for the empty PCI or ISA expansion slot in which you plan to install the NIC card.

3.  Remove the network card from the anti-static bag. Handle the top corners of the network card with both hands. Align the tabs of the network card with the slot, and gently rock the card front to rear to insert it into the expansion slot. Finally, secure the card to the case with a screw.

4.  Restart the computer. The Windows 95 setup hardware detection will automatically determine the adapter driver for your network card. Windows 95 might ask you to supply your computer name and workgroup name. Select a computer name for your PC, and use a specific workgroup name provided by your lab instructor.

5.  Double-click the Network Neighborhood icon on the desktop. If you find other computer names displayed in the window, the network card is working properly. If you do not find other computer names, Windows 95 might have installed an incorrect driver for your network card. If so, you will need to perform the following steps to add an adapter driver:

    1.  Click the Start button, select Settings, and then select Control Panel.
    2.  Double-click the Network icon. A network dialog box will appear.
    3.  Click the Add button. Select adapter and click on the Add button once again.
    4.  Click the Have Disk button. Insert the network card's driver disk into the floppy drive. Click OK. The Windows 95 setup will install the driver.
    5.  Windows 95 might ask you to reboot your system. After you restart the computer, follow the instructions in the beginning of this exercise to check whether your network card is working properly.

## Reflection:
Write in your journal the steps that you used to install a network card. Also write what precautions you took and why they were important.

# Cisco Labs - Semester 1 – Networking Fundamentals
## _LAB 1.1.4 – NIC INSTALLATION – ANSWERS_

1. Turn off your computer and unplug the power cable. Use a static mat and wrist strap to ground yourself.

2. Remove the cover from the computer. Remove the dust plate from the computer case for the empty PCI or ISA expansion slot in which you plan to install the NIC card.

3. Remove the network card from the anti-static bag. Handle the top corners of the network card with both hands. Align the tabs of the network card with the slot and gently rock the card front to rear to insert it into the expansion slot. Finally, secure the card to the case with a screw.

4. Plug a straight-through wired network patch cable into the back of the NIC. The cable should connect to a hub or switch with other PCs in a workgroup. The green link light on the back of the NIC should come on when the PC is restarted, indicating a good connection with the hub or switch.

5. Restart the computer. The Windows 95/98 setup hardware detection will automatically determine the adapter driver for your network card. Windows may ask you to supply your computer name and workgroup name. Select a computer name for your PC, and use a specific workgroup name provided by your lab instructor.

6. Double-click the Network Neighborhood icon on the desktop. If you find other computer names displayed in the window, the network card is working properly. If you do not find other computer names, then Windows might have installed an incorrect driver for your network card. If so, you will need to perform the following steps to add an adapter driver:

   1. Click the Start button, select Settings, then select Control Panel.
   2. Double-click the Network icon. A network dialog box will appear.
   3. Click the Add button. Select adapter and click on the Add button again.
   4. Click the Have Disk button. Insert the network card's driver disk into the floppy drive. Click OK. The Windows setup will install the driver.
   5. Windows might ask you to reboot your system. After you restart the computer, follow the instructions in the beginning of this exercise to check whether your network card is working properly.

## Reflection:
Write in your journal the steps that you used to install a network card. Also write what precautions you took and why they were important.

Be sure to write in your journal about the proper care that must be taken when working on the inside of PCs (for example, anti-static precautions, changing one thing at a time, working with the power off, using the proper tools). Also record any problems that might have occurred, such as incorrect drivers.

**Cisco Labs - Semester 1 – Networking Fundamentals**
## *LAB 1.2.1.1 – TCP/IP NETWORK SETTINGS - OVERVIEW*
### *(Estimated time: 45 minutes)*

## Objectives:
This lab will focus on your ability to accomplish the following tasks:
- Use the Windows Network icon in Control Panel to determine current network settings
- Use the WINIPCFG.EXE utility (with Windows 95 or 98) to determine network settings
- Identify the type of client software being used and record related settings
- Determine the computer name and domain name
- Determine the NIC manufacturer and driver
- Identify what network (layer 3) protocols are bound to the NIC (in use)
- Determine the Internet Protocol (IP) layer 3 address
- Determine the subnet mask and IP address of the default gateway (router)
- Determine whether Domain Name System (DNS), Dynamic Host Configuration Protocol (DHCP) and Windows Internet Name Service (WINS) are being used and the IP addresses of the servers providing these services
- Determine the Media Access Control (MAC) or hardware address of the workstation NIC
- Use the Windows System Device Manager to verify that the NIC is working properly
- Document all findings in this lab

## Background:
This lab will help you become familiar with the network settings required to connect your PC to a local-area network and to gain access to the Internet (World Wide Web - WWW) and intranet (internal local web servers). The purpose of this lab is to discover what your workstation's network settings are and how they are used. You will review Network Interface Card (NIC) configuration and drivers and TCP/IP protocol settings for a typical Windows client workstation in a server-based Ethernet network. This information is very valuable any time you have a problem logging on to a network or when you must set up a new workstation. This lab will focus on the Windows 95 or 98 client.

## Tools / Preparation:
Before you begin, the teacher or lab assistant will have a typical desktop Pentium-based (or comparable) PC available. The desktop policies must be set to allow access to the Network icon in Control Panel and either the Run command or the DOS command prompt in order to run the WINIPCFG.EXE utility. The PC should be a classroom/lab computer configured to access the web-based Cisco curriculum and assessment system. You can work individually or in teams. Before beginning this lab, you should read the *Cisco Networking Academy Program: First-Year Companion Guide*, Chapter 2. You should also review semester 1 on-line Lessons 1 through 4. The following resources will be required:

- PC workstation with monitor, keyboard, mouse, and power cords
- Windows operating system (Windows 95, 98, NT or 2000) installed on PC
- NIC installed and Cat 5 patch cable with connection to the Internet
- Browser software installed (Netscape Navigator 3.0 or higher or Internet Explorer 4.0 or higher)
- Apple QuickTime browser and ShockWave Macromedia browser plug-ins

# Cisco Labs - Semester 1 – Networking Fundamentals
## *LAB 1.2.1.1 – TCP/IP NETWORK SETTINGS - WORKSHEET*

### Step 1 - Determine the network settings for your workstation.

**Task:** Boot (start) the PC, log in to the network and use the following procedures to determine the network settings for your workstation.

**Explanation:** The primary tools you will use for gathering this information are 1) the Network icon in Control Panel and 2) the WINIPCFG.EXE utility (Windows 95 or 98) or IPCONFIG.EXE (Windows NT) and 3) the System icon in Control Panel. You will use these tools to verify your network settings and that the NIC is functioning properly. The following procedures focus primarily on a Windows NT server-based network. Answers will vary depending on the PC you are using and the network you are on.

### Step 2 - Use Control Panel / Network to determine the workstation computer name, NT domain name, network client, the network layer 3 protocols in use, and information about the NIC.

**Task:** Click on Start, select Settings and then Control Panel. Double-click the Network icon. Click the Identification tab to find the computer name and the domain name (Windows NT). Click the Configuration tab and note what networking components are installed.

**Explanation:** The Network Client has an icon that looks like a computer, the NIC icon looks like a NIC and the Protocols have an icon that looks like a network cable connection. There might be more than one of each of these.

1. Record your findings in the table below.

| Computer (NetBIOS) Name | |
|---|---|
| NT Domain Name | |
| Network Client Type | |
| NIC installed (driver name) | |
| 1$^{st}$ Protocol installed | |
| 2$^{nd}$ Protocol installed | |
| Other network components | |
| Other network components | |

### Step 3 - Use Control Panel / Network to check the TCP/IP-related settings, such as IP address information, DHCP, and DNS.

**Task:** Click the TCP/IP protocol while on the Network Configuration tab and then click Properties.

**Explanation:** Click the tab indicated in the table, and record your findings below.

# Cisco Labs - Semester 1 – Networking Fundamentals
## _LAB 1.2.1.1 – TCP/IP NETWORK SETTINGS - WORKSHEET_

1.  Record your findings in the table below.

| Tab | Type of Information | Findings |
|-----|---------------------|----------|
| IP Addr. | How does the workstation get its IP address? | If "obtain IP address automatically" button is selected, go to worksheet Step 4. |
| IP Addr. | Workstation IP Address | |
| IP Addr. | Workstation Subnet Mask | |
| Gateway | Default Gateway | |
| DNS Cfg. | Is DNS enabled? | |
| DNS Cfg. | DNS Server IP address | |
| WINS Cfg. | Is WINS enabled? | |
| WINS Cfg. | WINS Server IP address | |

## Step 4 – Using WINIPCFG.EXE utility

**Task:** You can run WINIPCFG.EXE from the Start / Run command or from the DOS command prompt (IPCONFIG.EXE must be run from the DOS prompt). This exercise will focus on the WINIPCFG.EXE utility. To run it from the Start menu, click Start and Run, then type in WINIPCFG in the window. To run it from the DOS prompt, click Start, Programs, MS DOS Prompt and then type WINIPCFG at the command line. If you enter WINIPCFG/ALL you will get much more information, including the MAC address.

**Explanation:** The WINIPCFG.EXE utility can be used to check TCP/IP-related settings as well as the MAC address of the NIC installed (also called the hardware address). When the TCP/IP protocol is installed on Windows 95 or 98, the graphical WINIPCFG.EXE utility is included with it. Windows NT uses a different utility, IPCONFIG.EXE, to give similar results. If your workstation obtains its IP address automatically (a DHCP client), you must use one of these utilities to determine its IP address and subnet mask. Be sure to select the proper NIC or Ethernet adapter.

1.  Record your findings in the table below.

| | |
|---|---|
| Workstation IP Address | |
| Workstation Subnet Mask | |
| Workstation MAC Address | |
| Default Gateway (Router) | |
| DHCP Server | |
| DNS Server IP address | |
| WINS Server IP address | |

**Cisco Labs - Semester 1 – Networking Fundamentals**

## *LAB 1.2.1.1 – TPC/IP NETWORK SETTINGS – WORKSHEET*

**Step 5 - Use Control Panel / System / Device Manager to verify that the NIC and drivers are functioning properly.**

**Task:** Click on Start, select Settings and then Control Panel. Double-click the System icon, click the Device Manager tab and then click the plus sign on the Network Adapter icon. Select the desired adapter and click Properties. Click the General tab to see the Adapter Manufacturer and check the status. Click the Driver tab to see the version of the driver and files being used.
**Explanation:** You can also find the operating system version, the CPU type and the amount of RAM installed.

1. Record you findings in the table below.

| | |
|---|---|
| **Network Adapter (NIC) Manufacturer** | |
| **Is the Network Adapter working properly?** | |
| **Date of the Driver** | |
| **List one of the driver files** | |

# Cisco Labs - Semester 1 – Networking Fundamentals
## *LAB 1.2.1.1 – TCP/IP NETWORK SETTINGS – ANSWERS*

**Step 2**

1.  Record your findings in the table below.

| Computer (NetBIOS) Name | W1-005 |
|---|---|
| NT Domain Name | Domain1 |
| Network Client Type | Client for Microsoft networks (and/or Novell Client) |
| NIC installed (driver name) | 3-COM Fast Etherlink 10/100 (or other NIC mfg) |
| 1$^{st}$ Protocol installed | TCP/IP |
| 2$^{nd}$ Protocol installed | IPX/SPX-compatible protocol (if there are Novell servers) |
| Other network components | |
| Other network components | |

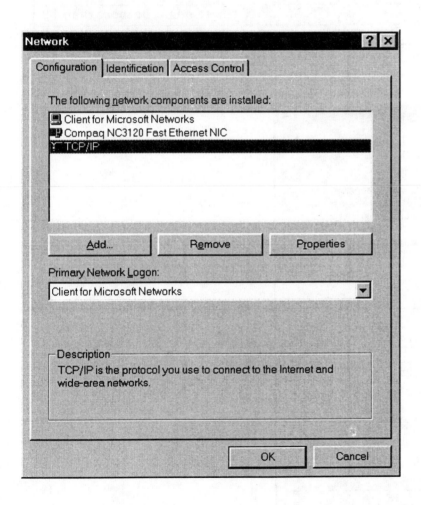

# Cisco Labs - Semester 1 – Networking Fundamentals
## *LAB 1.2.1.1 – TCP/IP NETWORK SETTINGS – ANSWERS*

## Step 3

1. Record your findings in the table below.

| TAB | Type of Information | Findings |
|-----|---------------------|----------|
| IP Addr. | How does the workstation get its IP address? | If "obtain IP address automatically" is selected, DHCP is enabled and you must use the WINIPCFG.EXE utility from step 3 to determine IP address and subnet mask. |
| IP Addr. | Workstation IP Address | 175.38.227.122 |
| IP Addr. | Workstation Subnet Mask | 255.255.255.0 |
| Gateway | Default Gateway | 175.38.227.1 |
| DNS Cfg. | Is DNS enabled? | Yes |
| DNS Cfg. | DNS Server IP address | 175.38.227.10 (there might be more than 1) |
| WINS Cfg. | Is WINS enabled? | Yes |
| WINS Cfg. | WINS Server IP address | 175.38.227.11 |

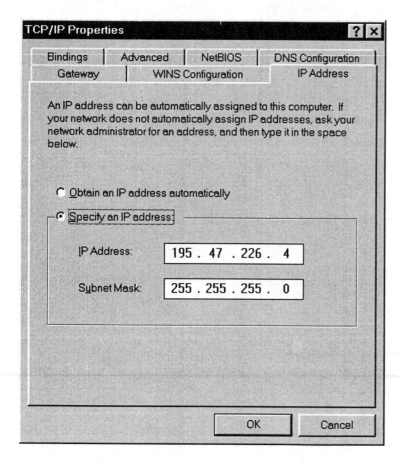

**Cisco Labs - Semester 1 – Networking Fundamentals**
## *LAB 1.2.1.1 – TCP/IP NETWORK SETTINGS – ANSWERS*

### Step 4

1.  Record your findings in the table below (your answers will vary).

| | |
|---|---|
| **Workstation IP Address** | 175.38.227.122 |
| **Workstation Subnet Mask** | 255.255.255.0 |
| **Workstation MAC Address** | 00-08-C7-5B-A6-AB |
| **Default Gateway** | 175.38.227.1 |
| **DHCP Server** | 175.38.227.15 |
| **DNS Server IP address** | 175.38.227.10 (can be more than 1) |
| **WINS Server IP address** | 175.38.227.11 (primary and secondary) |

### Step 5

1.  Record your findings in the table below.

| | |
|---|---|
| **Network Adapter (NIC) Manufacturer** | Compaq NC3120 Fast Ethernet NIC |
| **Is the Network Adapter working properly?** | Yes |
| **Date of the Driver** | 4-23-99 |
| **List one of the driver files** | E100BNT.SYS |

**Cisco Labs - Semester 1 – Networking Fundamentals**
## *LAB 1.2.1.2 – PC SOFTWARE - OVERVIEW*
### *(Estimated time: 30 minutes)*

## Objectives:

This lab will focus on your ability to accomplish the following tasks:
- Determine the PC operating system and version number.
- Identify the manufacturer and version number of the BIOS the computer is running
- Learn how to access the CMOS settings for the computer
- Check browser software setup including version and necessary plug-ins

## Background:

This lab will help you become familiar with the PC operating system, Basic Input Output System (BIOS) and application software configuration. You will verify that the PC is configured properly to run the Cisco Online Curriculum and practice exams that are multimedia-based. This includes the operating system, video settings, browser and plug-ins required. For some of you, this lab will be a review.

## Tools / Preparation:

Before you begin, the teacher or lab assistant will have a typical desktop Pentium-based (or comparable) PC available with the following software installed. The PC should be a classroom computer configured to access the web-based Cisco curriculum and assessment system. You can work individually or in teams. Before you begin this lab you should read the A+ or PC hardware maintenance training materials. The following resources will be required:

- PC workstation with monitor, keyboard, mouse, and power cords
- Windows operating system (Windows 95, 98, NT or 2000) installed on PC
- NIC installed and Cat 5 patch cable with connection to the Internet
- Browser software installed (Netscape Navigator 3.0 or higher or Internet Explorer 4.0 or higher)
- Apple QuickTime browser plug-in for use with training videos (can be downloaded from www.apple.com)
- ShockWave Macromedia browser plug-in for use with practice quizzes (can be downloaded from www.macromedia.com)

**Notes:** _____

_____

_____

_____

_____

# Cisco Labs - Semester 1 – Networking Fundamentals
## *LAB 1.2.1.2 – PC SOFTWARE – WORKSHEET*

### Step 1 – PC software overview

**Task:** Before booting the PC, determine the manufacturer and model number.
**Explanation:** Boot (start) the PC and use the following procedures to determine the BIOS. Answers will vary depending on the PC. You can "cold boot" the PC by turning it off and on again. You can "warm boot" it by holding down the Ctrl and Alt keys and pressing the Delete key. Be sure to shut down Windows properly before rebooting by clicking Start and Shutdown.

1.  What is PC manufacturer and model? _____

### Step 2 – operating system

**Task:** Determine the operating system and version.
**Explanation:** You can check the operating system by watching the screen as the computer boots, or by clicking Start, Help after it has finished booting. To verify the exact version number, click Start, Settings, Control Panel, then double-click the System icon. This will also show the manufacturer, model, CPU and amount of RAM in the PC.

1.  What operating system (OS) and version is the computer running? _____

### Step 3 – CMOS setup

**Task:** Determine the keys to press to enter CMOS setup. Then determine the BIOS manufacturer and version number.
**Explanation:** While booting the system, watch the screen to see what keystroke(s) are required to enter the CMOS Setup mode. CMOS setup can be used to change settings such as the boot sequence (floppy, CD or hard disk) and power saver options. As the system is booting you should also see who makes the Basic Input Output System (BIOS) and what version it is.

1.  How would you access the CMOS setup to change settings? _____

2.  Who is the BIOS manufacturer? _____

### Step 4 – Verify browser software and plug-ins.

**Task:** Determine the browser software and version and check for the plug-ins required to view the Cisco on-line computer-based curriculum.
**Explanation:** Start the browser (Netscape or Internet Explorer) on the computer and determine the following information. Start one of the lessons from the Cisco on-line computer-based curriculum and run a movie clip and take a sample quiz. QuickTime (from Apple Computer) is required to run the videos and ShockWave (from Macromedia) is required to run the sample quizzes.

**Cisco Labs - Semester 1 – Networking Fundamentals**
## *LAB 1.2.1.2 – PC SOFTWARE – WORKSHEET*


1. What is the browser software and version? _____

2. Is the QuickTime plug-in on this computer? _____

3. Is the ShockWave plug-in on this computer? _____

4. Does the sound work when playing the videos? _____

**Step 5 - Verify your video settings.**

**Task:** Click on Start, Settings, Control Panel and then double-click the Display icon. Click the Settings tab.
**Explanation:** The display settings allow you to confirm that you have at least 800 x 600 resolution with 256 colors.

1. Record the settings on your computer below:

| Screen area (resolution) | |
|---|---|
| Colors | |

# Cisco Labs - Semester 1 – Networking Fundamentals
## *LAB 1.2.1.2 – PC SOFTWARE – ANSWERS*

### Step 1

1. What is PC manufacturer and model? **Compaq Desktop**

### Step 2

1. What operating system (OS) and version is the computer running? **Windows 98 Second Edition 400.10.2222A**

### Step 3

1. How would you access the CMOS setup to change settings? **Press F10 when the message is displayed at boot-up**

2. Who is the BIOS manufacturer? **XYZ BIOS v4.56**

### Step 4

1. What is the browser software and version? **Netscape Navigator version 4.6 or Internet Explorer version 5.0.**

2. Is the QuickTime plug-in on this computer? **Yes**

3. Is the ShockWave plug-in on this computer? **Yes**

4. Does the sound work when playing the videos? **Yes**

### Step 5

1. Record the settings on your computer below:

| Screen area (resolution) | 800 x 600 (super VGA) |
|---|---|
| Colors | 256 |

# Cisco Labs - Semester 1 – Networking Fundamentals
## *LAB 1.2.2 – WEB BROWSER LITERACY - OVERVIEW*
### *(Estimated time: 20 minutes)*

## Objectives:
- Learn how to use a web browser to access Internet sites
- Become familiar with the concept of a URL
- Use a search engine to locate information on the Internet
- Access selected web sites to learn the definitions of networking terms
- Use hyperlinks to jump from the current web site to other web sites

## Background:
A web browser is a very powerful tool that many people use every day to surf around different sites (cyber places) on the World Wide Web. With a web browser you can find anything from airline flight information to the directions on how to get to a specific address. A browser is a client application program or software that is loaded on the PC to gain access to the Internet and local web pages.

The name of a web sight such as **www.cisco.com** is also referred to as a Universal Resource Locator (URL). This URL points to the World Wide Web server (WWW) in the Cisco domain (CISCO) under the Commercial domain (COM). The www also refers to an HTTP or Hypertext Transfer Protocol server. You can also type in a slash after the web site name and then the name of a web page to get to a specific location on a web site. When you type in the URL or name of a web site, your browser makes a request of a Domain Name Server (DNS) in order to convert the URL to an IP address. The IP address is how the server (www.cisco.com) is actually contacted.

Web browsers can provide access to a number of search engines, such as www.yahoo.com, www.excite.com, www.lycos.com and www.metacrawler.com among others. You can use these search engines directly by typing in their URL or you can click on Search from the Netscape or Internet Explorer menu. There are also a number of web sites that provide definitions of networking and computer-related terms and acronyms. These can be used to help learn more about networking and to do research on the Internet. Two of these are www.whatis.com and www.webopedia.com. Most web sites contain "hyperlinks," which are words that are underlined and highlighted. By clicking on a hyperlink you will "jump" to another page on the current site or to a page on another web site.

## Tools / Preparation:
Before you begin, the teacher or lab assistant will have a typical desktop Pentium-based (or comparable) PC available with the following software installed. The PC should be a classroom computer configured to access the web-based Cisco curriculum and assessment system. You should also review semester 1 On-line Lesson 1. The following resources will be required:

- A computer running Windows 95/98
- Netscape or Internet Explorer software CD-ROM (if not already installed on the computer)
- Access to the Internet via an Internet Service Provider (ISP) using a local-area network (LAN) or dial-up

# Cisco Labs - Semester 1 – Networking Fundamentals
## *LAB 1.2.2 – WEB BROWSER LITERACY - WORKSHEET*

1.  Install Netscape or Internet Explorer on your computer (if it has not already been done).

2.  If you are on a LAN, start the web browser (either Netscape or Internet Explorer). If you are using a modem to make the connection, you must dial your ISP before you can start your web browser.

3.  What version of Netscape or Internet Explorer are you using? _____
    _____

4.  After you start your browser, click and highlight the Location field (with Netscape) or Address field (with Internet Explorer). Press the Delete key to delete the current address.

5.  When your Location or Address field is empty, type in **www.cisco.com** to get to the Cisco web site. This is how you can navigate from one site to another on the World Wide Web (WWW).

6.  Load a new page (type in a new location, for example, **www.nba.com**). Notice the status on the bottom bar of your browser. What do you see? _____
    _____

7.  Each of the buttons on top of your browser has a function. Click on the Back button. What did it do? _____

8.  Click on the Forward button. Does it take you to the NBA web site? _____

9.  Try clicking on the Reload or Refresh button. What do you think they do? _____
    _____

10. Type in a new web site address and click the Stop button. What happens? _____
    _____

11. Enter the URL for a search engine such as www.metacrawler.com. Search for the word BROWSER. What was the result? _____
    _____

12. Enter the URL for www.webopedia.com. Enter the keyword BROWSER. What was the result?
    _____. What other hyperlinks were available?
    _____
    _____

## Reflection Questions:

1.  Identify a way in which you can navigate from one site to another. _____
    _____

2.  If you see the same graphics or text the next time you go to the NBA site, what should you do to ensure that you could look at updated news? _____

# Cisco Labs - Semester 1 – Networking Fundamentals
## *LAB 1.2.2 – WEB BROWSER LITERACY – ANSWERS*

1. Install Netscape or Internet Explorer on your computer (if it has not already been done).

2. If you are on a LAN, start the web browser (either Netscape or Internet Explorer). If you are using a modem to make the connection, you must dial your ISP before you can start your web browser.

3. What version of Netscape or Internet Explorer are you using? **Netscape 4.6 or Internet Explorer 5.0 (Click the Help menu, then About to find out the exact product name and version)**

4. After you start your browser, click and highlight the Location field (with Netscape) or Address field (with Internet Explorer). Press the Delete key to delete the current address.

5. When your Location or Address field is empty, type in **www.cisco.com** to get to the Cisco web site. This is how you can navigate from one site to another on the World Wide Web (WWW).

6. Load a new page (type in a new location, for example, **www.nba.com**). Notice the status on the bottom bar of your browser. What do you see? **You should see the status of the web page that is loading (i.e. percentage done; contacting host; starting Java; and so on).**

7. Each of the buttons on top of your browser has a function. Click the Back button. What did it do? **Takes you back to the Cisco web site or the previous web site you were at.**

8. Click the Forward button. Does it take you to the NBA web site? **Yes**

9. Try clicking on the Reload or Refresh button. What do you think they do? **They reload everything, which prevents your browser from loading old pages from its cache.**

10. Type in a new web site address and click the Stop button. What happens? **It will stop everything from loading.**

11. Enter the URL for a search engine such as www.metacrawler.com. Search for the word BROWSER. What was the result? **Showed search results and several possible web sites where information on browsers can be obtained, including download sites.**

12. Enter the URL for www.webopedia.com. Enter the keyword BROWSER. What was the result? **A brief definition of a browser was displayed**. What other hyperlinks were available? **Links to many other web sites, including Internet Explorer and Netscape Navigator were available. The latest version of these browsers can be downloaded from the sites.**

## Reflection Questions:

1. Identify a way in which you can navigate from one site to another. **Type in a web site that you want to go to in the location or address field of your browser.**

2. If you see the same graphics or text the next time you go to the NBA site, what should you do to ensure that you could look at updated news? **Press the Refresh or Reload button**

**Cisco Labs - Semester 1 – Networking Fundamentals**
## *LAB 1.2.3 – BASIC TROUBLESHOOTING - OVERVIEW*
### *(Estimated time: 30 minutes)*

## Objectives:
- Learn the proper sequence for troubleshooting computer- and network-related problems
- Become familiar with some of the more common hardware and software problems
- Given a basic problem situation, be able to troubleshoot and resolve the problem

## Background:
The ability to effectively troubleshoot computer-related problems is an important skill. The process of identifying the problem and trying to solve it requires a systematic step-by-step approach. This lab will introduce some basic hardware- and software-related problems to solve and will help you become more familiar with PC components and the software required to use the Cisco curriculum. The process of trying to solve a problem is fairly straightforward. Some of the suggestions here are more than will be required to solve basic hardware and software problems, but they will help provide a framework and guidelines when more complex problems arise.

### Step 1 – Gather information:
- Observe the symptoms and try to characterize or identify the problem.
- Try to describe what is happening or not happening using proper terminology.
- Ask a coworker if they have encountered a similar problem.
- Get the opinions of others who might have more experience.
- Check web sites and troubleshooting knowledge databases.

### Step 2 – Isolate the problem:
- Is it hardware- (check for lights and noises) or software- (errors on screen) related?
- Use substitution to isolate the problem if there is more than one component. (If the monitor does not work, it could be the monitor, video adapter, or cables.)
- Is it local (this workstation only) or remote (possible network-wide problem)?
- Does it affect this software only or more than one application?
- Is this the first time it has happened, or has it happened before?
- Was anything changed recently?

### Step 3 – Select one or more possible causes and identify potential solutions:
- Rank them in order of most likely to least likely cause.
- Check the simplest possible causes first (Is the power turned on?).
- Check the easiest-to-check problems first (try a system reboot).
- Verify hardware first, then software (Do any lights come on?).
- Start with the physical, then move to logical (check the NIC before the IP address).
- Troubleshoot from the bottom up. Always check OSI layer 0 first (the power cord layer!). Note: There is no OSI layer 0, but it is pretty important to check.

### Step 4 – Test the most likely solution based on your best guess, and check the results.

### Step 5 – When you think you have found the problem and corrected it, double-check to make sure everything still works.

# Cisco Labs - Semester 1 – Networking Fundamentals
## *LAB 1.2.3 – BASIC TROUBLESHOOTING - WORKSHEET*

## Tools / Preparation:

Before you begin, the teacher or lab assistant will have a typical desktop Pentium-based (or comparable) PC available. The PC should be a classroom computer configured to access the web-based Cisco curriculum and assessment system. You should also review semester 1 on-line Lesson 1. The following resources will be required:

- A computer running Windows 95/98
- Netscape or Internet Explorer software CD-ROM (if not already installed on the computer)
- Access to the Internet via an Internet Service Provider (ISP) using a LAN or dial-up

1. Work in teams of two. Team member A (or the instructor) will select two problems from the list of common hardware- and software-related problems (see answer section) and introduce the problems into the computer. The desired goal will be to run one of the videos from the semester 1 on-line curriculum. Team member A (or the instructor) should create the hardware- or software-related problems with the computer while the other is out of the room and then turn off the computer and monitor.

2. When team member B identifies the problems and corrects them, switch places and have the other introduce some new problems.

3. Each team member solving the problem should fill in the table based on the symptoms observed, problems identified and solutions to the problem.

### Team Member A

|  | Symptom observed | Problem identified | Solution |
|---|---|---|---|
| 1st problem |  |  |  |
| 2nd problem |  |  |  |

### Team Member B

|  | Symptom observed | Problem identified | Solution |
|---|---|---|---|
| 1st problem |  |  |  |
| 2nd problem |  |  |  |

## Cisco Labs - Semester 1 – Networking Fundamentals
## *LAB 1.2.3– BASIC TROUBLESHOOTING - ANSWERS*

The following are some of the potential problems that can be introduced with this lab.

## COMMON PC HARDWARE- AND SOFTWARE-RELATED PROBLEMS

| Prob. No. | Category | Symptoms | Problem Description | Solution |
|---|---|---|---|---|
| 1 | PC Hardware | Monitor does not display anything | Power cord disconnected at wall outlet | Plug monitor into outlet |
| 2 | PC Hardware | Monitor does not display anything | Power cord disconnected at monitor | Verify that it is plugged solidly into the monitor |
| 3 | PC Hardware | Monitor does not display anything | Video card damaged | Open computer and replace with working card |
| 4 | PC Hardware | Monitor does not display anything | Monitor video output not connected to computer | Verify that the cable is connected to the PC system unit video DB15 adapter |
| 5 | PC Hardware | Monitor does not display anything | Brightness or contrast adjustment needs | Adjust brightness and/or contrast accordingly |
| 6 | PC Hardware | Can't use mouse or keyboard | Mouse or keyboard disconnected | Verify they are plugged securely into the correct ports on the back of the PC |
| 7 | PC Hardware | Can't hear videos | Speakers not plugged in | Connect speaker to sound card |
| 8 | PC Software | Can't hear videos | Multimedia sound not enabled | Use Control Panel to add new hardware. Select sound card and install software. |
| 9 | PC Software | Can't hear videos | Sound muted | Double-click the speaker icon on task bar and remove muting |
| 10 | PC Software | Can't navigate through lessons | Java is not active in your browser | Find Preferences menu and make sure Java is set up |
| 11 | PC Software | Poor colors or screen size problem with lessons | Colors not set to 256 or resolution not set to 800 x 600 | Use Control Panel to change display settings |

**Cisco Labs - Semester 1 – Networking Fundamentals**
## *EXERCISE 1.3.6 – BINARY NUMBERING - OVERVIEW*
### *(Estimated time: 30 minutes)*

## Objectives:

This lab will focus on your ability to accomplish the following tasks:

- Identify the positions in a binary number and know the value of each

- Identify the positions in a decimal number and know the value of each

- Work with base 10 exponents (powers of 10) and understand how position defines value

- Work with base 2 exponents (powers of 2) and understand how position defines value

- Manually convert simple binary numbers and decimal numbers

- Manually convert 32-bit binary IP addresses and dotted decimal IP addresses

- Use the Windows Scientific Calculator to check your answers

- Describe the differences between binary and decimal numbering systems

## Background:

This lab will help you learn to work with the binary numbering system. You will convert binary numbers (base 2) to decimal numbers (Base 10) and decimal to binary. Computers and networking equipment such as routers work with binary numbers, a series of Bits (short for Binary Digits) that are either on (a binary 1) or off (a binary 0). They are encoded internally in the PC and on networking media (cables) as either electrical voltages on copper cable, such as Unshielded Twisted Pair (UTP), or as light pulses on fiber cable. The current version of the Internet Protocol (IPv4) uses a 32-bit address (usually divided into 4 "octets" or 8-bit bytes) to identify a particular network and a host on that network. Humans are more comfortable working with decimal numbers, so IP addresses are usually written as four decimal numbers separated by periods (dots), each representing an octet, to make them easier to read. This is referred to as "dotted decimal notation." Understanding binary numbers and how they relate to decimal numbers is critical to understanding IP addresses, subnets and network routing.

## Tools / Preparation:

This is primarily a written lab exercise, but you will use the Windows Scientific Calculator, so you will need access to a PC. You might want to refer to Lab 1.3 – PC Network Settings for some real IP addresses to convert. Before beginning this lab you should read the *Cisco Networking Academy Program: First-Year Companion Guide*, Chapter 5. You should also review semester 1 on-line Lesson 9. The following resources will be required:

- PC workstation with Windows operating system (Windows 95, 98, NT or 2000) installed on PC and access to the Windows Calculator.

## NOTES:

_____

_____

_____

_____

# Cisco Labs - Semester 1 – Networking Fundamentals
## *EXERCISE 1.3.6 – BINARY NUMBERING - WORKSHEET*

**Step 1.  Decimal Numbers**

**Explanation:** We are most familiar with "decimal" numbers (base 10). The decimal numbering system is based on the powers of 10. This exercise will help develop an understanding of the exponentiation or "powers" of numbers using the base 10 number system, which is what our arithmetic and money system is based on. With base 10, the right-most position has a value of 1 (same as base 2). Each position moving to the left is worth 10 times more. 10 to the zero power ($10^0$) is 1, 10 to the first power ($10^1$ or 10 x 1) is 10, 10 to the second power ($10^2$ or 10 x 10) is 100 and 10 to the third power ($10^3$ or 10 x 10 x 10) is 1000, and so on. Just multiply the number in each position times the value of each position (for example, 400 = 4 x $10^2$ or 4 x 100). Remember that any number to the zero power is 1.

**Decimal Number Conversion Example**
The following chart shows how the decimal number system represents the number 352,481. This will help in understanding the binary numbering system.

| Exponent | $10^6$ | $10^5$ | $10^4$ | $10^3$ | $10^2$ | $10^1$ | $10^0$ |
|---|---|---|---|---|---|---|---|
| Position | 7 | 6 | 5 | 4 | 3 | 2 | 1 |
| Value | 1000000 | 100000 | 10000 | 1000 | 100 | 10 | 1 |
| Number | 0 | 3 | 5 | 2 | 4 | 8 | 1 |
| | 0 x 1,000,000 | 3 x 100,000 | 5 x 10,000 | 2 x 1000 | 4 x 100 | 8 x 10 | 1 x 1 |

**The number 352,481 if read from right to left would be (1 x 1) + (8 x 10) + (4 x 100) + (2 x 1000) + (5 x 10,000) + (3 x 100,000) for a total of 352,481 (a 6-digit number).**

**Here is another way to look at it that makes it easier to add up the decimal number values:**

| Position of digit (from right) | Value of bit position ($10^X$ or 10 to the power of) | Number value from 0 to 9 | Calculation | Decimal Value |
|---|---|---|---|---|
| 1st Decimal Digit | $10^0$ or 1 | 1 | 1 x 1 | 1 |
| 2nd Decimal Digit | $10^1$ or 2 | 8 | 8 x 10 | 80 |
| 3rd Decimal Digit | $10^2$ or 4 | 4 | 4 x 100 | 400 |
| 4th Decimal Digit | $10^3$ or 8 | 2 | 2 x 1000 | 2000 |
| 5th Decimal Digit | $10^4$ or 16 | 5 | 5 x 10,000 | 52,000 |
| 6th Decimal Digit | $10^5$ or 32 | 3 | 3 x 100,000 | 300,000 |
| **Decimal Value (Total of 6 digits)** | | | | **352,481** |

**Cisco Labs - Semester 1 – Networking Fundamentals**
## *EXERCISE 1.3.6 – BINARY NUMBERING - WORKSHEET*

### Step 2.  Binary Numbers

**Explanation:** Binary means "two," and each digit in a binary number can only have two values (zero or one). It is also called a base 2 numbering system. Binary numbers are the key to understanding how routers work and how packets get from one workstation (host) to another server (host) on a TCP/IP network. Internet addresses are made up of 32 bits or four groups of 8 bits known as "octets." Each bit of each octet has a value based on its position. Of the 8 bits in an octet, the left-most bit is worth 128 ($2^7$) and the right-most bit is worth 1 ($2^0$). The value of each bit is based on the powers of 2.

The binary numbering system is based on the powers of 2. This exercise will help develop an understanding of exponentiation or "powers" of numbers using the base 2 number system, which is what all computers and data communications use. With base 2, the right-most position has a value of 1, as with base 10. Each position moving to the left is worth 2 times more. 2 to the zero power ($2^0$) is 1, and 2 to the first power ($2^1$ or 2 x 1) is 2. 2 to the second power ($2^2$ or 2 x 2) is 4 and 2 to the third power ($2^3$ or 2 x 2 x 2) is 8, and so on. Just multiply the number in each position (either a 0 or a 1) times the value of each position (for example, 8 = 1 x $2^3$ or 1 x 8) and add up the total. Remember, any number to the zero power is 1. Convert the following binary numbers to decimal numbers. In the first exercise you will convert a binary number to a decimal number. Starting from the right, the first binary digit is a zero, which is calculated as zero times $2^0$ (two to the zero power or 0 x 1 – anything to the zero power is 1). The second position from the left is also a zero, so this is zero times $2^1$ (or 0 x 2). The third binary number from the right is a 1. This is 1 times $2^2$ (two to the $2^{nd}$ power or 4).

### Binary Number Conversion Example
The following table shows the detail calculations (starting from the right side) to convert the binary number 10011100 into a decimal number.

| Position of digit (from right) | Value of bit position (2 to the power of) | Is bit a One (on) or a Zero (off)? | Calculation | Decimal Value |
|---|---|---|---|---|
| 1$^{st}$ Binary Digit | $2^0$ or 1 | 0 | 0 x 1 | 0 |
| 2$^{nd}$ Binary Digit | $2^1$ or 2 | 0 | 0 x 2 | 0 |
| 3$^{rd}$ Binary Digit | $2^2$ or 4 | 1 | 1 x 4 | 4 |
| 4$^{th}$ Binary Digit | $2^3$ or 8 | 1 | 1 x 8 | 8 |
| 5$^{th}$ Binary Digit | $2^4$ or 16 | 1 | 1 x 16 | 16 |
| 6$^{th}$ Binary Digit | $2^5$ or 32 | 0 | 0 x 32 | 0 |
| 7$^{th}$ Binary Digit | $2^6$ or 64 | 0 | 0 x 64 | 0 |
| 8$^{th}$ Binary Digit | $2^7$ or 128 | 1 | 1 x 128 | 128 |
| Decimal Value. (Sum total of 8 bits) | | | | 156 |

# Cisco Labs - Semester 1 – Networking Fundamentals
## *EXERCISE 1.3.6 – BINARY NUMBERING - WORKSHEET*

### Step 3.  Binary to Decimal Practice Exercises

**Task:** Practice converting the four binary octets of an IP address to the dotted decimal equivalent.

**Explanation:** Look at the binary number bit status. If there is a 1 in a position, add the value shown. If there is a 0 in a position, do not add it. Note that 8 bits cannot represent a decimal number greater than 255. (If all eight positions are ones, $128 + 64 + 32 + 16 + 8 + 4 + 2 + 1 = 255$.)

1.  Solve for the 1st, 2nd, 3rd, and 4th octet decimal value

| Exponent | $2^7$ | $2^6$ | $2^5$ | $2^4$ | $2^3$ | $2^2$ | $2^1$ | $2^0$ |
|---|---|---|---|---|---|---|---|---|
| Bit Position | 8 | 7 | 6 | 5 | 4 | 3 | 2 | 1 |
| Value | 128 | 64 | 32 | 16 | 8 | 4 | 2 | 1 |
| Binary Number Bit Status | 1 | 0 | 0 | 1 | 1 | 1 | 0 | 0 |

**1st Octet Decimal Value:** _____

| Exponent | $2^7$ | $2^6$ | $2^5$ | $2^4$ | $2^3$ | $2^2$ | $2^1$ | $2^0$ |
|---|---|---|---|---|---|---|---|---|
| Bit Position | 8 | 7 | 6 | 5 | 4 | 3 | 2 | 1 |
| Value | 128 | 64 | 32 | 16 | 8 | 4 | 2 | 1 |
| Binary number bit status | 1 | 1 | 1 | 0 | 0 | 0 | 1 | 1 |

**2nd Octet Decimal Value:** _____

| Exponent | $2^7$ | $2^6$ | $2^5$ | $2^4$ | $2^3$ | $2^2$ | $2^1$ | $2^0$ |
|---|---|---|---|---|---|---|---|---|
| Bit Position | 8 | 7 | 6 | 5 | 4 | 3 | 2 | 1 |
| Value | 128 | 64 | 32 | 16 | 8 | 4 | 2 | 1 |
| Binary number bit status | 0 | 1 | 1 | 1 | 0 | 0 | 0 | 0 |

**3rd Octet Decimal Value:** _____

| Exponent | $2^7$ | $2^6$ | $2^5$ | $2^4$ | $2^3$ | $2^2$ | $2^1$ | $2^0$ |
|---|---|---|---|---|---|---|---|---|
| Bit Position | 8 | 7 | 6 | 5 | 4 | 3 | 2 | 1 |
| Value | 128 | 64 | 32 | 16 | 8 | 4 | 2 | 1 |
| Binary number bit status | 1 | 1 | 0 | 1 | 1 | 0 | 1 | 0 |

**4th Octet Decimal Value:** _____

2.  Enter the dotted decimal octet values for all four octets for the above IP address:

10011100 . 11100011 . 01110000 . 11011010

_____ _____ _____ _____

# Cisco Labs - Semester 1 – Networking Fundamentals
## *EXERCISE 1.3.6 – BINARY NUMBERING - WORKSHEET*

### Step 4.  Decimal to Binary Practice Exercises

**Task:** Practice converting the following decimal values of the IP address 209.114.58.165 to the binary octet equivalent.

**Explanation:** Look at the decimal value and then subtract binary values starting from 128 (the highest value binary bit). If the number is larger than 128, put a 1 in the first position binary number bit status. Subtract 128 from the number, and then see if there is a 64 left. If there is, put a 1 there; otherwise put a 0 and see if there is a 32. Continue until all 8 bits are defined as either a zero or a 1.

1.  Solve the 1st, 2nd, 3rd and 4th octet decimal value to binary bit number

| Exponent | $2^7$ | $2^6$ | $2^5$ | $2^4$ | $2^3$ | $2^2$ | $2^1$ | $2^0$ |
|---|---|---|---|---|---|---|---|---|
| Bit Position | 8 | 7 | 6 | 5 | 4 | 3 | 2 | 1 |
| Value | 128 | 64 | 32 | 16 | 8 | 4 | 2 | 1 |
| Binary number bit status | | | | | | | | |

## 1st Octet Binary Value: 209

| Exponent | $2^7$ | $2^6$ | $2^5$ | $2^4$ | $2^3$ | $2^2$ | $2^1$ | $2^0$ |
|---|---|---|---|---|---|---|---|---|
| Bit Position | 8 | 7 | 6 | 5 | 4 | 3 | 2 | 1 |
| Value | 128 | 64 | 32 | 16 | 8 | 4 | 2 | 1 |
| Binary number bit status | | | | | | | | |

## 2nd Octet Binary Value: 114

| Exponent | $2^7$ | $2^6$ | $2^5$ | $2^4$ | $2^3$ | $2^2$ | $2^1$ | $2^0$ |
|---|---|---|---|---|---|---|---|---|
| Bit Position | 8 | 7 | 6 | 5 | 4 | 3 | 2 | 1 |
| Value | 128 | 64 | 32 | 16 | 8 | 4 | 2 | 1 |
| Binary number bit status | | | | | | | | |

## 3rd Octet Binary Value: 58

| Exponent | $2^7$ | $2^6$ | $2^5$ | $2^4$ | $2^3$ | $2^2$ | $2^1$ | $2^0$ |
|---|---|---|---|---|---|---|---|---|
| Bit Position | 8 | 7 | 6 | 5 | 4 | 3 | 2 | 1 |
| Value | 128 | 64 | 32 | 16 | 8 | 4 | 2 | 1 |
| Binary number bit status | | | | | | | | |

# Cisco Labs - Semester 1 – Networking Fundamentals
## *EXERCISE 1.3.6 – BINARY NUMBERING - WORKSHEET*

**4<sup>th</sup> Octet Binary Value: 165**

2. Enter the 8 binary bits (zeros and ones) octet values for all four octets for the IP address:

    **209**    .    **114**   .    **58**    .    **165**

    _____    _____    _____    _____

# Cisco Labs - Semester 1 – Networking Fundamentals
## *EXERCISE 1.3.6 – BINARY NUMBERING – ANWERS*

**Step 3.**

1. Solve for the 1st, 2nd, 3rd,and 4th octet Decimal value

## *CHECK ANSWERS WITH WINDOWS CALCULATOR:*

Use the Windows Calculator to check your answers. Click Start, Programs, Accessories, Calculator. Click View on the Calculator menu and then click the Scientific Button. To convert a binary number to decimal, first click the Binary button (Bin) and enter the binary number as 8 bits (zeros or ones). Click the Decimal button (Dec) to convert to decimal. To convert from decimal to binary, start by clicking the Decimal button, enter the decimal number and then click the Binary button to convert.

| Exponent | $2^7$ | $2^6$ | $2^5$ | $2^4$ | $2^3$ | $2^2$ | $2^1$ | $2^0$ |
|---|---|---|---|---|---|---|---|---|
| Bit Position | 8 | 7 | 6 | 5 | 4 | 3 | 2 | 1 |
| Value | 128 | 64 | 32 | 16 | 8 | 4 | 2 | 1 |
| Binary Number Bit Status | 1 | 0 | 0 | 1 | 1 | 1 | 0 | 0 |

## 1st Octet Decimal Value: 156

| Exponent | $2^7$ | $2^6$ | $2^5$ | $2^4$ | $2^3$ | $2^2$ | $2^1$ | $2^0$ |
|---|---|---|---|---|---|---|---|---|
| Bit Position | 8 | 7 | 6 | 5 | 4 | 3 | 2 | 1 |
| Value | 128 | 64 | 32 | 16 | 8 | 4 | 2 | 1 |
| Binary number bit status | 1 | 1 | 1 | 0 | 0 | 0 | 1 | 1 |

## 2nd Octet Decimal Value: 227

| Exponent | $2^7$ | $2^6$ | $2^5$ | $2^4$ | $2^3$ | $2^2$ | $2^1$ | $2^0$ |
|---|---|---|---|---|---|---|---|---|
| Bit Position | 8 | 7 | 6 | 5 | 4 | 3 | 2 | 1 |
| Value | 128 | 64 | 32 | 16 | 8 | 4 | 2 | 1 |
| Binary number bit status | 0 | 1 | 1 | 1 | 0 | 0 | 0 | 0 |

## 3rd Octet Decimal Value: 112

| Exponent | $2^7$ | $2^6$ | $2^5$ | $2^4$ | $2^3$ | $2^2$ | $2^1$ | $2^0$ |
|---|---|---|---|---|---|---|---|---|
| Bit Position | 8 | 7 | 6 | 5 | 4 | 3 | 2 | 1 |
| Value | 128 | 64 | 32 | 16 | 8 | 4 | 2 | 1 |
| Binary number bit status | 1 | 1 | 0 | 1 | 1 | 0 | 1 | 0 |

## 4th Octet Decimal Value: 218

2. Enter the dotted decimal octet values for all four octets for the IP address:

| 10011100 | . | 11100011 | . | 01110000 | . | 11011010 |
|---|---|---|---|---|---|---|
| **156** | . | **227** | . | **112** | . | **218** |

# Cisco Labs - Semester 1 – Networking Fundamentals
## *EXERCISE 1.3.6 – BINARY NUMBERING – ANSWERS*

**Step 4.**

1. Decimal to binary practice exercises.

| Exponent | $2^7$ | $2^6$ | $2^5$ | $2^4$ | $2^3$ | $2^2$ | $2^1$ | $2^0$ |
|---|---|---|---|---|---|---|---|---|
| Bit Position | 8 | 7 | 6 | 5 | 4 | 3 | 2 | 1 |
| Value | 128 | 64 | 32 | 16 | 8 | 4 | 2 | 1 |
| Binary number bit status | 1 | 1 | 0 | 1 | 0 | 0 | 0 | 1 |

**1<sup>st</sup> Octet Decimal Value: 209**

| Exponent | $2^7$ | $2^6$ | $2^5$ | $2^4$ | $2^3$ | $2^2$ | $2^1$ | $2^0$ |
|---|---|---|---|---|---|---|---|---|
| Bit Position | 8 | 7 | 6 | 5 | 4 | 3 | 2 | 1 |
| Value | 128 | 64 | 32 | 16 | 8 | 4 | 2 | 1 |
| Binary number bit status | 0 | 1 | 1 | 1 | 0 | 0 | 1 | 0 |

**2<sup>nd</sup> Octet Decimal Value: 114**

| Exponent | $2^7$ | $2^6$ | $2^5$ | $2^4$ | $2^3$ | $2^2$ | $2^1$ | $2^0$ |
|---|---|---|---|---|---|---|---|---|
| Bit Position | 8 | 7 | 6 | 5 | 4 | 3 | 2 | 1 |
| Value | 128 | 64 | 32 | 16 | 8 | 4 | 2 | 1 |
| Binary number bit status | 0 | 0 | 1 | 1 | 1 | 0 | 1 | 0 |

**3<sup>rd</sup> Octet Decimal Value: 58**

| Exponent | $2^7$ | $2^6$ | $2^5$ | $2^4$ | $2^3$ | $2^2$ | $2^1$ | $2^0$ |
|---|---|---|---|---|---|---|---|---|
| Bit Position | 8 | 7 | 6 | 5 | 4 | 3 | 2 | 1 |
| Value | 128 | 64 | 32 | 16 | 8 | 4 | 2 | 1 |
| Binary number bit status | 1 | 0 | 1 | 0 | 1 | 0 | 0 | 1 |

**4<sup>th</sup> Octet Decimal Value: 165**

2. Enter the 8 binary bits (zeros and ones) octet values for all four octets for the IP address:

| 209 | . | 114 | . | 58 | . | 165 |
|---|---|---|---|---|---|---|
| 11010001 | | 01110010 | | 00111010 | | 10100101 |

**Cisco Labs - Semester 1 – Networking Fundamentals**
## *EXERCISE 2.2.5 – OSI MODEL LAYERS - OVERVIEW*
### *(Estimated time: 20 minutes)*

## Objectives:

This lab will focus on your ability to accomplish the following tasks:

- Name the seven layers of the OSI model in order using a mnemonic (memory jogger)
- Describe the characteristics, functions and keywords relating to each layer
- Describe the packaging units used to encapsulate each layer
- Name several protocols and standards that operate at each layer

## Background:

This lab will help you develop a better understanding of the seven layers of the OSI model. You will identify the characteristics of each layer as well as the terminology at each layer. The OSI model was developed by the ISO to help provide a common framework for the development of both local-area networks (LANs) and wide-area networks (WANs). Most network architectures and companies do not adhere exactly to the ISO model but use it to describe their products and compare them to others. The OSI model helps us troubleshoot networking problems by breaking down the networking process (communication from hosts to servers) into distinct layers where functions must occur and identifying tools that can help isolate the problem. An understanding of the OSI model is essential to success in the world of networking. This lab focuses on the Ethernet network architecture and related physical devices.

## Tools / Preparation:

This is primarily a written lab exercise, but you will also identify physical devices that relate to the layers of the OSI model. Before you begin this lab, the teacher or lab assistant should have samples of typical networking components such as Network Interface Cards (NICs), hubs, cables, routers, switches, and so on. You can work individually or in teams. Before beginning this lab you should read the *Cisco Networking Academy Program: First-Year Companion Guide*, Chapter 2. You should also review semester 1 on-line Lesson 2. The following resources will be required:

- PC workstation with monitor, keyboard, mouse, and power cords
- Windows operating system (Windows 95, 98, NT or 2000) installed on PC
- NIC installed and Cat 5 patch cable with connection to the Internet
- Browser software installed (Netscape 4.6.1 or Internet Explorer 5.1 Flash Plug-in)
- Apple QuickTime and ShockWave Macromedia browser plug-ins
- Sample Ethernet and Token Ring NICs with different connectors (Coax, AUI, RJ45)
- Sample hubs, switches, and routers

**NOTES:** _____

_____

_____

# Cisco Labs - Semester 1 – Networking Fundamentals
## *EXERCISE 2.2.5 – OSI MODEL LAYERS – WORKSHEET*

### Step 1 – The OSI Model Layers – Functions and Devices

**Task:** Fill out the following charts based on your knowledge of the OSI model.
**Explanation:** Your understanding of the OSI model will greatly increase your ability to absorb and categorize networking information as you learn it.

1. List the 7 layers of the OSI model from the top to the bottom. Give a mnemonic word for each layer that can help you remember it and then list the keywords and phrases that describe the characteristics and function of each.

| Layer # | Name | Mnemonic | Key Words and Description of Function |
|---|---|---|---|
| 7 | | | |
| 6 | | | |
| 5 | | | |
| 4 | | | |
| 3 | | | |
| 2 | | | |
| 1 | | | |

2. List the 7 layers of the OSI model. List the encapsulation unit used to describe the data grouping at each layer and the corresponding devices or components that operate at this level.

| Layer # | Name | Encapsulation Unit or Logical Grouping | Devices or components that operate at this level |
|---|---|---|---|
| 7 | | | |
| 6 | | | |
| 5 | | | |
| 4 | | | |
| 3 | | | |
| 2 | | | |
| 1 | | | |

# Cisco Labs - Semester 1 – Networking Fundamentals
## *EXERCISE 2.2.5 – OSI MODEL LAYERS – ANSWERS*

## Step 1

1. List the 7 layers of the OSI model from the top to the bottom. Give a mnemonic word for each layer that can help you remember it and then list the key terms and phrases that describe the characteristics and function of each.

| Layer # | Name | Mnemonic | Key Words and Description of Function |
|---|---|---|---|
| 7 | Application | All | Network processes applications such as File, Print, Message, Database and Application services. Establishes availability of resources between two nodes. (FTP and Telnet are examples.) |
| 6 | Presentation | People | Data representation, coding (EBCDIC, ASCII), data transfer syntax, conversion, encryption, formatting and compression services. |
| 5 | Session | Seem | Interhost communication. Establishes, maintains and terminates connections between applications. |
| 4 | Transport | To | End-to-end connections. Segments and reassembles data in proper sequence. Setup and teardown of "virtual circuits" (connection-oriented). Can ensure segment delivery with error correction, recovery and flow control. |
| 3 | Network | Need | Network / host addresses and selection of best path through an internetwork (routing). Encapsulates upper-layer information into "packets." |
| 2 | Data Link | Data | Access to media. Adds frame header to upper-layer information which contains the hardware address of the destination device or next device on the path. The data link layer is divided into 2 sub-layers. 1) The Logical Link Control (LLC) and 2) The Media Access Control (MAC). |
| 1 | Physical | Processing | Binary transmission signals and encoding. Electrical (copper), light (fiber) and physical connections and media (cabling) between network devices. |

# Cisco Labs - Semester 1 – Networking Fundamentals
## *EXERCISE 2.2.5 – OSI MODEL LAYERS – ANSWERS*

2. List the 7 layers of the OSI model. List the encapsulation unit used to describe the logical grouping of bits at each layer and the concepts and physical devices that operate at each layer.

| Layer # | Name | Encapsulation Unit or Logical Grouping | Devices or components that operate at this layer |
|---|---|---|---|
| 7 | Application | Data | Software (gateways) |
| 6 | Presentation | Data | Software |
| 5 | Session | Data | Software |
| 4 | Transport | Segments | Router |
| 3 | Network | Packets, Datagrams | Router |
| 2 | Data Link | Frames | NIC (LLC and MAC), Bridge, Switch |
| 1 | Physical | Bits | NIC (Physical connectors – BNC, RJ45, and so on), Media (cable), Repeater, Hub, DCE and DTE |

**Cisco Labs - Semester 1 – Networking Fundamentals**
## *EXERCISE 2.3.4 – OSI MODEL and TCP/IP - OVERVIEW*
### *(Estimated time: 20 minutes)*

## Objectives:
This lab will focus on your ability to accomplish the following tasks:

- Describe the 4 layers of the TCP/IP model

- Relate the 7 layers of the OSI model to the 4 layers of the TCP/IP model

- Name the primary TCP/IP protocols and utilities that operate at each layer

## Background:
This lab will help you develop a better understanding of the seven layers of the OSI model as they relate to the most popular functioning networking model in existence, the TCP/IP model. The Internet is based on TCP/IP, which has become the standard language of networking. Although the TCP/IP model is the most widely used, the 7 layers of the OSI model are the ones most commonly used to describe and compare networking software and hardware from various vendors. It is very important to know both the OSI and TCP/IP models and to be able to relate (or map) the layers of one to the other. An understanding of the TCP/IP model and the protocols and utilities that operate at each layer is essential when troubleshooting.

## Tools / Preparation:
You can work individually or in teams. Before beginning this lab you should read the Networking Academy First Year Companion Guide, Chapters 1, 2 and 10. You should also review semester 1 on-line Lesson 2. The following resources will be required:

- PC workstation with monitor, keyboard, mouse, and power cords
- Windows operating system (Windows 95, 98, NT or 2000) installed on PC
- NIC installed and Cat 5 patch cable with connection to the Internet
- Browser software installed (Netscape 4.6.1 or Internet Explorer 5.1 Flash Plug-in)
- Apple QuickTime and ShockWave Macromedia browser plug-ins
- Sample Ethernet and Token Ring NICs with different connectors (Coax, AUI, RJ45)
- Sample hubs, switches, and routers

## NOTES: _____
_____
_____
_____
_____
_____

# Cisco Labs - Semester 1 – Networking Fundamentals
## *EXERCISE 2.3.4 – OSI MODEL and TCP/IP – WORKSHEET*

### Step 1 – The OSI model and associated TCP/IP protocol stack layers

**Task:** Fill out the following chart based on your knowledge of the OSI and TCP/IP models.
**Explanation:** Your understanding of the OSI model as it relates to the TCP/IP model will greatly increase your ability to absorb and categorize networking information as you learn it.

1. List the 7 layers of the OSI model from the top to the bottom with the proper name for each layer. List the TCP/IP layer number and its correct name in the next columns. Also list the term used for the encapsulation units, the related TCP/IP protocols/utilities and the devices that operate at each layer. NOTE: More than one OSI layer will be related to certain TCP/IP layers.

## OSI comparison with TCP/IP Protocol Stack

| OSI # | OSI Layer Name | TCP/IP # | TCP/IP Layer name | Encapsul. Units | TCP/IP Protocols at each TCP/IP layer | TCP Utilities |
|-------|----------------|----------|-------------------|-----------------|----------------------------------------|---------------|
| 7 | | | | | | |
| 6 | | | | | | |
| 5 | | | | | | |
| 4 | | | | | | |
| 3 | | | | | | |
| 2 | | | | | | |
| 1 | | | | | | |

# Cisco Labs - Semester 1 – Networking Fundamentals
## *EXERCISE 2.3.4 – OSI MODEL and TCP/IP – ANSWERS*

### Step 1 – The OSI model and associated TCP/IP protocol stack layer

**Task:** Fill out the following chart based on your knowledge of the OSI and TCP/IP models.
**Explanation:** Your understanding of the OSI model as it relates to the TCP/IP model will greatly increase your ability to absorb and categorize networking information as you learn it.

1. List the 7 layers of the OSI model from the top to the bottom with the proper name for each layer. List the TCP/IP layer number and its correct name in the next columns. Also list the term used for the encapsulation units, the related TCP/IP protocols/utilities and the devices that operate at each layer. NOTE: More than one OSI layer will be related to certain TCP/IP layers.

## OSI comparison with TCP/IP Protocol Stack

| OSI # | OSI Layer Name | TCP/IP # | TCP/IP Layer Name | Encapsul. Units | TCP/IP Protocols at each TCP/IP layer | TCP Utilities |
|---|---|---|---|---|---|---|
| 7 | Application | 4 | Application | Data | FTP, HTTP use TCP as transport<br><br>SMTP, DNS, and TFTP use UDP as transport | Telnet, Rlogin |
| 6 | Presentation | 4 | Application | Data | | |
| 5 | Session | 4 | Application | Data | | |
| 4 | Transport | 3 | Transport | Segments | TCP or UDP | |
| 3 | Network | 2 | Internet | Packets (datagrams) | IP, ICMP, ARP, RARP | Ping, Traceroute |
| 2 | Data Link (LLC and MAC) | 1 | Network (interface) | Frames | | |
| 1 | Physical | 1 | Network (interface) | Bits | | |

# Cisco Labs - Semester 1 – Networking Fundamentals
## *LAB 3.4.2 – BASIC LAN SETUP - OVERVIEW*
### *(Estimated time: 60 minutes)*

## Objectives:
- Create a simple LAN with two PCs using a single crossover cable to connect the workstations
- Create a simple LAN with two PCs using an Ethernet hub and two straight-thru cables to connect the workstations
- Connect the hub-based mini-LAN to the Internet if a connection is available
- Use the Control Panel / Network utility to verify and configure the network settings
- Use the ICMP Ping command to verify the TCP/IP connection between the two workstations
- Use the WINIPCFG.EXE utility to verify all IP configuration settings

## Background:
In this lab, you learn how to connect two PCs to create a simple peer-to-peer LAN or workgroup. The instructions for this lab focus on the Windows 95 or 98 operating system. You will share a folder on one workstation and connect to that folder from the other workstation. This lab is divided into three exercises as follows:

**Exercise A** – The two PCs (or workstations) will be connected directly to each other from one Network Interface Card (NIC) to the other NIC using a crossover cable. This can be useful to allow you to create a mini-lab for testing purposes with the need for a hub. Because the NICs on the workstations are directly connected, you will not be able to connect any additional workstations.

**Exercise B** – The two PCs will be connected with a hub between them. Using a hub allows for more than just two workstations to be connected, depending on the number of ports on the hub. Hubs can have anywhere from 4 to 24 ports.

Note: For both Exercises A and B, you will verify that the workstations are functioning and that network hardware is installed properly. You will also need to verify and configure all TCP/IP protocol network settings for the two workstations to communicate, such as IP address and subnet mask.

**Exercise C** (optional) – The two PCs attached to the hub will be connected to the Internet with another straight-thru cable connected to a live hub or switch. You will use your browser to access a web site.

## Tools / Preparation:
It is best to start with a fresh install of Windows 98. The workstations should have Network Interface Cards (NIC) installed with the proper drivers (floppy disk or CD) available. Before beginning this lab you should read *Cisco Networking Academy Program: First-Year Companion Guide*, Chapters 1 and 2. You should also review semester 1 on-line Lesson number 1. The following resources will be required:
- Two Pentium-based workstations with a NIC in each (NIC drivers should be available)
- Exercise A – One CAT5 Crossover cable to connect the workstations without a hub
- Exercise B – An Ethernet hub (4 or 8 port) and two CAT5 straight-wired cables
- Exercise C – A connection to the Internet if available with a third straight-thru cable on the hub
- Windows 98 CD-ROM to do fresh install or to use when network setting changes are made

# Cisco Labs - Semester 1 – Networking Fundamentals
## *LAB 3.4.2 – BASIC LAN SETUP - WORKSHEET*

In this lab, you will set up a small peer-to-peer Ethernet LAN workgroup using two workstations. Answer the following questions with each step as you check and/or configure the necessary components.

**Note:** Steps 1 and 2 (physical LAN connections) will be different between exercises A and B. The steps from 3 on should be the same because they relate only to the workstations and should be performed on both workstations.

### Step 1 – Check local-area network (LAN) connections
**Task:** Verify the cables
**Explanation:**
**Exercise A** – A single CAT 5 crossover cable is used to connect the workstations together. Verify that the pins are wired as a crossover by holding both RJ45 connectors side by side with the clip down and inspect them. Pairs 2 and 3 should be reversed. Refer to Lab 5.3.4.1 for correct wire color and pin locations.

**Exercise B** – Check each of the two CAT 5 cables from each workstation to the hub. Verify that the pins are wired straight through by holding the two RJ45 connectors for each cable side by side with the clip down and inspect them. All pins should have the same color wire on the same pin at both ends of the cable. (Pin 1 should match pin 1 and pin 8 should match pin 8, and so on.) Refer to Lab 5.3.4.1 for correct pin locations.

1.  Are the cable(s) wired correctly? _____

### Step 2 – Plug in and connect the equipment
**Task:** Check the workstations (and hub for exercise B)
**Explanation:**
**Exercises A** – Check to make sure that the NICs are installed correctly in each workstation. Plug in the workstations and turn them on.

**Exercise B** – Plug the hub or its AC adapter into a power outlet. Plug the straight through cable from workstation 1 into port 1 of the hub and the cable from workstation 2 into port 2 of the hub. After the workstations have booted, check the green link light on the back of each NIC and the green lights on ports 1 and 2 of the hub to verify that they are communicating. This also verifies a good physical connection between the hub and the NICs in the workstations (OSI Layers 1 and 2). If the link light is not on, it usually indicates a bad cable connection or an incorrectly wired cable, or the NIC or hub might not be functioning correctly.

1.  Are the NIC and hub link lights on? _____

# Cisco Labs - Semester 1 – Networking Fundamentals
## *LAB 3.4.2 – BASIC LAN SETUP - WORKSHEET*

### Step 3 – Network Adapters and Protocols

**Task:** Check the Network Adapter (NIC): Use the Control Panel, System, Device Manager utility to verify that the Network Adapter (NIC) is functioning properly for both workstations. Double-click Network Adapters and then right-click the NIC adapter in use. Click Properties to see if the device is working properly.

**Explanation:** If there is a problem with the NIC or driver, the icon will show a yellow circle with an exclamation mark in it with (possible resource conflict) or a red X indicating a serious problem (device could cause Windows to lock up).

1. What does the NIC properties screen say about the Network Adapter?

_____

### Step 4 – Check the TCP/IP Protocol Settings

**Task:** Use the Control Panel, Network utility and select the TCP/IP protocol from the Configuration Tab and click Properties. Check the IP address and subnet mask for both workstations on the IP Address tab.

**Explanation:** The IP addresses can be set to anything as long as they are compatible and on the same network. Record the existing settings before making any changes in case they need to be set back (for instance, they might be DHCP clients now). For this lab, use the Class C network address of 200.150.100.0 and set workstation 1 to the static IP address 200.150.100.1 and set workstation 2 to 200.150.100.2. Set the default subnet mask on each workstation to 255.255.255.0.

1. Have the IP addresses and subnet mask been set? _____

### Step 5 – Check the TCP/IP Settings with the WINIPCFG Utility

**Task:** Use the winipcfg.exe command to see your TCP/IP settings on one screen. Click on Start, Programs and then select the MS-DOS Prompt.

**Explanation:** Enter the winipcfg /all command (you do not need the .exe because this is an executable command) to see all TCP/IP-related settings for your workstation.

1. Using the results of the winipcfg command, fill in the blanks for each workstation:

| Workstation 1 Name: | Workstation 2 Name: |
|---|---|
| IP Address: | IP Address: |
| Subnet Mask: | Subnet Mask: |
| MAC (Hardware) Address: | MAC (Hardware) Address: |

### Step 6 – Check the network connection with the Ping Utility

**Task:** Use the Ping command to check for basic TCP/IP connectivity. Click on Start, Programs and then the MS-DOS Prompt. Enter the Ping command followed by the IP address of the other workstation.

**Explanation:** This will verify that you have a good OSI Layers 1 through 3 connection.

1. What was the result of the Ping command?_____

_____

**Cisco Labs - Semester 1 – Networking Fundamentals**
## *LAB 3.4.2 – BASIC LAN SETUP - WORKSHEET*

**Step 7 – Windows Networking Options**

    **Task:** Check Network Configuration: Use the Control Panel, Network utility, Configuration tab and check to be sure that you have the following networking components installed:

1. Microsoft Family or Microsoft Windows Logon Client (small computer icon)
2. The NIC adapter (small NIC icon)
3. The TCP/IP Protocol (small network cable connection icon)

There might be other adapters and protocols listed, but these are the ones required for this lab. Click on the Access Control tab and verify that that the Share Level Access Control button is selected. Select the Microsoft Family or Windows client and click Properties. Click the Identification tab and enter a name for the first computer of PC1. Name the other computer PC2. The Workgroup should be WORKGROUP and the Computer Description is optional.

    **Explanation:** You will need to reboot the computer and insert the Windows 98 CD when prompted.

1. List the networking components installed:

| | |
|---|---|
| **Client (computer icon)** | |
| **Adapter (NIC icon)** | |
| **Protocol (net connection icon)** | |
| **Other Client / Adapter / Protocol** | |

**Step 8 – Check File and Print Sharing**

    **Task:** Use the Control Panel, Network utility, Configuration tab and click the File and Print Sharing button. On the workstation that will have the folder to be shared, check the box that says, "I want to be able to give others access to my files" to allow each workstation to share its folders. You can also check the box that says, "I want to be able to allow others to print to my printers" to allow the other workstation to print if you have a shared printer attached to one of the workstations.

**Step 9 – File Folders and Sharing Options**

    **Task:** Set up a file folder to share: On workstation one, use Windows Explorer to create a folder to be shared Called "Testfolder." Using Windows Explorer, My Computer or Network Neighborhood, select the folder and right-click to share it. Enter the name of the share and click OK. From the other workstation, click on Network Neighborhood and select the first workstation and the shared folder.

    **Explanation:** You can map a drive to the shared folder if you wish. While working in the shared folder on the other workstation, create a new document and save it. If you have a printer shared, you might want to print the document.

1. Document the results of the folder sharing and file creating process:

_____

_____

_____

# Cisco Labs - Semester 1 – Networking Fundamentals
## *LAB 3.4.2 – BASIC LAN SETUP – ANSWERS*

### Step 1

1. Are the cable(s) wired correctly? **Yes. They are wired crossed over (if no hub is being used with Exercise A) or they are wired straight through (if a hub is being used with exercise B).**

### Step 2

1. Are the NIC and hub link lights on? **Yes. The green link light on both NICs is on and the link lights on both hub ports are on (if using a hub with exercise B).**

### Step 3

1. What does the NIC properties screen say about the Network Adapter? **Lists the name of the controller, the manufacturer, the device type and status: This device is working properly.**

### Step 4

1. Have the IP addresses and subnet mask been set? **Yes**

### Step 5

1. Using the results of the winipcfg /all command, fill in the blanks for each workstation:

| Workstation 1 Name: PC1 | Workstation 2 Name: PC2 |
|---|---|
| IP Address: 200.150.100.1 | IP Address: 200.150.100.2 |
| Subnet Mask: 255.255.255.0 | Subnet Mask: 255.255.255.0 |
| Adapter (MAC) Address: 00-08-C7-26-C5-A8 | Adapter (MAC) Address: 00-08-C7-48-AD-F3 |

### Step 6

1. What was the result of the Ping command? (Ping from 200.150.100.1 to 200.150.100.2 using the Windows 98 operating system.)
   **Pinging 200.150.100.2 with 32 bytes of data:**

   | | | |
   |---|---|---|
   | **Reply from 200.150.100.2:** | **Bytes = 32** | **Time = 1ms  TTL = 255** |
   | **Reply from 200.150.100.2:** | **Bytes = 32** | **Time = 1ms  TTL = 255** |
   | **Reply from 200.150.100.2:** | **Bytes = 32** | **Time = 1ms  TTL = 255** |
   | **Reply from 200.150.100.2:** | **Bytes = 32** | **Time = 1ms  TTL = 255** |

### Step 7

1. List the networking components installed (answers will vary):

| Client (computer icon) | Windows Family (or Windows Logon) |
|---|---|
| Adapter (NIC icon) | Compaq NC3120 Fast Ethernet NIC |
| Protocol (net connection icon) | TCP / IP |
| Other Client / Adapter / Protocol | There should be no others – Remove them if they are present |

### Step 9

1. Document the results of the folder sharing and file creating process:
   **The folder on PC1 was shared and PC2 was able to connect to the shared folder and create a document in it.**

**Cisco Labs - Semester 1 – Networking Fundamentals**

## *LAB 4.2.1 – SAFE HANDLING and USE OF A MULTIMETER - OVERVIEW*

### *(Estimated time: 15 minutes)*

## Objectives:

- Learn how to use or handle a multimeter correctly.

## Background:

A multimeter is a powerful electrical testing tool that can detect voltage levels, resistance levels and open/closed circuits. It can check both Alternating Current (AC) and Direct Current (DC) voltage. Open and closed circuits are indicated by resistance measurements in Ohms. Each computer and networking device consists of millions of circuits and small electrical components. A multimeter can be used to debug electrical problems within a computer/networking device or between networking devices.

## Tools / Preparation:

Prior to starting the lab, the teacher or lab assistant should have several multimeters available (one for each team of two students) and various batteries for testing. Work in teams of two. You should review semester 1 on-line Lesson 4. The following resources will be required:

- A digital multimeter (Fluke 12B or similar) for each team

- A manual for the multimeter

- A battery (for example, a 9v, 1.5V or lantern; it doesn't matter) for each team to test.

## Cisco Labs - Semester 1 – Networking Fundamentals
# *LAB 4.2.1 – SAFE HANDLING and USE OF A MULTIMETER - WORKSHEET*

**Note: The multimeter is a sensitive piece of electronic test equipment. Be sure that you do not drop it or throw it around. Be careful not to accidentally nick or cut the red or black wire leads (probes). Because it is possible to check high voltages, extra care should be taken when doing so to avoid electrical shock.**

Perform the following steps to become familiar with the handling of the multimeter:

**Step 1.** Insert the red and black leads (probes) into the proper jacks on the meter. The black probe should go in the COM jack and the red probe should go in the + (plus or positive) jack.

**Step 2.** Turn on the multimeter (click/turn to the on button). What model of multimeter are you working with? _____
What action must you take to turn the meter on?

_____

**Step 3.** Switch or turn to different measurements (for example, voltage, ohms, and so on). How many different switch positions does the multimeter have? _____
What are they? _____

_____

**Step 4.** Switch or turn the multimeter to the voltage measurement. What is the symbol for this? _____

**Step 5.** Put the tip of the red (positive) lead on one end of a battery (+ side), and put the tip of the black (negative) lead on the other end of a battery. Is any number showing up on the multimeter? _____ If not, make sure you switch to the correct type of measurement (Vol, voltage, or V). If the voltage is negative, reverse your leads.


## Reflection

Questions:

1. Name one thing that you should not do to a multimeter.

2. Name one important function of a multimeter.

3. If you get a negative voltage when measuring a battery, why is that?

**Cisco Labs - Semester 1 – Networking Fundamentals**
## *LAB 4.2.1 – SAFE HANDLING and USE OF A MULTIMETER - ANSWERS*

**Note: The multimeter is a sensitive piece of electronic test equipment. Be sure that you do not drop it or throw it around. Be careful not to accidentally nick or cut the red or black wire leads (probes). Because it is possible to check high voltages, extra care should be taken when doing so to avoid electrical shock.**

Perform the following steps to become familiar with the handling of the multimeter:

**Step 1.** Insert the red and black leads (probes) into the proper jacks on the meter. The black probe should go in the COM jack and the red probe should go in the + (plus or positive) jack.

**Step 2.** Turn on the multimeter (click/turn to the on button). What model of multimeter are you working with? **Fluke 12B digital multimeter**
What action must you take to turn the meter on? **With the Fluke 12B, you must move the rotary switch to a position other than OFF, depending on what kind of test you want to perform.**

**Step 3.** Switch or turn to different measurements (i.e. voltage, ohms, and so on). How many different switch positions does the multimeter have? **Three**
What are they? **Off, V (voltage), Ohms/Capacitance (check the manual if you do not know the meaning of the symbols shown)**

**Step 4.** Switch or turn the multimeter to the voltage measurement. What is the symbol for this? **V**

**Step 5.** Put the tip of the red (positive) lead on one end of a battery (+ side), and put the tip of the black (negative) lead on the other end of a battery. Is any number showing up on the multimeter? **Yes**
If not, make sure you switch to the correct type of measurement (Vol, voltage, or V). If the voltage is negative, reverse your leads.

## Reflection

Questions:

1. Name one thing that you should not do to a multimeter.

2. Name one important function of a multimeter.

3. If you get a negative voltage when measuring a battery, why is that?

# Cisco Labs - Semester 1 – Networking Fundamentals
## *LAB 4.2.2 – RESISTANCE MEASUREMENTS - OVERVIEW*
### *(Estimated time: 30 minutes)*

## Objectives:

- Demonstrate your ability to measure resistance and continuity with the multimeter.

## Background:

The digital multimeter is a versatile testing and troubleshooting device. In this lab, you will learn how to perform resistance measurements, and related measurements called continuity. Resistance is measured in Ohms (indicated by the Greek letter Omega or $\Omega$). Copper wires (conductors) such as those commonly used in network cabling (UTP and coax) normally have very low resistance or "good" continuity (the wire is continuous) if you check them from end to end. If there is a break in the wire, it is called "open," which creates very high resistance (air has nearly infinite resistance, indicated by the infinity symbol or $\infty$, a sideways 8). The multimeter has a battery in it, which it uses to test the resistance of a conductor (wire) or insulator (wire sheathing). When the probes are applied to the ends of a conductor, the battery current flows and the meter measures the resistance it encounters. If the battery in the multimeter is low or dead, you must replace it or you will not be able to take resistance measurements.

With this lab you will test common networking materials so that you can become familiar with them and their resistance characteristics. You will first learn to use the resistance setting on the multimeter. As you measure small resistances, you should also note the continuity feature.
The instructions provided are for the Fluke 12B. Other meters will function in a similar way.

## Tools / Preparation:

Prior to starting the lab, the teacher or lab assistant should have several multimeters available (one for each team of two students) and various networking-related items for testing resistance. Work in teams of two. You should review semester 1 on-line Lesson 4. The following resources will be required:

- Fluke 12B multimeter or equivalent
- 1000 Ohm resistor
- 10,000 Ohm resistor
- Pencil for creating graphite paths on paper
- Cat 5 jack
- Small (0.2m or appx 6 to 8 inches) section of Cat 5 UTP solid cable
- BNC terminated coaxial cable
- Unconnected DB9 to RJ45 adapter
- Terminated Cat 5 UTP patch cable

# Cisco Labs - Semester 1 – Networking Fundamentals
## *LAB 4.2.2 – RESISTANCE MEASUREMENTS - WORKSHEET*

**Step 1.** Move the rotary selector to the Omega symbol for Ohms (red Ω) in order to measure resistance. Press the button that has the Ohms symbol (red Ω) on it to select between resistance measurements and continuity.

**Resistance Measurements:** The screen will show Ω (ohms), KΩ (kilohms = thousands of Ohms) or MΩ (megohms = millions of Ohms). Use the Range button to change the range of resistance to be measured based on what resistance you expect to get. If you expect low resistance (less than 10 ohms), select a low scale (like Ω). If you expect a high reading (over 10,000 ohms), select a high scale (like KΩ). If the resistance reading is over the range selected, the OL or Over Limit indicator will be displayed on the screen. The resistance setting is for measuring exact amounts of resistance

**Continuity Measurements:** The screen will show a diode symbol, which is a small black triangle pointing to a vertical bar. A diode is an electronic device that either passes or blocks electrical current. You might see a small sound symbol next to it, which means that when there is good continuity (no resistance), the beep will sound. The continuity setting is used when you just want to know if there is a good path for electricity and don't care about the exact amount of resistance.

**Step 2.** Check the following resistances. Turn the meter off when finished or battery will drain.

| Item to Measure the resistance of | Set Selector and range scale to | Resistance reading |
|---|---|---|
| 1000 Ω Resistor | | |
| 10 kΩ Resistor | | |
| Graphite marking from a pencil on a piece of paper | | |
| Cat 5 jack | | |
| 0.2 m section of Cat 5 UTP solid cable | | |
| Touch red and black probe contacts together | | |
| Your own body (touch the tips of the probes with your fingers) | | |
| BNC terminated coaxial cable | | |
| Unconnected DB9 to RJ45 adapter | | |
| Terminated Cat 5 UTP patch cable | | |

**Reflection Question:** What purpose might the multimeter serve in maintaining and troubleshooting a computer network? _____

# Cisco Labs - Semester 1 – Networking Fundamentals
## *LAB 4.2.2 – RESISTANCE MEASUREMENTS - ANSWERS*

**Step 1.** Move the rotary selector to the Omega symbol for Ohms (red Ω) in order to measure resistance. Press the button that has the Ohms symbol (red Ω) on it to select between resistance measurements and continuity.

**Resistance Measurements:** The screen will show Ω (ohms), KΩ (kilohms = thousands of Ohms) or MΩ (megohms = millions of Ohms). Use the Range button to change the range of resistance to be measured based on what resistance you expect to get. If you expect low resistance (less than 10 ohms), select a low scale (like Ω). If you expect a high reading (over 10,000 ohms), select a high scale (like KΩ). If the resistance reading is over the range selected, the OL or Over Limit indicator will be displayed on the screen. The resistance setting is for measuring exact amounts of resistance.

**Continuity Measurements:** The screen will show a diode symbol, which is a small black triangle pointing to a vertical bar. A diode is an electronic device that either passes or blocks electrical current. You might see a small sound symbol next to it, which means that when there is good continuity (no resistance), the beep will sound. The continuity setting is used when you just want to know if there is a good path for electricity and don't care about the exact amount of resistance.

**Step 2.** Check the following resistances. Turn the meter off when finished or battery will drain.

| Item to Measure the resistance of | Set Selector and range scale to | Resistance reading |
|---|---|---|
| 1000 Ω Resistor | KΩ with range display of 0.L | About 1000 Ohms |
| 10 kΩ Resistor | KΩ with range display of 0.L | About 10,000 Ohms |
| Graphite marking from a pencil on a piece of paper | KΩ with range display of 0.L | From 10,000 to 100,000 Ohms, depending on the length of the mark and how hard you press (longer marks = higher resistance reading) |
| Cat 5 jack | Ω with range display of 0L | Less than 0.3Ω contact resistance; Over Limit (OL) on insulator |
| 0.2 m section of Cat 5 UTP solid cable | Ω with range display of 0L | Less than 0.3Ω contact resistance; Over Limit (OL) on insulator |
| Touch red and black probe contacts together | Ω with range display of 0L | Less than 0.2Ω (the harder you press, the lower the resistance reading) |
| Your own body (touch the tips of the probes with your fingers) | MΩ with range display of 0L | Stable readings will be hard to obtain, but depending on sweatiness and grip, from 100,000 (100kΩ) to 1,000,000 (MΩ) readings are typical |
| BNC terminated coaxial cable | Diode symbol (continuity scale) | Should show nearly 0 resistance or beeping sound |
| Unconnected DB9 to RJ45 adapter | Diode symbol (continuity scale) | Should show nearly 0 resistance or beeping sound (you can use the console cable adapter) |
| Terminated Cat 5 UTP patch cable | Diode symbol (continuity scale) | Less than 0.3 W contact resistance on the wire; Over Limit (OL) on insulator |

# Cisco Labs - Semester 1 – Networking Fundamentals
## *LAB 4.2.3 – VOLTAGE MEASUREMENTS - OVERVIEW*
### *(Estimated time: 30 minutes)*

## Objectives:

- Demonstrate your ability to measure voltage safely with the multimeter

## Background:

The digital multimeter is a versatile testing and troubleshooting device. In this lab, you will learn how to perform both Direct Current (DC) and Alternating Current (AC) voltage measurements. Voltage is measured in either AC or DC volts (indicated by a V). Voltage is the pressure that moves electrons through a circuit from one place to another. Voltage differential is essential to the flow of electricity. The voltage differential between a cloud in the sky and the earth is what causes lightning to strike. **NOTE: It is very important to be careful when taking voltage measurements because it is possible to receive an electrical shock.**

**Direct Current (DC):** DC voltage rises to a set level and then stays at that level and flows in one direction (positive or negative). Batteries produce DC voltage and are commonly rated at 1.5v or 9v (flashlight batteries) and 6v (lantern and vehicle batteries). Typically the battery in your car or truck is a 12v battery. When an electrical "load" such as a light bulb or motor is placed between the positive (+) and negative (-) terminals of a battery, electricity flows.

**Alternating Current (AC):** AC voltage rises above zero (positive) and then falls below zero (negative) and actually changes direction very rapidly. The most common example of AC voltage is the wall outlet in your house or business. These outlets provide approximately 120 volts of AC directly to any electrical appliance that is plugged in, such as a computer, toaster or television. Some devices, such as small printers and laptop computers, have a transformer (small black box) that plugs into a 120V AC wall outlet and then converts the AC voltage to DC voltage for use by the device. Some AC outlets can provide a higher voltage of 220V for use by devices and equipment with heavier requirements, such as clothes dryers and arc welders.

## Tools / Preparation:

Prior to starting the lab, the teacher or lab assistant should have several multimeters available (one for each team of students) and various items for testing voltage. Work in teams of two. You should review semester 1 on-line Lesson 4. The following resources will be required:

**Required voltage measurement items:**
- Fluke 12B multimeter (or equivalent)
- An assortment of batteries: A cell, C cell, D cell, 9 Volts, 6 V lantern
- Duplex wall outlet (typically 120v)
- Power supply (for laptop or other networking electrical device)

**Optional voltage measurement items:**
- A lemon with a galvanized nail stuck in one side and a piece of uninsulated copper wire stuck in the opposite side
- Solar cell with leads attached
- Homemade generator (wire wound around a pencil 50 times and a magnet)

**Cisco Labs - Semester 1 – Networking Fundamentals**
## *LAB 4.2.3 – VOLTAGE MEASUREMENTS - WORKSHEET*

**Step 1.** Move the rotary selector to the V symbol for voltage (black V) in order to be able to measure voltage. Press the button that has the VDC and VAC symbol to select between Direct Current (DC) and Alternating Current (AC) measurements.

**Direct Current Measurements:** The screen will show a V (voltage) with a series of dots and a line over the top. There are several scales available depending on the voltage to be measured. They start from millivolts (abbreviated mV = 1000th of a volt) to voltages up to hundreds of volts. Use the Range button to change the range of DC voltage to be measured based on what voltage you expect to measure. Batteries (less than 15 volts) can typically be measured accurately with the VDC scale and 0.0 range. DC voltage measurements can be used to determine if batteries are good or if there is voltage coming out of an AC adapter (transformer or converter). These are common and are used with hubs, modems, laptops, printers and other peripherals. These adapters can take wall outlet AC voltage and step it down to lower AC voltages for the device attached or can convert the AC voltage to DC and step it down. Check the back of the adapter to see what the input (AC) and output voltages (AC or DC) should be.

**Alternating Current Measurements:** The screen will show a V (voltage) with a tilde (~) after it. This represents alternating current. There are several scales available depending on the voltage to be measured. They start from millivolts (abbreviated mV = 1000th of a volt) to voltage up to hundreds of volts. Use the Range button to change the range of AC voltage to be measured based on what voltage you expect to measure. Voltage from power outlets (120v or greater) can typically be measured accurately with the VAC scale and 0.0 range. AC voltage measurements are useful in determining if there is adequate voltage coming from an AC outlet to power the equipment plugged in.

Use a Fluke 12B multimeter (or equivalent) to measure the voltage of each of the following:

**Step 2.** Check the following voltages. Be sure to turn the meter off when finished.

| Item to Measure the Voltage of | Set Selector and range scale to | Voltage reading |
|---|---|---|
| Batteries: A cell (AA, AAA), C cell, D cell, 9 Volts, 6 V lantern | | |
| Duplex wall outlet (typically 120v) | | |
| Power supply (converts AC to lower AC or DC) for laptop, mobile phone or other networking electrical device | | |
| (Optional) A lemon with a galvanized nail stuck in one side and a piece of uninsulated copper wire stuck in the opposite side | | |

**Reflection Question:** Why might you want to measure voltage when troubleshooting a network?

# Cisco Labs - Semester 1 – Networking Fundamentals
## *LAB 4.2.3 – VOLTAGE MEASUREMENTS - ANSWERS*

**Step 1.** Move the rotary selector to the V symbol for voltage (black V) in order to be able to measure voltage. Press the button that has the VDC and VAC symbol select between Direct Current (DC) and Alternating Current (AC) measurements.

**Direct Current Measurements:** The screen will show a V (voltage) with a series of dots and a line over the top. There are several scales available depending on the voltage to be measured. They start from millivolts (abbreviated mV = 1000th of a volt) to voltages up to hundreds of volts. Use the Range button to change the range of DC voltage to be measured based on what voltage you expect to measure. Batteries (less than 15 volts) can typically be measured accurately with the VDC scale and 0.0 range. DC voltage measurements can be used to determine if batteries are good or if there is voltage coming out of an AC adapter (transformer or converter). These are common and are used with hubs, modems, laptops, printers and other peripherals. These adapters can take wall outlet AC voltage and step it down to lower AC voltages for the device attached or can convert the AC voltage to DC and step it down. Check the back of the adapter to see what the input (AC) and output voltages (AC or DC) should be.

**Alternating Current Measurements:** The screen will show a V (voltage) with a tilde (~) after it. This represents alternating current. There are several scales available depending on the voltage to be measured. They start from millivolts (abbreviated mV = 1000th of a volt) to voltage up to hundreds of volts. Use the Range button to change the range of AC voltage to be measured based on what voltage you expect to measure. Voltage from power outlets (120v or greater) can typically be measured accurately with the VAC scale and 0.0 range. AC voltage measurements are useful in determining if there is adequate voltage coming from an AC outlet to power the equipment plugged in.

Use a Fluke 12B multimeter (or equivalent) to measure the voltage of each of the following:

**Step 2.** Check the following voltages. Be sure to turn the meter off when finished.

| Item to Measure the Voltage of | Set Selector and range scale to | Voltage reading |
|---|---|---|
| Batteries: A cell (AA, AAA), C cell, D cell, 9 Volts, 6 V lantern | **VDC range display of 0.0** | **Good AA battery is 1.6v or higher** |
| Duplex wall outlet (typically 120v) | **VAC range display of 0.0** | **120v or higher** |
| Power supply (converts AC to DC) for laptop, or other networking electrical device) | **VDC or VAC range display of 0.0 (read back of adapter to check for what output should be)** | **From 4 to 20 VAC or VDC (will vary)** |
| (Optional) A lemon with a galvanized nail stuck in one side and a piece of uninsulated copper wire stuck in the opposite side | **VDC range display of 0.0** | **Varies** |

**Reflection Question:** Why might you want to measure voltage when troubleshooting a network?

# Cisco Labs - Semester 1 – Networking Fundamentals
## *LAB 4.2.4 – SERIES CIRCUITS - OVERVIEW*
### *(Estimated time: 30 minutes)*

## Objective:

• Build series circuits and explore their basic properties.

## Background:

One of the most basic concepts in electronics is that of a continuous loop through which electrons flow, and which is called a circuit. Throughout networking there are references to ground loop circuit, circuit versus packet switching, and virtual circuits, in addition to all the real circuits formed by networking media and networking devices. One of the fundamental electrical circuits is the series circuit. While most networking devices and networks are built from very complex circuits that are beyond the scope of the lessons included in this course, the process of building some series circuits will help you with some of the terminology and concepts of networking. This lab will also help increase your overall understanding of some of the most basic electrical circuit building blocks.

## Tools / Preparation:

Prior to starting the lab, the teacher or lab assistant should have several multimeters available (one for each team of students) and various items for testing voltage. Work in teams of two. You should review semester 1 on-line Lesson 4. The following resources will be required:

• Fluke 12B multimeter (or equivalent)
• Light switch
• Wire cutters/stripper
• Copper wire
• 2 light bulbs (6v) with bulb bases
• 6-Volt lantern battery

# Cisco Labs - Semester 1 – Networking Fundamentals
## *LAB 4.2.4 – SERIES CIRCUITS - WORKSHEET*

**Step 1.** Measure the resistances of all devices and components except the battery. Measure the voltage of the battery. All resistances should be less than 1 Ω (Ohm), except the light bulbs. All the devices except the battery should register continuity (with the tone), indicating a short circuit or a conducting path.

**Check the following resistances. Turn the meter off when finished or it will drain the battery.**

| Item to Measure the resistance of | Set Selector and range scale to | Resistance reading |
|---|---|---|
| Pieces of wire to connect components | | |
| Light switch | | |
| Light bulbs | | |

**Step 2.** Measure the voltage of the battery, unloaded (with nothing attached to it).

| Item to Measure the Voltage of | Set Selector and range scale to | Voltage reading |
|---|---|---|
| Lantern battery: (6 V) with no load | | |

**Step 3.** Build a series circuit, one device at a time (use 1 battery, 1 switch, 1 bulb and connecting wires). Connect the battery positive lead to the end of one wire and connect the negative lead to the other wire. If the switch is turned on, the bulb should light. Disconnect one thing and see that the circuit is broken. Did the bulb go out? _____

**Step 4.** Measure the battery voltage while the circuit is running. The switch should be turned on and the light bulb should be lit. What was the voltage of the battery with the light bulb on? _____

**Step 5.** Add the second bulb in series and measure the battery voltage again. What was the voltage of the battery with the light bulb on? _____

**Reflection Question:** How do series circuits apply to networking?

_____

_____

# Cisco Labs - Semester 1 – Networking Fundamentals
## *LAB 4.2.4 – SERIES CIRCUITS - ANSWERS*

**Step 1.** Measure the resistances of all devices and components except the battery. Measure the voltage of the battery. All resistances should be less than 1 Ω (Ohm), except the light bulbs. All the devices except the battery should register continuity (with the tone), indicating a short circuit or a conducting path.

**Check the following resistances. Turn the meter off when finished or it will drain the battery.**

| Item to Measure the resistance of | Set Selector and range scale to | Resistance reading: |
|---|---|---|
| Pieces of wire to connect components | Ω with range display of 0L | Less than 1 Ohm |
| Light switch | Ω with range display of 0L | Less than 1 Ohm |
| Light bulbs | Ω with range display of 0L | Between 10 and 15 Ohms |

**Step 2.** Measure the voltage of the battery, unloaded (with nothing attached to it).

| Item to Measure the Voltage of | Set Selector and range scale to | Voltage reading |
|---|---|---|
| Lantern battery (6 V) with no load | VDC range display of 0.0 | 6.0 v or higher |

**Step 3.** Build a series circuit, one device at a time (use 1 battery, 1 switch, 1 bulb and connecting wires). Connect the battery positive lead to the end of one wire and connect the negative lead to the other wire. If the switch is turned on, the bulb should light. Disconnect one thing and see that the circuit is broken. Did the bulb go out? **Yes**

**Step 4.** Measure the battery voltage while the circuit is running. The switch should be turned on and the light bulb should be lit. What was the voltage of the battery with the light bulb on? **6.0 +**

**Step 5.** Add the second bulb in series and measure the battery voltage again. What was the voltage of the battery with the light bulb on? **Should be slightly less than Step 4.**

**Reflection Question:** How do series circuits apply to networking?
**Computer networks and networking devices contain millions of circuits. An understanding of basic series circuit terminology helps us understand these networks and devices without having to know everything about how the more complex circuits work.**

# Cisco Labs - Semester 1 – Networking Fundamentals
## *LAB 4.2.5 – COMMUNICATIONS CIRCUIT - OVERVIEW*
### *(Estimated time: 50 minutes)*

## Objective:

- Design, build, and test a simple, complete, fast, and reliable communication system, using common materials.

## Background:

For reliable communications to take place on a network, many things must be defined ahead of time, including the physical method of signaling and the meaning of each signal or series of signals. With this lab, you will create a very simple physical network and agree on some basic rules for communication in order to send and receive data. This will be a digital network based on the American Standard Code for Information Interchange (ASCII). It will be somewhat similar to the old telegraph Morse code-based systems where the only means of communicating over long distances was by sending a series of dots and dashes as electrical signals over wires between locations. Although the technology used will be simpler than real systems, many of the key concepts of data communications between computers will arise. This lab will also help to clarify the functions of the layers of the OSI model.

## Tools / Preparation:

Prior to starting the lab, the teacher or lab assistant should have several multimeters available (one for each team of students) and various items for construction of a simple communication network. Work in teams of 2 to 4. The following resources will be required. Be sure to review the purpose of each of the required items listed below because it will help in designing your network. Review semester 1 on-line Lesson 4 prior to starting this lab.

| Network construction item required | Purpose |
|---|---|
| Fluke 12B multimeter (or equivalent) | For testing communication connections |
| 20' Cat 5 UTP cable | For the physical communications lines (the cabling medium) |
| ASCII chart | To help with coding and interpretation of signals (If you do not have a hardcopy of the 7-bit ASCII code chart, search the Internet for the words "ACSII chart" and you will find several listed.) |
| Light switch | To activate the signaling device in order to create the digital on/off (binary) signals |
| Light bulbs (6v) with bulb bases | To act as the signaling device |
| 6-Volt lantern battery | To power the signaling device |
| Wire cutters/stripper | To adjust the length and prepare the ends of the communication lines |

# Cisco Labs - Semester 1 – Networking Fundamentals
## *LAB 4.2.5 – COMMUNICATIONS CIRCUIT - WORKSHEET*

**Lab Goals:**

Your group must design, build, and test a communications circuit with another team. You must communicate as much data as possible, quickly and with as few errors as possible. Spoken, written, or miscellaneous non-verbal communication of any kind is not allowed–only communication over the wire. You will agree as a team on the physical connections and on the coding you will use. One of the main goals is to send a message to the other team and have them interpret what you intended without them knowing ahead of time what your message was. Keep the OSI model in mind as you design your system.

1. Layer 1 issues–You must connect 2 pairs of wire in order to have communication in both directions (half or full duplex).

2. Layer 2 issues–You must communicate some sort of frame start and stop sequence. This is a sequence of bits that is different than the character and number bits you will be transmitting.

3. Layer 3 issues–You must invent an addressing scheme (for hosts and networks) if it is more than point-to-point communication.

4. Layer 4 issues–You must include some form of control to regulate quality of service (for example, error correction, acknowledgment, windowing, flow controls, and so on).

5. Layer 5 issues–You must implement some way of synchronizing or pausing long conversations.

6. Layer 6 issues–You must use some means of data representation (for example, ASCII encoded as optical bits).

7. Layer 7 issues–You must be able to communicate an idea supplied by your instructor or come up with a message on your own.

## Reflection Questions:

1. What issues arose as you tried to build your communications system that you think apply to data communications between computers?

_____

_____

_____

_____

2. Analyze your communications system in terms of the OSI layers.

_____

_____

_____

_____

_____

# Cisco Labs - Semester 1 – Networking Fundamentals
## *LAB 4.2.5 – COMMUNICATIONS CIRCUIT - ANSWERS*

## Reflection Questions:

1. What issues arose as you tried to build your communications system that you think apply to data communications between computers? Answers should include most of the following:

- **The issue of medium (Cat 5 was chosen).**

- **The issue of signaling (optical pulses from the light bulbs being turned on and off).**

- **The issue of encoding (what do the flashes of light represent).**

- **The issue of throughput (how many bits per second can they communicate).**

- **The issue of standards (if two groups do not communicate standards).**

- **The issue of simplex versus half-duplex versus full duplex communications.**

- **The issue of framing and error correction (how the start of a frame was indicated, how did the other team indicate whether they received the frame or not).**

- **The issue of scalability – how will more nodes be added to the network.**

2. Analyze your communications system in terms of the OSI layers.

**Answers should include a reference to each layer of the OSI model and a brief discussion of how the team dealt with the concerns of that layer.**

# Cisco Labs - Semester 1 – Networking Fundamentals
## *LAB 5.3.1 – BASIC CABLE TESTER - OVERVIEW*
### *(Estimated time: 30 minutes)*

## Objective:

- Use a cable tester to verify that a straight-through or crossover path cable is good or bad

## Background:

**UTP Ethernet Cabling:** Cabling is one of the most critical areas of network design and implementation. Cabling is expected to last from 10 to 15 years. The quality of cable and connections is a major factor in reducing network problems and time spent troubleshooting. Unshielded Twisted Pair (UTP) copper cable is the most common in use in today's Ethernet networks. There are various categories (CAT 3, CAT 5, CAT 5e, and so on) but all of them contain 8 wires or conductors and use RJ45 connectors. A UTP patch cable in a network is usually wired as a straight-through or crossover. In order to follow proper specifications, all 8 conductors must be used even though with most earlier versions of Ethernet, not all 8 conductors were used. You will create these cables in the future labs. In this lab, you will work with several cables that have already been made and will test them for basic continuity (breaks in wires) and shorts (2 or more wires touching) using a basic cable tester (refer to the lab on resistance measurements).

**Basic Cable Testers:** There are a number of very simple and inexpensive basic cable testers available (less than $100). They usually consist of one or two small boxes with RJ45 jacks in them to plug the cables to be tested into. Many of these are designed specifically to test only the Ethernet UTP type of cable. The testers will have more than one jack to allow for testing of straight-through or crossover cable. Both ends of the cable are plugged in to the proper jacks, and the tester will test all 8 wires and indicate whether the cable is good or bad. If any of the eight wires has a break or is shorted to any of the other wires, the cable is bad. The simple testers might just have a single light to indicate this; others might have eight lights to tell you which wire is bad. These testers have internal batteries and are doing continuity checks on the wires.

**Advanced Cable Testers:** Advanced cable testers, such as the Fluke 620 LAN CableMeter, are sophisticated cable testers that have basic cable testing functions and much more. You will use an advanced cable tester in future labs to do wire maps, and so on. If an inexpensive basic cable tester is unavailable, the Fluke (or equivalent) is more than adequate. Advanced cable testers can cost from hundreds to thousands of dollars.

## Tools / Preparation:

Prior to starting the lab, the teacher or lab assistant should have several basic cable testers available (one for each team of students) or several Fluke cable meters and various lengths of wire with induced problems. Work in teams of two. Before beginning this lab, you might want to read the *Cisco Networking Academy Program: First-Year Companion Guide*, Chapter 8. You should also review semester 1 on-line Lesson 5. The following resources will be required:
- Basic cable tester
- Advanced cable tester (Fluke 620 or equivalent)
- 2 lengths of *good* CAT 5 cable (one crossover and one straight-through; use different colors or labels)

# Cisco Labs - Semester 1 – Networking Fundamentals
## *LAB 5.3.1 – BASIC CABLE TESTER - WORKSHEET*

If you are using a basic cable tester, refer to the instructions from the manufacturer and insert the ends of the cable to be tested into the jacks accordingly. If you are using the Fluke 620, use the following instructions to test the four cables. Insert the RJ45 from one end of the cable into the UTP/FTP jack on the tester and turn the dial to test. All conductors will be tested to verify they are not broken or shorted. (Note: This test does not verify that the pins are connected correctly from one end to the other.)

**Step 1.** 1st Cable test–Insert the cable into the RJ45 jack(s) of the cable tester.
    a. What is the color or cable number of this cable? _____
    b. What category type of cable is it (CAT 3, CAT 5, and so on)? _____
    c. How is the cable wired (straight-through or crossover)? _____
    d. How long is the cable? _____
    e. Did the cable test OK? _____

**Step 2.** 2nd Cable test–Insert the cable into the RJ45 jack(s) of the cable tester.
    a. What is the color or cable number of this cable? _____
    b. What category type of cable is it (CAT 3, CAT 5, and so on)? _____
    c. How is the cable wired (straight-through or crossover)? _____
    d. How long is the cable? _____
    e. Did the cable test OK? _____

**Step 3.** 3rd Cable test–Insert the cable into the RJ45 jack(s) of the cable tester.
    a. What is the color or cable number of this cable? _____
    b. What category type of cable is it (CAT 3, CAT 5, and so on)? _____
    c. How is the cable wired (straight-through or crossover)? _____
    d. How long is the cable? _____
    e. Did the cable test OK? _____

**Step 4.** 4th Cable test–Insert the cable into the RJ45 jack(s) of the cable tester.
    a. What is the color or cable number of this cable? _____
    b. What category type of cable is it (CAT 3, CAT 5, and so on)? _____
    c. How is the cable wired (straight-through or crossover)? _____
    d. How long is the cable? _____
    e. Did the cable test OK? _____

**Answers:**
**Answers will vary depending on the cables being tested and the problems they have.**

**Cisco Labs - Semester 1 – Networking Fundamentals**
## *LAB 5.3.2 – STRAIGHT-THROUGH CABLE - OVERVIEW*
### *(Estimated time: 30 minutes)*

## Objective:
- Build a straight-through Ethernet patch cable to T568-B (or T568-A) standards for connection from workstation to hub/switch or patch panel to hub/switch.

## Background:
In this lab, you will learn how to build a Category 5 (CAT 5) Unshielded Twisted Pair (UTP) Ethernet network patch cable (or patch cord) and test it for good connections (continuity) and correct pinouts (correct color of wire on the right pin). This will be a 4-pair (8 wires) "straight through" cable, which means that the color of wire on pin 1 on one end of the cable will be the same as pin 1 on the other end. Pin 2 will be the same as pin 2, and so on. It will be wired to EIA/TIA 568-B or A standards for 10Base-T Ethernet, which determines what color wire is on each pin. T568-B (also called AT&T specification) is more common, but many installations are also wired to T568-A (also called ISDN).

This patch cable will conform to the structured cabling standards and is considered to be part of the "horizontal" cabling, which is limited to 99 meters total between workstation and hub or switch. It can be used in a workstation area to connect the workstation NIC to the wall plate data jack, or it can be used in the wiring closet to connect the patch panel (horizontal cross connect) to an Ethernet hub or switch. Patch cables are wired straight thru because the cable from the workstation to the hub or switch is normally crossed over automatically at the switch or the hub. Note that the ports on most hubs have an X next to them. This means the send and receive pairs will be crossed when the cabling reaches the switch. The pinouts will be T568-B, and all 8 conductors (wires) should be terminated with RJ45 modular connectors (only 4 of the 8 wires are used for 10/100Base-T Ethernet; all 8 are used for 1000Base-T Ethernet).

## Tools / Preparation:
Prior to starting the lab, the teacher or lab assistant should have a spool of Cat 5 Unshielded Twisted Pair (UTP) cable, RJ45 (8-pin) connectors, an RJ45 crimping tool and an Ethernet/RJ45 continuity tester available. Work individually or in teams. Before beginning this lab you might want to read the *Cisco Networking Academy Program: First-Year Companion Guide*, Chapter 8. You should also review semester 1 on-line Lesson 5. The following resources will be required:

- Two to three foot length of Cat 5 cabling (one per person or one per team)
- Four RJ45 connectors (two extra for spares)
- RJ45 Crimping Tools to attach the RJ45 connectors to the cable ends
- Ethernet cabling continuity tester that can test straight through or crossover type cables (T568-A or T568-B)
- Wire cutters

# Cisco Labs - Semester 1 – Networking Fundamentals
## _LAB 5.3.2 – STRAIGHT-THROUGH CABLE - WORKSHEET_

### Step 1 – Cabling Information

**Explanation:** Instructions are provided here for building a T568-A or T568-B cable. Either can be used as long as all connections (pinouts) from the workstation to the wiring closet and terminating electronics (hubs or switches) are consistent. If cables are to be built for an existing network, it is important to keep the same standard that already exists (either T568-A or B). A patch cable that is wired "straight through" will have the same color of wire on the same pin (1–8) at both ends. A straight through patch cable (T568-A or B) can be used to connect a PC workstation to a wall plate in a work area, or it can be used to connect from a patch panel in a wiring closet to a hub or a switch. A PC can also be connected directly to a port on a hub or switch with this cable. If a cable will be used to connect from an "Uplink" port on one hub to a "crossover" front port on another hub, a straight-through cable should be used.

### Step 2 – Create a T568-B straight-through patch panel cable.

**Task:** Use the following tables and diagrams and steps to create a T568-B patch panel cable.
**Explanation:** Both cable ends should be wired the same when looking at the conductors. Only four wires are used with 10Base-T or 100Base-TX Ethernet.

**T568-B Cabling**

| Pin # | Pair # | Function | Wire Color | Used with 10/100 Base-T Ethernet? | Used with 100Base-T4 and 1000Base-T Ethernet? |
|---|---|---|---|---|---|
| 1 | 2 | Transmit | White / Orange | Yes | Yes |
| 2 | 2 | Receive | Orange / White | Yes | Yes |
| 3 | 3 | Transmit | White / Green | Yes | Yes |
| 4 | 1 | Not used | Blue / White | No | Yes |
| 5 | 1 | Not used | White / Blue | No | Yes |
| 6 | 3 | Receive | Green / White | Yes | Yes |
| 7 | 4 | Not used | White / Brown | No | Yes |
| 8 | 4 | Not used | Brown / White | No | Yes |

**Diagram showing both T568-A and T568-B cabling wire colors**

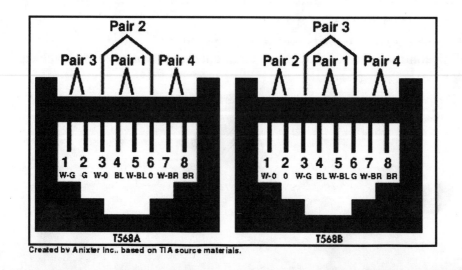

Created by Anixter Inc., based on TIA source materials.

# Cisco Labs - Semester 1 – Networking Fundamentals
## *LAB 5.3.2 – STRAIGHT-THROUGH CABLE - WORKSHEET*

1.  Determine the distance between devices, or device and plug, and then add at least 12" to it. The maximum length for this cord is 3 m; standard lengths are 6' and 10'.

2.  Cut a piece of stranded Cat 5 unshielded twisted-pair cable to a determined length. You will use stranded cable for patch cables because it is more durable when bent repeatedly. Solid wire is fine for cable runs that are punched down into jacks.

3.  Strip 2" of jacket off one end of the cable.

4.  Hold the 4 pairs of twisted cables tightly where the jacket was cut away, and then reorganize the cable pairs into the order of the 568-B wiring standard. Take care to maintain the twists because this provides noise cancellation (orange pair, green pair, blue pair, brown pair).

5.  Hold the jacket and cable in one hand, untwist a short length of the green and blue pairs, and reorder them to reflect the 568-B wiring color scheme. Untwist and order the rest of the wire pairs according to the color scheme.

6.  Flatten, straighten, and line up the wires, then trim them in a straight line to within 1/2"–3/4" from the edge of the jacket. Be sure not to let go of the jacket and the wires, which are now in order! You should minimize the length of untwisted wires because overly-long sections that are near connectors are a primary source of electrical noise.

7.  Place an RJ45 plug on the end of the cable, with the prong on the underside and the orange pair at the top of the connector.

8.  Gently push the plug onto the wires until you can see the copper ends of the wires through the end of the plug. Make sure the end of the jacket is inside the plug and all wires are in the correct order. If the jacket is not inside the plug, it will not be properly strain-relieved and will eventually cause problems. If everything is correct, crimp the plug hard enough to force the contacts through the insulation on the wires, thus completing the conducting path.

9.  Repeat Steps 3–8 to terminate the other end of the cable, using the same scheme to finish the straight through cable.

10. Test the finished cable and have the instructor check it. How can you tell if your cable is functioning properly? _____

**Answers: <u>There are several methods that can be used to check the cable.</u>**
Have the instructor check your cable and verify it using one or more of these tests:
**Visual Test:** Inspect the cable ends visually. Hold the RJ45 connectors side by side. The same color wire should be on the same pin. This is not a conclusive test but is a good start.
**Cable Test:** You can test the cable with a cable tester to verify the wires have continuity (no breaks) and are not shorted.
**Functional Test**: You can connect your cable from a workstation to a hub and verify that you can see other workstations. This is the ultimate test but requires more setup and configuration time.

# Cisco Labs - Semester 1 – Networking Fundamentals
## *LAB 5.3.3 – ROLLOVER CABLE - OVERVIEW*
### *(Estimated time: 30 minutes)*

## Objective:
* Build a rollover cable for connection from a workstation to the console port on a router or switch

## Background:
In this lab, you learn how to build a Category 5 (CAT 5) Unshielded Twisted Pair (UTP) console rollover cable and test it for good connections (continuity) and correct pinouts (correct wire on the right pin). This will be a 4-pair (8 wires) "rollover" cable.

This cable should be approximately 10 feet in length but can be as long as 25 feet. It can be used to connect a workstation or dumb terminal to the console port on the back of a router or Ethernet switch in order to be able to configure the router or switch. This cable uses an asynchronous serial interface to the router or switch (8 data bits, no parity, and 2 stop bits). Both ends of the cable you build will have RJ45 connectors on them. One end plugs directly into the RJ45 console management port on the back of the router or switch, and the other end plugs into an RJ45-to-DB9 terminal adapter. This adapter converts the RJ45 to a 9-pin female D connector that plugs into the DB9 serial port male adapter on the back of a PC running terminal emulation software such as HyperTerminal. A DB25 terminal adapter is also available to connect with a dumb terminal that has a 25-pin connector.

A rollover cable uses 8 pins but is different from the straight-through cable or crossover cable that you will build in other labs. With a rollover cable, pin 1 on one end connects to pin 8 on the other end. Pin 2 connects to pin 7, pin 3 connects to pin 6, and so on. This is why it is referred to as a rollover, because the pins on one end are all reversed on the other end as though one end of the cable was just rotated or rolled over.

A flat black rollover cable comes with each new router or switch, along with the terminal adapters for both DB9 and DB25 connections to terminals or PC serial ports. It is approximately 8 feet long. This lab will enable you to build another cable if the one that comes with the router or switch is damaged or lost. It will also allow you to connect to routers or switches from workstations that are more than 8 feet away by building your own longer cables.

## Tools / Preparation:
Prior to starting the lab, the teacher or lab assistant should have a spool of Cat 5 Unshielded Twisted Pair (UTP) cable, RJ45 (8-pin) connectors, an RJ45 crimping tool and a continuity tester available. Work individually or in teams. Before beginning this lab you might want to read the *Cisco Networking Academy Program: First-Year Companion Guide*, Chapter 8. You should also review semester 1 on-line Lesson 5. The following resources will be required:

* 10 to 20 foot length of Cat 5 cabling (one per person or one per team)
* Four RJ45 connectors (two extra for spares)
* RJ45 crimping tools to attach the RJ45 connectors to the cable end
* An RJ45 to DB9 female terminal adapter (available from Cisco)
* Cabling continuity tester
* Wire cutters

# Cisco Labs - Semester 1 – Networking Fundamentals
## *LAB 5.3.3 – ROLLOVER CABLE - WORKSHEET*

### Step 1. Review Cable Connections and Pin Locations
Use the following table as a reference to answer the following questions and to help you create a rollover console cable.

### Questions:
1. Which signal on the Router port (column 1 of the table) will be used to transmit data to the PC when the PC is first connected and HyperTerminal is started (this is what displays the router prompt on the workstation)? _____

2. Which pin is this connected to on the router end of the RJ45 cable? _____

3. Which pin is this connected to on the other end of the RJ45 cable? _____

4. Which pin is this connected to in the DB9 connector? _____

5. Which console device signal does this connect to? _____

6. What would happen if pin 3 on the left cable end were attached to pin 3 as with a straight-through cable? _____
_____

### Rollover Console Cable Table
For connecting from a router or switch console port to a PC workstation running HyperTerminal terminal emulation software. Console port signaling and cabling using an RJ45 rollover and DB9 adapter.

| Router or switch Console port (DTE) | RJ45 to RJ45 Rollover Cable (left end) | RJ45 to RJ45 Rollover Cable (right end) | RJ45 to DB9 Adapter | Console Device (PC workstation serial port) |
|---|---|---|---|---|
| Signal | From RJ45 Pin No. | To RJ45 Pin No. | DB9 Pin No. | Signal |
| RTS | 1 | 8 | 8 | CTS |
| DTR | 2 | 7 | 6 | DSR |
| TxD | 3 | 6 | 2 | RxD |
| GND | 4 | 5 | 5 | GND |
| GND | 5 | 4 | 5 | GND |
| RxD | 6 | 3 | 3 | TxD |
| DSR | 7 | 2 | 4 | DTR |
| CTS | 8 | 1 | 7 | RTS |

Signal Legend: RTS = Request To Send, DTR = Data Terminal Ready, TxD = Transmit Data, GND = Ground (one for TxD and one for RxD), RxD = Receive Data, DSR = Data Set Ready, CTS = Clear To Send

# Cisco Labs - Semester 1 – Networking Fundamentals
## *LAB 5.3.3 – ROLLOVER CABLE - WORKSHEET*

**Step 2. Use the following steps to build the rollover console cable.**

1.  Determine the distance between devices, and then add at least 12" to it. Make your cable about 10 feet unless you are connecting to a router or switch from a greater distance. The maximum length for this cable is about 8m (approximately 25 feet).

2.  Strip 2" of jacket off one end of the cable.

3.  Hold the 4 pairs of twisted cables tightly where the jacket was cut away, and then reorganize the cable pairs and wires into the order of the 568-B wiring standard. You can order them in any sequence but use the 568-B sequence to become more familiar with it.

4.  Flatten, straighten, and line up the wires, and then trim them in a straight line to within 1/2"-3/4" from the edge of the jacket. Be sure not to let go of the jacket and the wires, which are now in order!

5.  Place an RJ45 plug on the end of the cable, with the prong on the underside and the orange pair at the top of the connector.

6.  Gently push the plug onto the wires until you can see the copper ends of the wires through the end of the plug. Make sure the end of the jacket is inside the plug and all wires are in the correct order. If the jacket is not inside the plug, it will not be properly strain-relieved and will eventually cause problems. If everything is correct, crimp the plug hard enough to force the contacts through the insulation on the wires, thus completing the conducting path.

7.  Repeat Steps 2-6 to terminate the other end of the cable, but reversing every pair of wires as indicated in the table above (pin 1 to pin 8, pin 2 to pin 7, pin 3 to pin 6, and so on).

8.  Test the finished cable and have the instructor check it. How can you tell if your cable is functioning properly?

_____
_____
_____
_____
_____

# Cisco Labs - Semester 1 – Networking Fundamentals
## *LAB 5.3.3 – ROLLOVER CABLE - ANSWERS*

**Step 1. Review Cable Connections and Pin Locations**
Use the following table as a reference to help create a rollover console cable.

**Questions:**
1.  Which signal on the Router port (column 1 of the table) will be used to transmit data (showing the router prompt, and so on) to the PC when the PC is first connected and HyperTerminal is started? **TxD**

2.  Which Pin is this connected to on the router end of the RJ45 cable? **3**

3.  Which pin is this connected to on the other end of the RJ45 cable? **6**

4.  Which pin is this connected to in the DB9 connector? **2**

5.  Which console device signal does this connect to? **RxD**

6.  What would happen if Pin 3 on the left cable end were attached to pin 3 as with a straight-through cable? **Transmit Data (TxD) from the router would be connected to the Transmit Data (TxD) on the workstation, and they would never communicate.**


**Step 2. Use the following steps to build the rollover console cable.**

8.  Test the finished cable and have the instructor check it. How can you tell if your cable is functioning properly? **There are several methods that can be used to check the cable.**

**Visual Test:** The cable ends can be visually inspected and should be wired exactly opposite when looking at the conductors and holding the RJ45 connectors side by side with the clip facing down. If you hold the RJ45 connectors end to end with the clip facing down, the wire colors should match. Pinouts are listed in the table.

**Cable Test:** You can test the cable with a cable tester to verify the wires have continuity (no breaks) and are not shorted.

**Functional Test**: You can connect your rollover cable to the RJ45-to-DB9 terminal adapter and connect a workstation to the router to verify that you can see the router console prompts. This is the ultimate test and also requires that HyperTerminal be set up properly on the workstation (8 data bits, no parity, 2 stop bits).

# Cisco Labs - Semester 1 – Networking Fundamentals
## LAB 5.3.4 – CROSSOVER CABLE - OVERVIEW
### (Estimated time: 30 minutes)

## Objective:
- Build a crossover Ethernet patch cable to T568-B (OR T568-A) standards for connection from workstation to workstation or from switch to switch.

## Background:
In this lab you will learn how to build a Category 5 (CAT 5) Unshielded Twisted Pair (UTP) Ethernet crossover network cable and test it for good connections (continuity) and correct pinouts (correct color of wire on the right pin). This will be a 4-pair (8 wires) "crossover" cable, which means that pairs 2 and 3 on one end of the cable will be reversed on the other end. It will be wired to EIA/TIA 568-B and A standards for 10Base-T Ethernet, which determines what color wire is on each pin. The pinouts will be T568-A on one end and T568-B on the other end. All eight conductors (wires) should be terminated with RJ45 modular connectors.

This patch cable will conform to the structured cabling standards and, if it is used between hubs or switches, is considered to be part of the "vertical" cabling, also know as backbone cable. A crossover cable can be used as a backbone cable to connect two or more hubs or switches in a LAN or to connect two isolated workstations to create a mini-LAN. This will allow you to connect two workstations together or a server and a workstation without the need for a hub between them. This can be helpful for training and testing. If you want to connect more than two workstations, you will need a hub or a switch.

## Tools / Preparation:
Prior to starting the lab, the teacher or lab assistant should have a spool of Cat 5 Unshielded Twisted Pair (UTP) cable, RJ45 (8-pin) connectors, an RJ45 crimping tool and an Ethernet/RJ45 continuity tester available. Work individually or in teams. Before beginning this lab you might want to read the *Cisco Networking Academy Program: First-Year Companion Guide*, Chapter 8. You should also review semester 1 on-line Lesson 5. The following resources will be required:

- Two to three foot length of Cat 5 cabling (one per person or one per team)
- Four RJ45 connectors (two extra for spares)
- RJ45 crimping tools to attach the RJ45 connectors to the cable ends
- Ethernet cabling continuity tester that can test crossover type cables (T568-A to T568-B)
- Wire cutters

# Cisco Labs - Semester 1 – Networking Fundamentals
## *LAB 5.3.4 – CROSSOVER CABLE - WORKSHEET*

### Step 1. Create a crossover patch panel cable.

Use the following tables and diagrams and steps to create a crossover cable. One end of the cable should be wired to the T568-A standard and the other end to the T568-B standard. This crosses the transmit and receive pairs (2 and 3) to allow communication to take place. Only four wires are used with 10Base-T or 100Base-TX Ethernet.

### T568-A Cabling

| Pin # | Pair # | Function | Wire Color | Used with 10Base-T and 100 Base-TX Ethernet? | Used with 100Base-T4 and 1000Base-T Ethernet? |
|---|---|---|---|---|---|
| 1 | 3 | Transmit | White / Green | Yes | Yes |
| 2 | 3 | Receive | Green / White | Yes | Yes |
| 3 | 2 | Transmit | White / Orange | Yes | Yes |
| 4 | 1 | Not used | Blue / White | No | Yes |
| 5 | 1 | Not used | White / Blue | No | Yes |
| 6 | 2 | Receive | Orange / White | Yes | Yes |
| 7 | 4 | Not used | White / Brown | No | Yes |
| 8 | 4 | Not used | Brown / White | No | Yes |

### T568-B Cabling

| Pin # | Pair # | Function | Wire Color | Used with 10/100 Base-T Ethernet? | Used with 100Base-T4 and 1000Base-T Ethernet? |
|---|---|---|---|---|---|
| 1 | 2 | Transmit | White / Orange | Yes | Yes |
| 2 | 2 | Receive | Orange / White | Yes | Yes |
| 3 | 3 | Transmit | White / Green | Yes | Yes |
| 4 | 1 | Not used | Blue / White | No | Yes |
| 5 | 1 | Not used | White / Blue | No | Yes |
| 6 | 3 | Receive | Green / White | Yes | Yes |
| 7 | 4 | Not used | White / Brown | No | Yes |
| 8 | 4 | Not used | Brown / White | No | Yes |

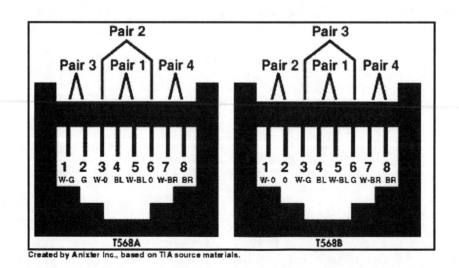

Created by Anixter Inc., based on TIA source materials.

# Cisco Labs - Semester 1 – Networking Fundamentals
## *LAB 5.3.4 – CROSSOVER CABLE – WORKSHEET*

1. Determine the distance between devices, or device and plug, and then add at least 12" to it. The maximum length for this cord is 3 m; standard lengths are 6' and 10'.

2. Cut a piece of stranded Cat 5 unshielded twisted-pair cable to the determined length. You will use stranded cable for patch cables because it is more durable when bent repeatedly. Solid wire is fine for cable runs that are punched down into jacks.

3. Strip 2" of jacket off one end of the cable.

4. Hold the 4 pairs of twisted cables tightly where the jacket was cut away, and then reorganize the cable pairs into the order of the 568-B wiring standard. Take care to maintain the twists because this provides noise cancellation (orange pair, green pair, blue pair, brown pair).

5. Hold the jacket and cable in one hand, untwist a short length of the green and blue pairs, and reorder them to reflect the 568-B wiring color scheme. Untwist and order the rest of the wire pairs according to the color scheme.

6. Flatten, straighten, and line up the wires, then trim them in a straight line to within 1/2"-3/4" from the edge of the jacket. Be sure not to let go of the jacket and the wires, which are now in order! You should minimize the length of untwisted wires because overly-long sections that are near connectors are a primary source of electrical noise.

7. Place an RJ45 plug on the end of the cable, with the prong on the underside and the orange pair at the top of the connector.

8. Gently push the plug onto the wires until you can see the copper ends of the wires through the end of the plug. Make sure the end of the jacket is inside the plug and all wires are in the correct order. If the jacket is not inside the plug, it will not be properly strain-relieved and will eventually cause problems. If everything is correct, crimp the plug hard enough to force the contacts through the insulation on the wires, thus completing the conducting path.

9. Repeat Steps 3-8 to terminate the other end of the cable, using the 568-A scheme to finish the crossover cable.

10. Test the finished cable and have the instructor check it. How can you tell if your cable is functioning properly? _____

**Answers: <u>There are several methods that can be used to check the cable.</u>**
Have the instructor check your cable and verify it using one or more of these tests:
**Visual Test:** Inspect the cable ends visually. Hold the RJ45 connectors side by side. The same color wire should be on the same pin. This is not a conclusive test but is a good start.
**Cable Test:** You can test the cable with a cable tester to verify the wires have continuity (no breaks) and are not shorted.
**Functional Test**: You can connect your cable from a workstation to a hub and verify that you can see other workstations. This is the ultimate test but requires more setup and configuration time.

## Cisco Labs - Semester 1 – Networking Fundamentals
# LAB 5.3.5 – CABLE TESTER - WIRE MAP - OVERVIEW
### (Estimated time: 45 minutes)

## Objectives:
- Demonstrate skill with a cable tester more advanced than a simple continuity/pin-out tester
- Use the wire mapping features of the tester to check for opens and shorts with UTP cable
- Perform wire mapping on cables, detecting faults that are not detectable with simple continuity measuring devices such as crossed and split pairs

## Background:
In this lab, you will learn the wire mapping features of the Fluke 620 LAN CableMeter (or its equivalent). Wire maps can be very helpful in troubleshooting cabling problems with UTP cable. Wire maps are not used with coaxial cable because there is only one wire and no map is needed. A wire map allows the network technician to verify which pins on one end of the cable are connected to which pins on the other end. With an understanding of the proper wiring connections, you can determine when a cable is wired improperly, depending on its intended use. You will learn how to use a cable tester to check for the proper installation of Unshielded Twisted Pair (UTP) Category 5 (CAT 5) according to EIA/TIA 568 cabling standards in an Ethernet network. You will test different cables using all four pairs to determine some problems that can occur from incorrect cabling installation and termination.

The cabling infrastructure (or cable plant) in a building is expected to last at least 10 years. Cabling-related problems are one of the most common causes of network failure. The quality of cabling components used, the routing and installation of the cable and quality of the connector terminations will be the main factors in determining how trouble-free the cabling will be.

## Tools / Preparation:
Prior to starting the lab, the teacher or lab assistant should have several correctly wired CAT 5 cables (both straight-through and crossover) to test. There should also be several CAT 5 cables created with problems such as poor connections and split pairs to test. Cables should be numbered to simplify the testing process and to maintain consistency. A cable tester should be available that can test at least continuity, cable length and wire map. Work individually or in teams. Before beginning this lab, you should read the *Cisco Networking Academy Program: First-Year Companion Guide*, Chapter 8. You should also review semester 1 on-line Lesson 5. The following resources will be required:

- CAT 5 straight-wired cables of different colors
- CAT 5 crossover-wired cable (T568A on one end and T568B on the other)
- CAT 5 straight-wired cables with open wire connections in the middle or one or more conductors shorted at one end of different colors and different lengths
- CAT 5 straight-wired cable with a split pair miswire
- Cable tester (Fluke 620 LAN CableMeter or similar) to test cable length, continuity, wire map

## Related Research Web Sites:
http://www.bicsi.org/techsem
http://www.fluke.com/

**Cisco Labs - Semester 1 – Networking Fundamentals**
## *LAB 5.3.5 – CABLE TESTER - WIRE MAP - WORKSHEET*

### Step 1. Set the Advanced Cable Tester for the Desired cable

These instructions pertain to the Fluke 620 LAN CableMeter. Turn the rotary switch selector on the tester to the WIRE MAP position. Press the SETUP button to enter the setup mode and observe the LCD screen on the tester. The first option should be CABLE. Press the UP or DOWN buttons until the desired cable type of UTP is selected. Press ENTER to accept that setting and go to the next one. Continue pressing the UP/DOWN arrows and pressing ENTER until the tester is set to the following cabling characteristics:

| Tester Option | Desired Setting |
|---|---|
| CABLE: | UTP |
| WIRING: | 10BASE-T or EIA/TIA 4PR |
| CATEGORY: | CAT 5 |
| WIRE SIZE | AWG 24 |
| CAL to CABLE? | NO |
| BEEPING: | ON or OFF |
| LCD CONTRAST | From 1 thru 10 (brightest) |

### Step 2. Set up the Cable to be Tested

For each cable to be tested with the following tests, place the near end of the cable into the RJ45 jack labeled UTP/FTP on the tester. Place the RJ45-RJ45 female coupler on the far end of the cable and then insert the Cable Identifier into the other side of the coupler. The coupler and the cable identifier are accessories that come with the Fluke 620 LAN CableMeter.

### Step 3. Perform Wire Map Testing

Using the tester's Wire Map function and a Cable ID unit, you can determine the wiring of both the near and far end of the cable. The top set of numbers displayed on the LCD screen is the near end and the bottom set is the far end. Perform a Wire Map test on each of the cables provided and fill in the following table based on the result for each CAT 5 cable tested. For each cable, write down the number and color, whether the cable is straight thru or crossover, the tester screen test results and what you think the problem is.

| Cable No. | Cable Color | How cable is wired (straight-through or crossover) | Tester Displayed Test Results (Note: refer to the Fluke manual for detailed description of test results for wire map) | Problem Description |
|---|---|---|---|---|
| 1 | | | Top:<br>Bot: | |
| 2 | | | Top:<br>Bot: | |
| 3 | | | Top:<br>Bot: | |
| 4 | | | Top:<br>Bot: | |
| 5 | | | Top:<br>Bot: | |

# Cisco Labs - Semester 1 – Networking Fundamentals
## *LAB 5.3.5 – CABLE TESTER - WIRE MAP - ANSWERS*

### Step 1. Set the Advanced Cable Tester for the Desired cable

These instructions pertain to the Fluke 620 LAN Cablemeter. Turn the rotary switch selector on the tester to the WIRE MAP position. Press the SETUP button to enter the setup mode and observe the LCD screen on the tester. The first option should be CABLE. Press the UP or DOWN buttons until the desired cable type of UTP is selected. Press ENTER to accept that setting and go to the next one. Continue pressing the UP/DOWN arrows and pressing ENTER until the tester is set to the following cabling characteristics:

| Tester Option | Desired Setting |
|---|---|
| CABLE | UTP |
| WIRING | 10BASE-T or EIA/TIA 4PR |
| CATEGORY | CAT 5 |
| WIRE SIZE | AWG 24 |
| CAL to CABLE? | NO |
| BEEPING | ON or OFF |
| LCD CONTRAST | From 1 thru 10 (brightest) |

### Step 2. Set up the Cable to be Tested

For each cable to be tested with the following tests, place the near end of the cable into the RJ45 jack labeled UTP/FTP on the tester. Place the RJ45-RJ45 female coupler on the far end of the cable and then insert the Cable Identifier into the other side of the coupler. The coupler and the cable identifier are accessories that come with the Fluke 620 LAN CableMeter:

### Step 3. Perform Wire Map Testing.

Using the tester's Wire Map function and a Cable ID unit, you can determine the wiring of both the near and far end of the cable. The top set of numbers displayed on the LCD screen is the near end and the bottom set is the far end. Perform a Wire Map test on each of the cables provided and fill in the following table based on the result for each CAT 5 cable tested. For each cable, write down the number and color, whether the cable is straight-through or crossover, the tester screen test results and what you think the problem is. (Your answers might vary.)

| Cable No. | Cable Color | How cable is wired (straight-through or crossover) | Tester Displayed Test Results (Note: refer to the Fluke manual for detailed description of test results for wire map) | | Problem Description |
|---|---|---|---|---|---|
| 1 | Red | Straight-through | Top: 1 2  3 6  4 5  7 8 <br> Bot: 1 2  3 6  4 5  7 8 | ID <br> #1 | Wire is OK for a straight-through cable |
| 2 | Blue | Straight-through | Top: 1 2  3 6  o <br> Bot: 1 2  3 6 | ID <br> #1 | Open (o means wire no. 2 open) |
| 3 | Yellow | Straight-through | Top: **2 3**  1  6 <br> Bot: | ID <br> #1 | Short (wires 2 & 3 touching - near end) |
| 4 | Green | Straight-through | Top: **1 3  2 6** <br> Bot: **1 3  2 6** | ID <br> #1 | Split Pair |
| 5 | Orange | Crossover | Top: 1 2  3 6  4 5  7 8 <br> Bot: 3 6  1 2  4 5  7 8 | ID <br> #1 | Wire is OK for a crossover cable |

**Cisco Labs - Semester 1 – Networking Fundamentals**
## *LAB 5.3.6 – STRAIGHT-THROUGH CABLE TESTER - OVERVIEW*
*(Estimated time: 45 minutes)*

## Objectives:
- Demonstrate skill with a cable tester more advanced than a simple continuity/pin-out tester
- Use the Test feature of the tester to check for opens and shorts with coax and UTP cable
- Understand the use of the Cable ID feature

## Background:
In this lab, you will learn the Cable Test – Pass / Fail features of the Fluke 620 LAN CableMeter (or its equivalent). Basic cable tests can be very helpful in troubleshooting cabling problems with UTP and coaxial cable. You will learn how to use a cable tester to check for the proper installation of Unshielded Twisted Pair (UTP) and Coaxial (Thinnet) for an Ethernet network. You will test different cables to determine some problems that can occur from incorrect cabling installation and termination.

The cabling infrastructure (or cable plant) in a building is expected to last at least 10 years. Cabling-related problems are one of the most common causes of network failure. The quality of cabling components used, the routing and installation of the cable and quality of the connector terminations will be the main factors in determining how trouble-free the cabling will be.

## Tools / Preparation:
Prior to starting the lab, the teacher or lab assistant should have several correctly wired CAT 5 cables (both straight-through and crossover) to test. There should also be several CAT 5 cables created with problems and a coaxial cable to test. Cables should be numbered to simplify the testing process and to maintain consistency. A cable tester should be available that can do a basic cable test for UTP and coax. Work individually or in teams. Before beginning this lab, you should read the *Cisco Networking Academy Program: First-Year Companion Guide*, Chapter 8. You should also review semester 1 on-line Lesson 5. The following resources will be required:

- CAT 5 straight-through and crossover wired cables of different colors (some good and some bad)
- CAT 5 straight-through and crossover wired cables with open wire connections in the middle or one or more conductors shorted at one end of different colors and different lengths
- Coax cable with a short in it
- Cable tester (Fluke 620 LAN CableMeter or similar) to test cable length, continuity, wire map

## Related Research Web Sites:
Here are several web sites where you can get additional information on cabling standards:
http://www.bicsi.org/techsem
http://www.fluke.com/

**Cisco Labs - Semester 1 – Networking Fundamentals**
## *LAB 5.3.6 ¬STRAIGHT-THROUGH CABLE TESTER - WORKSHEET*

### Step 1. Set the Advanced Cable Tester for the Desired cable (UTP or COAX)

These instructions pertain to the Fluke 620 LAN CableMeter. Turn the rotary switch selector on the tester to the TEST position. Press the SETUP button to enter the setup mode and observe the LCD screen on the tester. The first option should be CABLE. Press the UP or DOWN buttons until the desired cable type of UTP or COAX (thinnet) is selected. Press ENTER to accept that setting and go to the next one. Continue pressing the UP/DOWN arrows and pressing ENTER until the tester is set to the following cabling characteristics, depending on the type of cable you will be testing:

| Tester Option | Desired Setting - UTP | Desired Setting - COAX |
| --- | --- | --- |
| CABLE | UTP | COAX |
| WIRING | 10BASET or EIA/TIA 4PR | 10BASE2 or RG58 (thinnet) |
| CATEGORY | CAT 5 | N/A |
| WIRE SIZE | AWG 24 | N/A |
| CAL to CABLE? | NO | NO |
| BEEPING | ON or OFF | ON or OFF |
| LCD CONTRAST | From 1 thru 10 (brightest) | From 1 thru 10 (brightest) |

### Step 2. Set up the Cable to be Tested (UTP or COAX)

For each UTP cable to be tested with the following tests, place the near end of the cable into the RJ-45 jack labeled UTP/FTP on the tester. Place the RJ-45-RJ-45 female coupler on the far end of the cable and then insert the Cable Identifier into the other side of the coupler. The coupler and the cable identifier are accessories that come with the Fluke 620 LAN CableMeter. Multiple Cable IDs with different numbers can be purchased to help in identifying which cable you are working with. For coax cables, insert one end of the BNC connector into the jack labeled COAX on the tester. Coax cables should not have a terminating resistor.

### Step 3. Perform Basic Cable Test – Pass/Fail Function

Using the tester's Test function and a Cable ID unit (for UTP), you can determine the functionality of the cable. Perform a basic cable test on each of the cables provided and fill in the following table based on the result for each cable tested. For each cable, write down the number and color, whether the cable is straight-through or crossover or coaxial, the tester screen test results and what you think the problem is. The Cable ID can be used to identify a particular cable by moving it to another cable.

| Cable No. | Cable Color | How cable is wired (UTP or coax) | Tester Displayed Test Results (Note: refer to the Fluke manual for detailed description of test results) | Problem Description |
| --- | --- | --- | --- | --- |
| 1 | | | | |
| 2 | | | | |
| 3 | | | | |
| 4 | | | | |

# Cisco Labs - Semester 1 – Networking Fundamentals
## *LAB 5.3.6 – STRAIGHT-THROUGH CABLE TESTER - ANSWERS*

### Step 1. Set the Advanced Cable Tester for the Desired cable (UTP or COAX)

These instructions pertain to the Fluke 620 LAN CableMeter. Turn the rotary switch selector on the tester to the TEST position. Press the SETUP button to enter the setup mode and observe the LCD screen on the tester. The first option should be CABLE. Press the UP or DOWN buttons until the desired cable type of UTP or COAX (thinnet) is selected. Press ENTER to accept that setting and go to the next one. Continue pressing the UP/DOWN arrows and pressing ENTER until the tester is set to the following cabling characteristics:

| Tester Option | Desired Setting - UTP | Desired Setting - COAX |
|---|---|---|
| CABLE | UTP | COAX |
| WIRING | 10BASET or EIA/TIA 4PR | 10BASE2 or RG58 (thinnet) |
| CATEGORY | CAT 5 | N/A |
| WIRE SIZE | AWG 24 | N/A |
| CAL to CABLE? | NO | NO |
| BEEPING | ON or OFF | ON or OFF |
| LCD CONTRAST | From 1 thru 10 (brightest) | From 1 thru 10 (brightest) |

### Step 2. Set up the Cable to be Tested (UTP or COAX)

For each UTP cable to be tested with the following tests, place the near end of the cable into the RJ-45 jack labeled UTP/FTP on the tester. Place the RJ-45-RJ-45 female coupler on the far end of the cable and then insert the Cable Identifier into the other side of the coupler. The coupler and the cable identifier are accessories that come with the Fluke 620 LAN CableMeter. Multiple Cable IDs with different numbers can be purchased to help in identify which cable you are working with. For coax cables, insert one end of the BNC connector into the jack labeled COAX on the tester. Coax cables should not have a terminating resistor.

### Step 3. Perform Basic Cable Test – Pass/Fail Function

Using the tester's Test function and a Cable ID unit (for UTP), you can determine the functionality of the cable. Perform a basic cable test on each of the cables provided and fill in the following table based on the result for each cable tested. For each cable, write down the number and color, whether the cable is straight-through or crossover or coaxial, the tester screen test results and what you think the problem is. The Cable ID can be used to identify a particular cable by moving it to another cable. (Your answers might vary.)

| Cable No. | Cable Color | How cable is wired (UTP or coax) | Tester Displayed Test Results (Note: refer to the Fluke manual for detailed description of test results) | | | Problem Description |
|---|---|---|---|---|---|---|
| 1 | Red | Straight-through UTP | Top: PASS<br>Bot:  7' | | ID<br>#1 | Wire is OK for a straight-through |
| 2 | Blue | Straight-through UTP | Top: FAIL<br>Bot:  1 2 | **SHORT** | ID #1<br><8' | Short (wires 1 & 2 touching appx. 8') |
| 3 | Yellow | Straight-through UTP | Top: FAIL<br>Bot:  1 2 | **OPEN** | ID #1<br>@7' | Open (wires 1 and 2 open at far end 7') |
| 4 | Black | Thinnet Coax (RG58) – No cable ID used | COAX | **SHORT** | < 12' | Center conductor touching braided sheathing appx 12' |

# Cisco Labs - Semester 1 – Networking Fundamentals
## *LAB 5.3.7 – CABLE TESTER - LENGTH- OVERVIEW*
### *(Estimated time: 45 minutes)*

## Objectives:
- Demonstrate skill with a cable tester more advanced than a simple continuity/pin-out tester
- Use the Length features of the tester to check for opens and shorts with coax and UTP cable

## Background:
In this lab, you will learn the Cable Length feature of the Fluke 620 LAN CableMeter (or its equivalent). Cable length tests can be very helpful in troubleshooting cabling problems with UTP and coaxial cable. You will learn how to use a cable tester to check the length of Ethernet cabling to verify that it is within the standards specified and that the wires inside are the same length (for UTP). You will test different cables including UTP and Coax to determine their length.

The cabling infrastructure (or cable plant) in a building is expected to last at least 10 years. Cabling-related problems are one of the most common causes of network failure. The quality of cabling components used, the routing and installation of the cable and quality of the connector terminations will be the main factors in determining how trouble-free the cabling will be.

## Tools / Preparation:
Prior to starting the lab, the teacher or lab assistant should have several correctly wired CAT 5 cables (both straight-through and crossover) and several Coaxial (thinnet) cables to test. Cables should be numbered to simplify the testing process and to maintain consistency. A cable tester should be available that can do cable length tests for UTP and coax. Work individually or in teams. Before beginning this lab you should read the *Cisco Networking Academy Program: First-Year Companion Guide*, Chapter 8. You should also review semester 1 on-line Lesson 5. The following resources will be required:

- CAT 5 straight-through or crossover cables of different colors (some good and some bad)
- Coax (thinnet) cables of different lengths
- Cable Tester (Fluke 620 LAN CableMeter or similar) to test cable length

## Related Research Web Sites:
Here are several web sites where you can get additional information on cabling standards:
http://www.bicsi.org/techsem
http://www.fluke.com/

# Cisco Labs - Semester 1 – Networking Fundamentals
## _LAB 5.3.7 – CABLE TESTER - LENGTH - WORKSHEET_

### Step 1. Set the Advanced Cable Tester for the Desired cable (UTP or COAX)

These instructions pertain to the Fluke 620 LAN CableMeter. Turn the rotary switch selector on the tester to the LENGTH position. Press the SETUP button to enter the setup mode and observe the LCD screen on the tester. The first option should be CABLE. Press the UP or DOWN buttons until the desired cable type of UTP or COAX (thinnet) is selected. Press ENTER to accept that setting and go to the next one. Continue pressing the UP/DOWN arrows and pressing ENTER until the tester is set to the following cabling characteristics, depending on the type of cable you will be testing:

| Tester Option | Desired Setting - UTP | Desired Setting - COAX |
|---|---|---|
| CABLE | UTP | COAX |
| WIRING | 10BASET or EIA/TIA 4PR | 10BASE2 or RG58 (thinnet) |
| CATEGORY | CAT 5 | N/A |
| WIRE SIZE | AWG 24 | N/A |
| CAL to CABLE? | NO | NO |
| BEEPING | ON or OFF | ON or OFF |
| LCD CONTRAST | From 1 thru 10 (brightest) | From 1 thru 10 (brightest) |

### Step 2. Set up the Cable to be Tested (UTP or COAX)

For each UTP cable to be tested with the following tests, place the near end of the cable into the RJ45 jack labeled UTP/FTP on the tester. Place the RJ45-RJ45 female coupler on the far end of the cable and then insert the Cable Identifier into the other side of the coupler. The coupler and the cable identifier are accessories that come with the Fluke 620 LAN CableMeter. For coax cables, insert one end of the BNC connector into the jack labeled COAX on the tester. Coax cables should not be terminated. If tested with a terminating resistor (50Ω), the display will be the resistance of the cable plus the terminating resistor.

### Step 3. Perform Cable Length Test Function

Using the tester's Test function and a Cable ID Unit (for UTP), you can determine the functionality of the cable. Perform a basic cable test on each of the cables provided and fill in the following table based on the result for each CAT 5 cable tested. For each cable, write down the number and color, whether the cable is straight-through or crossover or coaxial, the tester screen test results and what you think the problem is. For UTP cables, press the down arrow or up arrow to see all pairs.

| Cable No. | Cable Color | How cable is wired (UTP or coax) | Tester Displayed Test Results (Note: refer to the Fluke manual for detailed description of test results) | Problem |
|---|---|---|---|---|
| 1 | | | | |
| 2 | | | | |
| 3 | | | | |

# Cisco Labs - Semester 1 – Networking Fundamentals
## _LAB 5.3.7 – CABLE TESTER - LENGTH - ANSWERS_

### Step 1. Set the Advanced Cable Tester for the Desired cable (UTP or COAX)

These instructions pertain to the Fluke 620 LAN CableMeter. Turn the rotary switch selector on the tester to the LENGTH position. Press the SETUP button to enter the setup mode and observe the LCD screen on the tester. The first option should be CABLE Press the UP or DOWN buttons until the desired cable type of UTP or COAX (thinnet) is selected. Press ENTER to accept that setting and go to the next one. Continue pressing the UP/DOWN arrows and pressing ENTER until the tester is set to the following cabling characteristics, depending on the type of cable you will be testing:

| Tester Option | Desired Setting - UTP | Desired Setting - COAX |
|---|---|---|
| CABLE | UTP | COAX |
| WIRING | 10BASET or EIA/TIA 4PR | 10BASE2 or RG58 (thinnet) |
| CATEGORY | CAT 5 | N/A |
| WIRE SIZE | AWG 24 | N/A |
| CAL to CABLE? | NO | NO |
| BEEPING | ON or OFF | ON or OFF |
| LCD CONTRAST | From 1 thru 10 (brightest) | From 1 thru 10 (brightest) |

### Step 2. Set up the Cable to be Tested (UTP or COAX)

For each UTP cable to be tested with the following tests, place the near end of the cable into the RJ45 jack labeled UTP/FTP on the tester. Place the RJ45-RJ45 female coupler on the far end of the cable and then insert the Cable Identifier into the other side of the coupler. The coupler and the cable identifier are accessories that come with the Fluke 620 LAN CableMeter. For coax cables, insert one end of the BNC connector into the jack labeled COAX on the tester. Coax cables should not be terminated. If tested with a terminating resistor (50Ω), the display will be the resistance of the cable plus the terminating resistor.

### Step 3. Perform Cable Length Test Function

Using the tester's Test function and a Cable ID unit (for UTP), you can determine the functionality of the cable. Perform a basic cable test on each of the cables provided and fill in the following table based on the result for each CAT 5 cable tested. For each cable, write down the number and color, whether the cable is straight-through or crossover or coaxial, the tester screen test results and what you think the problem is. For UTP cables, press the down arrow or up arrow to see all pairs.

| Cable No. | Cable Color | How cable is wired (UTP or coax) | Tester Displayed Test Results (Note: refer to the Fluke manual for detailed description of test results) | | Problem |
|---|---|---|---|---|---|
| 1 | Red | Straight-through UTP | 1 2<br>3 6<br>4 5<br>7 8 | 7'<br>7'<br>7'<br>7' | Wire is OK for a straight-through. All 4 pairs are 7' long. |
| 2 | Blue | Straight-through UTP | 1 2<br>3 6<br>4 5<br>7 8 | 12'<br>12'<br>12'<br>12' | Wire is OK for a straight-through. All 4 pairs are 12' long. |
| 3 | Black | Thinnet Coax (RG58) | COAX | 8' | Wire is OK for coax – 8' long. |

**Cisco Labs - Semester 1 – Networking Fundamentals**
## *LAB 7.6.2 – NETWORK DISCOVERY - OVERVIEW*
### *(Estimated time: 20 minutes)*

## Objective:

- Use Network Inspector (or equivalent) software to perform network discovery

## Background:

One of the most powerful tools for troubleshooting computer networks is Network Management software. There are many fine programs for performing various network discovery, monitoring, and analysis tasks. In this lab you will explore a basic network management application: Fluke Network Inspector 3.0 (or equivalent). You will use the Network Inspector to perform a process called network discovery. As the number of computers, servers, printers, switches, and routers on a network grows, it can be difficult to keep track of all the relevant characteristics of the devices. Such information as MAC addresses, IP addresses, and topologies is crucial for troubleshooting a network. You will use Network Inspector to perform a network discovery on an Ethernet 10Base-T (or 100Base-TX) network.

## Tools / Preparation:

Each PC must be running Windows 95, 98, or NT, Microsoft TCP/IP stack, and Winsock 2.0. Fluke Network Inspector 3.0 (or equivalent) must be installed on each PC. During the installation of the software you must specify which network adapter (NIC, dial-up, and so on) you wish to monitor. Specify the NIC that attaches the PC to an Ethernet. The PCs should be on either a 10Base-T or 100Base-TX Ethernet network that preferably includes servers, switches, routers, and printers (this will make the network discovery more interesting). Before beginning this lab, you should read the *Cisco Networking Academy Program: First-Year Companion Guide*, Chapter 19. You should also review semester 1 on-line Lesson 7. The following resources will be required:

- PC with Windows 95, 98, or NT, Microsoft TCP/IP stack, and Winsock 2.0.
- Fluke Network Inspector 3.0 software

**Cisco Labs - Semester 1 – Networking Fundamentals**
## *LAB 7.6.2 – NETWORK DISCOVERY - WORKSHEET*

1. If you have not done so already, install Network Inspector software (the "Agent" and the "Console") on your PC. How will you know this step was done correctly?

   _____

2. Make sure you are connected to a working Ethernet network. What are some signs that you are on the network? _____

   _____

3. Open Fluke Network Inspector Agent. You will be prompted to do something. What are you prompted to do and why do you suppose you must do this? Click OK when finished.

   _____

4. Now the Agent will prompt you with a status screen. Click on the tabs and write down what are the major categories of things you can control about the Agent. Under the database/address tab, click on "overwrite" so that the new data you are collecting will be stored in the database. Click Apply. _____

5. Start the Agent. What is the status shown? What does the status change to after a few minutes? What do you suppose is happening? Minimize the Agent.

   _____

   _____

6. Open Fluke Network Inspector Console. What do you see? _____

   _____

7. Allow the Agent to run for a few minutes. What do you see? _____

8. Stop the Agent and minimize the Agent screen. What significant information about the network have you obtained? Write down a few complete lines of the database.

   _____

   _____

   _____

9. In the left of the Control Panel, click each of the "Devices" and explain briefly what they are: "Fluke Tools," "Key Devices," "Utilization Sources," "SNMP Agents," "Servers," "Routers," "Switches," "Printers," and "Hosts."

   _____

   _____

   _____

10. Close the Agent and the Console. You have begun using a very powerful piece of software.

**Reflection:** Imagine you have earned your CCNA and are working in a medium-sized company. Write in your journal what value you see in using Network Management software.

   _____

   _____

# Cisco Labs- Semester 1 – Networking Fundamentals
## *LAB 7.6.2 – NETWORK DISCOVERY - ANSWERS*

1. If you have not done so already, install Network Inspector software (the "Agent" and the "Console") on your PC. How will you know you are done with this step? **The icons for both programs should appear in your Program Directory Menu.**

2. Make sure you are connected to a working Ethernet network. What are some signs that you are on the network? **The link light on your NIC is lit and the other LED is indicating network traffic. You examine your cable run and note that you are connected to a hub or switch. You are able to send and receive e-mail and access the Internet (if your network is connected). You can "ping" other machines' IP addresses. And so on.**

3. Open Fluke Network Inspector Agent. You will be prompted to do something. What are you prompted to do and why do you suppose you must do this? Click OK when finished. **You will be prompted to decide which interface, specifically which Network Interface Adapter, you want to study. Many PCs will have multiple adapters installed (perhaps one for modem, one for Ethernet, and others); you must choose one for the software to study.**

4. Now the Agent will prompt you with a status screen. Click on the tabs and write down what are the major categories of things you can control about the Agent. Under the database/address tab, click on "overwrite" so that the new data you are collecting will be stored in the database. Click Apply. **Agent, Database/Address, SNMP, Problems, Advanced, About**

5. Start the Agent. What is the status shown? What does the status change to after a few? What do you suppose is happening? Minimize the Agent. **The status first changes from "stop" to "start pending," then "running." The agent is discovering your network.**

6. Open Fluke Network Inspector Console. What do you see? **You see the console interface and the database being filled with discovered devices.**

7. Allow the Agent to run for a few minutes. What do you see? **The database has filled with information.**

8. Stop the Agent and minimize the Agent screen. What significant information about the network have you obtained? Write down a few complete lines of the database. **You obtain icons indicating the type of device, device identifier names, IP addresses, IPX addresses (if any), NetBIOS addresses (if any), and MAC addresses. All crucial information for managing your network.**

**Cisco Labs - Semester 1 – Networking Fundamentals**
## *LAB 7.6.2 – NETWORK DISCOVERY - ANSWERS*

9. In the left of the control panel, click each of the "Devices" and explain briefly what they are: "Fluke Tools," "Key Devices," "Utilization Sources," "SNMP Agents," "Servers," "Routers," "Switches," "Printers," and "Hosts." **Fluke Tools – other Fluke hardware devices that can be attached at other points in the network to help study it; Key Devices – servers, switches, routers; Utilization sources – which devices are causing network traffic; SNMP Agents – devices that use the Simple Network Management Protocol to report network information; Servers – computers that provide services to client computers; Routers – Layer 3 path determination and switching devices; Switches – Layer 2 multiport bridges; Printers – common peripheral devices; Hosts – PCs on the network.**

10. Close the Agent and the Console. You have begun using a very powerful piece of software.

**Reflection:** Imagine you have earned your CCNA and are working in a medium-sized company. Write in your journal what value you see in using Network Management software.
**As a newly hired CCNA, one of the first tasks you might be given is to study the existing network. No doubt some amount of sneakernet is in order – walk around, talk to people, look in wiring closets. But, network discovery will greatly assist you in documenting and studying the current status of the network.**

# Cisco Labs - Semester 1 – Networking Fundamentals
## *LAB 7.6.3 – NETWORK INSPECTOR PROBLEM LOG - OVERVIEW*
### *(Estimated time: 20 minutes)*

## Objective:

- Use Network Inspector (or equivalent) software problem logging function to monitor network management information such as errors, warnings and changes

## Background:

Network Management is an important part of a networking professional's responsibilities. One of the most common network management tasks is keeping track of IP addresses. You have been reading about IP addresses and subnets. The Network Analysis software will allow you to get the "big picture" of how IP addresses are assigned on your networks and subnetworks. It will also allow you to access detailed information from the problem log for errors (such as incorrect subnet mask), warnings (such as incorrect IP address), and changes (such as IP address change).

## Tools / Preparation:

Each PC must be running Windows 95, 98, or NT, Microsoft TCP/IP stack, and Winsock 2.0. Fluke Network Inspector 3.0 (or equivalent) must be installed on each PC. During the installation of the software you must specify which network adapter (NIC, dial-up, and so on) you wish to monitor. Specify the NIC that attaches the PC to an Ethernet. The PCs should be on either a 10Base-T or 100Base-TX Ethernet network that preferably includes servers, switches, routers, and printers (this will make the network discovery more interesting). Before beginning this lab, you should read the *Cisco Networking Academy Program: First-Year Companion Guide*, Chapter 19. You should also review semester 1 on-line Lesson 7. The following resources will be required:

- PC with Windows 95, 98, or NT, Microsoft TCP/IP stack, and Winsock 2.0
- Fluke Network Inspector 3.0 software

**Cisco Labs - Semester 1 – Networking Fundamentals**
## *LAB 7.6.3 – NETWORK INSPECTOR PROBLEM LOG - WORKSHEET*

1. Make sure you are connected to the network. How can you verify this? _____
   _____

2. Log into Network Inspector Agent, set the Database tab to overwrite, and start the agent running.
   _____

3. Open Network Inspector Console, and watch until network discovery appears to have stopped.
   Stop the agent. _____

4. Go to Help / About the problem log and troubleshooting problems / errors, warnings and changes
   that can be discovered – does a list appear? _____
   _____

5. Review the list. Choose 3 errors, 3 warnings, and 3 changes that you believe are important, and
   describe them in your own words. _____
   _____
   _____
   _____

6. Return to database view. Are there any errors, warnings, and changes that have appeared? If your
   instructor tells you to, try starting and stopping the agent again, rediscovering the network, and
   seeing if the instructor has caused any errors, warnings, or changes. Note these changes in your
   journal. _____
   _____

7. Can you draw a topology of the network based on the IP addresses and subnetwork information
   obtained? Go ahead and try. _____
   _____

## Reflection:
Imagine you are a network administrator. Describe how this software would be useful to you.
_____
_____
_____
_____
_____
_____

# Cisco Labs - Semester 1 – Networking Fundamentals
## *LAB 7.6.3– NETWORK INSPECTOR PROBLEM LOG - ANSWERS*

1. Make sure you are connected to the network. How can you verify this? **The link light on your NIC is lit and the other LED is indicating network traffic. You examine your cable run and note that you are connected to a hub or switch. You are able to send and receive e-mail and access the Internet (if your network is connected). You can "ping" other machines' IP addresses. And so on.**

2. Log into Network Inspector Agent, set Database tab to overwrite, and start the agent running. **The agent should indicate it is running.**

3. Open Network Inspector Console, and watch until network discovery appears to have stopped. Stop the agent. **Depending on the size of your network, this might take a few seconds.**

4. Go to Help / About the problem log and troubleshooting problems / errors, warnings and changes that can be discovered – does a list appear? **Yes, 3 lists appear detailing the errors, warnings, and changes that can be discovered. Many of these are common network management problems.**

5. Review the list. Choose 3 errors, 3 warnings, and 3 changes that you believe are important, and describe them in your own words. **Students should use the online help to obtain these descriptions.**

6. Return to database view. Are there any errors, warnings, and changes that have appeared? If your instructor tells you to, try starting and stopping the agent again, rediscovering the network, and seeing if the instructor has caused any errors, warnings, or changes. Note these changes in your journal.

7. Can you draw a topology of the network based on the IP addresses and subnetwork information obtained? **Go ahead and try. Yes, topology information can be obtained by grouping hosts by subnet and inferring things like router ports and switch placement. (Note that if you have NI 4.0, you can obtain this topology automatically.)**

**Reflection**:
Imagine you are a network administrator. Describe how this software would be useful to you. **Network administrators often have to keep track of dozens or hundreds of computers, on several or more subnetworks, with routers, switches, and servers all around the network. Even in a well-designed and well-run network, keeping track of all of the IP addresses, MAC addresses, descriptions, and topology of these devices can be a challenge. Network Inspector and other network management software make this task easier, especially as users' needs (and hence the network topology) change.**

## Cisco Labs - Semester 1 – Networking Fundamentals
## *LAB 7.6.4 – PROTOCOL INSPECTOR FRAME STATS - OVERVIEW*
### *(Estimated time: 35 minutes)*

## Objective:

- Use Protocol Inspector (or equivalent) software to examine some simple network utilization and frame statistics, in order to make more real the concept of frame flow as the heartbeat of the LAN

## Background:

Protocol analysis software, often called protocol "sniffers," allows an in-depth view of the amazing diversity of network processes. Protocol analysis software often lets you study protocols at various layers of the OSI model, especially layers 2, 3, 4, 5, and 7. In this lab you will focus on layer 2 information. You have been studying frames, the layer 2 protocol data unit (PDU). Frames might seem like an abstract thing, hard to imagine, but they are constantly being sent and received by your PC on a network. One feature of protocol analysis software is the ability to gather statistics about frames on the "wire" in real time so you can see some of the frame processes occurring. This is one indication of the health of a network, and helps in troubleshooting network problems. Most protocol analyzers can capture frames to and from a host based on MAC address, IP address and the type of traffic to be monitored. Be warned that this is an amazingly powerful piece of software with many features, so you will learn them in small labs.

## Tools / Preparation:

Each PC must be running Windows 95, 98, or NT, Microsoft TCP/IP stack, and Winsock 2.0. Fluke Protocol Inspector 3.0 (or equivalent) must be installed on each PC. During the installation of the software, you must specify which network adapter (NIC, dial-up, and so on) you wish to monitor. Specify the NIC that attaches the PCs to an Ethernet. The PCs should be on either a 10Base-T or 100Base-TX Ethernet network that preferably includes servers, switches, routers, and printers and a connection to a web server, or preferably the Internet (this will make the protocol analysis more interesting). Before beginning this lab, you should read the *Cisco Networking Academy Program: First-Year Companion Guide*, Chapter 19. You should also review semester 1 on-line Lesson 7. The following resources will be required:

- PC with Windows 95, 98, or NT, Microsoft TCP/IP stack, and Winsock 2.0
- Fluke Protocol Inspector 3.0 software

**Cisco Labs - Semester 1 – Networking Fundamentals**
## *LAB 7.6.4 – PROTOCOL INSPECTOR FRAME STATS - WORKSHEET*

1. Make sure the PC is connected to your local-area network (LAN), which preferably is connected to the Internet. What are some ways to determine if your PC is connected to the LAN?

   _____

   _____

2. Install the protocol analysis software onto your computer (unless you have already done so). For Protocol Inspector, you must be sure that you have installed the correct NDIS 802.3 module as a Resource in Protocol Inspector. You will probably need to see several NDIS 802.3 modules as resources, corresponding to different installed adapters on your PC. The Protocol Inspector can only look at one of these adapters at a time, which you must choose. Open the Protocol Inspector program. Do you see multiple adapters in the resource window? (Your instructor might need to specify which one. Note that if you are doing captures and you see no traffic whatsoever, you are probably looking at the wrong resource.)

   _____

3. Choose the correct module with a double-click. Describe the 2 graphs and the 6 tabs that appear. Write down and explain everything that appears in the Description tab.

   _____

   _____

4. Click the start button (1$^{st}$ line of icons, 3$^{rd}$ icon from the left) and see if the utilization graph increases above zero (displayed as blue sections on the graph). This indicates network traffic (perhaps switch or router or DNS updates). If after about 20 seconds you don't see anything, that's OK; click the stop button. You are about to start your own traffic.

   _____

   _____

5. In another window, open your e-mail program and prepare to send a simple e-mail to yourself. But don't send it yet! _____

6. Click the start button. Watch the utilization graph as your e-mail is transmitted and then received. Check your e-mail until you get the second blue "bump" indicating receipt of the e-mail, then click the stop icon. If your network is such that the delay for receipt of e-mails is too long for class time, just watching the transmitted e-mail is fne._____

7. Check the RX tab. Look at the MAC counters column. What types of frames were received? What does each type mean? Look at the errors column (7 are listed). Imagine what the different types of frame errors are, and put, in your own words, what you think they mean. Frame types include broadcast (to all MAC addresses), multicast (to a group of MAC addresses), or unicast (to one MAC address). _____

   _____

8. At the top left of the window there should be two lines of icons. On the second line of icons, 6$^{th}$ from the left, is the Detail View icon. Click it and describe what happens.

   _____

   _____

**Cisco Labs - Semester 1 – Networking Fundamentals**
## *LAB 7.6.4 – PROTOCOL INSPECTOR FRAME STATS - WORKSHEET*

9.  From detail view, stop the capture. On the first line of icons, select the yellow "file cabinet," 8th from the left of "Capture View." What happens? _____

    _____

10. Take a view, scrolling down looking at all the frames and all of the protocols involved in a simple e-mail. _____

11. Now try out the other views: MAC statistics, Frame Size Distribution Monitor, Protocol statistics, Network Layer Host Table, Application Layer Host Table, Host Matrix, Network Layer Matrix. Comment on each. _____

    _____

    _____

**Reflection:**

1.  Has this program given you a new perspective on frames? Explain. _____

    _____

2.  Does the number of protocol frames for even a simple e-mail request surprise you? Why or why not? _____

    _____

3.  Did this lab change the way you view the functioning of computer networks? Explain.

    _____

    _____

    _____

Cisco Labs - Semester 1 – Networking Fundamentals
## *LAB 7.6.4 – PROTOCOL INSPECTOR FRAME STATS - ANSWERS*

1. Make sure the PC is connected to your local-area network (LAN), which preferably is connected to the Internet. What are some ways to determine if your PC is connected to the LAN? **The link light on your NIC is lit and the other LED is indicating network traffic. You examine your cable run and note that you are connected to a hub or switch. You are able to send and receive e-mail and access the Internet (if your network is connected). You can "ping" other machines' IP addresses. And so on.**

2. Install the protocol analysis software onto your computer (unless you have already done so). For Protocol Inspector, you must be sure that you have installed the correct NDIS 802.3 module as a Resource in Protocol Inspector. You will probably need to see several NDIS 802.3 modules as resources, corresponding to different installed adapters on your PC. The Protocol Inspector can only look at one of these adapters at a time, which you must choose. Open the Protocol Inspector program. Do you see multiple adapters in the resource window? (Your instructor might need to specify which one. Note that if you are doing captures and you see no traffic whatsoever, you are probably looking at the wrong resource.)

3. Choose the correct module with a double-click. Describe the 2 graphs and the 6 tabs that appear. Write down and explain everything that appears in the Description tab. **Two graphs – utilization and errors – appear. 6 tabs – monitor, RX, TX, Alarm, Alarm Log, and Description – appear.**

4. Click the start button (1st line of icons, 3rd icon from the left) and see if the utilization graph increases above zero (displayed as blue sections on the graph). This indicates network traffic (perhaps switch or router or DNS updates). If after about 20 seconds you don't see anything, that's OK; click the stop button. You are about to start your own traffic. **Depending on network conditions, you might or might not see traffic. Most likely on the classroom network this will not be an issue.**

5. In another window, open your e-mail program and prepare to send a simple e-mail to yourself. But don't send it yet! **E-mail, Browsers, or any applications that use the network adapter you selected are fine.**

6. Click the start button. Watch the utilization graph as your e-mail is transmitted and then received. Check your e-mail until you get the second blue "bump" indicating receipt of the e-mail, then click the stop icon. **If your network is such that the delay for receipt of e-mails is too long for class time, just watching the transmitted e-mail is fine.**

7. Check the RX tab. Look at the MAC counters column. What types of frames were received? What does each type mean? Look at the errors column (7 are listed). Imagine what the different types of frame errors are, and put, in your own words, what you think they mean. Frame types include broadcast (to all MAC addresses), multicast (to a group of MAC addresses), or unicast (to one MAC address). **Frame errors include CRC alignment (frame accuracy measurements), undersize frames (for Ethernet, less than 64 bytes), oversize frames (for Ethernet, >1518 bytes), fragments (parts of collided frames), jabbers (frames larger than 1518 bytes and with bad CRC values), collisions (two frames on the same medium at the same time), and packets dropped.**

**Cisco Labs - Semester 1 – Networking Fundamentals**
## *LAB 7.6.4 – PROTOCOL INSPECTOR FRAME STATS - ANSWERS*

8.  At the top left of the window there should be two lines of icons. On the second line of icons, 6th from the left, is the Detail View icon. Click it and describe what happens. **An entirely new window, with many more icons on top and the monitor view still running, is opened.**

9.  From detail view, stop the capture. On the first line of icons, select the yellow "file cabinet" 8th from the left of "Capture View." What happens? **A large, complex database appears. This will be studied in later labs.**

10. Take a view, scrolling down looking at all the frames and all of the protocols involved in a simple e-mail.

11. Now try out the other views: MAC statistics, Frame Size Distribution Monitor, Protocol statistics, Network Layer Host Table, Application Layer Host Table, Host Matrix, Network Layer Matrix. Comment on each. **Each view gives a different graphical representation of the communication "conversations" that have occurred and been captured.**

## Reflection:

1.  Has this program given you a new perspective on frames? Explain.
    **Hopefully the students now see frames as a more tangible part of computer network operation.**

2.  Does the number of protocol frames for even a simple e-mail request surprise you? Why or why not? **There's no right answer to this question; for many students it might be surprising that the operations that appear simple have a much more complex layer.**

3.  Did this lab change the way you view the functioning of computer networks? Explain.
    **Hopefully the students will now be wondering about all of the different protocols that they have glimpsed in the database. Chapters 10 – 15 will focus on these details. Use this moment in the course to contextualize what they have learned and what is forthcoming.**

# Cisco Labs - Semester 1 – Networking Fundamentals
## *LAB 9.2.12 – RJ45 JACK INSTALL - OVERVIEW*
### *(Estimated time: 45 minutes)*

## Objectives:
- Learn the correct process for terminating (punching down) an RJ45 jack
- Learn the correct procedure for installing the jack in a wall plate

## Background:
In this lab, you will learn to wire an RJ45 data jack for installation in a wall plate using a punch-down tool. These skills are useful when you must install a small amount of cabling in an office or residence. A punch tool is a device that uses spring-loaded action to push wires between metal pins, while at the same time skinning the sheath away from the wire. This ensures that the wire makes a good electrical connection with the pins inside the jack. The punch tool also cuts off any extra wire.

You will work with CAT 5 cabling and CAT 5 rated T568-B jacks. A CAT 5 straight-wired patch cable with an RJ45 connector will normally plug into this data jack (or outlet) to connect a PC in a work area to the network. It is important that you use CAT 5 rated jacks and patch panels with CAT 5 cabling in order to support higher-speed versions of Ethernet such as Fast Ethernet, which is 100Mbps. The process of punching down wires into a data jack in an office area is the same as punching them down in a patch panel in a wiring closet such as a Main Distribution Facility (MDF) or Intermediate Distribution Facility (IDF).

## Tools / Preparation:
Prior to starting the lab, the teacher or lab assistant should have a spool of Cat 5 Unshielded Twisted Pair (UTP) cable, several RJ45 data jacks, a 110 Punch down tool and an Ethernet/RJ45 continuity tester available. Work individually or in teams. *Cisco Networking Academy Program: First-Year Companion Guide* Chapter 8 and semester 1 on-line Lesson 9 should be reviewed prior to starting this lab. The following resources will be required:

- Two to three foot length of CAT 5 cabling (one per person or one per team).
- Two CAT 5 RJ45 data jacks (one extra for spare). If RJ45 data jacks are installed on both ends of the cable, the installation can be tested by inserting cable with RJ45 connectors and a simple cable continuity tester.
- CAT 5 wall plate.
- 110 type punch-down tool.
- Wire cutters.

# Cisco Labs- Semester 1 – Networking Fundamentals
## *LAB 9.2.12 – RJ45 JACK INSTALL - WORKSHEET*

**Use the following procedure and diagram below to punch down the wires into the RJ45 jack and install the jack into the wall plate:**

**Step 1.** Remove the jacket 1" from the end of the cable.

**Step 2.** Position wires in the proper channels on the jack, according to the color chart below.

**Step 3.** Use the 110 punch-down tool to push conductors into the channels. Make sure that you position the cut side of the punch-down tool so that it faces the outside of the jack, or you will cut the wire you are trying to punch down. (Note: If you tilt the handle of the punch tool a little to the outside, it will cut better.) If any wire remains attached after you have used the punch tool, simply twist the ends gently to remove them, then place the clips on the jack, and tighten them. Note: Make sure that no more than .5" of untwisted wire is between the end of the cable jacket and the channels on the jack.

**Step 4.** Snap the jack into its faceplate by pushing it in from the back side. Make sure, when you do this, that the jack is right-side up (clip faces down when wall plate is mounted).

**Step 5.** Use the screws to attach the faceplate to either the box, or to the bracket. If you have surface-mounted the box, keep in mind that it might hold 1'–2' of excess cable. Then you need to either slide the cable through its tie-wraps, or pull back the raceway that covers it, in order to push the rest of the excess cable back into the wall. If you have flush-mounted the jack, all you need to do is push the excess cable back into the wall.

**Category 5 568-B jack wiring color scheme**
Hold the jack with the 8-pin jack receptacle (the part the RJ45 connector goes into) facing up or away from you while looking at the wire channels or slots. There should be four wire channels on each side.

| 8-pin receptacle | |
|---|---|
| White Green | White Blue |
| Green | Blue |
| White Brown | White Orange |
| Brown | Orange |

# Cisco Labs - Semester 1 – Networking Fundamentals
## *LAB 9.2.12 – RJ45 JACK INSTALL - ANSWERS*

**Use the following procedure and diagram below to punch down the wires into the RJ45 jack and install the jack into the wall plate:**

**Step 1.** Remove the jacket 1" from the end of the cable.

**Step 2.** Position wires in the proper channels on the jack, according to the color chart below.

**Step 3.** Use the 110 punch-down tool to push conductors into the channels. Make sure that you position the cut side of the punch-down tool so that it faces the outside of the jack, or you will cut the wire you are trying to punch down. (Note: If you tilt the handle of the punch tool a little to the outside, it will cut better.) If any wire remains attached after you have used the punch tool, simply twist the ends gently to remove them, then place the clips on the jack, and tighten them. Note: Make sure that no more than .5" of untwisted wire is between the end of the cable jacket and the channels on the jack.

**Step 4.** Snap the jack into its faceplate by pushing it in from the back side. Make sure, when you do this, that the jack is right-side up (clip faces down when wall plate is mounted).

**Step 5.** Use the screws to attach the faceplate to either the box, or to the bracket. If you have surface-mounted the box, keep in mind that it might hold 1'–2' of excess cable. Then you need to either slide the cable through its tie-wraps, or pull back the raceway that covers it, in order to push the rest of the excess cable back into the wall. If you have flush-mounted the jack, all you need to do is push the excess cable back into the wall.

**Category 5 568-B jack wiring color scheme**
Hold the jack with the 8-pin jack receptacle (the part the RJ45 connector goes into) facing up or away from you while looking at the wire channels or slots. There should be four wire channels on each side.

| 8-pin receptacle | |
|---|---|
| White Green | White Blue |
| Green | Blue |
| White Brown | White Orange |
| Brown | Orange |

**Instructor note:**
**The most common error is that students will have the blade facing the wrong way, and cut off the wire inside the jack instead of trimming the excess wire from outside the jack. You might want to point out that this same procedure is used to punch down into a patch panel, another necessary skill for cable installation.**

**Cisco Labs - Semester 1 – Networking Fundamentals**
## *LAB 9.5.1 – DEMO CABLE INSTALLATION - OVERVIEW*
### *(Estimated time: 50 minutes)*

## Objective:

- To learn three crucial cable installation skills: stringing, running, and mounting Cat 5 cable

## Background:

How you do this lab depends on your instructor's choice of project. You can simply string, run, and mount some cable temporarily for practice. Or, you might actually be wiring some or part of your lab. Or you might be doing your structured cabling project, installing networks in some other part of the school or some small business. Regardless of where you are doing your project, you should follow the same professional standards. These were described in Learning Objective 9.4. Assume that one end of your cable run will terminate, via punchdown, in an RJ45 jack. Assume the other end of your cable run will terminate, via punchdown, in an RJ45 Patch panel. Assume you will put the cable in raceway, in ceilings, around obstructions–various conditions you will likely encounter.

## Tools / Preparation:

Basic materials include spools of Cat 5 cable, wire cutter/strippers, punchdown tools, raceway, various mounting consumables like cable ties, cable label, surface mounts, RJ45 jacks and outlets, rack-mounted patch panels, a mock wall, fish tape and telepole, safety goggles, a ladder. The actual complete list and quantity of materials depends heavily on your actual project. Use the Cost Calculator, available on the Community Server, for a complete lab list and estimated quantities and costs. In other words, actual tools and preparation depend heavily on local conditions and resources. Before beginning this lab you should read the *Cisco Networking Academy Program: First-Year Companion Guide*, Chapter 8. You should also review semester 1 on-line Lesson 9. The following resources will be required:

### Equipment / Tools
- Wire cutter/strippers
- Fish tape
- Telepole
- Safety goggles
- Ladder
- Punchdown tools

### Consumables
- Cat 5 cable
- Raceway
- Cable ties
- Cable label
- Surface mounts
- RJ45 jacks and outlets
- Rack-mounted patch panels
- Mock wall (2x4 with drywall)

**Cisco Labs- Semester 1 – Networking Fundamentals**
## *LAB 9.5.1 – DEMO CABLE INSTALLATION - WORKSHEET*

Before starting the lab, you and your group should plan your cable run. Walk from where the RJ45 jack and outlet will be to where the patch panel will be. Look for hazards, obstructions, light fixtures, difficult-to-reach places, and places where cable and raceway will be difficult to mount. Prepare a plan, which includes a diagram of your entire run, the total lengths of cable and raceway you will need, and how you plan to actually install the cable (for example, will you need a ladder to reach a high point in the room?). After your plan is approved by your instructor, follow the procedures your instructor has described for you and your team to demonstrate the following procedures/techniques:

1. Fish cable from above.

2. Fish cable from below.

3. String cable through a dropped ceiling space.

4. Wall mount cable by using tie-wraps.

5. Wall mount cable by using decorative raceway.

6. Wall mount cable by using gutter.

7. Mount cable by using a ladder rack.

8. String cable by using a telepole.

9. String cable by using fish tape.

10. String cable using pull string.

# Cisco Labs- Semester 1 – Networking Fundamentals
## *LAB 9.5.1 – DEMO CABLE INSTALLATION - ANSWERS*

**Proper technique is described in the curriculum, learning objectives 9.4. Safety must be emphasized first, then professional installation (quality punchdowns, proper cable routing and mounting procedures). It is probably most efficient to have the students demonstrate their skills in teams.**

**There is considerable flexibility with this lab, and there are many options for how to run the cable. Answers will vary considerably. The necessary tools and samples of components should be available for demonstration. Some or all of the following cabling tasks can be demonstrated by the instructor and performed by the students, depending on the resources and facilities available. The main things to look for are clean and neat cable runs with no kinks and good connections. At a minimum, the students should punch down an RJ45 jack and run a piece of cable to a patch panel to simulate a cable run from a workstation from a PC workstation to an IDF or MDF.**

1.  Fish cable from above.

2.  Fish cable from below.

3.  String cable through a dropped ceiling space.

4.  Wall mount cable by using tie-wraps.

5.  Wall mount cable by using decorative raceway.

6.  Wall mount cable by using gutter.

7.  Mount cable by using a ladder rack.

8.  String cable by using a telepole.

9.  String cable by using fish tape.

10. String cable using pull string.

# Cisco Labs - Semester 1 – Networking Fundamentals
## *LAB 9.7.13 – DEMO CABLE TESTING - OVERVIEW*
### *(Estimated time: 50 minutes)*

## Objective:

- Use the Fluke 620 (or equivalent) to perform cable verification experiments on newly installed cable runs

## Background:

In lab 9.5.1.1, you were supposed to do a cable installation. As part of that lab, or as part of a project, you should complete the cable run installation by punching down into an RJ45 jack on one end and a patch panel on the other. In this lab, you are called upon to test this cable run. There are a wide variety of tests and a wide variety of equipment that you could use. In this lab you will learn two techniques, one using a simple cable continuity meter and the other using a more sophisticated cable test meter.

Students should demonstrate the ability to use simple continuity-level cable testers. Instructors should at least demonstrate cable testing to the level of a Fluke 620 Cablemeter or equivalent. If more Fluke meters (or equivalent) are available, training all students on these meters will give them enhanced professional skills. If available (perhaps on loan from your regional academy or a local cable installation company), demonstrate the use of the higher-end cable testers–they are truly remarkable devices that measure many of the cable parameters discussed throughout the curriculum.

## Tools / Preparation:

You should be familiar with the use of the Fluke 620 and basic cable testers from the Lesson 5 labs on media. Before beginning this lab you should read the *Cisco Networking Academy Program: First-Year Companion Guide*, Chapter 8. You should do the Lesson 5 labs and also review semester 1 on-line Lessons 5 and 9. The following resources will be required:

- One completely installed but untested cable run (RJ45 wall jack to cable to patch panel) per student group
- Fluke 620 Cablemeter or equivalent
- Common RJ45 cable continuity meter
- Journals
- Tools and materials for lab 9.5.1.1 if the cable run fails the test and must be redone
- High-end cable testers (attenuation, NEXT, FEXT) if one can be borrowed from a local company or regional academy

**Cisco Labs - Semester 1 – Networking Fundamentals**
*LAB 9.7.13 – DEMO CABLE TESTING - WORKSHEET*

You should be able to take the cable run created in Lab 9.5.1.1 and test it. Your instructor will demonstrate some of the tests that can be performed with a cable tester. In some instances, the tests will indicate that problems exist. You will be asked to outline how you would determine what the problem is, and describe how you would fix it.

1. Complete a cable run: _____

2. Use the Fluke 620 Meter on Wire Map to test the installation: _____

3. Identify any faults as near-end, along the cable, or far-end: _____

4. Correct the faults: _____

5. Retest until the cable run passes on the Fluke Meter: _____

6. Label the cable run (alphanumeric identification) as passed and record in your journal: _____

7. (Optional) Using the continuity meter, test two straight-through patch cords – one can be short, but the other must make up the entire rest of the distance from jack to patch panel. Test both patch cables on the continuity tester: _____

8. (Optional) Connect both cables to the continuity tester. If all of the light pairs (1 to 1, 2 to 2, 3 to 3, and so on; up to 8 to 8) light up, you have demonstrated at least the continuity.

9. (Optional) Perform high-end tests on the cable run with more expensive test equipment.

# Cisco Labs - Semester 1 – Networking Fundamentals
## *LAB 9.7.13 – DEMO CABLE TESTING - ANSWERS*

**You should be able to take the cable run created in Lab 9.5.1.1 and test it by connecting a workstation with a NIC to an RJ45 straight-through patch cable and then into the wall plate (RJ45 jack). Connect another RJ45 straight-through patch cable from the patch panel to a hub or switch and make sure the switch is plugged in. If the link lights on the NIC and the hub or switch come on, you have a good connection. You can also use the Fluke CableMeter or a basic cable tester to verify the cable run is good using the following steps. Results will vary depending on the resources and facilities available.**

1.  Complete a cable run.

2.  Use the Fluke 620 Meter on Wire Map to test the installation.

3.  Identify any faults as near-end, along the cable, or far-end.

4.  Correct the faults.

5.  Retest until the cable run passes on the Fluke Meter.

6.  Label the cable run (alphanumeric identification) as passed and record in your journal.

7.  (Optional) Using the continuity meter, test two straight-through patch cords–one can be short, but the other must make up the entire rest of the distance from jack to patch panel. Test both patch cables on the continuity tester.

8.  (Optional) Connect both cables to the continuity tester. If all of the light pairs (1 to 1, 2 to 2, 3 to 3, and so on; up to 8 to 8) light up, you have demonstrated at least the continuity.

9.  (Optional) Perform high-end tests on the cable run with more expensive test equipment.

# Cisco Labs - Semester 1 – Networking Fundamentals
## *LAB 10.4.1. – IP ADDRESSING - OVERVIEW*
### *(Estimated time: 30 minutes)*

## Objectives:
This lab will focus on your ability to accomplish the following tasks:

- Name the five different classes of IP addresses

- Describe the characteristics and use of the different IP address classes

- Identify the class of an IP address based on the network number

- Determine which part (octet) of an IP address is the network ID and which part is the host ID

- Identify valid and invalid IP host addresses based on the rules of IP addressing

- Define the range of addresses and default subnet mask for each class

## Background:
This lab will help you develop an understanding of IP addresses and how TCP/IP networks operate. IP addresses are used to uniquely identify individual TCP/IP networks and hosts (computers and printers) on those networks in order for devices to communicate. Workstations and servers on a TCP/IP network are called "hosts," and each will have a unique IP address, which is referred to as its "host" address. TCP/IP is the most widely used protocol in the world. The Internet or World Wide Web uses only IP addressing. In order for a host to access the Internet, it must have an IP address.

In its basic form, the IP address has two parts: a Network Address and a Host Address. The network portion of the IP address is assigned to a company or organization by the Internet Network Information Center (InterNIC). Routers use the IP address to move data packets between networks. IP Addresses are 32 bits long (with current version IPv4) and are divided into 4 octets of 8 bits each. They operate at the network Layer 3 of the OSI model (the Internetwork layer of the TCP/IP model) and are assigned statically (manually) by a network administrator or dynamically (automatically) by a Dynamic Host Configuration Protocol (DHCP) Server. The IP address of a workstation (host) is a "logical address," meaning it can be changed. The MAC address of the workstation is a 48-bit "physical address," which is burned into the NIC and cannot change unless the NIC is replaced. The combination of the logical IP address and the physical MAC address help route packets to their proper destination.

There are five different classes of IP addresses, and depending on the class, the network and host part of the address will use a different number of bits. In this lab, you will work with the different classes of IP addresses and become familiar with the characteristics of each. The understanding of IP addresses is critical to your understanding of TCP/IP and internetworks in general.

## Tools / Preparation:
This is primarily a written lab exercise but you might want to use Control Panel/Network to review some real network IP addresses. Before beginning this lab you should read the *Cisco Networking Academy Program: First-Year Companion Guide*, Chapter 5. You should also review semester 1 on-line Lesson 10. The following resources will be required:

- PC workstation with Windows operating system (Windows 95, 98, NT or 2000) installed on PC and access to the Windows Calculator

## Cisco Labs - Semester 1 – Networking Fundamentals
## *LAB 10.4.1 – IP ADDRESSING - WORKSHEET*

**Step 1 – Review IP Address classes and Their Characteristics**

**Explanation:** There are five classes of IP addresses (A through E). Only the first three classes are used commercially. We will discuss a class A network address in the table to get started. The first column is the class of IP address. The second column is the first octet, which must fall within the range shown for a given class of address. The class A address must start with a number between 1 and 126. The first bit of a class A address is always a zero, meaning the High Order Bit (HOB) or the 128 bit cannot be used. 127 is reserved for loopback testing. The first octet alone defines the network ID for a class A network address. The default subnet mask uses all binary ones (decimal 255) to mask the first 8 bits of the class A address. The default subnet mask helps routers and hosts determine if the destination host is on this network or another one. Because there are only 126 class A networks, the remaining 24 bits (3 octets) can be used for hosts. Each class A network can have $2^{24}$ (2 to the $24^{th}$ power) or over 16 million hosts. It is common to subdivide the network into smaller groupings called subnets using a custom subnet mask, which will be discussed in the next lab.

The network or host portion of the address cannot be all ones or all zeros. As an example, the class A address of 118.0.0.5 is a valid IP address because the network portion (first 8 bits, equal to 118) is not all zeros and the host portion (the last 24 bits) is not all zeros or all ones. If the host portion were all zeros it would be the network address itself. If the host portion were all ones, it would be a broadcast for the network address. The value of any octet can never be greater than decimal 255 or binary 11111111.

| Cls | 1st Octet Decimal Range | 1st Octet High Order Bits | Network / Host ID (N=Network, H=Host) | Default Subnet Mask | Number of Networks | Hosts per Network (usable addresses) |
|---|---|---|---|---|---|---|
| A | 1 – 126* | 0 | N.H.H.H | 255.0.0.0 | 126 $(2^7 - 2)$ | 16,777,214 $(2^{24} - 2)$ |
| B | 128 – 191 | 1 0 | N.N.H.H | 255.255.0.0 | 16,382 $(2^{14} - 2)$ | 65,534 $(2^{16} - 2)$ |
| C | 192 – 223 | 1 1 0 | N.N.N.H | 255.255.255.0 | 2,097,150 $(2^{21} - 2)$ | 254 $(2^8 - 2)$ |
| D | 224 – 239 | 1 1 1 0 | Reserved for Multicasting | | | |
| E | 240 – 254 | 1 1 1 1 0 | Experimental; used for research | | | |

* Class A address 127 cannot be used and is reserved for loopback and diagnostic functions.

# Cisco Labs - Semester 1 – Networking Fundamentals
## *LAB 10.4.1 – IP ADDRESSING - WORKSHEET*

### Step 2 – Basic IP addressing
**Task:** Use the IP address chart and your knowledge of IP address classes to answer the following questions.

1. What is the decimal and binary range of the first octet of all possible class B IP addresses?
   Decimal:    From: _____    To: _____
   Binary:     From: _____    To: _____

2. Which octet(s) represent the network portion of a class C IP address? _____

3. Which octet(s) represent the host portion of a class A IP address? _____

### Step 3 – Determine the host and network portion of the IP address.
**Task:** With the following IP host addresses, indicate the Class of each address, the Network Address or ID, the Host portion, the Broadcast Address for this network and the default Subnet Mask.

**Explanation:** The host portion will be all zeros for the network ID. Enter just the octets that make up the host. The host portion will be all ones for a broadcast. The network portion of the address will be all ones for the subnet mask.

1. Fill in the following table:

| Host IP Address | Addr. Class | Network Address | Host Address | Network Broadcast Address | Default Subnet Mask |
|---|---|---|---|---|---|
| 216.14.55.137 | | | | | |
| 123.1.1.15 | | | | | |
| 150.127.221.244 | | | | | |
| 194.125.35.199 | | | | | |
| 175.12.239.244 | | | | | |

2. Given an IP address of **142.226.0.15**

   a. What is the binary equivalent of the second octet? _____
   b. What is the class of the address? _____
   c. What is the network address of this IP address? _____
   d. Is this a valid IP host address (Y/N)? _____
   e. Why or why not? _____
   _____
   _____
   _____

# Cisco Labs - Semester 1 – Networking Fundamentals
## *LAB 10.4.1 – IP ADDRESSING – WORKSHEET*

3. What is the maximum number of hosts you can have with a class C network address? _____

4. How many class B networks are there? _____

5. How many hosts can each class B network have? _____

6. How many octets are there in an IP address? _____ How many bits per octet? _____

**Step 4 – Determine which IP host addresses are valid for commercial networks.**
> **Task:** For the following IP host addresses determine which are valid for commercial networks. Why or why not?
>
> **Explanation:** Valid means it could be assigned to a workstation, server, printer, router interface, and so on.

1. Fill in the following table.

| IP Host address | Valid Address? (Yes / No) | Why or Why not |
|---|---|---|
| 150.100.255.255 | | |
| 175.100.255.18 | | |
| 195.234.253.0 | | |
| 100.0.0.23 | | |
| 188.258.221.176 | | |
| 127.34.25.189 | | |
| 224.156.217.73 | | |

# Cisco Lab - Semester 1 – Networking Fundamentals
## *LAB 10.4.1 – IP ADDRESSING – ANSWERS*

### Step 2
1.  What is the decimal and binary range of the first octet of all possible class B IP addresses?
    Decimal:   From: **128**         To: **191**
    Binary:    From: **10000000**    To: **10111111**

2.  Which octet(s) represent the network portion of a class C IP address? **The first three octets**

3.  Which octet(s) represent the host portion of a class A IP address? **The last three octets**

### Step 3
1.  Fill in the following table:

| Host IP Address | Addr. Class | Network Address | Host Address | Network Broadcast Address | Default Subnet Mask |
|---|---|---|---|---|---|
| 216.14.55.137 | C | 216.14.55.0 | 137 | 216.14.55.255 | 255.255.255.0 |
| 123.1.1.15 | A | 123.0.0.0 | 1.1.15 | 123.255.255.255 | 255.0.0.0 |
| 150.127.221.244 | B | 150.127.0.0 | 221.244 | 150.127.255.255 | 255.255.0.0 |
| 194.125.35.199 | C | 194.125.35.0 | 199 | 194.125.35.255 | 255.255.255.0 |
| 175.12.239.244 | B | 175.12.0.0 | 239.244 | 175.12.255.255 | 255.255.0.0 |

2.  Given an IP address of **142.226.0.15**

a.  What is the binary equivalent of the second octet? **11100010**
b.  What is the class of the address? **Class B**
c.  What is the network address of this IP address? **142.226.0.0 (First two octets followed by zeros)**
d.  Is this a valid IP host address? **Yes**
e.  Why or why not? **The network part of the address (the first 2 octets or 16 bits) is 142.226, which is a valid class B address. The host part (last 2 octets or 16 bits) is 0.15 or 00000000.00001111. Because all 16 bits of the host ID are not all zeros or all ones it is a valid host address.**

3.  What is the maximum number of hosts you can have with a class C network address? **254**
    **The host portion of the address cannot be all ones (11111111 binary or 255 decimal) or all zeros (00000000 binary or 0 decimal). There are 8 bits or $2^8 = 265$ minus 2 = 254.**

4.  How many class B networks are there? **16,382**
    **Although there are 16 bits in the first two octets for networks, the first two bits are always 10 and do not change. That leaves 14 bits or $2^{14}$ minus 2 = 16,382.**

## Cisco Labs - Semester 1 – Networking Fundamentals
## *LAB 10.4.1 – IP ADDRESSING – ANSWERS*

5.  How many hosts can each class B network have? <u>**65,534**</u>
    <u>**There are 16 bits left in the host portion of the address and you cannot use the all zeros (network address) or all ones (broadcast address) value. That means 16 bits or $2^{16}$ minus 2 = 65,534.**</u>

6.  How many octets are there in an IP address? <u>**4**</u> How many bits per octet? <u>**8**</u>

**Step 4**

1.  Fill in the following table:

| IP Host address | Valid Address? (Yes / No) | Why or Why not |
|---|---|---|
| 150.100.255.255 | No | 150.100.0.0.is a Class B network. This is a broadcast address for a Class B (host portion 3$^{rd}$ and 4$^{th}$ octets is all ones) and cannot be used for a host address. |
| 175.100.255.18 | Yes | 175.100.0.0 is a Class B network. The host portion is the 3$^{rd}$ and 4$^{th}$ octets (16 bits taken together) 11111111.00010010 and is not all zeros or all ones. It is valid even though the 3$^{rd}$ octet is all ones. |
| 195.234.253.0 | No | 195.234.253.0 is a Class C network. This is the network address or ID for this network and cannot be used for a host address because all the host bits are zeros. |
| 100.0.0.23 | Yes | 100.0.0.0 is a Class A network. The host portion of the address is the 2$^{nd}$, 3$^{rd}$ and 4$^{th}$ octets (24 bits taken together) 00000000.00000000.00010111 and is not all zeros or all ones. It is valid even though the 2$^{nd}$ and 3$^{rd}$ octets are all zeros. |
| 188.258.221.176 | No | This would be a Class B network but is invalid because the 2$^{nd}$ octet is greater than 255. No octet can be greater than 255 (all ones) in any IP address (network or host). |
| 127.34.25.189 | No | This would be a Class A network, but is invalid because 127 can't be used in the first octet because it is reserved for diagnostic testing. |
| 224.156.217.73 | No | This is a Class D network, and Class D is reserved for multicasting and can't be used as a commercial IP address. |

# Cisco Labs- Semester 1 – Networking Fundamentals
## *LAB 10.6.6 – SUBNET MASK 1 - OVERVIEW*
### *(Estimated time: 45 minutes)*

## Objectives:
This lab will focus on Class C subnet masks and your ability to accomplish the following tasks:

- Cite some reasons why a subnet mask would be needed.

- Distinguish between a default subnet mask and a custom subnet mask.

- Determine the subnets available with a particular IP network address and subnet mask.

- Given a network address and requirements for how many subnets and hosts, be able to determine what subnet mask should be used.

- Given a network address and a subnet mask, be able to determine the number of subnets and hosts per subnet that can be created as well as useable subnets and useable number of hosts.

- Use the "ANDing" process to determine if a destination IP address is local or remote.

- Identify valid and invalid IP host addresses based on a given a network number and subnet mask.

## Background:
This lab will help you understand the basics of IP subnet masks and their use with TCP/IP networks. The subnet mask can be used to split up an existing network into "subnetworks" or "subnets." This can be done to 1) reduce the size of the broadcast domains (create smaller networks with less traffic), 2) to allow LANs in different geographical locations to communicate or 3) for security reasons to separate one LAN from another. Routers separate subnets, and the router determines when a packet can go from one subnet to another. Each router a packet goes through is considered a "hop." Subnet masks help workstations, servers and routers in an IP network determine if the destination host for the packet they want to send is on their own network or another network. Default subnet masks were discussed in a prior lab. This lab will review the default subnet mask and then focus on custom subnet masks, which will use more bits than the default subnet mask by "borrowing" these bits from the host portion of the IP address. This creates a three-part address: 1) The original network address assigned by InterNIC, 2) The subnet address made up of the bits borrowed and 3) the host address made up of the bits left after borrowing some for subnets.

## Tools / Preparation:
This is primarily a written lab exercise, but you might want to use Control Panel / Network to review some real network IP addresses. Before beginning this lab you should read the *Cisco Networking Academy Program: First-Year Companion Guide*, Chapter 5. You should also review semester 1 on-line Lesson 10. The following resources will be required:

- PC workstation with Windows operating system (Windows 95, 98, NT or 2000) installed on the PC and access to the Windows Calculator.

## Notes:

_____

_____

_____

# Cisco Labs - Semester 1 – Networking Fundamentals
## *LAB 10.6.6 – SUBNET MASK 1 - WORKSHEET*

### Step 1 – IP Address Basics

**Explanation:** IP network addresses are assigned by the Internet Network Information Center (InterNIC). If your organization has a class A IP network address, the first octet (8 bits) is assigned by InterNIC and your organization can use the remaining 24 bits to define up to 16,777,214 hosts on your network. This is a lot of hosts! It is not possible to put all of these hosts on one physical network without separating them with routers and subnets. A workstation might be on one network or subnet and a server might be on another network or subnet. When the workstation needs to retrieve a file from the server it will need to use its subnet mask to determine the network or subnet that the server is on. The purpose of a subnet mask is to help hosts and routers determine the network location where a destination host can be found. Refer to the following table to review IP address classes, default subnet masks and the number of networks and hosts that can be created with each class of network address.

| Adr Cls | 1<sup>st</sup> Octet Decimal Range | 1<sup>st</sup> Octet High Order Bits | Network / Host ID (N=Network, H=Host) | Default Subnet Mask | Number of Networks | Hosts per Network (usable addresses) |
|---|---|---|---|---|---|---|
| A | 1 – 126* | 0 | N.H.H.H | 255.0.0.0 | 126 $(2^7 - 2)$ | 16,777,214 $(2^{24} - 2)$ |
| B | 128 – 191 | 1 0 | N.N.H.H | 255.255.0.0 | 16,382 $(2^{14} - 2)$ | 65,534 $(2^{16} - 2)$ |
| C | 192 – 223 | 1 1 0 | N.N.N.H | 255.255.255.0 | 2,097,150 $(2^{21} - 2)$ | 254 $(2^8 - 2)$ |
| D | 224 – 239 | 1 1 1 0 | Reserved for Multicasting | | | |
| E | 240 – 254 | 1 1 1 1 0 | Experimental; used for research | | | |

### Step 2 – The "ANDing" process

**Explanation:** Hosts and routers use the "ANDing" process to determine if a destination host is on the same network or not. The ANDing process is done each time a host wants to send a packet to another host on an IP network. If you want to connect to a server, you might know the IP address of the server you want to connect to or you can just enter the host name (for example, www.cisco.com), and a Domain Name Server (DNS) will convert the host name to an IP address. First, the source host will compare (AND) its own IP address to its own subnet mask. The result of the ANDing is to identify the network where the source host resides. It will then compare the destination IP address to its own subnet mask. The result of the 2<sup>nd</sup> ANDing will be the network that the destination host is on. If the source network address and the destination network address are the same, they can communicate directly. If the results are different, they are on different networks or subnets and will need to communicate through routers or might not be able to communicate.

# Cisco Labs - Semester 1 – Networking Fundamentals
## *LAB 10.6.6 – SUBNET MASK 1 - WORKSHEET*

ANDing depends on the subnet mask. Subnet masks are always all ones. A default subnet mask for a Class C network is 255.255.255.0 or 11111111.11111111.11111111.00000000. This is compared to the source IP address bit for bit. The first bit of the IP address is compared to the first bit of the subnet mask and the second bit to the second, and so on. If the two bits are both ones, the **ANDing result is a ONE**. If the two bits are a zero and a one or two zeros, the **ANDing result is a ZERO**. Basically, this means that a combination of 2 ones results in a ONE, anything else is a zero. The result of the ANDing process is the network or subnet number that the source or destination address is on.

### Step 3 – Two Class C networks using the default subnet mask

**Explanation:** This example will show how a Class C default subnet mask can be used to determine which network a host is on. A default subnet mask does not break an address into subnets. If the default subnet mask is used, the network is not being "subnetted." Host X (source) on network 200.1.1.0 has an IP address of 200.1.1.5 and wants to send a packet to host Z (destination) on network 200.1.2.0 and has an IP address of 200.1.2.8. All hosts on each network are connected to hubs or switches and then to a router. Remember that with a Class C network address InterNIC assigns the first 3 octets (24 bits) as the network address, so these are two different Class C networks. This leaves one octet (8 bits) for hosts, so each Class C network could have up to 254 hosts ($2^8 = 256 - 2 = 254$).

**Source net:    200.1.1.0**
**Subnet mask:  255.255.255.0**

**Destination net: 200.1.2.0**
**Subnet mask:  255.255.255.0**

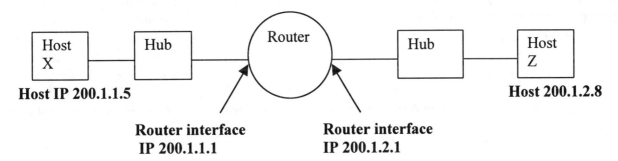

The ANDing process will help the packet get from host 200.1.1.5 on network 200.1.1.0 to host 200.1.2.8 on network 200.1.2.0 using the following steps.

**a.    Host X compares its own IP address to its own subnet mask using the ANDing process.**

| | |
|---|---|
| **Host X IP address 200.1.1.5** | 11001000.00000001.00000001.00000101 |
| **Subnet Mask 255.255.255.0** | 11111111.11111111.11111111.00000000 |
| **ANDing Result (200.1.1.0)** | 11001000.00000001.00000001.00000000 |

Note: The result of step 3a of the ANDing process is the network address of host X, which is 200.1.1.0.

# Cisco Labs - Semester 1 – Networking Fundamentals
## *LAB 10.6.6 – SUBNET MASK 1 - WORKSHEET*

**b.** **Next, host X compares the IP address of the Host Z destination to its own subnet mask using the ANDing process.**

| | |
|---|---|
| **Host Z IP address 200.1.2.8** | 11001000.00000001.00000010.00001000 |
| **Subnet Mask 255.255.255.0** | 11111111.11111111.11111111.00000000 |
| **ANDing Result (200.1.2.0)** | 11001000.00000001.00000010.00000000 |

NOTE: The result of step3b ANDing process is the network address of host Z, which is 200.1.2.0.

Host X compares the ANDing results from step A and the ANDing results from step B, and they are different. Host X now knows that host Z is not in its local-area network (LAN), and it must send the packet to its "Default Gateway," which is the IP address of the router interface of 200.1.1.1 on network 200.1.1.0. The router will then repeat the ANDing process to determine which router interface to send the packet out.

## Step 4 – One Class C network using a Custom subnet mask

**Explanation:** This example uses a single Class C network address (200.1.1.0) and will show how a Class C custom subnet mask can be used to determine which subnetwork (or subnet) a host is on and to route packets from one subnetwork to another. Remember that with a Class C network address InterNIC assigns the first 3 octets (24 bits) as the network address. This leaves 8 bits (one octet) for hosts, so each Class C network could have up to 254 hosts ($2^8 = 256 – 2 = 254$).

Perhaps you want less than 254 hosts (workstations and servers) all on one network and you want to create two subnetworks and separate them with a router for security reasons or to reduce traffic. This will create smaller independent broadcast domains and can improve network performance and increase security because these subnetworks will be separated by a router. Assume you will need at least 2 subnetworks and at least 50 hosts per subnetwork. Because you only have one Class C network address, you have only 8 bits in the fourth octet available for a total of 254 possible hosts, so you must create a custom subnet mask. You will use the custom subnet mask to "borrow" bits from the host portion of the address. The following steps will help accomplish this:

a. The first step to "subnetting" is to determine how many subnets are needed. In this case you will need 2 subnetworks. To see how many bits you should borrow from the host portion of the network address, add the bit values from right to left until the total is equal to or greater than the number of subnets you will need. Because we need two subnets, add the one bit and the two bit, which equals three. This is over the number of subnets we need, so we need to borrow at least two bits from the host address starting from the left side of the octet that contains the host address.

# Cisco Labs - Semester 1 – Networking Fundamentals
## *LAB 10.6.6 – SUBNET MASK 1 - WORKSHEET*

**Network address: 200.1.1.0**

| **4th octet Host address bits:** | 1 | 1 | 1 | 1 | 1 | 1 | 1 | 1 |
|---|---|---|---|---|---|---|---|---|
| **Host address bit values (from right)** | 128 | 64 | 32 | 16 | 8 | 4 | **2** | **1** |

(Add bits starting from the right side (the 1 and the 2) until you get more than the number of subnets needed.)

b.  After we know how many bits to borrow, we take them from the left side of the first octet of the host address. Every bit we borrow from the host leaves fewer bits for the hosts. Even though we increase the number of subnets, we decrease the number of hosts per subnet. Because we need to borrow two bits from the left side, we must show that new value in our subnet mask. Our existing default subnet mask was 255.255.255.0 and our new "custom" subnet mask is 255.255.255.192. The 192 comes from the value of the first two bits from the left (128 + 64 = 192). These bits now become 1s and are part of the overall subnet mask. This leaves 6 bits for host IP addresses or $2^6 = 64$ hosts per subnet.

| **4th Octet borrowed bits for subnet:** | **1** | **1** | 0 | 0 | 0 | 0 | 0 | 0 |
|---|---|---|---|---|---|---|---|---|
| **Subnet bit values: (from left side)** | **128** | **64** | 32 | 16 | 8 | 4 | 2 | 1 |

With this information you can build the following table. The first two bits are the subnet binary value. The last 6 bits are the host bits. By borrowing 2 bits from the 8 bits of the host address you can create 4 subnets with 64 hosts each. The 4 networks created are the "0" net, the "64" net, the "128" net and the "192" net. The "0" net and the "192" net are considered unusable. This is because the "0" net has all zeros in the subnet portion of the address and the 192 net has all ones in the subnet portion of the address.

| Subnet No. | Subnet bits borrowed Binary value | Subnet bits Decimal Value | Host bits possible binary values (range) (6 bits) | Subnet / Host Decimal range | Useable? |
|---|---|---|---|---|---|
| 0 Subnet | 00 | 0 | 000000 – 111111 | 0 – 63 | NO |
| 1st Subnet | 01 | 64 | 000000 – 111111 | 64 – 127 | YES |
| 2nd Subnet | 10 | 128 | 000000 – 111111 | 128 – 191 | YES |
| 3rd Subnet | 11 | 192 | 000000 – 111111 | 192 – 254 | NO |

Notice that the first subnet always starts at 0 and, in this case, increases by 64, which is the number of hosts on each subnet. One way to determine the number of hosts on each subnet or the start of each subnet is to take the remaining host bits to the power of 2. Because we borrowed two of the 8 bits for subnets and have six bits left, the number of hosts per subnet is $2^6$ or 64. Another way to figure the number of host per subnet or the "increment" from one subnet to the next is to subtract the subnet mask value in decimal (192 in the fourth octet) from 256 (which is maximum number of possible combinations of 8 bits), which equals 64. This means you start at 0 for the first network and add 64 for each additional subnetwork. If we take the second subnet (the 64 net) as an example the IP address of 200.1.1.64 cannot be used for a host ID because it is the "network ID" of the "64" subnet (host portion is all zeros) and the IP address of 200.1.1.127 cannot be used because it is the broadcast address for the 64 net (host portion is all ones).

# Cisco Labs - Semester 1 – Networking Fundamentals
## *LAB 10.6.6 – SUBNET MASK 1 - WORKSHEET*

### Step 5 – One Class C network using a Custom Subnet Mask

**Task:** Use the following information and the previous examples to answer the following subnet-related questions.

**Explanation:** Your company has applied for and received a Class C network address of 197.15.22.0. You want to subdivide your physical network into 4 subnets, which will be interconnected by routers. You will need at least 25 hosts per subnet. You will need to use a Class C custom subnet mask and will have a router between the subnets to route packets from one subnet to another. Determine the number of bits you will need to borrow from the host portion of the network address and then the number of bits left for host addresses. (Hint: There will be 8 subnets.)

1. Fill in the table below and answer the following questions:

| Subnet No. | Subnet bits borrowed Binary value | Subnet bits Decimal and Subnet No. | Host bits possible binary values (range) (6 bits) | Subnet / Host Decimal range | Use? |
|---|---|---|---|---|---|
| 0 Subnet | | | | | |
| 1st Subnet | | | | | |
| 2nd Subnet | | | | | |
| 3rd Subnet | | | | | |
| 4th Subnet | | | | | |
| 5th Subnet | | | | | |
| 6th Subnet | | | | | |
| 7th Subnet | | | | | |

**NOTES:**

_____

_____

_____

_____

_____

_____

_____

_____

_____

_____

# Cisco Labs - Semester 1 – Networking Fundamentals
## *LAB 10.6.6 – SUBNET MASK 1 - WORKSHEET*

**QUESTIONS: Use the table you just developed to help answer the following questions:**

1. Which octet(s) represent the network portion of a Class C IP address? _____

2. Which octet(s) represent the host portion of a Class C IP address? _____

3. What is the binary equivalent of the Class C network address in the scenario (**197.15.22.0**)?

Decimal network address:      _____ . _____. _____ . _____
Binary network address:      _____ . _____ . _____ . _____

4. How many high-order bits were borrowed from the host bits in the fourth octet? _____

5. What subnet mask must you use (show the subnet mask in decimal and binary)?

Decimal subnet mask:      _____ . _____ . _____ . _____
Binary subnet mask:      _____ . _____ : _____ . _____

6. What is the maximum number of subnets that can be created with this subnet mask? _____

7. What is the maximum number of useable subnets that can be created with this mask? _____

8. How many bits were left in the 4$^{th}$ octet for host IDs? _____

9. How many hosts per subnet can be defined with this subnet mask? _____

10. What is the maximum number of hosts that can be defined for all subnets with this scenario (assuming you cannot use the lowest and highest subnet numbers and cannot use the lowest and highest host ID on each subnet)? _____

11. Is **197.15.22.63** a valid host IP address with this scenario? _____

12. Why or why not? _____

13. Is **197.15.22.160** a valid host IP address with this scenario? _____

14. Why or why not? _____

15. Host A has an IP address of **197.15.22.126**. Host B has an IP address of **197.15.22.129**. Are these hosts on the same subnet? _____ Why? _____
_____

# Cisco Labs - Semester 1 – Networking Fundamentals
## *LAB 10.6.6 – SUBNET MASK 1 – ANSWERS*

**Step 5**

1. Fill in the table below and answer the following questions:

| Subnet No. | Subnet bits borrowed Binary value | Subnet bits Decimal and Subnet No. | Host bits possible binary values (range) (6 bits) | Subnet / Host Decimal range | Use? |
|---|---|---|---|---|---|
| 1<sup>st</sup> Subnet | 000 | 0 (197.15.22.0) | 00000 – 11111 | 0 – 31 | NO |
| 2<sup>nd</sup> Subnet | 001 | 32 (197.15.22.32 | 00000 – 11111 | 32 – 63 | YES |
| 3<sup>rd</sup> Subnet | 010 | 64 (197.15.22.64) | 00000 – 11111 | 64 – 95 | YES |
| 4<sup>th</sup> Subnet | 011 | 96 (197.15.22.96) | 00000 – 11111 | 96 – 127 | YES |
| 5<sup>th</sup> Subnet | 100 | 128 (197.15.22.128) | 00000 – 11111 | 128 – 159 | YES |
| 6<sup>th</sup> Subnet | 101 | 160 (127.15.22.160) | 00000 – 11111 | 160 – 191 | YES |
| 7<sup>th</sup> Subnet | 110 | 192 (127.15.22.192) | 00000 – 11111 | 192 – 223 | YES |
| 8<sup>th</sup> Subnet | 111 | 224 (127.15.22.224) | 00000 – 11111 | 224 – 255 | NO |

**NOTES:**

# Cisco Labs - Semester 1 – Networking Fundamentals
## *LAB 10.6.6 – SUBNET MASK 1 – ANSWERS*

**QUESTIONS: Use the table above to help answer the following questions:**

1.  Which octet(s) represent the network portion of a class C IP address? **$1^{st}$, $2^{nd}$ and $3^{rd}$**

2.  Which octet(s) represent the host portion of a class C IP address? **$4^{th}$**

3.  What is the binary equivalent of the class C network address in the scenario (**197.15.22.0**)?
    Decimal network address:       **197.**        **15.**        **22.**        **0**
    Binary network address:       **11000101.**   **00001111.**   **00010110.**   **00000000**

4.  How many high-order bits were borrowed from the host bits in the fourth octet? **3 bits**

5.  What subnet mask must you use (show the subnet mask in decimal and binary)?
    Decimal subnet mask:       **255 .**        **255 .**        **255.**        **224**
    Binary subnet mask:       **11111111.**   **11111111.**   **11111111.**   **11100000**

6.  What is the maximum number of subnets that can be created with this subnet mask? **$2^3$ or 8 subnets**

7.  What is the maximum number of useable subnets that can be created with this mask? **$2^3 - 2$ or 6 useable subnets**

8.  How many bits were left in the $4^{th}$ octet for host IDs? **5 bits**

9.  How many hosts per subnet can be defined with this subnet mask? **$2^5 = 32 - 2 = 30$ hosts per subnet**

10. What is the maximum number of hosts that can be defined for all subnets with this scenario (assuming you cannot use the lowest and highest subnet numbers and cannot use the lowest and highest host ID on each subnet)? **6 useable subnets with 30 useable hosts per subnet = 180 actual host addresses**

11. Is 197.15.22.63 a valid host IP address with this scenario? **NO**

12. Why or why not? **It cannot be used for a host because it is the broadcast address for the .32 subnet.**

13. Is **197.15.22.160** a valid host IP address with this scenario? **NO**

14. Why or why not? **It cannot be used for a host because it is the network address of the .160 subnet.**

15. Host A has an IP address of **197.15.22.126**. Host B has an IP address of **197.15.22.129**. Are these hosts on the same subnet? **NO.** Why? **The 197.15.22.126 host address is on the 197.15.22..98 subnetwork and the 197.15.22.129 host address is on the 197.15.22.128 subnetwork, so they are on different subnets.**

# Cisco Labs - Semester 1 – Networking Fundamentals
## *LAB 10.7.7– SUBNET MASK 2 - OVERVIEW*
### *(Estimated time: 45 minutes)*

## Objectives:
This lab will focus on your ability to accomplish the following tasks:

- Work with a more complex Class C subnet scenario.

- Determine the subnets available with a particular IP network address and subnet mask.

- Given a network address and requirements for how many subnets and hosts, be able to determine what subnet mask should be used.

- Given a network address and a subnet mask, be able to determine the number of subnets and hosts per subnet that can be created as well as useable subnets and useable number of hosts.

- Assign IP addresses and subnet masks to hosts and router interfaces.

- Use the "ANDing" process to move an IP packet from a local host to a remote host through a router.

## Background:
This lab will build on Lab Subnet Mask 1 and help develop a better understanding of IP subnet masks using a real-world example with additional worksheet exercises based on foundations established in the prior lab. This lab will focus on a Class C network with three subnets and using a custom subnet mask.

## Tools / Preparation:
This is primarily a written lab exercise but you will want to use Control Panel / Network some real network IP addresses and the basics covered in the prior lab. Before beginning this lab you should read the *Cisco Networking Academy Program: First-Year Companion Guide*, Chapter 5. You should also review semester 1 on-line Lesson 10. The following resources will be required:

- PC workstation with Windows operating system (Windows 95, 98, NT or 2000) installed on the PC and access to the Windows Calculator.

## Notes:

_____

_____

_____

_____

_____

_____

_____

_____

# Cisco Labs - Semester 1 – Networking Fundamentals
## *LAB 10.7.7– SUBNET MASK 2 - WORKSHEET*

### Step 1 – IP Address – Basics

**Explanation:** For reference, the IP addressing table from the prior lab is included here. IP network addresses are assigned by the Internet Network Information Center (InterNIC). You will work with a Class C.

| Adr Cls | 1st Octet Decimal Range | 1st Octet High Order Bits | Network / Host ID (N=Network, H=Host) | Default Subnet Mask | Number of Networks | Hosts per Network (usable addresses) |
|---|---|---|---|---|---|---|
| A | 1 – 126* | 0 | N.H.H.H | 255.0.0.0 | 126 $(2^7 - 2)$ | 16,777,214 $(2^{24} - 2)$ |
| B | 128 – 191 | 1 0 | N.N.H.H | 255.255.0.0 | 16,382 $(2^{14} - 2)$ | 65,534 $(2^{16} - 2)$ |
| C | 192 – 223 | 1 1 0 | N.N.N.H | 255.255.255.0 | 2,097,150 $(2^{21} - 2)$ | 254 $(2^8 - 2)$ |
| D | 224 – 239 | 1 1 1 0 | Reserved for Multicasting | | | |
| E | 240 – 254 | 1 1 1 1 0 | Experimental; used for research | | | |

### Step 2 – Class C network address with 3 subnets.

**Task:** Use the following information and use the information from the worksheet in the prior lab to help determine your valid subnets and host IP addresses. Do **not** use subnet zero or the last subnet.

**Explanation:** Your company has a Class C network address of 200.10.57.0. You want to subdivide your physical network into 3 subnets (A, B and C) using a router as shown in the diagram at the end of the worksheet. You will need at least 20 hosts per subnet. Answer the following questions.

1.  What is the binary equivalent of the Class C network address **200.10.57.0** in the exercise?

    _____ . _____ . _____ . _____

2.  Which octet(s) represent the network portion and which octet(s) represent the host portion of this Class C network address?

    _____

3.  How many bits must you borrow from the host portion of the network address in order to provide at least 3 subnets and at least 20 hosts per subnet? _____

4.  What will the subnet mask be (using dotted decimal notation) based on the number of bits borrowed in Step 3?

    _____ . _____ . _____ . _____

5.  What is the binary equivalent of the subnet mask previously?

    _____ . _____ . _____ . _____

# Cisco Labs - Semester 1 – Networking Fundamentals
## *LAB 10.7.7 – SUBNET MASK 2 - WORKSHEET*

### Step 3 – Class C network address with 3 subnets

**Task:** Use the diagram below to fill in the blanks and answer the following questions.

**Explanation:** Be sure to specify all four octets for subnet address and subnet mask. The same subnet mask should be used for all hosts, router interfaces and subnets. Having a common subnet mask will allow hosts and routers to determine which subnet the IP packet is intended for. Router interfaces will usually be numbered first when assigning IP addresses and hosts will receive higher numbers.

1. Fill in the following table for each of the possible subnets that can be created by borrowing 3 bits for subnets from the fourth octet (host octet). Identify the Network Address, the Subnet Mask, the Subnetwork Address, the range of possible host IP addresses for each subnet, the broadcast address of each subnet and also indicate whether the subnet is useable or not. You will only use 3 of these subnets for the exercise.

| SN # | Network Address | Subnet Mask | Subnetwork Address | Range of possible Host IP Addresses | Broadcast Address | Use ? |
|---|---|---|---|---|---|---|
| 0 | | | | | | |
| 1st | | | | | | |
| 2nd | | | | | | |
| 3rd | | | | | | |
| 4th | | | | | | |
| 5th | | | | | | |
| 6th | | | | | | |
| 7th | | | | | | |

2. Assign an IP address and subnet mask to router interface A and write it down here.

    _____ / _____

3. Assign an IP address and subnet mask to router interface B and write it down here.

    _____ / _____

4. Assign an IP address and subnet mask to router interface C and write it down here.

    _____ / _____

5. Assign a host IP address to Host X on Subnet A and assign an IP address to Host Z on Subnet C (answers can vary). Describe the steps (using ANDing) for the process of sending an IP packet from Host X to host Z through the router. Remember, when ANDing two 1s together, the result is a 1. ANDing any other combination (1 and 0, 0 and 1 or 0 and 0) results in a zero. Also, when ANDing two network IP addresses together the result of the ANDing process will be the network (or subnetwork) address of the destination IP address in the packet. Use the information from the diagram above and the prior lab to help assign IP addresses and subnet masks.

_____

_____

_____

_____

**Cisco Labs- Semester 1 – Networking Fundamentals**
## *LAB 10.7.7 – SUBNET MASK 2 - WORKSHEET*

6.  What is the result of the ANDing process for Host X?
    **Decimal Host X IP addr:** _____ . _____ . _____ . _____
    **Binary Host X  IP addr:** _____ . _____ . _____ . _____
    **Binary Subnet Mask:** _____ . _____ . _____ . _____
    **Binary ANDing Result:** _____ . _____ . _____ . _____
    **Decimal ANDing Result:** _____ . _____ . _____ . _____

7.  What is the result of the ANDing process for Host Z?
    **Decimal Host Z IP addr:** _____ . _____ . _____ . _____
    **Binary Host Z  IP addr:** _____ . _____ . _____ . _____
    **Binary Subnet Mask:** _____ . _____ . _____ . _____
    **Binary ANDing Result:** _____ . _____ . _____ . _____
    **Decimal ANDing Result:** _____ . _____ . _____ . _____

8.   The decimal ANDing result from question 6 is the network/subnet that Host X is on. The result from question 7 is the network/subnet that Host Z is on. Are Host X and Host Z on the same network/subnet? _____

9.  What will Host X now do with the packet? _____

10. Fill in the blanks in the following diagram with the correct network and IP addresses.

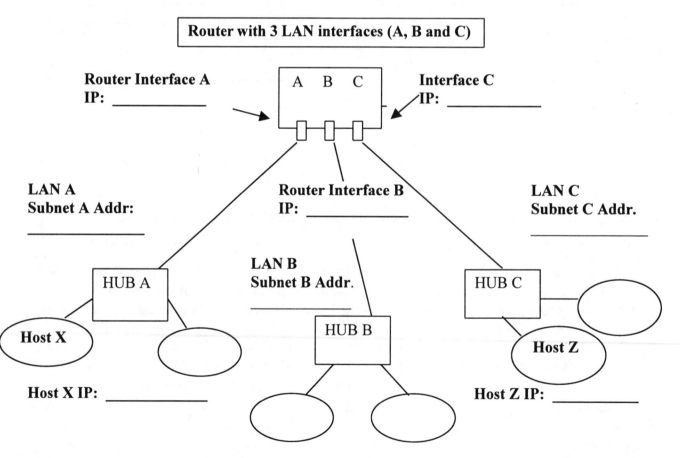

# Cisco Labs - Semester 1 – Networking Fundamentals
## *LAB 10.7.7 – SUBNET MASK 2 – ANSWERS*

**Step 2**

1. What is the binary equivalent of the class C network address 200.10.57.0 in the exercise?
   **11001000 . 00001010 . 00111001 . 00000000**

2. Which octet(s) represent the network portion and which octet(s) represent the host portion of this class C network address? **The first three octets are the network and the 4th octet is the host.**

3. How many bits must you borrow from the host portion of the network address in order to provide at least 3 subnets and at least 20 hosts per subnet? **3 bits ($2^3 - 2 = 6$) will create 8 possible subnets of which 6 are useable (not counting the first and the last subnet).**

4. What will the subnet mask be (using dotted decimal notation) based on the number of bits borrowed in Step 3? **255 . 255 . 255 . 224**
   **(The first 3 bit are borrowed from the left side of the host address. 128 + 64 + 32 = 224)**

5. What is the binary equivalent of the subnet mask previously?
   **11111111 . 11111111 . 11111111 . 11100000**
   **(The first three octets (24 bits of all 1s) mask the original network address. The first 3 bits of the host portion 4th octet are all 1s and mask the subnet number. The last 5 bits of 0s are reserved for host Ids.)**

**Step 3**

1. Fill in the following table:

| SN # | Network Address | Subnet mask | Subnetwork Address | Range of possible Host IP Addresses | Broadcast Address | Use ? |
|---|---|---|---|---|---|---|
| 1st | 200.10.57.0 | 255.255.255.224 | 200.10.57.0 | 200.10.57.1 – 30 | 200.10.57.31 | N |
| 2nd | 200.10.57.0 | 255.255.255.224 | 200.10.57.32 | 200.10.57.33 – 62 | 200.10.57.63 | Y |
| 3rd | 200.10.57.0 | 255.255.255.224 | 200.10.57.64 | 200.10.57.65 – 94 | 200.10.57.95 | Y |
| 4th | 200.10.57.0 | 255.255.255.224 | 200.10.57.96 | 200.10.57.97 – 126 | 200.10.57.127 | Y |
| 5th | 200.10.57.0 | 255.255.255.224 | 200.10.57.128 | 200.10.57.129 – 158 | 200.10.57.159 | Y |
| 6th | 200.10.57.0 | 255.255.255.224 | 200.10.57.160 | 200.10.57.161 – 190 | 200.10.57.191 | Y |
| 7th | 200.10.57.0 | 255.255.255.224 | 200.10.57.192 | 200.10.57.193 – 222 | 200.10.57.223 | Y |
| 8th | 200.10.57.0 | 255.255.255.224 | 200.10.57.224 | 200.10.57.225 – 254 | 200.10.57.255 | N |

## Cisco Labs - Semester 1 – Networking Fundamentals
### *LAB 10.7.7 – SUBNET MASK 2 – ANSWERS*

2. Assign an IP address and subnet mask to router interface A and write it down here.
   **200.10.57.33      /      255.255.255.224**
   **(The first subnet you can use is the .32 net. The first useable IP address for a host or router interface on the .32 net is .33 because the .32 is reserved for the address of the subnet itself, the lowest numbers are reserved for router interfaces. The subnet mask will be the same for all interfaces and subnets.)**

3. Assign an IP address and subnet mask to router interface B and write it down here.
   **200.10.57.65     / 255.255.255.224**

4. Assign an IP address and subnet mask to router interface C and write it down here.
   **200.10.57.97     / 255.255.255.224**

5. Assign a host IP address to Host X on Subnet A and assign an IP address to Host Z on Subnet C (answers might vary). Describe the steps (using ANDing) in the process of sending an IP packet from Host X to host Z through the router. **Host X = 200.10.57.34 (.33 was used for the router interface on subnet A), Host Z = 200.10.57.98 (.97 was used for the router interface on subnet C). Host X compares (ANDs) the subnet mask to its own IP address and comes up with its own network/subnet address of 200.10.57.32. It then compares the subnet mask to the IP address of the destination host (200.10.57.98) and comes up with the network/subnet address of the target network (200.10.57.96). Because the two do not match, host X must assume that the destination host is not on its network, and it sends the packet to its "Default Gateway" or the nearside port of the router. The router goes through the same process on its incoming interface A and determines that network 200.10.57.96 is on its C interface. The router forwards the packet to interface C and because the router also knows the MAC address of hosts directly attached to its interfaces such as host Z, it forwards the packet to the 200.10.57.96 network/subnet LAN and host Z picks it up.**

6. What is the result of the ANDing process for host X?

| | | | |
|---|---|---|---|
| **Decimal Host X IP addr: 200 .** | **10 .** | **57 .** | **34** |
| **Binary Host X IP addr:** 11001000 . | 00001010 . | 00111001 . | 00100110 |
| **Binary Subnet Mask:** 11111111 . | 11111111 . | 11111111 . | 11100000 |
| **Binary ANDing Result:** 11001000 . | 00001010 . | 00111001 . | 00100000 |
| **Decimal ANDing Result:** 200 . | 10 . | 57 . | 32 |

7. What is the result of the ANDing process for host Z?

| | | | |
|---|---|---|---|
| **Decimal Host Z IP addr: 200 .** | **10 .** | **57 .** | **98** |
| **Binary Host Z IP addr:** 11001000 . | 00001010 . | 00111001 . | 01100110 |
| **Binary Subnet Mask:** 11111111 . | 11111111 . | 11111111 . | 11100000 |
| **Binary ANDing Result:** 11001000 . | 00001010 . | 00111001 . | 00100000 |
| **Decimal ANDing Result:** 200 . | 10 . | 57 . | 96 |

# Cisco Labs - Semester 1 – Networking Fundamentals
## *LAB 10.7.7 – SUBNET MASK 2 – ANSWERS*

8. The decimal ANDing result from questions 11 is the network/subnet that Host X is on. The result from question 12 is the network/subnet that Host Z is on. Are Host X and Host Z on the same network/subnet? **NO**

9. What will Host X do with the packet? **Because the destination Host Z is not on the Host X local-area network, Host X will send the packet to the "Default Gateway," which is the IP address of Interface A on the router.**

10. When the router receives the packet from Host X and compares its interface A IP address and the destination address for host Z with the subnet mask, which router interface will it send the packet out of to get the packet to Host Z? **Interface C**

**Router with 3 LAN interfaces (A, B and C)**

**Router Interface A**
**IP:  200.10.57.33**

A  B  C

**Router Interface C**
**IP:  200.10.57.97**

**LAN A**
**Subnet A Addr:**
**200.10.57.32**

**Router Interface B**
**IP:  200.10.57.65**

**LAN C**
**Subnet C Addr.**
**200.10.57.96**

**LAN B**
**Subnet B Addr.**
**200.10.57.64**

HUB A

HUB C

**Host X**

HUB B

**Host Z**

**Host X IP:  200.10.57.34**

**Host Z IP:  200.10.57.98**

## Cisco Labs - Semester 1 – Networking Fundamentals
# *LAB 11.9.1 – PROTOCOL INSPECTOR and ARP - OVERVIEW*
### *(Estimated time: 20 minutes)*

## Objective:

- Use Protocol Inspector (or equivalent) software to study ARP requests and replies

## Background:

Protocol analysis software has a featured called capture. This feature allows all frames through an interface to be captured for analysis. With this feature, we can peek in on the Address Resolution Protocol process. You might have found ARP a bit abstract. With the protocol analyzer we can see just how important ARP is to the normal functioning of a network.

## Tools / Preparation:

- Each PC must be running Windows 95, 98, or NT, Microsoft TCP/IP stack, and Winsock 2.0. Fluke Protocol Inspector 3.0 (or equivalent) must be installed on each PC. During the installation of the software you must specify which network adapter (NIC, dial-up, and so on) you wish to monitor. Specify the NIC that attaches the PCs to an Ethernet. The PCs should be on either a 10BaseT or 100BaseTX Ethernet network that preferably includes servers, switches, routers, printers, and a connection to a web server, or preferably the Internet (this will make the protocol analysis more interesting). Before beginning this lab, you should read the *Cisco Networking Academy Program: First-Year Companion Guide*, Chapter 19. You should also review semester 1 on-line Lessons 7 and 11.

## Cisco Labs - Semester 1 – Networking Fundamentals
## *LAB 11.9.1 – PROTOCOL INSPECTOR and ARP - WORKSHEET*

1.  Open Protocol Inspector (or equivalent) software. _____
    _____

2.  Go to detail view. What do you see? _____
    _____

3.  Start a capture. What happens? _____
    _____

4. Open an MS-DOS window. _____

5.  Using arp –a examine the contents of the ARP table. What do you see? _____
    _____

6.  Using arp –d a.b.c.d delete all entries in the ARP table. Use arp –a to re-examine the ARP table. What has happened? _____

7.  Use ping a.b.c.d to trigger an ARP frame. What happens? Ping your own machine or another machine on the network. _____
    _____

8.  Stop the capture. What happens? _____
    _____

9.  Study the ARP frames, ping frames, and statistics using various views, especially the detail view. Describe the various views and what you learned about ARP. _____
    _____
    _____

10. Start another capture to examine the network you are on.

11. Use the network for a minute or so (sending e-mails, requesting web pages, and so on) over some period of time (say two minutes) and see in detail how many ARP frames occur. Are any occurring? If so, why? _____
    _____

## Reflection:
Why is ARP necessary for LANs to function? _____
_____
_____
_____

# Cisco Labs - Semester 1 – Networking Fundamentals
## *LAB 11.9.1 – PROTOCOL INSPECTOR and ARP - ANSWERS*

1. Open Protocol Inspector (or equivalent) software. **Students should be experienced with this step from the earlier lab.**

2. Go to detail view. What do you see? **A brand new window, with the monitoring graph, and many more icons indicating the powerful capabilities of this software.**

3. Start a capture. What happens? **The monitor graph indicates any network traffic that is detected. It might be somewhat flat ("quiet") depending on your network's configuration.**

4. Open an MS-DOS window. **In Windows, go to START – PROGRAMS – MS-DOS PROMPT.**

5. Using arp –a examine the contents of the ARP table. What do you see? **You should see the contents of your PCs ARP table, which includes MAC addresses and their associated IP addresses.**

6. Using arp –d a.b.c.d delete all entries in the ARP table. Use arp –a to re-examine the ARP table. What has happened? **The ARP table should be empty.**

7. Use ping a.b.c.d to trigger an ARP frame. What happens? Ping your own machine or another machine on the network. **The ping should be successful, and you should notice specific activity on the monitoring graph.**

8. Stop the capture. What happens? **The monitor graph indicates you are no longer capturing frames. Now you will use the database (the detail view) to study the ARP in detail.**

9. Study the ARP frames, ping frames, and statistics using various views, especially the detail view. Describe the various views and what you learned about ARP. **This is an excellent opportunity to take various views of two important network protocols, ARP and ping. The graphs provide an interesting look at the frames involved in these network processes.**

10. Start another capture to examine the network you are on.

11. Use the network for a minute or so (sending e-mails, requesting web pages, and so on) over some period of time (say two minutes) and see in detail how many ARP frames occur. Are any occurring? If so, why? **On an active network there will be ARPs occurring for various reasons: workstations logging on and off, other protocols requiring ARP information.**

## Reflection:
Why is ARP necessary for LANs to function? **ARP is necessary for local delivery of information on a LAN. Having the destination IP address is not sufficient; the destination MAC is required as well. ARP indicates the MAC address – IP address bindings.**

# Cisco Labs - Semester 1 – Networking Fundamentals
## *LAB 12.4.1 – PROTOCOL INSPECTOR and TCP - OVERVIEW*
### *(Estimated time: 30 minutes)*

## Objective:

• Use Protocol Inspector (or equivalent) software to view dynamic TCP operations

## Background:

Protocol analysis software has a feature called capture. This feature allows all frames, through an interface, to be captured for analysis. With this feature, we can peek in on Transmission Control Protocol (TCP) as it moves segments filled with user data across the network. You might have found TCP to be a bit abstract, but with the protocol analyzer we can see just how important TCP is to network processes (such as e-mail and web-browsing).

## Tools / Preparation:

Each PC must be running Windows 95, 98, or NT, Microsoft TCP/IP stack, and Winsock 2.0. Fluke Protocol Inspector 3.0 (or equivalent) must be installed on each PC. During the installation of the software you must specify which network adapter (NIC, dial-up, and so on) you wish to monitor. Specify the NIC that attaches the PCs to an Ethernet. The PCs should be on either a 10Base-T or 100Base-TX Ethernet network. Preferably, this should include servers, switches, routers, printers, and a connection to a web server, or ideally the Internet. Before beginning this lab, you should read *Cisco Networking Academy Program: First-Year Companion Guide*, Chapter 19. You should also review semester 1 on-line Lessons 7 and 11. The following resources will be required:

• PC with Windows 95, 98, or NT, Microsoft TCP/IP stack, and Winsock 2.0
• Fluke Protocol Inspector 3.0 software
• Browser and e-mail applications installed and running

**Cisco Labs- Semester 1 – Networking Fundamentals**
## LAB 12.4.1 – PROTOCOL INSPECTOR and TCP - WORKSHEET

1.  Open protocol inspector and your browser. _____

2.  Go to detail view. _____
    _____

3.  Start a capture. _____

4.  Request a web page: _____

5.  Watch the monitor view while the web page is requested and delivered. _____
    _____

6.  Stop the capture. _____

7.  Study the TCP frames, HTTP frames, and statistics using various views, especially the detail view.
    _____
    _____
    _____

8.  Using the detail view, explain what evidence it provides about a) TCP handshakes b) TCP acknowledgements c) TCP segmentation and segment size d) TCP sequence numbers and e) TCP sliding windows.
    _____
    _____
    _____
    _____
    _____

## Reflection:

Did this lab help you to visualize the TCP protocol in action? Why or why not?

_____
_____
_____

**Cisco Labs - Semester 1 – Networking Fundamentals**
*LAB 12.4.1 – PROTOCOL INSPECTOR and TCP - ANSWERS*

1. Open protocol inspector and your browser. **Students should be familiar with this from earlier labs**.

2. Go to detail view. **Again, students should be familiar with this from earlier labs. By this lab they should have basic proficiency in navigating the Protocol Inspector.**

3. Start a capture.

4. Request a web page. **Using a browser, either go to a www address or enter an IP address.**

5. Watch the monitor view while the web page is requested and delivered. **The monitor view should show bursts of activity corresponding to the web page request and reply.**

6. Stop the capture. **Stop the information flowing into the database**.

7. Study the TCP frames, HTTP frames, and statistics using various views, especially the detail view. **Going line by line through the Capture View Database can be intimidating, but this is just an overview look to get a flavor of the information available and the "back and forth" nature of TCP. The curriculum details various TCP characteristics, but without actually acting them out (in class) and seeing them (with a Protocol Analyzer) TCP can be very abstract.**

8. Using the detail view, explain what evidence it provides about a) TCP Handshakes b) TCP acknowledgements c) TCP segmentation and segment size d) TCP sequence numbers and e) TCP sliding windows.
   **a) look at the beginnings of the TCP sequences b) look at the back and forth nature of the TCP conversation c) look at the byte size of the TCP frames d) look at the sequence numbers for each TCP frame and e) look at the variations in the byte size of the frames (?)**

**Reflection:**

Did this lab help you to visualize the reality of the TCP protocol in action? Why or why not? **Hopefully, the students will associate their HTTP request with the many TCP operations that occurred.**

# Semester 2 Labs

# Cisco Labs – Semester 2 – Router Configuration
## *LAB 2.1.1.2 – ROUTER CHARACTERISTICS – OVERVIEW*
### *(Estimated time: 30 minutes)*

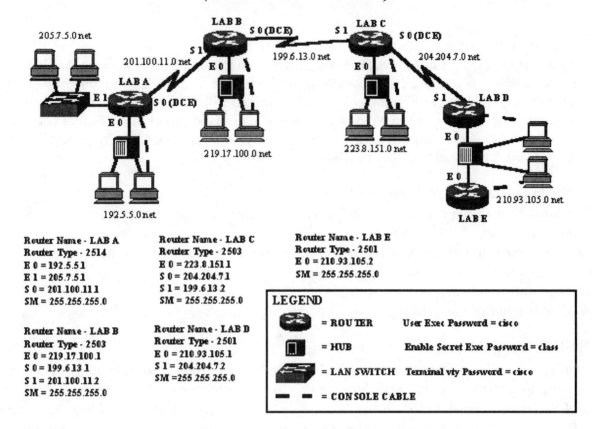

Router Name - LAB A
Router Type - 2514
E 0 = 192.5.5.1
E 1 = 205.7.5.1
S 0 = 201.100.11.1
SM = 255.255.255.0

Router Name - LAB C
Router Type - 2503
E 0 = 223.8.151.1
S 0 = 204.204.7.1
S 1 = 199.6.13.2
SM = 255.255.255.0

Router Name - LAB E
Router Type - 2501
E 0 = 210.93.105.2
SM = 255.255.255.0

Router Name - LAB B
Router Type - 2503
E 0 = 219.17.100.1
S 0 = 199.6.13.1
S 1 = 201.100.11.2
SM = 255.255.255.0

Router Name - LAB D
Router Type - 2501
E 0 = 210.93.105.1
S 1 = 204.204.7.2
SM = 255.255.255.0

**LEGEND**

= ROUTER  User Exec Password = cisco

= HUB  Enable Secret Exec Password = class

= LAN SWITCH  Terminal vty Password = cisco

= CONSOLE CABLE

## Objectives:
- Determine the model number of a Cisco router and what physical interfaces (ports) it has
- Identify the cables attached to the router and what they connect to
- Check and/or modify HyperTerminal configuration parameters
- Connect to the router as its console using the PC and HyperTerminal program
- Determine the IOS version and filename
- Determine the CPU type, amount of RAM, NVRAM, and Flash memory

## Background:
In this lab you will examine a Cisco router to gather information about its physical characteristics and begin to relate Cisco router products to their function. You will determine the model number and features of a specific Cisco router, including which interfaces are present and to which cabling and devices they are connected.

A router is basically a dedicated microcomputer. It has a Central Processing Unit (CPU), an operating system (Cisco IOS), RAM, and ROM inside. Routers do not have disk drives, keyboards, or monitors. One of the ways to configure or program the router is to connect directly to it with a PC or a dumb terminal. The PC provides a monitor and keyboard for the router, which is referred to as its "console." The PC becomes the console, which allows you to enter commands and communicate directly with the router. In this lab, you will work with a PC workstation using the Windows HyperTerminal (terminal emulation) program to act as a console to the router, and you will configure the proper PC serial port settings in order to connect to and communicate with it.

## Cisco Labs – Semester 2 – Router Configuration
## *LAB 2.1.1.2 – ROUTER CHARACTERISTICS – OVERVIEW*

## Tools / Preparation:

Prior to starting the lab, the teacher or lab assistant will need to check that a router is available and that a PC workstation is connected as a console with HyperTerminal installed and properly configured to access the router. The router should be exposed with all sides clearly visible so that all physical connections and cables can be inspected. Work in teams of two or more. Before beginning this lab, you should review Chapters 3 and 4 in the *Cisco Networking Academy Program: First-Year Companion Guide* and semester 2 on-line Chapter 2.

### The following resources will be required:

- Windows PC with HyperTerminal installed and configured to access the router
- Cisco router (16xx or 25xx model)
- Console cable (roll-over) connecting the PC serial port to the router console port
- CAT 5 Ethernet cable attached to an Ethernet port
- Ethernet hub or switch
- WAN cable attached to a serial port

## Web Site Resources:

- **Routing basics** – http://www.cisco.com/univercd/cc/td/doc/cisintwk/ito_doc/routing.htm
- **General information on routers** – http://www.cisco.com/univercd/cc/td/doc/pcat/#2
- **2500 series routers** – http://www.cisco.com/warp/public/cc/cisco/mkt/access/2500/index.shtml
- **1600 series routers** – http://www.cisco.com/warp/public/cc/cisco/mkt/access/1600/index.shtml
- **Terms and acronyms** – http://www.cisco.com/univercd/cc/td/doc/cisintwk/ita/index.htm
- **IP routing protocol IOS command summary** –
  http://www.cisco.com/univercd/cc/td/doc/product/software/ios120/12cgcr/rbkixol.htm

## Notes:

_____
_____
_____
_____
_____
_____
_____
_____
_____
_____
_____
_____

## Cisco Labs – Semester 2 – Router Configuration
## *LAB 2.1.1.2 – ROUTER CHARACTERISTICS – WORKSHEET*

**Step 1 – Examine the router.**

1. What is the model number? _____

2. Do you see a console port? (Y/N) _____    What port is it connected to on the console terminal (PC workstation)? _____

3. What type of cable is the console cable, and is it a roll-over, cross-connect, or straight-through cable? _____

**Step 2 – Record all router interfaces, connectors, and cables.**

**Explanation:** If the port has a cable attached, identify the cable type, connector, and the device attached to the other end. (If a port does not have a cable, you should be able to identify the connector type that would be used.)

4. Fill in the following table.

| Router Interface / Port Identifier | Cable Type / Connector | Device and Port to Which the Cable Is Connected |
|---|---|---|
| | | |
| | | |
| | | |
| | | |
| | | |
| | | |
| | | |

**Step 3 – Review the workstation's HyperTerminal configuration.**

**Explanation:** Click Start/Programs/Accessories/Communications/HyperTerminal. Right-click the icon that is defined for console access to the Cisco router, and then click Properties. The icon might be named **Cisco.ht** or something similar. If one does not exist, you can create it using the settings shown in the answers to the worksheet. On the Properties screen, click the Phone Number tab, and then click the Configure button.

**Cisco Labs – Semester 2 – Router Configuration**
## *LAB 2.1.1.2 – ROUTER CHARACTERISTICS – WORKSHEET*

5. Fill in the following table with the information indicated.

| Configuration Option | Current Setting(s) |
|---|---|
| COM port | |
| Bits per second | |
| Data bits | |
| Parity | |
| Stop bits | |
| Flow control | |

**Step 4 – Display IOS version and other important information related to RAM, NVRAM, and Flash memory with the show version command.**

**Task:** Connect to the console port on the router, and enter the **show version** command.
**Explanation:** The router will return information about the IOS and memory.

6. What is the IOS version? _____

7. What is the name of the system image (IOS) file? _____

8. From where was the router IOS image booted? _____

9. What type of processor (CPU) and how much RAM does this router have? _____
_____

10. How many Ethernet interfaces does this router have? _____

11. How many serial interfaces? _____

12. The router backup configuration file is stored in Non-Volatile Random Access Memory (NVRAM). How much NVRAM does this router have? _____

13. The router operating system (IOS) is stored in Flash memory. How much flash memory does this router have? _____

# Cisco Labs – Semester 2 – Router Configuration
## *LAB 2.1.1.2 – ROUTER CHARACTERISTICS – ANSWERS*

### Step 1
1. Examine the router. What is the model number? **Cisco 2514 (answers will vary)**

2. Do you see a console port? **Yes**    What port is it connected to on the console terminal (PC workstation)? **9-pin serial COM1 port with an RJ45 converter**

3. What type of cable is the console cable? Is it a roll-over, cross-connect, or straight-through cable? **The cable is a roll-over (pin 1 to pin 8, pin 2 to pin 7, and so on)**

### Step 2
4. Fill in the following table. (These are examples.)

| Router Interface / Port Identifier | Cable Type / Connector | Device and Port to Which the Cable Is Connected |
|---|---|---|
| Console | Roll-over, RJ45 | PC serial port com1 (9-Pin) |
| AUX | None | Used for modem with remote dial-in |
| E0 (AUI0) | CAT 5 Unshielded Twisted Pair (UTP) and 8-pin RJ45 or DB15 | Ethernet hub or switch |
| BRI0 | Not used, RJ45 | Basic Rate Interface ISDN |
| To0 (DB9) | Not used, connector female | Token Ring interface |
| S0 (synchronous) | Serial cable DB60 to V.35 | WAN link connection to other router |
| S1 (synchronous) | Not used | WAN link connection |

### Step 3
5. Fill in the following table with the information indicated.

| Configuration Option | Current Setting(s) |
|---|---|
| COM port | Direct to COM1 |
| Bits per second | 9600 |
| Data bits | 8 |
| Parity | None |
| Stop bits | 2 |
| Flow control | Hardware |

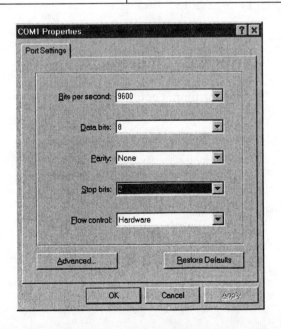

# Cisco Labs – Semester 2 – Router Configuration
## *LAB 2.1.1.2 – ROUTER CHARACTERISTICS – ANSWERS*

**Step 4 – Display IOS version and other important information related to RAM, NVRAM, and Flash memory with the show version command (refer to the show version output listed following the questions).**

6.  What is the IOS version? **Version 11.1(5)**
7.  What is the name of the system image (IOS) file? **flash:igs-j-l.111-5**
8.  From where was the router IOS image booted? **Flash memory**
9.  What type of processor (CPU) and how much RAM does this router have? **cisco 2500 (68030) processor (revision N) with 6144K/2048K bytes of memory**
10. How many Ethernet interfaces does this router have? **1 Ethernet/IEEE 802.3 interface**
11. How many serial interfaces? **2 serial network interfaces**
12. The router backup configuration file is stored in Non-Volatile Random Access Memory (NVRAM). How much NVRAM does this router have? **32K bytes of non-volatile configuration memory**
13. The router operating system (IOS) is stored in Flash memory. How much flash memory does this router have? **8192K bytes of processor board system Flash (read-only)**

## **Results of show version command** (output generated by a Cisco 2501 router)

```
Lab-D> show version
Cisco Internetwork Operating System Software
IOS (tm) 3000 Software (IGS-J-L), Version 11.1(5), RELEASE SOFTWARE (fc1)
Copyright (c) 1986-1996 by cisco Systems, Inc.
Compiled Mon 05-Aug-96 11:48 by mkamson
Image text-base: 0x0303794C, data-base: 0x00001000

ROM: System Bootstrap, Version 11.0(10c), SOFTWARE
ROM: 3000 Bootstrap Software (IGS-BOOT-R), Version 11.0(10c), RELEASE SOFTWARE (fc1)

Router uptime is 15 minutes
System restarted by power-on
System image file is "flash:igs-j-l.111-5", booted via flash

cisco 2500 (68030) processor (revision N) with 6144K/2048K bytes of memory.
Processor board ID 05645767, with hardware revision 00000000
Bridging software.
SuperLAT software copyright 1990 by Meridian Technology Corp).
X.25 software, Version 2.0, NET2, BFE and GOSIP compliant.
TN3270 Emulation software (copyright 1994 by TGV Inc).
1 Ethernet/IEEE 802.3 interface.
2 Serial network interfaces.
32K bytes of non-volatile configuration memory.
8192K bytes of processor board System flash (Read ONLY)

Configuration register is 0x2102
```

# Cisco Labs – Semester 2 – Router Configuration
## *LAB 2.2.10.1 – ROUTER LAB SETUP – OVERVIEW*
### *(Estimated time: 30 minutes)*

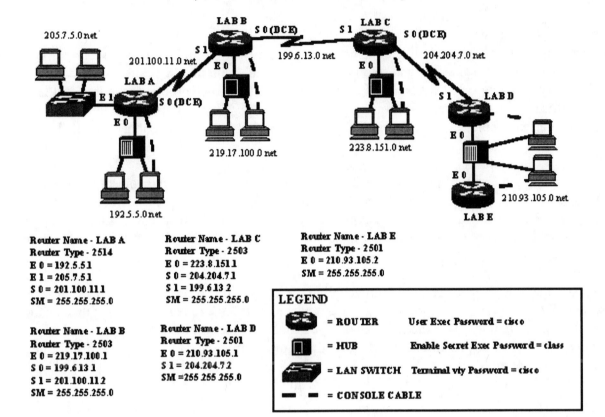

Router Name - LAB A
Router Type - 2514
E 0 = 192.5.5.1
E 1 = 205.7.5.1
S 0 = 201.100.11.1
SM = 255.255.255.0

Router Name - LAB C
Router Type - 2503
E 0 = 223.8.151.1
S 0 = 204.204.7.1
S 1 = 199.6.13.2
SM = 255.255.255.0

Router Name - LAB E
Router Type - 2501
E 0 = 210.93.105.2
SM = 255.255.255.0

Router Name - LAB B
Router Type - 2503
E 0 = 219.17.100.1
S 0 = 199.6.13.1
S 1 = 201.100.11.2
SM = 255.255.255.0

Router Name - LAB D
Router Type - 2501
E 0 = 210.93.105.1
S 1 = 204.204.7.2
SM = 255.255.255.0

**LEGEND**

| | | |
|---|---|---|
| = ROUTER | User Exec Password = cisco |
| = HUB | Enable Secret Exec Password = class |
| = LAN SWITCH | Terminal vty Password = cisco |
| = CONSOLE CABLE | |

## Objectives:
- Set up the Cisco lab equipment according to the semester 2 topology diagram shown above or analyze the physical connections of an existing lab setup
- Document the cabling and connections between devices
- Draw a diagram of your lab equipment setup

## Background:
This lab will help you develop an understanding of how the Cisco lab routers are set up and connected for the Semester 2 topology (see the diagram above). You will examine and document the physical connections between these routers and the other lab hardware components such as hubs, switches, and workstations. This lab will utilize the standard setup consisting of five routers, four hubs, one switch, and at least five workstations, plus all associated cabling and adapters. The next lab, 2.2.10.2, will give you an opportunity to document the IP addressing and internal IOS configuration of the routers if they are already configured. If they are not configured, instructions will be provided to configure and test them.

# Cisco Labs – Semester 2 – Router Configuration
## *LAB 2.2.10.1 – ROUTER LAB SETUP – OVERVIEW*

## Tools / Preparation:

Prior to starting this lab, you will need to have the equipment from the standard five-router lab available (routers, hubs, switch, and so on). The routers and hubs should be disconnected and stacked. Each cabling type (WAN, LAN, console, power) should be grouped together. If it is not possible to start with equipment disconnected, you should review the steps of the lab with the equipment already connected. This will familiarize you with the physical connections and device interfaces.

The routers may be preconfigured by the instructor or lab assistant with the correct IP interface settings, and so on. The workstations may also be preconfigured to have the correct IP address settings prior to starting the lab. The next lab, 2.2.10.2, will provide instructions for analyzing and configuring the routers and workstations using IOS commands if they are not already configured. The routers and workstations should be labeled as indicated in this lab.

Start with the routers, switches, hubs, and cabling disconnected if possible. Your team will need to connect them according to the topology diagram in the overview at the beginning of this lab and then document your findings. This lab requires that you assemble the routers into the standard lab topology or as close as possible, depending on the equipment you have. Work in teams of three or more. Before beginning this lab, you should review Chapters 3 and 4 in the *Cisco Networking Academy Program: First-Year Companion Guide* and semester 2 on-line Chapter 2.

## The following resources will be required:

- 5 PC workstations (minimum) with Windows operating system and HyperTerminal installed
- 5 Cisco routers (model 1600 series or 2500 series with IOS 11.2 or later)
- 4 Ethernet hubs (10Base-T with 4 to 8 ports)
- 1 Ethernet switch (Cisco Catalyst 1900 or comparable)
- 5 serial console cables to connect the workstation to the router console port (with RJ45 to DB9 converters)
- 3 sets of V.35 WAN serial cables (DTE male/ DCE female) to connect from router to router
- CAT5 Ethernet cables wired straight through to connect routers and workstations to hubs and switches
- AUI (DB15) to RJ45 Ethernet transceivers (the quantity depends on the number of routers with AUI ports) to convert router AUI interfaces to 10Base-T RJ45

**Cisco Labs – Semester 2 – Router Configuration**
## *LAB 2.2.10.1 – ROUTER LAB SETUP – WORKSHEET*

## Web Site Resources:
- **Routing basics** – http://www.cisco.com/univercd/cc/td/doc/cisintwk/ito_doc/routing.htm
- **General information on routers** – http://www.cisco.com/univercd/cc/td/doc/pcat/#2
- **2500 series routers** – http://www.cisco.com/warp/public/cc/cisco/mkt/access/2500/index.shtml
- **1600 series routers** – http://www.cisco.com/warp/public/cc/cisco/mkt/access/1600/index.shtml
- **Terms and acronyms** – http://www.cisco.com/univercd/cc/td/doc/cisintwk/ita/index.htm
- **IP routing protocol IOS command summary** –
  http://www.cisco.com/univercd/cc/td/doc/product/software/ios120/12cgcr/rbkixol.htm

## Notes:
_____
_____
_____
_____
_____
_____

# Cisco Labs – Semester 2 – Router Configuration
## *LAB 2.2.10.1 – ROUTER LAB SETUP – WORKSHEET*

### Step 1 – Plan router lab LAN/WAN arrangement.

A. When setting up the lab equipment from scratch, you will need to give some thought to the questions listed below. Even if you are starting with an existing assembled lab setup, you should review all steps and answer all questions to become more familiar with how the routers are connected. Even though you might not actually be connecting the equipment, you should locate, examine, and document the cabling and physical connections between routers, hubs, and workstations.

- Where should the PCs be placed?
- Where should the routers be placed?
- Where should the switch and hubs be placed?
- How should the Ethernet, serial, and power cables be run?
- How many outlets and power strips will be needed?
- Which PC connects to which router?
- Which PC connects to which hub or switch?
- Which router connects to which hub or switch?
- How should devices and cabling be labeled?

### Step 2 – Arrange lab equipment.

Your arrangement of the routers and equipment will vary depending on space and physical setup of your lab area. The goal is to group each combination of router/hub/workstation closely because they can represent separate LANs and geographical locations in the real world. It is easier to see the relationships between equipment with this arrangement. Equipment should be positioned so that all interfaces are facing the same direction and so that cabling and connections can be accessed easily.

A. **Table or work surface setup** – If you are setting the routers out over tables or desks, place the labeled routers side by side in order from left to right (Lab-A, Lab-B...). Place the switch on top of router Lab-A. Place hub 1 on top of the switch and hubs 2, 3, and 4 on top of routers B, C, and D. Place router Lab-D with its hub on top of Lab-E because they are connected to the same LAN. Workstations should be located close to or on the tables for the routers and hubs to which they connect.

B. **Single rack setup** – If you have a single 19-inch network equipment rack, mount the first router, Lab-A, up high in the rack, and mount the switch just above it. Mount the other routers in the rack in sequence from top to bottom with about 4 to 6 inches between each router. Place a hub on top of the switch above router Lab-A and on top of routers B, C, and D. Workstations should be spread out around the rack to allow workspace and will be numbered from left to right.

C. **Multiple rack setup** – If you have multiple racks, put a router and hub in each rack from top to bottom and left to right, depending on how many racks you have. Place workstations as close to the routers as possible while still allowing workspace.

# Cisco Labs – Semester 2 – Router Configuration
## *LAB 2.2.10.1 – ROUTER LAB SETUP – WORKSHEET*

**Step 3 – Connect serial WAN cabling.**
Next you will connect serial cables (DCE-DTE) between routers. With this lab setup, the router interface serial 0 (S0) is connected to the DCE cable. DCE refers to Data Circuit-Terminating Equipment (or Data Communications Equipment) connections and represents the clocking end of the synchronous WAN link. The DCE cable has a large female V.35 (34-pin) connector on one end and a DB60 connector on the other end that attaches to the router serial interface. Interface serial 1 (S1) is connected to the DTE (Data Terminal Equipment) cable. The DTE cable has a large male V.35 connector on one end and a DB60 on the other end that attaches to the router serial interface. Cables are also labeled as DCE or DTE.

1. Examine the cables and connections on the routers, and document the connections in this table:

| From Router Name | Interface | To Router Name | Interface |
|---|---|---|---|
| | | | |
| | | | |
| | | | |

**Step 4 – Connect the router Ethernet cabling.**
For routers that have an AUI (Attachment Unit Interface) Ethernet 0 (E0) or E1 port, you will need an external transceiver that converts the DB15 AUI to an RJ45 10Base-T connector. The 2500 series routers usually have an AUI port. The 1600 series has both AUI and RJ45 ports, and you can use the RJ45 port without the need for the external transceiver. All Ethernet cabling from routers to hubs or switches must be Category 5 (Cat 5) and wired straight-through (pin 1 to pin 1, pin 2 to pin 2, and so on). Connect the Ethernet cabling as indicated in the diagram, and then label the cabling at each end. Hubs should be numbered Hub 1, Hub 2, and so on.

2. Record the router Ethernet interfaces in use and which hub (or switch) they attach to in this table:

| From Router Name | Router Interface | To Which Ethernet Device |
|---|---|---|
| Lab-A | | |
| Lab-A | | |
| Lab-B | | |
| Lab-C | | |
| Lab-D | | |
| Lab-E | | |

**Step 5 – Connect the workstation Ethernet cabling.**
Place the PCs at their planned locations and label them (WS-1, WS-2…) from left to right according to the diagram. Run straight-through CAT 5 cables from each PC to where the switch and hubs are located. Connect the Ethernet cabling as indicated, and then label the cables at each end depending on what device and interface they connect to. The following table shows the connections for all 10 workstations. Connect at least one workstation to each hub or switch.

## Cisco Labs – Semester 2 – Router Configuration
## *LAB 2.2.10.1 – ROUTER LAB SETUP – WORKSHEET*

3.  Indicate which Ethernet device each workstation connects to in this table:

| From Workstation | To Which Ethernet Device |
|---|---|
| WS-1 | |
| WS-2 | |
| WS-3 | |
| WS-4 | |
| WS-5 | |
| WS-6 | |
| WS-7 | |
| WS-8 | |
| WS-9 | |
| WS-10 | |

### Step 6 – Connect the console workstations to routers.
Connect one end of the roll-over cables from workstations 4, 6, 8, 9, and 10 to the console interface of routers Lab-A, B, C, D, and E. Connect the other end of each of the roll-over cables to an RJ45-to-DB9 serial connector. Connect the serial connector to the serial ports of the five workstations. Label the cables at each end.

4.  What type of cable is the console cable? _____

### Step 7 – Connect power cords to all devices.
Plug in and turn on all devices. Verify all of them are activated by checking their indicator lights.

5.  Are the link lights for the switch, the hubs, and the Network Interface Cards (NICs) in the workstations on? _____ Are the OK lights on the back of the routers on? _____

### Step 8 – Draw your lab diagram.

6.  In the space provided below, or in your engineering journal, redraw the router lab diagram to match your physical setup. Label all LAN (Ethernet) and WAN (serial) interfaces and cabling.

# Cisco Labs – Semester 2 – Router Configuration
## *LAB 2.2.10.1 – ROUTER LAB SETUP – ANSWERS*

1. Examine the cables and connections on the routers, and document the connections in this table:

| From Router Name | Interface | To Router Name | Interface |
|---|---|---|---|
| Lab-A | S0 (DCE) | Lab-B | S1 (DTE) |
| Lab-B | S0 (DCE) | Lab-C | S1 (DTE) |
| Lab-C | S0 (DCE) | Lab-D | S1 (DTE) |

2. Record the router Ethernet interfaces in use and which hub (or switch) they attach to in this table:

| From Router Name | Router Interface | To Which Ethernet Device |
|---|---|---|
| Lab-A | E0 | Hub # 1 |
| Lab-A | E1 | Switch |
| Lab-B | E0 | Hub # 2 |
| Lab-C | E0 | Hub # 3 |
| Lab-D | E0 | Hub # 4 |
| Lab-E | E0 | Hub # 4 |

3. Indicate which Ethernet device each workstation connects to in this table:

| From Workstation | To Which Ethernet Device |
|---|---|
| WS-1 | Switch |
| WS-2 | Switch |
| WS-3 | Hub # 1 |
| WS-4 | Hub # 1 |
| WS-5 | Hub # 2 |
| WS-6 | Hub # 2 |
| WS-7 | Hub # 3 |
| WS-8 | Hub # 3 |
| WS-9 | Hub # 4 |
| WS-10 | Hub # 4 |

4. What type of cable is the console cable? **Roll-over (pin 1 to pin 8, pin 2 to pin 7, and so on)**

5. Are the link lights for the switch, the hubs, and the Network Interface Cards (NICs) in the workstations on? **Yes** Are the OK lights on the back of the routers on? **Yes**

6. Draw your lab diagram.
**The lab diagrams might vary, depending on what type of equipment is present. Focus should be on the physical components and on the communications links between them, including LAN (Ethernet) and WAN (serial) connections.**

# LAB 2.2.10.2 – ROUTER LAB CONFIGURATION – OVERVIEW
### (Estimated time: 30 minutes)

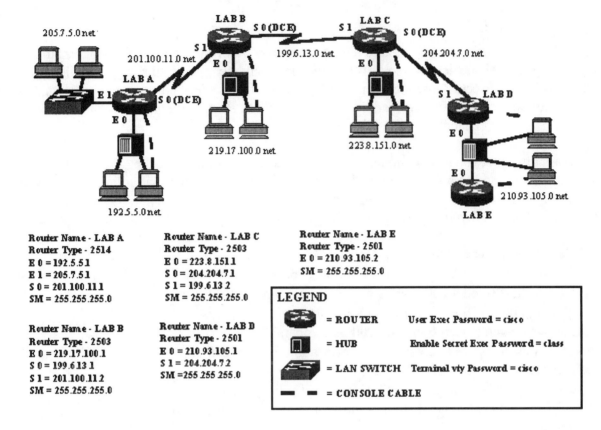

**Router Name - LAB A**
Router Type - 2514
E 0 = 192.5.5.1
E 1 = 205.7.5.1
S 0 = 201.100.11.1
SM = 255.255.255.0

**Router Name - LAB C**
Router Type - 2503
E 0 = 223.8.151.1
S 0 = 204.204.7.1
S 1 = 199.6.13.2
SM = 255.255.255.0

**Router Name - LAB E**
Router Type - 2501
E 0 = 210.93.105.2
SM = 255.255.255.0

**Router Name - LAB B**
Router Type - 2503
E 0 = 219.17.100.1
S 0 = 199.6.13.1
S 1 = 201.100.11.2
SM = 255.255.255.0

**Router Name - LAB D**
Router Type - 2501
E 0 = 210.93.105.1
S 1 = 204.204.7.2
SM = 255.255.255.0

**LEGEND**

| | | |
|---|---|---|
| = ROUTER | User Exec Password = cisco |
| = HUB | Enable Secret Exec Password = class |
| = LAN SWITCH | Terminal vty Password = cisco |
| = CONSOLE CABLE | |

## Objectives:
- Analyze the routers in an existing lab setup and document the IOS configuration
- Use the **show running-config** command at each router to determine attached IP network numbers, interfaces, IP addresses, and subnet mask information for the local-area networks (LANs) and wide-area networks in use
- Use Control Panel/Network or the **winipcfg.exe** utility at each workstation to determine IP address, subnet mask, and default gateway settings
- Use the **Ping** command to test the router and workstation connections
- Use IOS commands to configure routers to the standard lab setup (optional)

## Background:
This lab will help you develop an understanding of how the Cisco lab routers and workstations are configured for the Semester 2 topology (see the diagram above). You will use IOS commands to examine and document the IP network configurations of each router. You will also check the IP configuration of each workstation to ensure that there is full connectivity between all nodes in the lab setup. If the routers are not already configured, you can (optionally) use the instructions at the end of the worksheet to configure each router. This will require additional time and probably some assistance from your instructor or a lab assistant because you have not covered this material in the text, labs, or online chapters yet.

## Cisco Labs – Semester 2 – Router Configuration
# *LAB 2.2.10.2 – ROUTER LAB CONFIGURATION – OVERVIEW*

## Tools / Preparation:

Prior to starting this lab you will need to have the equipment for the standard five-router lab available (routers, hubs, switch, cables, and so on). The routers should be preconfigured by the instructor or lab assistant with the correct IP interface, settings, and so on if possible. The workstations should also be preconfigured to have the correct IP address settings prior to starting the lab. The routers, hubs, and workstations should be labeled.

This lab assumes that you have completed the prior lab, 2.2.10.1, and that the lab equipment (routers, hub, workstations, and so on) is assembled and connected in the standard lab topology. Work in teams of three or more. Before beginning this lab, you should review Chapters 12 and 13 in the *Cisco Networking Academy Program: First-Year Companion Guide* and semester 2 on-line Chapter 2.

## The following resources will be required:

- 5 PC workstations (minimum) with Windows operating system and HyperTerminal installed
- 5 Cisco routers (model 1600 series or 2500 series with IOS 11.2 or later)
- 4 Ethernet hubs (10Base-T with 4 to 8 ports)
- 1 Ethernet switch (Cisco Catalyst 1900 or comparable)
- 5 serial console cables to connect the workstation to the router console port (with RJ45 to DB9 converters)
- 3 sets of V.35 WAN serial cables (DTE male/ DCE female) to connect from router to router
- CAT5 Ethernet cables wired straight through to connect routers and workstations to hubs and switches
- AUI (DB15) to RJ45 Ethernet transceivers (the quantity depends on the number of routers with AUI ports) to convert router AUI interfaces to 10Base-T RJ45

## Web Site Resources:

- **Routing basics** – http://www.cisco.com/univercd/cc/td/doc/cisintwk/ito_doc/routing.htm
- **General information on routers** – http://www.cisco.com/univercd/cc/td/doc/pcat/#2
- **2500 series routers** – http://www.cisco.com/warp/public/cc/cisco/mkt/access/2500/index.shtml
- **1600 series routers** – http://www.cisco.com/warp/public/cc/cisco/mkt/access/1600/index.shtml
- **Terms and acronyms** – http://www.cisco.com/univercd/cc/td/doc/cisintwk/ita/index.htm
- **IP routing protocol IOS command summary** –
  http://www.cisco.com/univercd/cc/td/doc/product/software/ios120/12cgcr/rbkixol.htm

## Notes: _____

_____

_____

_____

_____

# Cisco Labs – Semester 2 – Router Configuration
## *LAB 2.2.10.2 – ROUTER LAB CONFIGURATION – WORKSHEET*

**Step 1 – Verify that all physical connections are correct.**
Review the standard Semester 2 lab diagram in the overview section of this lab or the diagram you created in the prior lab and check all physical devices, cables, and connections. Verify that the routers have been configured correctly (physically and internally) by the instructor or lab assistant.

**Step 2 – Examine and document current router configurations. (If the routers have not been configured, skip to step 5.)**

**A. Log on to the first router, Lab-A.**
Verify that you have a good console connection from the workstation to the router, and start the HyperTerminal program (Start/Programs/Accessories/Communications). Enter the password **cisco** if prompted to enter user mode. The prompt should be **Lab-A>**.
**B. Enter privileged exec mode.**
Type **enable** at the router prompt. Enter the password **class** if prompted. The prompt should now be **Lab-A#**.
**C. Gather information about the router.**
Physically examine each router and make note of the interfaces (E0, S0, and so on) you see.
Enter the **show running-config** command (abbreviated **sh run**) to gather information. The router will respond with the active configuration file currently in RAM.

1. Fill in the table below with IP interface information for each of the five routers.

**Cisco Lab Router IP Configuration (answers from router diagram – your answers may vary)**

| Router Name | Lab-A | Lab-B | Lab-C | Lab-D | Lab-E |
|---|---|---|---|---|---|
| **Model Number** | | | | | |
| **Interface E0 IP Address** | | | | | |
| **Interface E0 Subnet Mask** | | | | | |
| **Interface E1 IP Address** | | | | | |
| **Interface E1 Subnet Mask** | | | | | |
| **Interface S0 IP Address** | | | | | |
| **Interface S0 Subnet Mask** | | | | | |
| **Interface S0 Clock Rate** | | | | | |
| **Interface S1 IP Address** | | | | | |
| **Interface S1 Subnet Mask** | | | | | |
| **Other Interface(s)** | | | | | |

**Cisco Labs – Semester 2 – Router Configuration**
## *LAB 2.2.10.2 – ROUTER LAB CONFIGURATION – WORKSHEET*

2. With the information gathered from the **show running-config** command at router Lab-A, answer the following questions:

   a. What is the routing protocol used? _____

   b. What are the networks that are directly connected to the interfaces?
   
   _____

   c. What is the clock rate of interface S0 on router Lab-A? _____

   d. What is the password for Telnet lines VTY 0 through 4? _____

**Step 3 – Examine and document the workstation configurations. (If the workstations have not been configured, skip to step 6.)**

**A. Verify the workstation IP configuration.**
Click Start/Settings/Control Panel. Double-click the Network icon. Select the TCP/IP protocol and click the Properties button. For each workstation, click the IP Address tab and record the current settings for IP address and subnet mask in the table below. Click the Gateway tab and record the IP address of the default gateway in the table. (This should be the IP address of the E0 router interface that the hub is connected to for each workstation.) You can also use the **winipcfg.exe** utility at the DOS command prompt to verify settings at each workstation.

3. Fill in the IP configuration with information obtained from each workstation.

| Workstation # | Workstation IP Address | Workstation Subnet Mask | Default Gateway IP Address |
|---|---|---|---|
| 1 | | | |
| 2 | | | |
| 3 | | | |
| 4 | | | |
| 5 | | | |
| 6 | | | |
| 7 | | | |
| 8 | | | |
| 9 | | | |
| 10 | | | |

**Cisco Labs – Semester 2 – Router Configuration**
## *LAB 2.2.10.2 – ROUTER LAB CONFIGURATION – WORKSHEET*

### Step 4 – Test the router lab connectivity.

**A. Ping from router to router.**
Begin with router Lab-A and use the console workstation connection to it. Start the HyperTerminal program and ping the S1 interface of router Lab-B. This will verify that the WAN link between Lab-A and Lab-B is OK. Ping the serial interfaces of the other routers.
**Lab-A> ping 201.100.11.2**

    4.  Was the ping from router Lab-A to Lab-B successful? _____

**B. Ping from workstation to router.**
Begin with a workstation connected to the first hub. Click Start/Programs/MS-DOS Prompt and ping the S1 interface of router Lab-B. This will verify that the workstation's IP configuration and the WAN link between Lab-A and Lab-B is OK. Ping the serial interfaces of the other routers.
**C:\WINDOWS> ping 201.100.11.2**

    5.  Was the ping from router Lab-A to Lab-B successful? _____

### Step 5 – Configure the routers for the standard lab setup (optional).
If the routers need to be configured, refer to the answers section for the necessary steps. You will need to obtain assistance from your instructor or lab assistant.

### Step 6 – Configure the workstations for the standard lab setup (optional).
If the workstations need to be configured, refer to the answers section for the necessary steps. You will need to obtain assistance from your instructor or lab assistant.

# Cisco Labs – Semester 2 – Router Configuration
## *LAB 2.2.10.2 – ROUTER LAB CONFIGURATION – ANSWERS*

1. Fill in the table below with IP interface information for each of the five routers.

**Cisco Lab Router IP Configuration (answers from router diagram – your answers may vary)**

| Router Name | Lab-A | Lab-B | Lab-C | Lab-D | Lab-E |
|---|---|---|---|---|---|
| Model Number | 2514 | 2503 | 2503 | 2501 | 2501 |
| Interface E0 IP Address | 192.5.5.1 | 219.17.100.1 | 223.8.151.1 | 210.93.105.1 | 210.93.105.2 |
| Interface E0 Subnet Mask | 255.255.255.0 | 255.255.255.0 | 255.255.255.0 | 255.255.255.0 | 255.255.255.0 |
| Interface E1 IP Address | 205.7.5.1 | Not Present | Not Present | Not Present | Not Present |
| Interface E1 Subnet Mask | 255.255.255.0 | Not Present | Not Present | Not Present | Not Present |
| Interface S0 IP Address | 201.100.11.1 | 199.6.13.1 | 204.204.7.1 | Not Used | Not Used |
| Interface S0 Subnet Mask | 255.255.255.0 | 255.255.255.0 | 255.255.255.0 | Not Used | Not Used |
| Interface S0 * Clock Rate | 56000 | 56000 | 56000 | Not Used | Not Used |
| Interface S1 IP Address | Not Used | 201.100.11.2 | 196.6.13.2 | 204.204.7.2 | Not Used |
| Interface S1 Subnet Mask | Not Used | 255.255.255.0 | 255.255.255.0 | 255.255.255.0 | Not Used |
| Other Interface(s) | Console, AUX | ISDN BRI0, Console, AUX | ISDN BRI0, Console, AUX | Console, AUX | Console, AUX |

**\* Note: Clock rate must be set on the DCE end (S0) of the WAN link between routers.**

2. With the information gathered from the **show running-config** command at router Lab-A, answer the following questions:

   a. What is the routing protocol used? **RIP (Routing Information Protocol)**

   b. What are the networks that are directly connected to the interfaces?
   **192.5.5.0, 205.7.5.0, 201.100.11.0**

   c. What is the clock rate of interface S0 on router Lab-A? **56000**

   d. What is the password for Telnet VTY lines 0 through 4? **cisco**

# Cisco Labs – Semester 2 – Router Configuration
## *LAB 2.2.10.2 – ROUTER LAB CONFIGURATION – ANSWERS*

3. Fill in the IP configuration with information obtained from each workstation.

**Workstation IP Address Configuration**

| Workstation # | Workstation IP Address | Workstation Subnet Mask | Default Gateway IP Address |
|---|---|---|---|
| 1 | 192.5.5.11 | 255.255.255.0 | 192.5.5.1 |
| 2 | 192.5.5.12 | 255.255.255.0 | 192.5.5.1 |
| 3 | 205.7.5.11 | 255.255.255.0 | 205.7.5.1 |
| 4 | 205.7.5.12 | 255.255.255.0 | 205.7.5.1 |
| 5 | 219.17.100.11 | 255.255.255.0 | 219.17.100.1 |
| 6 | 219.17.100.12 | 255.255.255.0 | 219.17.100.1 |
| 7 | 223.8.151.11 | 255.255.255.0 | 223.8.151.1 |
| 8 | 223.8.151.12 | 255.255.255.0 | 223.8.151.1 |
| 9 | 210.93.105.11 | 255.255.255.0 | 210.93.105.1 |
| 10 | 210.93.105.12 | 255.255.255.0 | 210.93.105.2 |

4. Was the ping from router Lab-A to Lab-B successful? **Yes. If not, check connections and obtain assistance from instructor or lab assistant.**

5. Was the ping from router Lab-A to Lab-B successful? **Yes. If not, check connections and obtain assistance from instructor or lab assistant.**

6. Steps to configure the routers for the standard lab setup (optional)
**These are abbreviated instructions. You will need help from the instructor or lab assistant if you are not familiar with Cisco IOS configuration commands.**

From the PC that is connected to the console interface of a router, start HyperTerminal. Create a session that connects the PC's serial port to the router's console interface. Get to user exec mode (Router>). If the System Configuration dialog appears, press Ctrl-C to exit the dialog.

**A. Router Lab-A (2514) Basic Configuration Commands**
The following set of IOS commands can be used to configure router Lab-A. Explanations are provided for each command. Use these commands and the information provided in the table of answers for question 1, **Cisco Lab Router IP Configuration**, to configure the remaining four routers. The exact commands required to configure the other routers will vary somewhat, depending on which interfaces are in use and what IP addresses should be set on those interfaces.

**Cisco Labs – Semester 2 – Router Configuration**
## *LAB 2.2.10.2 – ROUTER LAB CONFIGURATION – ANSWERS*

### Router Lab-A (2514) Basic Configuration Commands (other routers will vary)

| Step Description / Explanation | Router Command Prompt | IOS Command |
|---|---|---|
| Enable privileged mode | Router> | Enable |
| Configure (the router) from terminal (keyboard) | Router# | Config T |
| **Name Router Lab-A** (the prompt will change) | Router(config)# | Hostname Lab-A |
| Set privileged mode encrypted (secret) password to class | Lab-A(config)# | Enable secret class |
| Set privileged mode text password (optional) | Lab-A(config)# | Enable password cisco |
| Disable DNS lookup | Lab-A(config)# | No ip domain-lookup |
|  |  |  |
| **Select E0 interface** | Lab-A(config)# | Interface Ethernet0 |
| Provide description for E0 (optional on any interface) | Lab-A(config-if)# | Description connected to LAN A |
| Set E0 IP address and subnet mask | Lab-A(config-if)# | Ip address  192.5.5.1  255.255.255.0 |
| Bring interface E0 up | Lab-A(config-if)# | No shutdown |
|  |  |  |
| **Select E1 interface** | Lab-A(config)# | Interface  Ethernet1 |
| Set E1 IP address and subnet mask | Lab-A(config-if)# | Ip address  205.7.5.1  255.255.255.0 |
| Bring interface E0 up | Lab-A(config-if)# | No shutdown |
|  |  |  |
| **Select S0 interface** | Lab-A(config-if)# | Interface  Serial0 |
| Set S0 IP address and subnet mask | Lab-A(config-if)# | ip address  201.100.11.1  255.255.255.0 |
| Set IGRP bandwidth metric | Lab-A(config-if)# | Bandwidth  56 |
| Set DCE clock synch at 56000 | Lab-A(config-if)# | Clock rate  56000 |
| Bring interface S0 up | Lab-A(config-if)# | no shutdown |
|  |  | ! |
| **Select S1 interface (not used)** | Lab-A(config-if)# | Interface  Serial1 |
| Set no IP address for S1 | Lab-A(config-if)# | No  ip  address |
| Administratively shut down S1 | Lab-A(config-if)# | Shutdown |
|  |  |  |
| Exit interface config mode | Lab-A(config-if)# | Exit |
|  |  |  |
| **Start RIP routing protocol** | Lab-A(config)# | Router  rip |
| Specify directly connected network for routing updates | Lab-A(config-router)# | Network  192.5.5.0 |
| Specify directly connected network for routing updates | Lab-A(config-router)# | Network  205.7.5.0 |
| Specify directly connected network for routing updates | Lab-A(config-router)# | Network  201.100.11.0 |
|  |  |  |
| Exit router config mode | Lab-A(config-router)# | Exit |

# Cisco Labs – Semester 2 – Router Configuration
## *LAB 2.2.10.2 – ROUTER LAB CONFIGURATION – ANSWERS*

## Router Lab-A (2514) Basic Configuration Commands – Continued

| Enable browser management | Lab-A(config)# | Ip http server |
|---|---|---|
| | | |
| **Define router host name table** | **N/A** | **N/A** |
| Specify host table entry for Lab-A (with interface IP addresses) | Lab-A(config)# | ip host Lab-A 192.5.5.1 205.7.5.1 201.100.11.1 |
| Specify host table entry for Lab-B (with interface IP addresses) | Lab-A(config)# | ip host Lab-B 219.17.100.1 199.6.13.1 201.100.11.2 |
| Specify host table entry for Lab-C (with interface IP addresses) | Lab-A(config)# | ip host Lab-C 223.8.151.1 204.204.7.1 199.6.13.2 |
| Specify host table entry for Lab-D (with interface IP addresses) | Lab-A(config)# | ip host LAB-D 210.93.105.1 204.204.7.2 |
| Specify host table entry Lab-E (with interface IP addresses) | Lab-A(config)# | ip host LAB-E 210.93.105.2 |
| | | |
| Disable classless IP routing | Lab-A(config)# | no ip classless |
| | | |
| **Configure console line** (direct attach to console port) | Lab-A(config)# | Line con 0 |
| Enable console login password checking | Lab-A(config-line)# | Login |
| Set user mode password for console connection login | Lab-A(config-line)# | Password cisco |
| **Configure telnet line** (virtual terminal or VTY) | Lab-A(config-line)# | Line vty 0 4 |
| Enable telnet login password checking | Lab-A(config-line)# | Login |
| Set user mode password for telnet connection login | Lab-A(config-line)# | Password cisco |
| | | |
| **Save the current running configuration to the startup configuration** | Lab-A# | Copy running-config startup-config |

**Common Problem:**
**You can't set the clock rate of the serial interface.**

Clock rate can be set only on DCE cables. DCE cable is the male-female cable. DTE is the male-male cable. Connect the DCE cable to the router serial interface that you want to set the clock rate to.

**Cisco Labs – Semester 2 – Router Configuration**
## *LAB 2.2.10.2 – ROUTER LAB CONFIGURATION – ANSWERS*

7.  Steps to configure the workstations for the standard lab setup (optional)
    **These are abbreviated instructions. You will need help from the instructor or lab assistant if you are unfamiliar with workstation TCP/IP configuration.**

    a.  Click Start/Settings/Control Panel. Double-click the Network icon. Select the TCP/IP protocol and click the Properties button. For each workstation, click the IP Address tab and enter the IP address and subnet mask found in the answers table to question 3, **Workstation IP address configuration.**

    b.  Click the Gateway tab and enter the IP address of the default gateway from the table. (This should be the IP address of the E0 router interface that the hub is connected to for each workstation.)

    c.  Click OK and then Yes to reboot the computer.

**Common Problem:**
**The PC can't ping anything other than what is in its own network.**

The gateway address has to be set. The gateway address of a PC has to be the IP address of the router interface that the PC is directly connected to. For example, WS-1's gateway address is Lab-A's Ethernet 0 IP address, which is 192.5.5.1.

# Cisco Labs – Semester 2 – Router Configuration
## *LAB 3.3.2.1 – ROUTER USER INTERFACE – OVERVIEW*
### *(Estimated time: 60 minutes)*

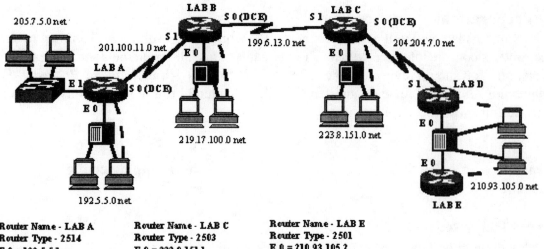

| Router Name - LAB A | Router Name - LAB C | Router Name - LAB E |
|---|---|---|
| Router Type - 2514 | Router Type - 2503 | Router Type - 2501 |
| E 0 = 192.5.5.1 | E 0 = 223.8.151.1 | E 0 = 210.93.105.2 |
| E 1 = 205.7.5.1 | S 0 = 204.204.7.1 | SM = 255.255.255.0 |
| S 0 = 201.100.11.1 | S 1 = 199.6.13.2 | |
| SM = 255.255.255.0 | SM = 255.255.255.0 | |

| Router Name - LAB B | Router Name - LAB D |
|---|---|
| Router Type - 2503 | Router Type - 2501 |
| E 0 = 219.17.100.1 | E 0 = 210.93.105.1 |
| S 0 = 199.6.13.1 | S 1 = 204.204.7.2 |
| S 1 = 201.100.11.2 | SM = 255.255.255.0 |
| SM = 255.255.255.0 | |

**LEGEND**

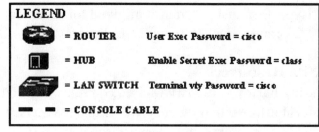

| = ROUTER | User Exec Password = cisco |
|---|---|
| = HUB | Enable Secret Exec Password = class |
| = LAN SWITCH | Terminal vty Password = cisco |
| = CONSOLE CABLE | |

## Objectives:
- Log into a router in both user and privileged modes
- Use several basic router commands to determine how the router is configured
- Become familiar with the router HELP facility
- Use the command history and editing features
- Log out of the router

## Background:
This lab will introduce the Cisco Internetwork Operating System (IOS) command-line user interface. You will log on to the router and use different levels of access to enter commands in user mode and privileged mode. You will become familiar with the commands available in each mode (user or privileged) and use the router HELP facility, history, and editing features. The IOS command interface is the most common method of configuring a Cisco router. You will see many commands available, especially in privileged mode. Do not be overwhelmed. As with many things, the 80/20 rule applies. You can do 80% of what you need to do on a daily basis with 20% of the tools available.

**Cisco Labs – Semester 2 – Router Configuration**
## *LAB 3.3.2.1 – ROUTER USER INTERFACE – OVERVIEW*

## Tools / Preparation:

Prior to starting this lab, you will need to connect a PC workstation with HyperTerminal to a router using the router's console interface with a roll-over cable. This lab should be done at the router console station. You should review Chapter 12 in the *Cisco Networking Academy Program: First-Year Companion Guide* and review semester 1 on-line Chapter 3 prior to starting this lab. You will need to be familiar with these commands:

- ?
- enable
- logout

- show ?
- show running-config
- exit

## Resources Required:

- PC with monitor, keyboard, mouse, and power cords
- Windows operating system (Windows 95, 98, NT, or 2000) installed on PC
- HyperTerminal program configured for router console access
- PC connected to the router console port with a roll-over cable

## Web Site Resources:

- **Routing basics** – http://www.cisco.com/univercd/cc/td/doc/cisintwk/ito_doc/routing.htm
- **General information on routers** – http://www.cisco.com/univercd/cc/td/doc/pcat/#2
- **2500 series routers** – http://www.cisco.com/warp/public/cc/cisco/mkt/access/2500/index.shtml
- **Terms and acronyms** – http://www.cisco.com/univercd/cc/td/doc/cisintwk/ita/index.htm
- **IP routing protocol IOS command summary** –
  http://www.cisco.com/univercd/cc/td/doc/product/software/ios120/12cgcr/rbkixol.htm

## Notes:

_____
_____
_____
_____
_____
_____
_____
_____
_____
_____
_____

# Cisco Labs – Semester 2 – Router Configuration
## *LAB 3.3.2.1 – ROUTER USER INTERFACE – WORKSHEET*

**Step 1 – Log on to router.**
   **Explanation:** Connect to the router and log in. Enter the password **cisco** if prompted.

   1.  What prompt did the router display? _____ What does it mean?
   _____

**Step 2 – Enter the help command.**
   **Task:** Enter the help command by typing **?** at the router prompt.
   **Explanation:** The router will respond with all of the available commands for user mode.

   2.  List eight available commands from the router response. Try to pick ones that might be more
       commonly used.

|  |  |
|--|--|
|  |  |
|  |  |
|  |  |

**Step 3 – Enter enable mode.**
   **Task:**
   a. From user EXEC mode, enter privileged mode by using the **enable** command.
   b. Enter the enable password **class**.
   **Explanation:** Entering the **enable** command and using the password **class** allows you privileged-
   mode access to the router.

   3.  Was **enable** one of the commands available from step 2? _____

   4.  What changed in the router prompt display, and what does it mean? _____
   _____

**Step 4 – Enter the help command.**
   **Task:** Enter the help command by typing **?** at the router prompt.
   **Explanation:** The router will respond with all of the available commands for privileged mode.

   5.  List ten available commands from the router response. Try to pick ones that might be more
       commonly used.

|  |  |
|--|--|
|  |  |
|  |  |
|  |  |
|  |  |

# Cisco Labs – Semester 2 – Router Configuration
## *LAB 3.3.2.1 – ROUTER USER INTERFACE – WORKSHEET*

**Step 5 – List all show commands.**
  **Task:** Enter the **show** command followed by a space and a **?**.
  **Explanation:** The router will respond with the available subcommands for **show**.

  6.  Is **running-config** one of the available commands from this user level? _____

**Step 6 – Look at the running router configuration.**
  **Task:** Enter **show running-config** at the router prompt.
  **Explanation:** Using the **show running-config** command displays the active configuration file for the router that is stored in RAM.

  6a. List six key pieces of information you can get from this command.

|  |  |
|---|---|
|  |  |
|  |  |
|  |  |

**Step 7 – Continue looking at the configuration.**
  **Task:** When the word **more** appears, press the spacebar.
  **Explanation:** When you press the spacebar, the router will display the next page of information.

  7.  What happened when you pressed the spacebar? _____

**Step 8 – Using the command history.**
  **Task:** Press the up arrow or Ctrl-P.
  **Explanation:** Ctrl-P or the up arrow lets you review your command history.

  8.  What happened at the router prompt?
  _____

**Step 9 – Exit the router.**
  **Task:** Enter **exit** at the router prompt.

# Cisco Labs – Semester 2 – Router Configuration
## *LAB 3.3.2.1 – ROUTER USER INTERFACE – ANSWERS*

1. What prompt did the router display? **router-name>** What does it mean? **You are at a user mode prompt that allows you to display some information without changing router configuration settings.**

2. List eight available commands from the router response.

| | |
|---|---|
| **Enable** | **Help** |
| **Exit** | **Ping** |
| **Logout** | **Show** |
| **Telnet** | **Traceroute** |

**User Mode Commands** (output generated by a Cisco 2514 router)

```
Lab-b>?
Exec commands:
  access-enable      Create a temporary access-list entry
  clear              Reset functions
  connect            Open a terminal connection
  disable            Turn off privileged commands
  disconnect         Disconnect an existing network connection
  enable             Turn on privileged commands
  exit               Exit from the EXEC
  help               Description of the interactive help system
  lat                Open a lat connection
  lock               Lock the terminal
  login              Log in as a particular user
  logout             Exit from the EXEC
  mrinfo             Request neighbor and version information from a multicast router
  mstat              Show statistics after multiple multicast traceroutes
  mtrace             Trace reverse multicast path from destination to source
  name-connection    Name an existing network connection
  pad                Open a X.29 PAD connection
  ping               Send echo messages
  ppp                Start IETF Point-to-Point Protocol (PPP)
  resume             Resume an active network connection
  rlogin             Open an rlogin connection
  show               Show running system information
  slip               Start Serial-Line IP (SLIP)
  systat             Display information about terminal lines
  telnet             Open a telnet connection
  terminal           Set terminal line parameters
  tn3270             Open a tn3270 connection
  traceroute         Trace route to destination
  tunnel             Open a tunnel connection
  where              List active connections
  x3                 Set X.3 parameters on PAD
  xremote            Enter XRemote mode
```

**Cisco Labs – Semester 2 – Router Configuration**
## *LAB 3.3.2.1 – ROUTER USER INTERFACE – ANSWERS*

3.  Is **enable** one of the commands? **Yes**

4.  What changed in the router prompt display, and what does it mean?
    **Router-name> changed to Router-name#, indicating that you are in privileged mode.**

5.  List ten available commands from the router response. (Note that the following global privileged mode commands are in alphabetical order and are some of the most common you will use with Cisco routers.)

| Clear | Help |
|-----------|------------|
| Configure | Ping |
| Copy | Reload |
| | Telnet |
| Erase | Traceroute |

**Privileged Mode Commands** (output generated by a Cisco 2514 router)

```
lab-b#?
Exec commands:
  access-enable      Create a temporary access-list entry
  access-template    Create a temporary access-list entry
  bfe                For manual emergency modes setting
  clear              Reset functions
  clock              Manage the system clock
  configure          Enter configuration mode
  connect            Open a terminal connection
  copy               Copy configuration or image data
  debug              Debugging functions (see also 'undebug')
  disable            Turn off privileged commands
  disconnect         Disconnect an existing network connection
  enable             Turn on privileged commands
  erase              Erase flash or configuration memory
  exit               Exit from the EXEC
  help               Description of the interactive help system
  lat                Open a lat connection
  lock               Lock the terminal
  login              Log in as a particular user
  logout             Exit from the EXEC
  mbranch            Trace multicast route down tree branch
  mrbranch           Trace reverse multicast route up tree branch
  mrinfo             Request neighbor and version information from a multicast router
  mstat              Show statistics after multiple multicast traceroutes
  mtrace             Trace reverse multicast path from destination to source
```

# Cisco Labs – Semester 2 – Router Configuration
## *LAB 3.3.2.1 – ROUTER USER INTERFACE – ANSWERS*

### Privileged Mode Commands – Continued (output generated by a Cisco 2514 router)

| | |
|---|---|
| name-connection | Name an existing network connection |
| no | Disable debugging functions |
| pad | Open a X.29 PAD connection |
| ping | Send echo messages |
| ppp | Start IETF Point-to-Point Protocol (PPP) |
| reload | Halt and perform a cold restart |
| resume | Resume an active network connection |
| rlogin | Open an rlogin connection |
| rsh | Execute a remote command |
| sdlc | Send SDLC test frames |
| send | Send a message to other tty lines |
| setup | Run the SETUP command facility |
| show | Show running system information |
| slip | Start Serial-Line IP (SLIP) |
| start-chat | Start a chat-script on a line |
| systat | Display information about terminal lines |
| tarp | TARP (Target ID Resolution Protocol) commands |
| telnet | Open a telnet connection |
| terminal | Set terminal line parameters |
| test | Test subsystems, memory, and interfaces |
| tn3270 | Open a tn3270 connection |
| traceroute | Trace route to destination |
| tunnel | Open a tunnel connection |
| undebug | Disable debugging functions (see also 'debug') |
| verify | Verify checksum of a Flash file |
| where | List active connections |
| which-route | Do OSI route table lookup and display results |
| write | Write running configuration to memory, network, or terminal |
| x3 | Set X.3 parameters on PAD |
| xremote | Enter XRemote mode |

6.  Enter **show** followed by a space then a **?**. Is **running-config** one of the available commands from this user level? <u>**Yes**</u>

6a. Enter **show running-config** at the router prompt. (This is the active configuration file for the router.) List six key pieces of information you can get from this command:

| | |
|---|---|
| Operating system version (11.1) | Interfaces and IP addresses (E0 and S0) |
| Name of router (lab-b) | Enable password (cisco) |
| Boot system image filename (igs-j-l.111-5) | Routing protocol (IGRP) |

# Cisco Labs – Semester 2 – Router Configuration
## *LAB 3.3.2.1 – ROUTER USER INTERFACE – ANSWERS*

**show running-config Command** (output generated by a Cisco 2514 router)

```
lab-b#show running-config

Building configuration...

Current configuration:
!
version 11.1
service slave-log
service udp-small-servers
service tcp-small-servers
!
hostname lab-b
!
boot system  igs-j-l.111-5
enable secret 5 $1$itif$vqTo8RC73KajshkzpFObr/
enable password cisco
!
interface Ethernet0
 ip address 192.5.5.1  255.255.255.0
!
interface Ethernet1
 ip address 205.7.5.1  255.255.255.0
!
interface Serial0
 ip address 201.100.11.1  255.255.255.0
 bandwidth 56
 no fair-queue
 clockrate 56000
!
interface Serial1
 no ip address
shutdown
!
router igrp 100
 network 201.100.11.0
network 192.5.5.0
 network 205.7.5.0
!
ip host LAB-A 192.5.5.1 201.100.11.1 205.7.5.1
ip host LAB-B 219.17.100.1 199.6.13.1 201.100.11.2
ip host LAB-C 223.8.151.1 204.204.7.1 199.6.13.2
ip host LAB-D 210.93.105.1 204.204.7.2
ip host LAB-E 210.93.105.2
```

# Cisco Labs – Semester 2 – Router Configuration
## *LAB 3.3.2.1 – ROUTER USER INTERFACE – ANSWERS*

**show running-config Command – Cont.** (output generated by a Cisco 2514 router)

```
no ip classless
!
!
line con 0
 exec-timeout 0 0
 password cisco
 login
line aux 0
line vty 0 4
 password cisco
 login
!
end
```

7. What happened when you pressed the spacebar? **Multiple screens are available as output.**

8. What happened at the router prompt? **Allows you to retrieve previous commands.**

# Cisco Labs – Semester 2 – Router Configuration
## *LAB 3.4.2.1 – ROUTER USER INTERFACE MODES – OVERVIEW*
### *(Estimated time: 20 minutes)*

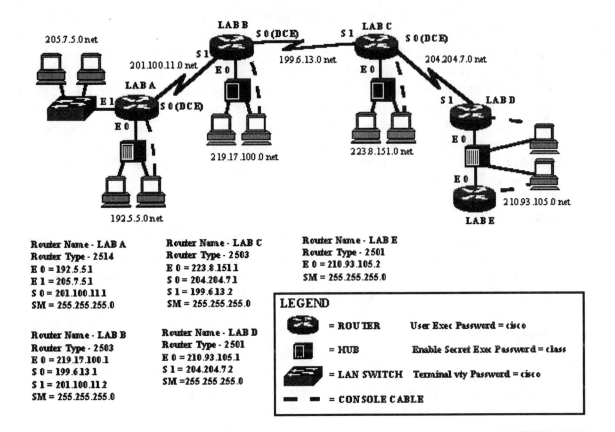

**Router Name - LAB A**
Router Type - 2514
E 0 = 192.5.5.1
E 1 = 205.7.5.1
S 0 = 201.100.11.1
SM = 255.255.255.0

**Router Name - LAB C**
Router Type - 2503
E 0 = 223.8.151.1
S 0 = 204.204.7.1
S 1 = 199.6.13.2
SM = 255.255.255.0

**Router Name - LAB E**
Router Type - 2501
E 0 = 210.93.105.2
SM = 255.255.255.0

**Router Name - LAB B**
Router Type - 2503
E 0 = 219.17.100.1
S 0 = 199.6.13.1
S 1 = 201.100.11.2
SM = 255.255.255.0

**Router Name - LAB D**
Router Type - 2501
E 0 = 210.93.105.1
S 1 = 204.204.7.2
SM = 255.255.255.0

**LEGEND**

= ROUTER      User Exec Password = cisco

= HUB         Enable Secret Exec Password = class

= LAN SWITCH  Terminal vty Password = cisco

= CONSOLE CABLE

## Objectives
- To identify the six basic and two optional router modes
- To become familiar with the router prompt for each mode
- Use several commands that will enter specific modes

## Background:
When using router operating systems such as Cisco IOS, you will have to know each of the different user modes a router has and what each one of them is for. Memorizing every command in all of the user modes would be time-consuming and pointless. Try to develop an understanding of what commands and functions are available with each of the modes. There are six main modes available with most routers:

1. User EXEC mode
2. Privileged EXEC mode (also known as enable mode)
3. Global configuration mode
4. Router configuration mode
5. Interface configuration mode
6. Subinterface configuration mode

# Cisco Labs – Semester 2 – Router Configuration
## *LAB 3.4.2.1 – ROUTER USER INTERFACE MODES – OVERVIEW*

In this lab you will work with the six most common modes listed above. Two other modes that are used less frequently are RXBoot mode and setup mode. RXBoot is a maintenance mode that can be used for password recovery. Setup mode presents an interactive prompted dialog at the console that helps a new user create a first-time basic configuration. Both RXBoot and setup modes will be covered in later labs. You can determine which mode you are in by looking at the prompt. Each of the modes will have a different prompt. Depending on which mode you are in, certain commands may or may not be available. You can always type a question mark (**?**) to see what commands you can use. The most common mistake made when working at the command line with different router modes is to enter a command and get an error when you are in the wrong mode. You need to be familiar with each mode and how to get in and out of each mode.

## Tools / Preparation:
Prior to starting this lab, you will need to connect a PC with HyperTerminal to a router using the router's console interface with a roll-over cable. Work individually or in teams. Before beginning this lab, you should read the *Cisco Networking Academy Program: First Year Companion Guide*, Chapters 12 and 15. You should also review on-line Chapter 3.

## Resources Required:
- PC with monitor, keyboard, mouse, and power cords
- Windows operating system (Windows 95, 98, NT, or 2000) installed on PC
- HyperTerminal program configured for router console access
- PC connected to the router console port with a roll-over cable

## Web Site Resources:
- **Routing basics** – http://www.cisco.com/univercd/cc/td/doc/cisintwk/ito_doc/routing.htm
- **General information on routers** – http://www.cisco.com/univercd/cc/td/doc/pcat/#2
- **2500 series routers** – http://www.cisco.com/warp/public/cc/cisco/mkt/access/2500/index.shtml
- **Terms and acronyms** – http://www.cisco.com/univercd/cc/td/doc/cisintwk/ita/index.htm
- **IP routing protocol IOS command summary** –
  http://www.cisco.com/univercd/cc/td/doc/product/software/ios120/12cgcr/rbkixol.htm

## Notes:
_____
_____
_____
_____
_____
_____
_____
_____

# Cisco Labs – Semester 2 – Router Configuration
## *LAB 3.4.2.1 – ROUTER USER INTERFACE MODES – WORKSHEET*

### Step 1 – Identify router modes, prompts, and functions.

For this lab, you and your group should try to discover what each of the modes are and what each of them does. Be sure to make note of what the prompts on the router look like in each of the modes. For example, when in interface config mode, the prompt is router(config-if)# (where router is the name of the router you are working with) .

1. Match the different router modes with their appropriate prompts (for example, 1-A, 2-B, and so on). Fill in the table by writing out the correct prompt, selecting from the list of choices provided below:

| Mode Description | Mode Prompts |
|---|---|
| 1. User EXEC mode | |
| 2. Privileged EXEC mode | |
| 3. Global configuration mode | |
| 4. Router configuration mode | |
| 5. Interface configuration mode | |

   A.  Router #
   B.  Router >
   C.  Router (config-if) #
   D.  Router (config-router) #
   E.  Router (config) #

2. Match the different router modes with their functionality. Fill in the table by writing the letter of the correct choice provided below:

| Mode Description | Mode Functions |
|---|---|
| 1. User EXEC mode | |
| 2. Privileged EXEC mode | |
| 3. Global configuration mode | |
| 4. Router configuration mode | |
| 5. Interface configuration mode | |

   A.  Detailed examination of router, debugging, and testing. Remote access.
   B.  Setting of IP addresses and subnet masks.
   C.  Simple configuration commands.
   D.  Limited examination of router. Remote access.
   E.  Routing protocols.

3. From the prompt shown below, write a command that will allow you to enter the mode listed:

| Desired Mode | Current Prompt | Command | Explanation |
|---|---|---|---|
| Privileged EXEC mode | Router> | | |
| Global config. mode | Router# | | |
| Interface config. mode | Router(config)# | | |
| Router config. mode | Router(config)# | | |

**Cisco Labs – Semester 2 – Router Configuration**
## *LAB 3.4.2.1 – ROUTER USER INTERFACE MODES –WORKSHEET*

### Step 2 – Diagram a router modes hierarchy.

4. In the space provided or in your Engineering Journal, draw a hierarchical diagram of the various router modes listed in the background section of this lab. At the top of the hierarchy you should have the initial router mode that comes up when you boot up the device. The bottom should have more specific modes. If two or more modes have equal priority, choose any order.

**Reflection:**

In your journal, describe what general function the following modes serve:
1. Config interface: _____
2. Enable mode: _____

Also answer the following:
1. What did you learn from this lab? _____
2. Where/when did you have difficulties? _____
3. How did you overcome them? _____
4. How can you apply what you learned in this lab toward future labs? _____

**Cisco Labs – Semester 2 – Router Configuration**
# _LAB 3.4.2.1 – ROUTER USER INTERFACE MODES – ANSWERS_

1. Match the different router modes with their appropriate prompts (for example, 1-A, 2-B, and so on). Fill in the table by writing out the correct prompt, selecting from the list of choices provided below:

| Mode Description | Mode Prompts |
|---|---|
| 1. User EXEC mode | **B. Router >** |
| 2. Privileged EXEC mode | **A. Router #** |
| 3. Global configuration mode | **E. Router (config) #** |
| 4. Router configuration mode | **D. Router (config-router) #** |
| 5. Interface configuration mode | **C. Router (config-if) #** |

A. Router #
B. Router >
C. Router (config-if) #
D. Router (config-router) #
E. Router (config) #

2. Match the different router modes with their functionality. Fill in the table by writing the letter of the correct choice provided below:

| Mode Description | Mode Functions |
|---|---|
| 1. User EXEC mode | **D. Limited examination of router. Remote access.** |
| 2. Privileged EXEC mode | **A. Detailed examination of router, debugging, and testing. Remote access.** |
| 3. Global configuration mode | **C. Simple configuration commands.** |
| 4. Router configuration mode | **E. Routing protocols.** |
| 5. Interface configuration mode | **B. Setting of IP addresses and subnet masks.** |

A. Detailed examination of router, debugging, and testing. Remote access.
B. Setting of IP addresses and subnet masks.
C. Simple configuration commands.
D. Limited examination of router. Remote access.
E. Routing protocols.

3. From the prompt shown below, write a command that will allow you to enter the mode listed:

| Desired Mode | Current Prompt | Command | Explanation |
|---|---|---|---|
| Privileged EXEC mode | Router> | **Enable** | **Enables priv. mode** |
| Global config. mode | Router# | **Configure T** | **Configure from terminal** |
| Interface config. mode | Router(config)# | **Interface Serial 0** | **Selects interface S0** |
| Router config. mode | Router(config)# | **Router rip** | **Enables RIP routing** |

**Cisco Labs – Semester 2 – Router Configuration**
## _LAB 3.4.2.1 – ROUTER USER INTERFACE MODES – ANSWERS_

**Router modes diagram**

4. In the space provided here or in your Engineering Journal, draw a hierarchical diagram of the various router modes listed in the background section of the lab. At the top of the hierarchy you should have the initial router mode that comes up when you boot up the device. The bottom should have more specific modes. If two or more modes have equal priority, choose any order.

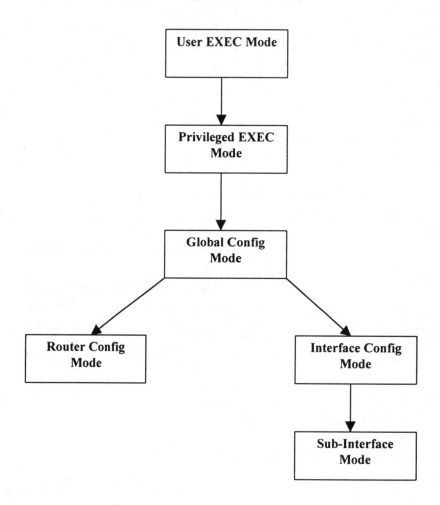

**Reflection:**

In your journal, describe the what general function the following modes serve:

1. Config interface: **Allows you to work with and configure a specific interface on a router.**
2. Enable mode: **Provides access to all available router commands and modes.**

Also answer the following:

1. What did you learn from this lab? _____
2. Where/when did you have difficulties? _____
3. How did you overcome them? _____
4. How can you apply what you learned in this lab toward future labs? _____

# Cisco Labs – Semester 2 – Router Configuration
## *LAB 4.5.2.1 – ROUTER SHOW COMMANDS – OVERVIEW*
### *(Estimated time: 90 minutes)*

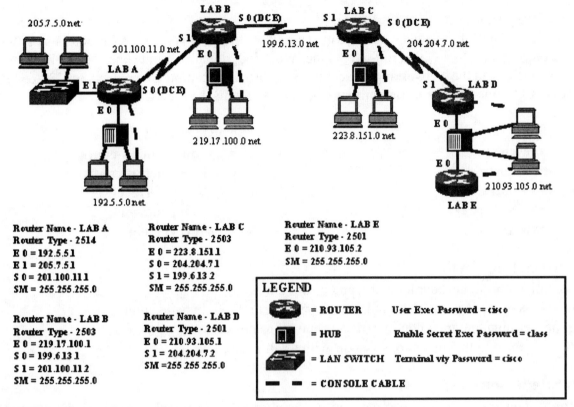

Router Name - LAB A
Router Type - 2514
E 0 = 192.5.5.1
E 1 = 205.7.5.1
S 0 = 201.100.11.1
SM = 255.255.255.0

Router Name - LAB C
Router Type - 2503
E 0 = 223.8.151.1
S 0 = 204.204.7.1
S 1 = 199.6.13.2
SM = 255.255.255.0

Router Name - LAB E
Router Type - 2501
E 0 = 210.93.105.2
SM = 255.255.255.0

Router Name - LAB B
Router Type - 2503
E 0 = 219.17.100.1
S 0 = 199.6.13.1
S 1 = 201.100.11.2
SM = 255.255.255.0

Router Name - LAB D
Router Type - 2501
E 0 = 210.93.105.1
S 1 = 204.204.7.2
SM = 255.255.255.0

LEGEND

= ROUTER        User Exec Password = cisco

= HUB           Enable Secret Exec Password = class

= LAN SWITCH    Terminal vty Password = cisco

= CONSOLE CABLE

## Objectives

- Become familiar with the basic router **show** commands
- Retrieve the current running configuration of the router in RAM using **show running-config**
- View the backup configuration file in NVRAM using **show startup-config**
- View the IOS file information using **show flash** and **show version**
- View the current status of the router interfaces using **show interface**
- View the status of any configured layer 3 protocol using **show protocol**

## Background:

This lab will help you become familiar with the router **show** commands. The show commands are the most important information-gathering commands available for the router. **show running-config** (or **show run**) is probably the single most valuable command to help determine the current status of a router, because it displays the active configuration file running in RAM. The **show startup-config** (or **show start**) command displays the backup configuration file that is stored in non-volatile RAM (NVRAM). This is the file that will be used to configure the router when it is first started or rebooted with the **reload** command.. All of the detailed router interface settings are contained in this file.

The **show flash** command is used to view the available flash memory and the amount used. Flash is where the Cisco Internetwork Operating System (IOS) file or image is stored.. The **show arp** command displays the router's IP to MAC to interface address mapping. The **show interface** command displays statistics for all interfaces configured on the router. **show protocol** displays global and interface-specific status of configured layer 3 protocols (IP, IPX, etc.).

**Cisco Labs – Semester 2 – Router Configuration**
## *LAB 4.5.2.1 – ROUTER SHOW COMMANDS – OVERVIEW*

## Tools / Preparation:

Prior to starting the lab, you will need to connect a PC with HyperTerminal to a router using the router's console interface with a roll-over cable. Work individually or in teams. Before beginning this lab, you should read the Networking Academy First Year Companion Guide, Chapter 13. You should also review On-line Chapter 4. Be familiar with the following **show** commands:

- **show ?**
- **show clock**
- **show hosts**
- **show users**
- **show history**
- **show arp**

- **show flash**
- **show running-config**
- **show startup-config**
- **show interface**
- **show protocol**
- **show version**

## Resources Required:

- PC with monitor, keyboard, mouse, and power cords
- Windows operating system (Windows 95, 98, NT, or 2000) installed on PC
- HyperTerminal program configured for router console access
- PC connected to the router console port with a roll-over cable

## Web Site Resources:

- **Routing basics** – http://www.cisco.com/univercd/cc/td/doc/cisintwk/ito_doc/routing.htm
- **General information on routers** – http://www.cisco.com/univercd/cc/td/doc/pcat/#2
- **2500 series routers** – http://www.cisco.com/warp/public/cc/cisco/mkt/access/2500/index.shtml
- **1600 series routers** – http://www.cisco.com/warp/public/cc/cisco/mkt/access/1600/index.shtml
- **Terms and acronyms** – http://www.cisco.com/univercd/cc/td/doc/cisintwk/ita/index.htm
- **IP routing protocol IOS command summary** –
  http://www.cisco.com/univercd/cc/td/doc/product/software/ios120/12cgcr/rbkixol.htm

## Notes:

_____
_____
_____
_____
_____
_____
_____
_____
_____
_____
_____
_____
_____

# Cisco Labs – Semester 2 – Router Configuration
## _LAB 4.5.2.1 – ROUTER SHOW COMMANDS – WORKSHEET_

**Step 1 – Log on to the router.**

**Explanation:** Connect to the router and log in. Enter the password **cisco** if prompted.

**Step 2 – Enter the help command.**

**Task:** Enter the help command by typing **?** at the router prompt.
**Explanation:** The router responds with all commands available in user mode.

1a. What did the router reply with? _____

1b. Are all router commands available at the current prompt? _____

2. Is **show** one of the options available? _____

**Step 3 – Display help for the show command.**

**Task:** Enter the **show ?** command.
**Explanation:** The router responds with the **show** subcommands available in user mode.

3. List three user mode **show** subcommands.

| show Subcommand | Description |
|---|---|
| | |
| | |
| | |

**Step 4 – Display IOS version and other important information with the show version command.**

**Task:** Enter the **show version** command.
**Explanation:** The router will return information about the IOS that is running in RAM.

4. With information from the **show version** command, answer these questions:
   a. What is the IOS version? _____
   b. What is the name of the system image (IOS) file? _____
   c. Where was the router IOS image booted from? _____
   d. What type of processor (CPU) and how much RAM does this router have? _____
   _____
   e. How many Ethernet interfaces does this router have? _____ How many serial interfaces? _____
   f. The router backup configuration file is stored in non-volatile random access memory (NVRAM). How much NVRAM does this router have? _____
   g. The router operating system (IOS) is stored in Flash memory. How much Flash memory does this router have? _____
   h. What is the configuration register set to? _____

# Cisco Labs – Semester 2 – Router Configuration
## *LAB 4.5.2.1 – ROUTER SHOW COMMANDS – WORKSHEET*

### Step 5 – Displaying the router's time and date.
**Task:** Enter the **show clock** command.
**Explanation:** The **show clock** command will show the current time and date.

5.  What information is displayed with **show clock**? _____

### Step 6 – Displaying a cached list of host names and addresses.
**Task:** Enter the **show hosts** command.
**Explanation:** The **show hosts** command displays a cached list of hosts and all of their interface IP addresses.

6.  What information is displayed with **show hosts**? _____

### Step 7 – Display users who are connected to the router.
**Task:** Enter the **show users** command.
**Explanation:** The **show users** command displays users who are connected to the router.

7.  What information is displayed with **show users**? _____

### Step 8 – Show the command buffer.
**Task:** Enter the **show history** command.
**Explanation:** The **show history** command displays a history of commands that have been entered.

8.  What information is displayed with **show history**? _____

### Step 9 – Enter privileged mode.
**Task:** a. From user EXEC mode, enter privileged EXEC mode using the **enable** command.
       b. Enter the enable password **class**.
**Explanation:** Enter enable mode from user EXEC mode.

9.
      a.     What command did you use to enter privileged mode? _____
      b.     How do you know if you are in privileged mode? _____

### Step 10 – Enter the help command.
**Task:** Enter the **show ?** command at the router prompt.
**Explanation:** The router responds with the **show** subcommands available for privileged mode.

10.
      a.     What did the router reply with? _____
      b.     How is this output different from the one you got in user mode in Step 3? _____
           _____

### Step 11 – Show the router ARP table.
**Task:** Enter the **show arp** command at the router prompt.

**Cisco Labs – Semester 2 – Router Configuration**
## *LAB 4.5.2.1 – ROUTER SHOW COMMANDS – WORKSHEET*

**Explanation:** The router will respond with its ARP table.
11. What is the ARP table? _____

**Step 12 – Show information about the Flash memory device.**
    **Task:** Enter **show flash** at the router prompt.
    **Explanation:** The router will respond with information about Flash memory and what IOS file(s) are stored there.
    12. Document the following information with **show flash**:
        a.   How much Flash memory is available and used? _____
        b.   What is the file that is stored in Flash memory? _____
        c.   What is the size in bytes of the Flash memory? _____

**Step 13 – Show information about the active configuration file.**
    **Task:** Enter **show running-config** (or **show run**) at the router prompt.
    **Explanation:** The router will display information on how it is currently configured.
    13. What important information is displayed with **show run**? _____
_____

**Step 14 – Show information about the backup configuration file.**
    **Task:** Enter **show startup-config** (or **show start**) at the router prompt.
    **Explanation:** The router will display information on the backup configuration file stored in NVRAM.
    14. What important information is displayed with **show start**, and where is this information kept?
_____

**Step 15 – Display statistics for all interfaces configured on the router.**
    **Task:** Enter **show interface** at the router prompt.
    **Explanation:** The router shows information about the configured interfaces.
    15a.  Find the following information for interface Ethernet 0 with **show interface**:
        1.   What is MTU? _____
        2.   What is rely? _____
        3.   What is load? _____
        4.   What is a runt? _____
        5.   What is a giant? _____

    15b.  Find the following information for interface serial0 with **show interface**:
        1.   What is the IP address and subnet mask? _____
        2.   What data link layer encapsulation is being used? _____
        3.   What does "Serial0 is up, line protocol is up" mean? _____

**Step 16 – Display the protocols configured on the router.**
    **Task:** Enter **show protocol** at the router prompt.
    **Explanation:** This command shows the global and interface-specific status of any configured layer 3 protocols.
    16. What important information is displayed? _____
    17. Enter **exit** at the router prompt.

# Cisco Labs – Semester 2 – Router Configuration
## _LAB 4.5.2.1 – ROUTER SHOW COMMANDS – ANSWERS_

1.
   a. What did the router reply with? **_Router-name>_**
   b. Are all router commands available at the current prompt? **No. Only user-mode commands are available.**

2. Is **show** one of the options available? **Yes**

3. List three user mode **show** commands.

| show Subcommand | Description |
|---|---|
| **show clock** | **Display the system clock** |
| **show hosts** | **IP domain-name, lookup style, nameservers, and host table** |
| **show version** | **IOS software version information and system hardware status** |

## User Mode show Commands (output generated by a Cisco 2501 router)

```
lab-b>show ?
  clock       Display the system clock
  history     Display the session command history
  hosts       IP domain-name, lookup style, nameservers, and host table
  kerberos    Show Kerberos Values
  modemcap    Show Modem Capabilities database
  ppp         PPP parameters and statistics
  rmon        rmon statistics
  sessions    Information about Telnet connections
  snmp        snmp statistics
  terminal    Display terminal configuration parameters
  users       Display information about terminal lines
  version     System hardware and software status
```

4. With information from the **show version** command, answer the following questions (answers will vary, depending on the router model and IOS version):
   a. What is the IOS version? **11.1(7)AA**
   b. What is the name of the system image (IOS) file? **c1600-nsy-l.111-7.AA**
   c. Where was the router IOS image booted from? **Flash memory**
   d. What type of processor (CPU) and how much RAM does this router have? **cisco CPA1600 (68360) processor (revision C) with 3584K/512KB of memory**
   e. How many Ethernet interfaces does this router have? **One** How many serial interfaces? **Two**
   f. The router backup configuration file is stored in non-volatile random access memory (NVRAM). How much NVRAM does this router have? **8KB of non-volatile configuration memory**
   g. The router operating system (IOS) is stored in Flash memory. How much Flash memory does this router have? **6144KB of processor board PCMCIA Flash (read-only) or approximately 6MB**
   h. What is the configuration register set to? **Configuration register is 0x102**

# Cisco Labs – Semester 2 – Router Configuration
## *LAB 4.5.2.1 – ROUTER SHOW COMMANDS – ANSWERS*

**Results of show version Command** (output generated by a Cisco 1601 router)

```
lab-c>show version
Cisco Internetwork Operating System Software
IOS (tm) 1600 Software (C1600-NSY-L), Version 11.1(7)AA, EARLY DEPLOYMENT RELEASE
SOFTWARE (fc2)
Copyright (c) 1986-1996 by cisco Systems, Inc.
Compiled Thu 24-Oct-96 05:24 by kuong
Image text-base: 0x080202B8, data-base: 0x02005000

ROM: System Bootstrap, Version 11.1(10)AA, EARLY DEPLOYMENT RELEASE SOFTWARE
(fc1)
ROM: 1600 Software (C1600-BOOT-R), Version 11.1(10)AA, EARLY DEPLOYMENT RELEASE
SOFTWARE (fc1)
lab-c uptime is 1 week, 2 days, 6 hours, 54 minutes
System restarted by reload
System image file is "flash:c1600-nsy-l.111-7.AA", booted via flash

cisco CPA1600 (68360) processor (revision C) with 3584K/512K bytes of memory.
Processor board ID 04176122
Bridging software.
X.25 software, Version 2.0, NET2, BFE and GOSIP compliant.
Authorized for CiscoPro software set only.
1 Ethernet/IEEE 802.3 interface.
2 Serial(sync/async) network interfaces.
System/IO memory with parity disabled
8K bytes of non-volatile configuration memory.
6144K bytes of processor board PCMCIA flash (Read ONLY)
Configuration register is 0x102
```

5. What information is displayed with **show clock**? **Time, day, month, year**

**Results of show clock Command** (output generated by a Cisco 2503 router)

```
lab-b>show clock
*22:17:53.250 UTC Mon Mar 1 1993
```

6. What information is displayed with **show hosts**? **A cached list of host names and IP
   addresses. Flags that tell how information was learned and its current status. Age,
   measured in hours, since the entry was referred to.**

**Results of show hosts command** (output generated by a Cisco 2503 router)

```
lab-b>show hosts
Default domain is not set
Name/address lookup uses domain service
Name servers are 255.255.255.255
Host            Flags    Age Type   Address(es)
```

# Cisco Labs – Semester 2 – Router Configuration
## *LAB 4.5.2.1 – ROUTER SHOW COMMANDS – ANSWERS*

**Results of show hosts Command – Continued** (output generated by a Cisco 2514 router)

| | | | | |
|---|---|---|---|---|
| LAB-A | (perm, OK) 22 | IP | 192.5.5.1 | 201.100.11.1 |
| LAB-B | (perm, OK) 22 | IP | 219.17.100.1 | 205.7.5.1 |
| | | | 199.6.13.1 | 201.100.11.2 |
| LAB-C | (perm, OK) 22 | IP | 223.8.151.1 | 204.204.7.1 |
| | | | 199.6.13.2 | |
| LAB-D | (perm, OK) 22 | IP | 210.93.105.1 | 204.204.7.2 |
| LAB-E | (perm, OK) 22 | IP | 210.93.105.2 | |

7.  What information is displayed with **show users**? **Shows all users connected to the router either directly or remotely.**

**Results of show users Command** (output generated by a Cisco 2514 router)

```
lab-b>show users
  Line    User    Host(s)        Idle Location

* 1 aux 0          idle            0
```

8.  What information is displayed with **show history**? **Shows up to the last 10 commands issued to the router.**

**Results of show history Command** (output generated by a Cisco 2501 router)

```
lab-b>show history
  show clock
  show users
  show history
```

9.
  a.  What command did you use to enter privileged mode? **Enable**
  b.  How do you know if you are in privileged mode? **The router prompt has a # instead of > after the router name.**

10.
  a.  What did the router reply with? **The router responds with the show subcommands available for privileged mode.**
  b.  How is this list different from the list you retrieved in Step 3, when you were in user mode? **Because you are in privileged mode, you have all show subcommands available to you.**

11. What is the arp table? **The arp table holds IP to MAC to interface mappings.**

12. Enter **show flash** at the router prompt.
  a.  How much Flash memory is available and used? **1506796 available, 6881812 bytes used**

# Cisco Labs – Semester 2 – Router Configuration
## *LAB 4.5.2.1 – ROUTER SHOW COMMANDS – ANSWERS*

    b.   What is the file that is stored in Flash memory? **The IOS file igs-j-l.111-5 is stored in Flash memory.**

    c.   What is the size in bytes of the Flash memory? **8192KB (8MB)**

**Results of show flash Command** (output generated by a Cisco 2514 router)

```
Lab-A#show flash

System flash directory:
File  Length   Name/status
  1   6881748  igs-j-l.111-5
[6881812 bytes used, 1506796 available, 8388608 total]
8192K bytes of processor board System flash (Read/Write)
```

13. What important information is displayed with **show run**? **The active configuration file**

**Results of show running-config Command**  (output generated by a Cisco 2514 router)

```
lab-A#show running-config
Building configuration....
Current configuration:
!
!
version 11.1
service slave-log
service udp-small-servers
service tcp-small-servers
!
hostname Lab-A
!
boot system igs-j-l.111-5
enable secret 5 $1$itif$vqTo8RC73KajshkzpFObr/
enable password cisco
!
interface Ethernet0
    ip address 192.5.5.1  255.255.255.0
!
interface Ethernet1
    ip address 205.7.5.1  255.255.255.0
!
interface Serial0
    ip address  210.100.11.1 255.255.255.0
    bandwidth 56
    no fair-queue
    clockrate 56000
!
```

# Cisco Labs – Semester 2 – Router Configuration
## *LAB 4.5.2.1 – ROUTER SHOW COMMANDS – ANSWERS*

## Results of show running-config Command - Cont. (output generated by a Cisco 2514)

```
    interface Serial1
    no ip address
    shut down
    !
router igrp 100
network 192.5.5.0
network 205.7.5.0
network 201.100.11.0
!
ip host Lab-A 192.5.5.1 205.7.5.1 201.100.11.1
ip host Lab-B 219.17.100.1 199.6.13.1 201.100.11.2
ip host Lab-C 223.8.151.1 204.204.7.1 199.6.13.2
ip host Lab-D 210.93.105.1 204.204.7.2
ip host Lab-E 210.93.105.2
no ip classless
!
line con 0
exec-timeout 0 0
password cisco
login
line aux 0
line vty 0 4
    password cisco
    login
end
```

14. What important information is displayed with **show start**, and where is this information kept?
    **The backup configuration file, startup-config, is stored in NVRAM.**

## Results of show startup-config Command (output generated by a Cisco 2514 router)

```
Lab-A#show startup-config
Using 960 out of 32762 bytes
!
version 11.1
service slave-log
service udp-small-servers
service tcp-small-servers
!
hostname Lab-A
!
```

**NOTE: The remainder of output should be the same as the show running-config command
unless changes have been made to the current running configuration that have not been copied
to the startup configuration.**

# Cisco Labs – Semester 2 – Router Configuration
## *LAB 4.5.2.1 – ROUTER SHOW COMMANDS – ANSWERS*

15a. Find the following information for interface Ethernet 0 with Show Interface:
1. What is the MTU? **Maximum Transmission Unit – Ethernet is 1500 bytes**
2. What is rely? **Reliability of the interface – 255/255 is 100% reliable**
3. What is load? **Load on the interface – 255/255 is completely saturated**
4. What is a runt? **An Ethernet packet that is less than the 64-byte minimum**
5. What is a giant? **An Ethernet packet that is greater than the 1500-byte maximum**

15b. Find the following information for interface serial0 with **show interface**:
1. What is the IP address and subnet mask? **199.6.13.1  255.255.255.0**
2. What data link layer encapsulation is being used? **HDLC (High-Level Data Link Control)**
3. What does "Serial0 is up, line protocol is up" mean? **"Serial0 is up" means that there is a carrier detect signal. "Line protocol is up" means that keepalive messages are being received.**

## Results of show interface Command (output generated by a Cisco 2514 router)

```
Lab-A#show interface
Ethernet0 is up, line protocol is up
  Hardware is Lance, address is 0000.0c3b.f3a6 (bia 0000.0c3b.f3a6)
  Internet address is 192.5.5.1/24
  MTU 1500 bytes, BW 10000 Kbit, DLY 1000 usec, rely 255/255, load 1/255
  Encapsulation ARPA, loopback not set, keepalive set (10 sec)
  ARP type: ARPA, ARP Timeout 04:00:00
  Last input 00:00:13, output 00:00:02, output hang never
  Last clearing of "show interface" counters never
  Queueing strategy: fifo
  Output queue 0/40, 0 drops; input queue 0/75, 0 drops
  5 minute input rate 0 bits/sec, 0 packets/sec
  5 minute output rate 0 bits/sec, 0 packets/sec
     27107 packets input, 15017900 bytes, 0 no buffer
     Received 172 broadcasts, 0 runts, 0 giants
     3 input errors, 3 CRC, 0 frame, 0 overrun, 0 ignored, 0 abort
     0 input packets with dribble condition detected
     37514 packets output, 2657602 bytes, 0 underruns
     0 output errors, 0 collisions, 1 interface resets
     0 babbles, 0 late collision, 0 deferred
     0 lost carrier, 0 no carrier
     0 output buffer failures, 0 output buffers swapped out
     10553 packets output, 1038298 bytes, 0 underruns
     0 output errors, 0 collisions, 1 interface resets
     0 babbles, 0 late collision, 0 deferred
     0 lost carrier, 0 no carrier
     0 output buffer failures, 0 output buffers swapped out
```

# Cisco Labs – Semester 2 – Router Configuration
## *LAB 4.5.2.1 – ROUTER SHOW COMMANDS – ANSWERS*

**Results of show interface Command – Cont.** (output generated by a Cisco 2514 router)

```
Serial0 is up, line protocol is up
  Hardware is HD64570
  Internet address is 210.100.11.1/24
  MTU 1500 bytes, BW 56 Kbit, DLY 20000 usec, rely 255/255, load 1/255
  Encapsulation HDLC, loopback not set, keepalive set (10 sec)
  Last input 00:00:00, output 00:00:07, output hang never
  Last clearing of "show interface" counters never
 Queueing strategy: fifo
 Output queue 0/40, 0 drops; input queue 0/75, 0 drops
  5 minute input rate 0 bits/sec, 0 packets/sec
  5 minute output rate 0 bits/sec, 0 packets/sec
    10513 packets input, 667585 bytes, 0 no buffer
    Received 10488 broadcasts, 0 runts, 0 giants
 0 input errors, 0 CRC, 0 frame, 0 overrun, 0 ignored, 0 abort
    10411 packets output, 643047 bytes, 0 underruns
    0 output errors, 0 collisions, 2 interface resets
    0 output buffer failures, 0 output buffers swapped out
    0 carrier transitions
    DCD=up  DSR=up  DTR=up  RTS=up  CTS=up
```

**Remainder of output truncated.**

16. What important information is displayed? **Global and interface-specific status of any configured level 3 protocols**

**Results of show protocol Command** (output generated by a Cisco 2514 router)

```
Lab-A#show protocol
Global values:
  Internet Protocol routing is enabled

Ethernet0 is up, line protocol is up
  Internet address is 192.5.5.1/24

Ethernet1 is up, line protocol is up
 Internet address is 205.7.5.1/24

Serial0 is up, line protocol is up
  Internet address is 199.6.13.1/24

Serial1 is administratively down, line protocol is down
```

17. Enter **exit** at the router prompt.

# Cisco Labs – Semester 2 – Router Configuration
## *LAB 4.6.2.1 – CDP NEIGHBORS – OVERVIEW*
### *(Estimated time: 30 minutes)*

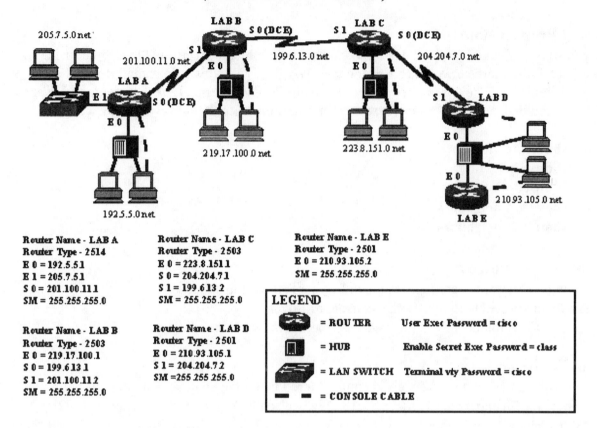

**Router Name - LAB A**
**Router Type - 2514**
E 0 = 192.5.5.1
E 1 = 205.7.5.1
S 0 = 201.100.11.1
SM = 255.255.255.0

**Router Name - LAB B**
**Router Type - 2503**
E 0 = 219.17.100.1
S 0 = 199.6.13.1
S 1 = 201.100.11.2
SM = 255.255.255.0

**Router Name - LAB C**
**Router Type - 2503**
E 0 = 223.8.151.1
S 0 = 204.204.7.1
S 1 = 199.6.13.2
SM = 255.255.255.0

**Router Name - LAB D**
**Router Type - 2501**
E 0 = 210.93.105.1
S 1 = 204.204.7.2
SM = 255.255.255.0

**Router Name - LAB E**
**Router Type - 2501**
E 0 = 210.93.105.2
SM = 255.255.255.0

**LEGEND**

| | | |
|---|---|---|
| = ROUTER | User Exec Password = cisco |
| = HUB | Enable Secret Exec Password = class |
| = LAN SWITCH | Terminal vty Password = cisco |
| = CONSOLE CABLE | |

## Objectives:

- Use CDP commands to get information about neighboring networks and routers
- Display information on how CDP is configured for its advertisement and discovery frame transmission
- Display CDP updates received on the local router

## Background:

In this lab you will use the **show cdp** command. Cisco Discovery Protocol (CDP) discovers and shows information about directly connected Cisco devices (routers and switches). CDP is a Cisco proprietary protocol that runs at the data link layer (layer 2) of the OSI model. This allows devices that may be running different network layer 3 protocols such as IP or IPX to learn about each other. CDP begins automatically upon a device's system startup. However, if you are using Cisco IOS Release 10.3 or a newer version of IOS, you must enable it on each of the device's interfaces by using the **cdp enable** command. Using the command **show cdp interface**, you will gather information CDP uses for its advertisement and discovery frame transmission. Use **show cdp neighbors** and **show cdp neighbors detail** to display the CDP updates received on the local router.

# Cisco Labs – Semester 2 – Router Configuration
## *LAB 4.6.2.1 – CDP NEIGHBORS – OVERVIEW*

## Tools / Preparation:
Prior to starting the lab, you will need to connect a PC with HyperTerminal to a router using the router's console interface with a roll-over cable. Work individually or in teams. Before beginning this lab, you should read the *Cisco Networking Academy Program: First Year Companion Guide*, Chapter 13. You should also review on-line Chapter 4. Be familiar with the following **show** commands:

- **show interface**
- **show cdp**
- **show cdp interface**
- **show cdp neighbors**
- **show cdp neighbors detail**

## Resources Required:
- PC with Windows operating system and HyperTerminal installed
- Router connected to the PC with a console roll-over cable
- At least three routers interconnected via Ethernet or WAN simulation cables

## Web Site Resources:
- **Routing basics** – http://www.cisco.com/univercd/cc/td/doc/cisintwk/ito_doc/routing.htm
- **General information on routers** – http://www.cisco.com/univercd/cc/td/doc/pcat/#2
- **2500 series routers** – http://www.cisco.com/warp/public/cc/cisco/mkt/access/2500/index.shtml
- **1600 series routers** – http://www.cisco.com/warp/public/cc/cisco/mkt/access/1600/index.shtml
- **Terms and acronyms** – http://www.cisco.com/univercd/cc/td/doc/cisintwk/ita/index.htm
- **IP routing protocol IOS command summary** –
  http://www.cisco.com/univercd/cc/td/doc/product/software/ios120/12cgcr/rbkixol.htm

## Notes:

_____
_____
_____
_____
_____
_____
_____
_____
_____
_____
_____
_____
_____
_____
_____

# Cisco Labs – Semester 2 – Router Configuration
## *LAB 4.6.2.1 – CDP NEIGHBORS – WORKSHEET*

**Step 1 – Log on to the router.**
   **Explanation:** Connect to the router and log in. Enter the password **cisco** if prompted.

**Step 2 – Gather information about the router you logged into by issuing the show interface command.**
   **Task:** Enter the **show interface** command at the router prompt.
   **Explanation:** The router shows information about the configured interfaces.

1. Document the following information about the router:

   a. What is the name of the router? _____

   b. List IP address and subnet mask of the interfaces.

| Interface | IP Address | Subnet Mask |
|---|---|---|
|  |  |  |
|  |  |  |
|  |  |  |
|  |  |  |

   c. List operational status of each interface.

| Interface | Interface Up or Down? (Carrier Detect Signal) | Line Protocol Up or Down? (Keepalives Being Received) |
|---|---|---|
|  |  |  |
|  |  |  |
|  |  |  |
|  |  |  |

**Step 3 – Display the values of the CDP timers, interface status, and encapsulation used.**
   **Task:** Enter the **show cdp interface** command at the router prompt.
   **Explanation:** The router responds with CDP information on all interfaces that have CDP enabled. Global CDP settings can be seen using the **show cdp** command by itself.

2. How often is the router sending CDP packets? _____

3. What is the holdtime value? _____

**Step 4 – Display the CDP updates received on the local router.**
   **Task:** Enter the **show cdp neighbors** command at the router prompt.
   **Explanation:** The router will respond with information about its neighbors that have CDP enabled.

**Cisco Labs – Semester 2 – Router Configuration**
## *LAB 4.6.2.1 – CDP NEIGHBORS – WORKSHEET*

4. Fill in the following table:

| Device and Port ID | Local Interface | Hold Time | Capability | Platform |
|---|---|---|---|---|
|  |  |  |  |  |
|  |  |  |  |  |
|  |  |  |  |  |

**Step 5 – Display details about CDP updates received on the local router.**
  **Task:** Enter **show cdp neighbors detail** from the router prompt.
  **Explanation:** The router will display the entry address(es), the IOS version, and the same information as the **show cdp neighbors** command.

5. Fill in the following table:

| | | | |
|---|---|---|---|
| **Neighbor device name** |  |  |  |
| **Neighbor device type** |  |  |  |
| **IP address of interface attached to your router** |  |  |  |
| **Port ID of your router that the neighbor is on** |  |  |  |
| **Port ID of neighbor router that your router is on** |  |  |  |
| **IOS version of neighbor router** |  |  |  |

**Step 6 – Telnet to your neighbor router and issue show cdp neighbor.**
  **Task:**
    a. Telnet to the neighboring router by entering **telnet *hostname of router or IP address***.
    b. Enter the password **cisco**.
    c. Enter **show cdp neighbor** at the router prompt you have telneted to.
  **Explanation:** The router will respond with information about its neighbors that have CDP enabled. **NOTE: Perform this step at router lab-b, lab-c, or lab-d, and telnet to your two neighbors on either side.**

# Cisco Labs – Semester 2 – Router Configuration
## *LAB 4.6.2.1 – CDP NEIGHBORS – WORKSHEET*

6.  Fill in the following tables:

**First neighbor**

| Device and Port ID | Local Interface | Hold Time | Capability | Platform |
|---|---|---|---|---|
| | | | | |
| | | | | |
| | | | | |

**Second neighbor**

| Device and Port ID | Local Interface | Hold Time | Capability | Platform |
|---|---|---|---|---|
| | | | | |
| | | | | |
| | | | | |

# Cisco Labs – Semester 2 – Router Configuration
## *LAB 4.6.2.1 – CDP NEIGHBORS – ANSWERS*

1.  Connect to the router and log in. Enter the password **cisco** if prompted. Gather information about the router you logged into by issuing the **show interface** command. Document the following information about the router:

    a.  What is the name of the router? **Lab-c**

    b.  List IP address and subnet mask of the interfaces.

| Interface | IP Address | Subnet Mask |
|---|---|---|
| **Ethernet 0** | **223.8.151.1** | **24 bits (255.255.255.0)** |
| **Serial 0** | **204.204.7.1** | **24 bits (255.255.255.0)** |
| **Serial 1** | **199.6.13.2** | **24 bits (255.255.255.0)** |
| | | |

    c.  List operational status of each interface.

| Interface | Interface Up or Down? (Carrier Detect Signal) | Line Protocol Up or Down? (Keepalives Being Received) |
|---|---|---|
| **Ethernet 0** | **Up** | **Up** |
| **Serial 0** | **Up** | **Up** |
| **Serial 1** | **Up** | **Up** |
| | | |

**Results of show interface Command** (output generated by a Cisco 1601 router)

```
lab-c>show interface
Ethernet0 is up, line protocol is up
  Hardware is QUICC Ethernet, address is 0060.474f.9bbd (bia 0060.474f.9bbd)
  Internet address is 223.8.151.1/24
  MTU 1500 bytes, BW 10000 Kbit, DLY 1000 usec, rely 255/255, load 1/255
  Encapsulation ARPA, loopback not set, keepalive set (10 sec)
  ARP type: ARPA, ARP Timeout 04:00:00
  Last input 2d02h, output 00:00:02, output hang never
  Last clearing of "show interface" counters never
  Queueing strategy: fifo
  Output queue 0/40, 0 drops; input queue 0/75, 0 drops
  5 minute input rate 0 bits/sec, 0 packets/sec
  5 minute output rate 0 bits/sec, 0 packets/sec
     7 packets input, 570 bytes, 0 no buffer
     Received 7 broadcasts, 0 runts, 0 giants
0 input errors, 0 CRC, 0 frame, 0 overrun, 0 ignored, 0 abort
     0 input packets with dribble condition detected
     100196 packets output, 10049637 bytes, 0 underruns
     0 output errors, 0 collisions, 1 interface resets
```

**Cisco Labs – Semester 2 – Router Configuration**
## *LAB 4.6.2.1 – CDP NEIGHBORS – ANSWERS*

## Results of show interface Command – Cont. (output generated by a Cisco 1601 router)

```
    0 babbles, 0 late collision, 0 deferred
    0 lost carrier, 0 no carrier
    0 output buffer failures, 0 output buffers swapped out
Serial0 is up, line protocol is up
  Hardware is QUICC Serial
  Internet address is 204.204.7.1/24
  MTU 1500 bytes, BW 56 Kbit, DLY 20000 usec, rely 255/255, load 1/255
  Encapsulation HDLC, loopback not set, keepalive set (10 sec)
  Last input 00:00:08, output 00:00:04, output hang never
  Last clearing of "show interface" counters never
  Input queue: 0/75/0 (size/max/drops); Total output drops: 0
  Queueing strategy: weighted fair
  Output queue: 0/64/0 (size/threshold/drops)
    Conversations  0/1 (active/max active)
Reserved Conversations 0/0 (allocated/max allocated)
5 minute input rate 0 bits/sec, 0 packets/sec
 5 minute output rate 0 bits/sec, 0 packets/sec
 129492 packets input, 8117948 bytes, 0 no buffer
    Received 126687 broadcasts, 0 runts, 0 giants
    0 input errors, 0 CRC, 0 frame, 0 overrun, 0 ignored, 0 abort
    103169 packets output, 6985930 bytes, 0 underruns
    0 output errors, 0 collisions, 7 interface resets
    0 output buffer failures, 0 output buffers swapped out
    18 carrier transitions
    DCD=up  DSR=up  DTR=up  RTS=up  CTS=up

Serial1 is up, line protocol is up
  Hardware is QUICC Serial
  Internet address is 199.6.13.2/24
  MTU 1500 bytes, BW 56 Kbit, DLY 20000 usec, rely 255/255, load 4/255
  Encapsulation HDLC, loopback not set, keepalive set (10 sec)
  Last input 00:00:00, output 00:00:02, output hang never
  Last clearing of "show interface" counters never
  Input queue: 0/75/0 (size/max/drops); Total output drops: 0
  Queueing strategy: weighted fair
  Output queue: 0/64/0 (size/threshold/drops)
    Conversations  0/3 (active/max active)
    Reserved Conversations 0/0 (allocated/max allocated)
  5 minute input rate 1000 bits/sec, 2 packets/sec
  5 minute output rate 1000 bits/sec, 2 packets/sec
107132 packets input, 5830048 bytes, 0 no buffer
    Received 102593 broadcasts, 0 runts, 0 giants
    1 input errors, 0 CRC, 1 frame, 0 overrun, 0 ignored, 0 abort
    104562 packets output, 6840784 bytes, 0 underruns
    0 output errors, 0 collisions, 6 interface resets
```

# Cisco Labs – Semester 2 – Router Configuration
## *LAB 4.6.2.1 – CDP NEIGHBORS – ANSWERS*

## Results of show interface Command – Cont. (output generated by a Cisco 1601 router)

| |
|---|
| 0 output buffer failures, 0 output buffers swapped out |
| 290 carrier transitions |
| DCD=up  DSR=up  DTR=up  RTS=up  CTS=up |

   2.  How often is the router sending CDP packets? **Every 60 seconds**

   3.  What is the hold time value? **180 seconds**

## Results of show cdp Command (output generated by a Cisco 2514 router)

| |
|---|
| lab-b>show cdp |
| Global CDP information: |
|       Sending CDP packets every 60 seconds |
|       Sending a holdtime value of 180 seconds |

   4.  Fill in the following table. (Answers may vary depending on lab setup. In this case, Lab-B is a 2514, and there is a Catalyst 1900 switch attached to the same Ethernet hub that Lab-B is attached to. Lab-A and Lab-C are Cisco 1600 models.)

| Device and Port ID | Local Interface | Hold Time | Capability | Platform |
|---|---|---|---|---|
| Lab-c, Serial1 | Serial0 | 166 | Router | CPA1600 |
| Lab-a, Serial0 | Serial1 | 151 | Router | CPA1600 |
| 00C01D 81259B, Port 1 | Ethernet1 | 136 | Trans Bridge Switch | 1900 |

## Results of show cdp neighbors Command (output generated by a Cisco 2514 router)

| |
|---|
| lab-b>show cdp neighbors |
| Capability Codes:  R - Router,  T - Trans Bridge,  B - Source Route Bridge |
|       S - Switch,  H - Host,  I - IGMP |

| Device ID | Local Intrfce | Holdtme | Capability | Platform | Port ID |
|---|---|---|---|---|---|
| lab-c | Ser 0 | 166 | R | CPA1600 | Ser 1 |
| lab-a | Ser 1 | 151 | R | 2500 | Ser 0 |
| 00C01D 81259B | Eth 1 | 136 | T S | 1900 | 1 |

**(Note: The last entry is the MAC address of a Cisco Catalyst 1900 Ethernet switch.)**

# Cisco Labs – Semester 2 – Router Configuration
## *LAB 4.6.2.1 – CDP NEIGHBORS – ANSWERS*

5. Fill in the following table:

| Neighbor device name | Lab-c | Lab-a | 00C01D81259B |
|---|---|---|---|
| Neighbor device type | Cisco CPA1600 | Cisco CPA1600 | Cisco 1900 switch |
| IP address of interface attached to your router | 199.6.13.2 | 201.100.11.1 | 205.7.5.2 |
| Port ID of your router that the neighbor is on | Serial0 | Serial1 | Ethernet1 |
| Port ID of neighbor router that your router is on | Serial1 | Serial0 | Port1 |
| IOS version of neighbor router | 11.1(7)AA | 11.1(7)AA | V5.35 |

**Results of show cdp neighbors detail Command** (output generated by a Cisco 2514 router)

```
lab-b>show cdp neighbors detail
Device ID: lab-c
Entry address(es):
  IP address: 199.6.13.2
Platform: cisco CPA1600,  Capabilities: Router
Interface: Serial0,  Port ID (outgoing port): Serial1
Holdtime : 142 sec

Version :
Cisco Internetwork Operating System Software
IOS (tm) 1600 Software (C1600-NSY-L), Version 11.1(7)AA, EARLY DEPLOYMENT RELEASE
SOFTWARE (fc2)
Copyright (c) 1986-1996 by cisco Systems, Inc.
Compiled Thu 24-Oct-96 05:24 by kuong

Device ID: lab-a
Entry address(es):
  IP address: 201.100.11.1
Platform: cisco CPA1600,  Capabilities: Router
Interface: Serial1,  Port ID (outgoing port): Serial0
Holdtime : 173 sec

Version :
Cisco Internetwork Operating System Software
IOS (tm) 1600 Software (C1600-NSY-L), Version 11.1(7)AA, EARLY DEPLOYMENT RELEASE
SOFTWARE (fc2)
Copyright (c) 1986-1996 by cisco Systems, Inc.
Compiled Thu 24-Oct-96 05:24 by kuong
Device ID: 00C01D 81259B
Entry address(es):
```

# Cisco Labs – Semester 2 – Router Configuration
## *LAB 4.6.2.1 – CDP NEIGHBORS – ANSWERS*

**Results of show cdp neighbors detail Command – Cont.** (output from a Cisco 2514 router)

```
 IP address: 205.7.5.2
Platform: cisco 1900,  Capabilities: Trans-Bridge Switch
Interface: Ethernet1,  Port ID (outgoing port): 1
Holdtime : 132 sec


Version :
V5.35
```

6.  Fill in the following tables:

**First neighbor**

| Device and Port ID | Local Interface | Hold Time | Capability | Platform |
|---|---|---|---|---|
| Lab-b, Serial1 | Serial0 | 142 | Router | CPA2500 |
|  |  |  |  |  |
|  |  |  |  |  |

**Results of telnet and show cdp neighbors Command** (output from a Cisco 1604 router)

```
Lab-b>telnet lab-a
Trying LAB-A (201.100.11.1)… Open




User Access Verification

Password:
lab-a>show cdp neighbors

Capability Codes:  R - Router,  T - Trans Bridge,  B - Source Route Bridge
       S - Switch,  H - Host,  I - IGMP

Device ID        Local Intrfce        Holdtme        Capability        Platform        Port ID
lab-b            Ser 0                142            R                 CPA2500         Ser 1
```

**Second neighbor**

| Device and Port ID | Local Interface | Hold Time | Capability | Platform |
|---|---|---|---|---|
| Lab-b, Serial0 | Serial1 | 142 | Router | CPA2500 |
| Lab-d, Serial1 | Serial0 | 151 | Router | CPA1600 |
|  |  |  |  |  |

# Cisco Labs – Semester 2 – Router Configuration
## *LAB 4.6.2.1 – CDP NEIGHBORS – ANSWERS*

**Results of telnet and show cdp neighbors Command** (output from a Cisco 1601 router)

```
Lab-b>telnet lab-c
Trying LAB-C (199.6.13.2)… Open



User Access Verification

Password:

lab-c>show cdp neighbors
Capability Codes:  R - Router,  T - Trans Bridge,  B - Source Route Bridge
        S - Switch,  H - Host,  I - IGMP


Device ID          Local Intrfce      Holdtme      Capability    Platform     Port ID
lab-b              Ser 1              142          R             CPA2500      Ser 0
lab-d              Ser 0              151          R             CPA1600      Ser 1
```

# Cisco Labs – Semester 2 – Router Configuration
## *LAB 4.7.2.1 – REMOTE TELNET ACCESS – OVERVIEW*
### *(Estimated time: 45 minutes)*

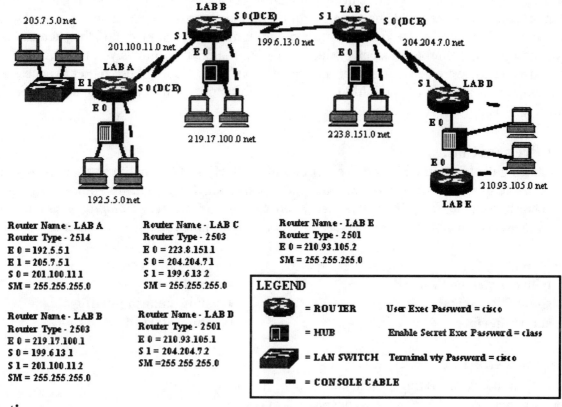

**Router Name - LAB A**
**Router Type - 2514**
**E 0 = 192.5.5.1**
**E 1 = 205.7.5.1**
**S 0 = 201.100.11.1**
**SM = 255.255.255.0**

**Router Name - LAB C**
**Router Type - 2503**
**E 0 = 223.8.151.1**
**S 0 = 204.204.7.1**
**S 1 = 199.6.13.2**
**SM = 255.255.255.0**

**Router Name - LAB E**
**Router Type - 2501**
**E 0 = 210.93.105.2**
**SM = 255.255.255.0**

**Router Name - LAB B**
**Router Type - 2503**
**E 0 = 219.17.100.1**
**S 0 = 199.6.13.1**
**S 1 = 201.100.11.2**
**SM = 255.255.255.0**

**Router Name - LAB D**
**Router Type - 2501**
**E 0 = 210.93.105.1**
**S 1 = 204.204.7.2**
**SM = 255.255.255.0**

**LEGEND**

| | | |
|---|---|---|
| = ROUTER | User Exec Password = cisco | |
| = HUB | Enable Secret Exec Password = class | |
| = LAN SWITCH | Terminal vty Password = cisco | |
| = CONSOLE CABLE | | |

## Objectives:

- Use the **telnet** command to remotely access other routers
- Verify that the application layer between source and destination is working properly
- Retrieve information about remote routers using **router show** commands
- Retrieve CDP information from routers not directly connected to you

## Background:

In this lab you will work with the **telnet** (remote terminal) utility to access routers remotely. You will **telnet** from your local router into another remote router in order to simulate being at the console on the remote router. This procedure will use your router's telnet client software and the remote router's telnet server software. You can also **telnet** from your workstation as a client into any router connected to your network. In addition, you can telnet into Cisco Ethernet switches. You cannot, however, telnet from a router or a workstation into another Windows client or server since the Windows operating system does not support the telnet server daemon. A daemon (pronounced demon) is a UNIX term that refers to a program running on a server that accepts requests for services. You can decide whether to allow others to telnet into your router, or you may require a password for incoming telnet sessions. Telnet connections are referred to as **line VTY 0 4** in the router configuration file. The router can support up to five simultaneous incoming telnet sessions (0 through 4).

# Cisco Labs – Semester 2 – Router Configuration
## *LAB 4.7.2.1 – REMOTE TELNET ACCESS – OVERVIEW*

Telnet is a good troubleshooting tool since it can be used to access remote routers to gather information when there are problems or when configuration changes are necessary. It also tests from the OSI Application layer of the source host down through its Physical layer and then across the network and back up the protocol stack of the destination router. This allows you to verify the application-layer software between source and destination hosts. You will use **telnet** to access a remote router and use **show cdp neighbors** to gather information from routers that are not directly connected to you.

## Tools / Preparation:

Prior to starting the lab, you will need to connect a PC with HyperTerminal to a router using the router's console interface with a roll-over cable. Work individually or in teams. Before beginning this lab, you should read the *Cisco Networking Academy Program: First Year Companion Guide*, Chapter 13. You should also review on-line Chapter 4. Be familiar with the following commands:

- **telnet ?**
- **telnet** *router-name or IP*
- **show CDP neighbors**
- **show interface**

- **show protocols**
- **enable**
- **show running-config**
- **show startup-config**

## Resources Required:

- PC with Windows operating system and HyperTerminal installed
- Router connected to the PC with a console roll-over cable
- At least three routers interconnected via Ethernet or WAN simulation cables

## Web Site Resources:

- **Routing basics** – http://www.cisco.com/univercd/cc/td/doc/cisintwk/ito_doc/routing.htm
- **General information on routers** – http://www.cisco.com/univercd/cc/td/doc/pcat/#2
- **2500 series routers** – http://www.cisco.com/warp/public/cc/cisco/mkt/access/2500/index.shtml
- **1600 series routers** – http://www.cisco.com/warp/public/cc/cisco/mkt/access/1600/index.shtml
- **Terms and acronyms** – http://www.cisco.com/univercd/cc/td/doc/cisintwk/ita/index.htm
- **IP routing protocol IOS command summary** –
  http://www.cisco.com/univercd/cc/td/doc/product/software/ios120/12cgcr/rbkixol.htm

## Notes:

_____
_____
_____
_____
_____

# Cisco Labs – Semester 2 – Router Configuration
## *LAB 4.7.2.1 – REMOTE TELNET ACCESS –WORKSHEET*

**Step 1 – Log onto the router.**
   **Task:** Connect to the router and log in. Enter the password **cisco** if prompted.

   1.  What prompt did the router display? _____

**Step 2 – Enter the help facility.**
   **Task:** Enter **telnet ?** at the router prompt.
   **Explanation:** The router will respond with help with the **telnet** command.

   2.  What did the router reply with? _____
   _____

**Step 3 – Telnet from router to router.**
   **Task:** Enter **telnet *router-name or IP address*** at the router prompt to connect to a remote router.
   **Explanation:** The router will prompt you for user access verification of the router you remotely access. Enter the password **cisco**.

   3.  What prompt did the router display? _____

**Step 4 – Show interfaces.**
   **Task:** Enter **show interface** at the router prompt.
   **Explanation:** The router will respond with information about its interfaces.

   4.  List the interfaces, their IP address, and subnet mask.

| Interface | IP Address | Subnet Mask |
|---|---|---|
| | | |
| | | |
| | | |
| | | |

**Step 5 – Show protocols.**
   **Task:** Enter **show protocols** at the router prompt.
   **Explanation:** This command shows the global and interface-specific status of any configured layer 3 protocols.

   5.  Fill in the table below with the information that was generated by the router you are remotely accessing.

| Interface | Is there a carrier detect signal? | Are the keepalive messages being received? |
|---|---|---|
| | | |
| | | |
| | | |

**Cisco Labs – Semester 2 – Router Configuration**
## *LAB 4.7.2.1 – REMOTE TELNET ACCESS –WORKSHEET*

**Step 6 – Enter privileged mode while connected to the remote router with telnet.**
   **Task:**
   a.   Enter **enable** at the command prompt.
   b.   Enter the password **class**.
   **Explanation:** You use the **enable** command to enter privileged EXEC mode.

6.   What prompt did the router display? _____ What mode are you in?
   _____

**Step 7 – Show information about the active configuration file of the remote router.**
   **Task:** Enter **show running-config** at the remote router prompt.
   **Explanation:** The remote router will display information on how it is currently configured.

7.   What file are you viewing on the remote router? _____ Where is
   this file stored? _____

**Step 8 – Show information about the backup configuration file of the remote router.**
   **Task:** Enter **show startup-config** at the router prompt.
   **Explanation:** The remote router will display information on the backup configuration file stored
   in NVRAM.

8.   What file are you viewing on the remote router? _____ Where is this file
   stored? _____

9.   What information do you see concerning the **line VTY** connections?
   _____

**Step 9 – Display the CDP updates received on the local router.**
   **Task:** Enter the **show cdp neighbors** command at the router prompt.
   **Explanation:** The router will respond with information about its neighbors that have CDP
   enabled.

10. List all device IDs that are connected to the remote router you have a telnet session with.
   _____
   _____

# Cisco Labs – Semester 2 – Router Configuration
## *LAB 4.7.2.1 – REMOTE TELNET ACCESS – ANSWERS*

1.  Connect to the router and log in. Enter the password **cisco** if prompted. What prompt did the router display? ***Router-Name>* (of local router)**

2.  Enter **telnet ?** at the router prompt. What did the router reply with? **WORD IP** *address or hostname of a remote system*

3.  Enter **telnet** *router-name or IP address* at the router prompt. The router will prompt you for user access verification of the router you remotely access. Enter the password **cisco**. What prompt did the router display? ***Router-Name>* (of remote router)**

4.  Enter **show interface** at the prompt of the remote router. List the interfaces, their IP address, and subnet mask from the remote router. (The following is for router Lab-C.)

| Interface | IP Address | Subnet Mask |
|---|---|---|
| Ethernet 0 | 223.8.151.1 | 24 bits (255.255.255.0) |
| Serial 0 | 204.204.7.1 | 24 bits (255.255.255.0) |
| Serial 1 | 199.6.13.2 | 24 bits (255.255.255.0) |
|  |  |  |

**telnet and show interface Command Output Generated by a Cisco 1600 Router**

```
lab-b>telnet lab-d
Trying LAB-D (210.93.105.1)... Open


User Access Verification

Password:
lab-D>show interface

Ethernet0 is up, line protocol is up
  Hardware is QUICC Ethernet, address is 0060.5cbc.033a (bia 0060.5cbc.033a)
  Internet address is 210.93.105.1/24
  MTU 1500 bytes, BW 10000 Kbit, DLY 1000 usec, rely 255/255, load 1/255
  Encapsulation ARPA, loopback not set, keepalive set (10 sec)
  ARP type: ARPA, ARP Timeout 04:00:00
  Last input 00:00:28, output 00:00:04, output hang never
  Last clearing of "show interface" counters never
  Queueing strategy: fifo
  Output queue 0/40, 0 drops; input queue 0/75, 0 drops
  5 minute input rate 0 bits/sec, 0 packets/sec
  5 minute output rate 0 bits/sec, 0 packets/sec
    13661 packets input, 4186769 bytes, 0 no buffer
    Received 12931 broadcasts, 0 runts, 0 giants
    0 input errors, 0 CRC, 0 frame, 0 overrun, 0 ignored, 0 abort
```

# Cisco Labs – Semester 2 – Router Configuration
## *LAB 4.7.2.1 – REMOTE TELNET ACCESS – ANSWERS*

**telnet and show interface Command Output Generated by a Cisco 1600 Router – Cont.**

```
      0 input packets with dribble condition detected
      113212 packets output, 10955040 bytes, 0 underruns
      0 output errors, 0 collisions, 1 interface resets
      0 babbles, 0 late collision, 4 deferred
      0 lost carrier, 0 no carrier
      0 output buffer failures, 0 output buffers swapped out
Serial0 is administratively down, line protocol is down
   Hardware is QUICC Serial
   MTU 1500 bytes, BW 1544 Kbit, DLY 20000 usec, rely 255/255, load 1/255
   Encapsulation HDLC, loopback not set, keepalive set (10 sec)
   Last input never, output never, output hang never
   Last clearing of "show interface" counters never
   Input queue: 0/75/0 (size/max/drops); Total output drops: 0
   Queueing strategy: weighted fair
   Output queue: 0/64/0 (size/threshold/drops)
      Conversations  0/0 (active/max active)
      Reserved Conversations 0/0 (allocated/max allocated)
   5 minute input rate 0 bits/sec, 0 packets/sec
   5 minute output rate 0 bits/sec, 0 packets/sec
      0 packets input, 0 bytes, 0 no buffer
      Received 0 broadcasts, 0 runts, 0 giants
      0 input errors, 0 CRC, 0 frame, 0 overrun, 0 ignored, 0 abort
      0 packets output, 0 bytes, 0 underruns
      0 output errors, 0 collisions, 6 interface resets
      0 output buffer failures, 0 output buffers swapped out
      0 carrier transitions
      DCD=down  DSR=down  DTR=down  RTS=down  CTS=down


Serial1 is up, line protocol is up
   Hardware is QUICC Serial
   Internet address is 204.204.7.2/24
   MTU 1500 bytes, BW 1544 Kbit, DLY 20000 usec, rely 255/255, load 1/255
   Encapsulation HDLC, loopback not set, keepalive set (10 sec)
   Last input 00:00:00, output 00:00:01, output hang never
   Last clearing of "show interface" counters never
   Input queue: 0/75/0 (size/max/drops); Total output drops: 0
   Queueing strategy: weighted fair
   Output queue: 0/64/0 (size/threshold/drops)
      Conversations  0/2 (active/max active)
      Reserved Conversations 0/0 (allocated/max allocated)
   5 minute input rate 1000 bits/sec, 2 packets/sec
   5 minute output rate 1000 bits/sec, 2 packets/sec
      88358 packets input, 6001075 bytes, 0 no buffer
      Received 86058 broadcasts, 0 runts, 0 giants
Note:  Output truncated.
```

# Cisco Labs – Semester 2 – Router Configuration
## *LAB 4.7.2.1 – REMOTE TELNET ACCESS – ANSWERS*

5.  Enter **show protocols** at the router prompt. Fill in the table below with the information that was generated by the router you are remotely accessing.

| Interface | Is there a carrier detect signal? | Are the keepalive messages being received? |
|---|---|---|
| Ethernet 0 | Yes | Yes |
| Serial 0 | No (administratively down) | No |
| Serial 1 | Yes | Yes |

**Output Generated by a Cisco 1600 Router**

```
lab-D>show protocols
Global values:
Internet Protocol routing is enabled
Ethernet0 is up, line protocol is up
  Internet address is 210.93.105.1/24
Serial0 is administratively down, line protocol is down
Serial1 is up, line protocol is up
  Internet address is 204.204.7.2/24
```

6.  Enter **enable** at the remote router prompt while connected to it with telnet. The router will prompt you for a password. Enter **class**. What prompt did the router display? ***Router-Name#*** What mode are you in? **Privileged EXEC mode**

7.  Enter **show running-config** at the router prompt. What file are you viewing on the remote router? **The active configuration file** Is this file stored in NVRAM? **No. The backup configuration file is stored in NVRAM.**

8.  Enter **show startup-config** at the router prompt. What file are you viewing on the remote router? **The backup configuration file**

9.  What information do you see concerning the **line VTY** connections?
    **line vty 0 4**      (refers to the five possible telnet sessions the router can support)
    **password cisco**   (defines the required password for any incoming telnet sessions)
    **login**              (prompts the user for the password when he attempts to connect)

10. Enter **show cdp neighbors** at the router prompt. List all device IDs that are connected to the remote router you have a telnet session with.

```
lab-D>show cdp neighbors
Capability Codes: R - Router, T - Trans Bridge, B - Source Route Bridge
        S - Switch, H - Host, I - IGMP, r - Repeater

Device ID     Local Intrfce     Holdtme     Capability     Platform     Port ID
Lab-C         Ser 1             165         R              CPA1600      Ser 0
Lab-E         Eth 0             176         R              CPA1600      Eth
```

# Cisco Labs – Semester 2 – Router Configuration
## *LAB 4.8.2.1 – ICMP PING – OVERVIEW*
### *(Estimated time: 30 minutes)*

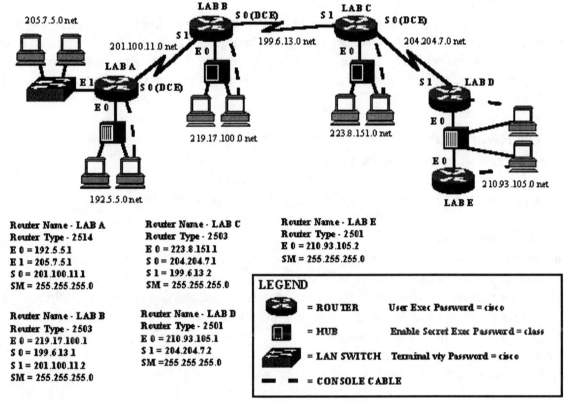

Router Name - LAB A
Router Type - 2514
E 0 = 192.5.5.1
E 1 = 205.7.5.1
S 0 = 201.100.11.1
SM = 255.255.255.0

Router Name - LAB C
Router Type - 2503
E 0 = 223.8.151.1
S 0 = 204.204.7.1
S 1 = 199.6.13.2
SM = 255.255.255.0

Router Name - LAB E
Router Type - 2501
E 0 = 210.93.105.2
SM = 255.255.255.0

Router Name - LAB B
Router Type - 2503
E 0 = 219.17.100.1
S 0 = 199.6.13.1
S 1 = 201.100.11.2
SM = 255.255.255.0

Router Name - LAB D
Router Type - 2501
E 0 = 210.93.105.1
S 1 = 204.204.7.2
SM = 255.255.255.0

**LEGEND**

= ROUTER    User Exec Password = cisco

= HUB    Enable Secret Exec Password = class

= LAN SWITCH    Terminal vty Password = cisco

= CONSOLE CABLE

## Objectives:

- Use the **ping** command to send ICMP datagrams to the target host
- Verify that the network layer between source and destination is working properly
- Retrieve information to evaluate the path-to-host reliability
- Determine delays over the path and whether the host can be reached or is functioning

## Background:

In this lab you will use ICMP (Internet Control Message Protocol). ICMP will give you the ability to diagnose basic network connectivity. Using **ping** *xxx.xxx.xxx.xxx* will send an ICMP packet to the specified host and then wait for a reply packet from that host. You can ping the host name of a router, but you must have a static host lookup table in the router or DNS server for name resolution to IP addresses.

Ping is an excellent tool for troubleshooting layers 1 though 3 of the OSI model. If you cannot connect to a host computer (such as a server) but you can ping the server's IP address, your problem is probably not with the physical cabling connections, the NICs, or the routers between you and the server. With this lab, you will also have a chance to see the differences between using the **ping** command from a router and from a workstation.

**Cisco Labs – Semester 2 – Router Configuration**
## *LAB 4.8.2.1 – ICMP PING – OVERVIEW*

## Tools / Preparation:
Prior to starting the lab, you will need to connect a PC with HyperTerminal to a router using the router's console interface with a roll-over cable. You should have access to the standard five-router lab if possible. Work individually or in teams. Before beginning this lab, you should read the *Cisco Networking Academy Program: First-Year Companion Guide*, Chapter 13, and you should also review on-line Chapter 4.

## Resources Required:
- PC with Windows operating system and HyperTerminal installed
- Router connected to the PC with a console roll-over cable
- At least three routers interconnected via Ethernet or WAN simulation cables

## Web Site Resources:
- **Routing basics** – http://www.cisco.com/univercd/cc/td/doc/cisintwk/ito_doc/routing.htm
- **General information on routers** – http://www.cisco.com/univercd/cc/td/doc/pcat/#2
- **2500 series routers** – http://www.cisco.com/warp/public/cc/cisco/mkt/access/2500/index.shtml
- **1600 series routers** – http://www.cisco.com/warp/public/cc/cisco/mkt/access/1600/index.shtml
- **Terms and acronyms** – http://www.cisco.com/univercd/cc/td/doc/cisintwk/ita/index.htm
- **IP routing protocol IOS command summary** –
  http://www.cisco.com/univercd/cc/td/doc/product/software/ios120/12cgcr/rbkixol.htm

## Notes:
_____
_____
_____
_____
_____
_____
_____
_____
_____
_____
_____
_____

# Cisco Labs – Semester 2 – Router Configuration
## *LAB 4.8.2.1 – ICMP PING – WORKSHEET*

**Step 1 – Log on to the router.**
   **Explanation:** Connect to the router and log in. Enter the password **cisco** if prompted.

1.
   a.    What prompt did the router display? _____
   b.    What does it mean? _____

**Step 2 – Display a cached list of host names and addresses.**
   **Task:** Enter **show host** at the router prompt.
   **Explanation:** The router will display information about host to Layer 3 (IP) address mappings, how this information was acquired, and the age of the entry.

2.  List four host names and the first IP address listed for each one.

| Host Name | IP Address |
|---|---|
|  |  |
|  |  |
|  |  |
|  |  |

**Step 3 – Test layer 3 addressing – ping from router to router.**
   **Task:** Enter **ping** *xxx.xxx.xxx.xxx* where *xxx.xxx.xxx.xxx* is an IP address from one of the other hosts listed above. Repeat with all IP addresses you listed.
   **Explanation:** The router sends an Internet Control Message Protocol (ICMP) packet to verify the hardware connection and network layer address. Since your PC is acting as the console to the router, you are pinging from your router to another router.

3.  Were you able to ping all the IP addresses? _____

4.  List four important pieces of information that you receive after issuing the **ping** command.
   _____
   _____
   _____
   _____

**Cisco Labs – Semester 2 – Router Configuration**
*__LAB 4.8.2.1 – ICMP PING – WORKSHEET__*

## Step 4 – Examine the output generated by the ping command.

5.  Look at the example of the **ping** command generated by a router.

> lab-b#ping 210.93.105.1
>
> Type escape sequence to abort.
> Sending 5, 100-byte ICMP Echoes to 210.93.105.1, timeout is 2 seconds:
> !!!.!
> Success rate is 80 percent (4/5), round-trip min/avg/max = 68/68/168 ms

  a.  What does the exclamation point (!) indicate? _____
  b.  What does the period (.) indicate? _____
  c.  What does the **ping** command test for? _____

## Step 5 – Access the workstation command prompt.
**Task:** From a Windows 95/98 or NT workstation, click Start/Programs/MS-DOS Command Prompt. This will open a command prompt window.
**Explanation:** Using the command prompt to ping the routers allows you to test that the TCP/IP stack and default gateway on the workstation are configured and working properly.

## Step 6 – Test the workstation default gateway.
**Task:** Using the command prompt, enter **ping** and the IP address of the workstation's default gateway. The default gateway is the nearside router interface IP address.
**Explanation:** By pinging your default gateway, you can test whether you can successfully send packets to and from the router that is directly connected to your LAN.

6.  Can you ping your default gateway? _____ (Hint: You may need to check the TCP/IP settings using the Windows Control Panel, Network icon.)

## Step 7 – Test layer 3 addressing from a workstation to a remote router.
**Task:** At the command prompt, enter **ping** and the IP address of a remote router.
**Explanation:** This will test layer 3 connectivity between your workstation and the remote router.

7.  Is the output from the workstation's **ping** command the same as the output from the **ping** command from a router? _____

## Step 8 – Test the connections to other remote routers.
**Task:** At the command prompt, enter **ping** and the IP address of another remote router.
**Explanation:** This will test layer 3 connectivity between your workstation and the other remote routers.

8.  List the differences between the router's **ping** command and the workstation's **ping** command.

_____

_____

_____

# Cisco Labs – Semester 2 – Router Configuration
## *LAB 4.8.2.1 – ICMP PING – ANSWERS*

1.

    a.  What prompt did the router display? ***Router Name>***

    b.  What does it mean? **You are at a user-mode prompt that allows you to display some information without changing router configuration settings.**

2.  List four host names and the first IP address listed.

| Host Name | IP Address |
|---|---|
| **Lab-a** | **192.5.5.1** |
| **Lab-c** | **223.8.151.1** |
| **Lab-d** | **210.93.105.1** |
| **Lab-e** | **210.93.105.2** |

```
lab-b>show host
Default domain is not set
Name/address lookup uses domain service
Name servers are 255.255.255.255

Host      Flags        Age   Type   Address(es)
LAB-A     (perm, OK)   22    IP     192.5.5.1   205.7.5.1   201.100.11.1
LAB-B     (perm, OK)   22    IP     219.17.100.1   199.6.13.1   201.100.11.2
LAB-C     (perm, OK)   22    IP     223.8.151.1   204.204.7.1 199.6.13.2
LAB-D     (perm, OK)   22    IP     210.93.105.1   204.204.7.2
LAB-E     (perm, OK)   22    IP     210.93.105.2
```

3.  Were you able to ping all the IP addresses? **Yes**

4.  List four important pieces of information that you received after issuing the **ping** command. **How many ICMP echoes were sent and how big the packets were, what the timeout duration is, what the success rate is, and what the minimum, average, and maximum round trip times are**

## Output Generated by a Cisco 2501 Router

```
lab-b#ping 204.204.7.1

Type escape sequence to abort.
Sending 5, 100-byte ICMP Echoes to 204.204.7.1, timeout is 2 seconds:
!!!!!
Success rate is 100 percent (5/5), round-trip min/avg/max = 36/36/36 ms
```

**Cisco Labs – Semester 2 – Router Configuration**
## *LAB 4.8.2.1 – ICMP PING – ANSWERS*

5.

    a.  What does the exclamation point (!) indicate? **The exclamation point (!) indicates each successful echo.**

    b.  What does the period (.) indicate? **The period (.) indicates the router has timed out waiting for a given packet echo from the ping target.**

    c.  What does the **ping** command test for? **Path-to-host reliability, delays over the path, and whether the host can be reached or is functioning**

6.  Can you ping your default gateway? **Yes. If you cannot, you will need to configure the networking properties on the workstation to make sure that the default gateway, IP address, and subnet mask are configured properly.**

7.  Is the output from the workstation's **ping** command the same as the output from the **ping** command from a router? **NO**

8.  List the differences between the router's **ping** command and the workstation's **ping** command. **The workstation's ICMP echo is 32 bytes of data instead of 100 bytes. There are four ICMP echos instead of five. It does not give minimum/average/maximum, only the time for each echo.**

## Output Generated by a Windows NT Workstation

```
C:\>ping 192.5.5.1

Pinging 192.5.5.1 with 32 bytes of data:

Reply from 192.5.5.1: bytes=32 time<10ms TTL=128
Reply from 192.5.5.1: bytes=32 time<10ms TTL=128
Reply from 192.5.5.1: bytes=32 time<10ms TTL=128
Reply from 192.5.5.1: bytes=32 time<10ms TTL=128

C:\>
```

# Cisco Labs – Semester 2 – Router Configuration
## *LAB 4.9.2.1 – TRACEROUTE COMMAND – OVERVIEW*
### *(Estimated time: 30 minutes)*

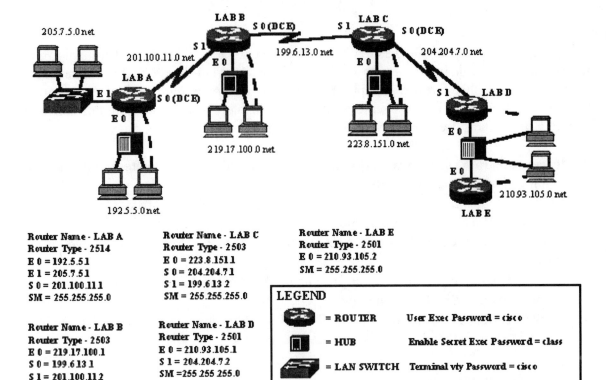

**Router Name - LAB A**
Router Type - 2514
E 0 = 192.5.5.1
E 1 = 205.7.5.1
S 0 = 201.100.11.1
SM = 255.255.255.0

**Router Name - LAB B**
Router Type - 2503
E 0 = 219.17.100.1
S 0 = 199.6.13.1
S 1 = 201.100.11.2
SM = 255.255.255.0

**Router Name - LAB C**
Router Type - 2503
E 0 = 223.8.151.1
S 0 = 204.204.7.1
S 1 = 199.6.13.2
SM = 255.255.255.0

**Router Name - LAB D**
Router Type - 2501
E 0 = 210.93.105.1
S 1 = 204.204.7.2
SM = 255.255.255.0

**Router Name - LAB E**
Router Type - 2501
E 0 = 210.93.105.2
SM = 255.255.255.0

**LEGEND**
= ROUTER    User Exec Password = cisco
= HUB    Enable Secret Exec Password = class
= LAN SWITCH    Terminal vty Password = cisco
= CONSOLE CABLE

## Objectives:
- Use the **traceroute** Cisco IOS command from source router to destination router
- Use the **tracert** Windows OS command from source workstation to destination router
- Use the **show ip route** command to display the router's routing table
- Verify that the network layer between source, destination, and each router along the way is working properly. Retrieve information to evaluate the end-to-end path reliability.
- Determine delays at each point over the path and whether the host can be reached

## Background:
In this lab you will use the IOS **traceroute** command. The **traceroute** command uses ICMP packets and the error message generated by routers when the packet exceeds its Time To Live (TTL). When you initiate the **traceroute** command to a target host, the router sends an ICMP echo-request packet with the TTL set to 1. The first router in the path to the target host receives the ICMP echo-request packet and sets the TTL to 0. The first router then sends an ICMP time-exceeded message back to the source. The source router then sends an ICMP echo-request packet with the TTL set to 2. The first router receives the ICMP echo request and sets the TTL to 1 and sends it to the next router in the path to the target host. The second router receives the ICMP echo request and sets the TTL to 0 and then sends an ICMP time-exceeded message back to the source. The source then sends an ICMP echo request with a TTL set to 3. This cycle continues until an ICMP echo reply is received from the target host or until an ICMP destination-unreachable message is received. This allows you to determine the last router to be reached in the path to the target host. This is a troubleshooting technique called fault isolation.

# Cisco Labs – Semester 2 – Router Configuration
## *LAB 4.9.2.1 – TRACEROUTE COMMAND – OVERVIEW*

## Tools / Preparation:

Prior to starting the lab, you will need to connect a PC workstation with HyperTerminal to a router using the router's console interface with a roll-over cable. This lab should be done at the router console station. You should review Chapter 13 in the *Cisco Networking Academy Program: First-Year Companion Guide* and review semester 2 on-line Chapter 4 prior to starting this lab. Work individually or in teams. Be familiar with the following commands:

- **traceroute ip** *xxx.xxx.xxx.xxx* (where *xxx.xxx.xxx.xxx* is the IP address of the host you want to trace) The **ip** after the command is the default and may be omitted.
- **traceroute** *hostname* (where *hostname* is a name that can be resolved to an IP address) **traceroute** is a Cisco IOS command.
- **tracert** *xxx.xxx.xxx.xxx* (where *xxx.xxx.xxx.xxx* is the IP address of the host you want to trace)
- **tracert** *hostname* (where *hostname* is a name that can be resolved to an IP address) **tracert** is a Windows 95/98 or NT command.
- **show ip route** This will show you the IP routing table. The directions that the router uses to determine how it will direct traffic across the network.

## Resources Required:

- PC with monitor, keyboard, mouse, and power cords
- Windows operating system (Windows 95, 98, NT, or 2000) installed on PC
- HyperTerminal program
- Access to multiple routers

## Web Site Resources:

- **Routing basics** – http://www.cisco.com/univercd/cc/td/doc/cisintwk/ito_doc/routing.htm
- **General information on routers** – http://www.cisco.com/univercd/cc/td/doc/pcat/#2
- **2500 series routers** – http://www.cisco.com/warp/public/cc/cisco/mkt/access/2500/index.shtml
- **1600 series routers** – http://www.cisco.com/warp/public/cc/cisco/mkt/access/1600/index.shtml
- **Terms and acronyms** – http://www.cisco.com/univercd/cc/td/doc/cisintwk/ita/index.htm
- **IP routing protocol IOS command summary** – http://www.cisco.com/univercd/cc/td/doc/product/software/ios120/12cgcr/rbkixol.htm

## Notes:

_____

_____

_____

_____

_____

_____

_____

**Cisco Labs – Semester 2 – Router Configuration**
## *LAB 4.9.2.1 – TRACEROUTE COMMAND – WORKSHEET*

**Step 1 – Log on to the router.**
   **Explanation:** Connect to the router and log in. Enter the password **cisco** if prompted.

   1.
       a.   What prompt did the router display? _____
       b.   What does it mean? _____

**Step 2 – Enter trace (the abbreviated form of traceroute).**
   **Task:** Enter **trace** at the router prompt.

   2.   What did the router respond with? _____

**Step 3 – Enter trace ?**
   **Task:** Enter **trace ?** at the router prompt.

   3.   What did the router respond with? _____

**Step 4 – Get help with the trace ip command**
   **Task:** Enter **trace ip ?** at the router prompt.

   4.   What did the router respond with? _____

**Step 5 – Trace the route from end router to end router.**
   **Task:** Enter **trace ip *xxx.xxx.xxx.xxx*** where *xxx.xxx.xxx.xxx* is the IP address of the target destination. **Note**: You will want to do this lab using one of the end routers and **trace ip** to the other end router (ip is the default).
   **Explanation:** The **trace** command is the ideal tool for finding where data is being sent in your network.

   5.
       a.   List the host name and IP address of the routers that the ICMP packet was routed through.

| Host Name | IP Address |
|-----------|------------|
|           |            |
|           |            |
|           |            |

**Step 6 – Trace the route to all other routers on your network.**
   **Task:** Repeat Step 5 with all other routers on your network.

# Cisco Labs – Semester 2 – Router Configuration
## *LAB 4.9.2.1 – TRACEROUTE COMMAND – WORKSHEET*

**Step 7 – Use tracert from an MS-DOS command prompt.**
   **Task:** From the console workstation, click Start/Programs/MS-DOS Command Prompt. An MS-DOS command prompt window will open up. Enter **tracert** and the same IP address that you used in Step 5.
   **Explanation:** By using the MS-DOS window, you will be using the TCP/IP stack of the workstation to begin the trace to the destination. The first hop will be your default gateway or the near side router interface on the LAN that the workstation is connected to.

   6.
      a.   List the host name and IP address of the router that the ICMP packet was routed through.

| Host Name | IP Address |
|---|---|
|  |  |
|  |  |
|  |  |
|  |  |

      b.   Why is there one more entry in the output of the **tracert** command when you trace from the computer command prompt to the target host? _____
      _____

**Step 8 – Trace a route over the Internet.**
   **Task:** From a Windows 95/98 or NT workstation that has Internet access, click on Start/Programs/MS-DOS Command Prompt. An MS-DOS command prompt window will open up. Enter **tracert www.cisco.com**.

   7.
      a.   What is the IP address of **www.cisco.com**?_____

      b.   How many hops did it take to get to **www.cisco.com**? If a packet passes through a router, it is considered one hop, and the TTL of the packet is decremented by 1.
      _____

**Step 9 – View the routing table of the router.**
   **Task:** From the router prompt, enter **show ip route**.
   **Explanation:** This will show you the router's routing table.

   8.   List the IP network number addresses that are directly connected to you.
   _____
   _____

# Cisco Labs – Semester 2 – Router Configuration
## *LAB 4.9.2.1 – TRACEROUTE COMMAND – ANSWERS*

1.
   a. What prompt did the router display? ***Router-name>***
   b. What does it mean? **You are at a user-mode prompt that allows you to display some information without changing router configuration settings.**

2. What did the router respond with? **% Incomplete command.**

3. What did the router respond with? **A list of subcommands and a description of the subcommands.**

4. What did the router respond with? **WORD Trace route to destination address or hostname.**

5. Traceroute from the router.
   a. List the host name and IP address of the routers that the ICMP packet was routed through.

| Host Name | IP Address |
|---|---|
| **Lab-B** | **201.100.11.2** |
| **Lab-C** | **199.6.13.2** |
| **Lab-D** | **204.204.7.2** |

**Results of trace ip Command** (output generated by a Cisco 1604 router)

```
LAB-A>trace ip 210.93.105.2

Type escape sequence to abort.
Tracing the route to LAB-E (210.93.105.2)

1 LAB-B (201.100.11.2)      36 msec      28 msec      24 msec
2 LAB-C (199.6.13.2)        36 msec      *            40 msec
3 LAB-D (204.204.7.2)       32 msec      30 msec      36 msec
4 LAB-E (210.93.105.2       38 msec      38 msec      40 msec
```

6. Tracert from the workstation.
   a. List the host name and IP address of the routers that the ICMP packet was routed through.

| Host Name | IP Address |
|---|---|
| **No DNS or host file configured** | **192.5.5.1** |
| **No DNS or host file configured** | **201.100.11.2** |
| **No DNS or host file configured** | **199.6.13.2** |
| **No DNS or host file configured** | **204.204.7.2** |

# Cisco Labs – Semester 2 – Router Configuration
## *LAB 4.9.2.1 – TRACEROUTE COMMAND – ANSWERS*

**Tracert Command** (output generated by Windows 95 workstation) **Note: The output does not include host names, only the IP address of the routers. If there was a DNS (Domain Name Server) or if you had the proper entries in a host file on the workstation, you would have entries like the output from question 5a.**

```
C:\>tracert 210.93.105.2

Tracing route to 210.93.105.2

1          2ms           2ms           2ms           192.5.5.1
2          30ms          29ms          29ms          201.100.11.2
3          55ms          56ms          57ms          199.6.13.2
4          79ms          80ms          79ms          204.204.7.2
5          94ms          93ms          93ms          210.93.105.2
```

   b.   Why is there one more entry in the output of the **tracert** command when you trace from the computer command prompt to the target host? **The first hop is to the default gateway or near side router interface of Lab-A router.**

7.  Trace a route over the Internet from a workstation.
   a.   What is the IP address of **www.cisco.com**? **198.133.219.25**
   b.   How many hops did it take to get to **www.cisco.com**? If a packet passes through a router, it is considered one hop, and the TTL of the packet is decremented by 1. **Usually 10 to 30 hops. The last entry is the target host. Your results will vary.**

**Results of tracert www.cisco.com command** (output generated by a Windows 98 workstation; answers will vary, depending on where your workstation is located)

```
Tracing route to www.cisco.com [198.133.219.25]
over a maximum of 30 hops:
1     1 ms     1 ms     1 ms  e0-xxx.college.edu [150.99.181.1]
2     5 ms     4 ms     3 ms  atm6-xxx.district.edu [150.99.25.254]
3     19 ms    5 ms     5 ms  216.90.195.185
4     14 ms    6 ms     6 ms  216.90.192.219
5     17 ms    15 ms    20 ms  sl-gw12-ana-1-1-1.sprintlink.net [144.228.207.205]
6     16 ms    17 ms    20 ms  sl-bb10-ana-0-2.sprintlink.net [144.232.1.65]
7     70 ms    48 ms    37 ms  sl-bb10-stk-6-0.sprintlink.net [144.232.8.89]
8     26 ms    26 ms    25 ms  sl-bb11-stk-8-0.sprintlink.net [144.232.4.106]
9     23 ms    23 ms    25 ms  sl-gw10-stk-8-0-0.sprintlink.net [144.232.4.78]
10    68 ms    63 ms    69 ms  sl-ciscopsn2-4-0-0.sprintlink.net [144.228.146.14]
11    34 ms    42 ms    40 ms  sty.cisco.com [192.31.7.1]
12    *        *        *      Request timed out.
13    *        *        *      Request timed out.
14    *        *        *      Request timed out.
15    46 ms    46 ms    38 ms  www.cisco.com [198.133.219.25]

trace complete
```

**Cisco Labs – Semester 2 – Router Configuration**
## *LAB 4.9.2.1 – TRACEROUTE COMMAND – ANSWERS*

8. List the IP networks that are directly connected to you. **201.100.11.0, 199.6.13.0, 219.17.100.0**

**Results of show ip route** (output generated by a Cisco 2514 router)

```
LAB-B>show ip route
Codes: C - connected, S - static, I - IGRP, R - RIP, M - mobile, B - BGP
    D - EIGRP, EX - EIGRP external, O - OSPF, IA - OSPF inter area
    E1 - OSPF external type 1, E2 - OSPF external type 2, E - EGP
    i - IS-IS, L1 - IS-IS level-1, L2 - IS-IS level-2, * - candidate default
    U - per-user static route

Gateway of last resort is not set

C   201.100.11.0/24      is directly connected,       Serial1
C   199.6.13.0/24        is directly connected,       Serial0
C   219.17.100.0/24      is directly connected,       Ethernet0
R   192.5.5.0/24         [120/1]    VIA   201.100.11.1  00:00:20    Serial1
R   205.7.5.0/24         [120/1]    VIA   201.100.11.1  00:00:20    Serial1
R   223.8.151.0/24       [120/1]    VIA   199.6.13.2    00:00:20    Serial0
R   204.204.7.0/24       [120/1]    VIA   199.6.13.2    00:00:20    Serial0
R   210.93.105.0/24      [120/1]    VIA   199.6.13.00:00:20         Serial0
```

# Cisco Labs – Semester 2 – Router Configuration
## *LAB 4.10.2.1 – SHOW INTERFACE and CLEAR COUNTERS – OVERVIEW*
### *(Estimated time: 30 minutes)*

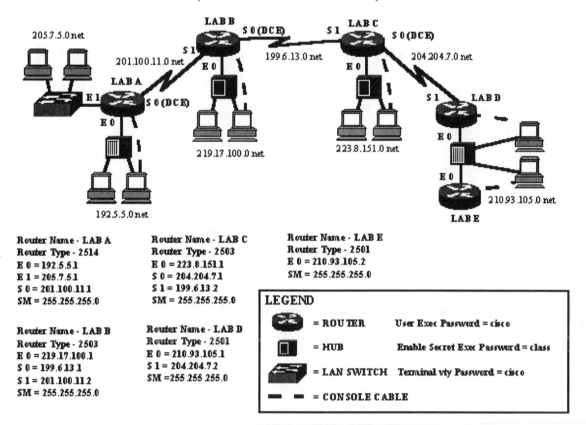

Router Name - LAB A
Router Type - 2514
E 0 = 192.5.5.1
E 1 = 205.7.5.1
S 0 = 201.100.11.1
SM = 255.255.255.0

Router Name - LAB B
Router Type - 2503
E 0 = 219.17.100.1
S 0 = 199.6.13.1
S 1 = 201.100.11.2
SM = 255.255.255.0

Router Name - LAB C
Router Type - 2503
E 0 = 223.8.151.1
S 0 = 204.204.7.1
S 1 = 199.6.13.2
SM = 255.255.255.0

Router Name - LAB D
Router Type - 2501
E 0 = 210.93.105.1
S 1 = 204.204.7.2
SM = 255.255.255.0

Router Name - LAB E
Router Type - 2501
E 0 = 210.93.105.2
SM = 255.255.255.0

**LEGEND**

| | | |
|---|---|---|
| = ROUTER | User Exec Password = cisco | |
| = HUB | Enable Secret Exec Password = class | |
| = LAN SWITCH | Terminal vty Password = cisco | |
| = CONSOLE CABLE | | |

## Objectives:

- Use the **show interface** command to display statistics for the router's interfaces
- Use the **clear counters** command to clear statistics for the router's interfaces

## Background:

In this lab you will use **show interface** and **clear counters**. The router keeps very detailed statistics about data traffic it has sent and received on its interfaces. This is very important in troubleshooting a network problem. The **clear counters** command resets the counters that are displayed when you issue the **show interface** command. By clearing the counters, you get a clearer picture of the current status of the network.

# Cisco Labs – Semester 2 – Router Configuration
## _LAB 4.10.2.1 – SHOW INTERFACE and CLEAR COUNTERS – OVERVIEW_

## Tools / Preparation:

Prior to starting the lab, you will need to connect a PC workstation with HyperTerminal to a router using the router's console interface with a roll-over cable. This lab should be done at the router console station. You should review Chapter 13 in the _Cisco Networking Academy Program: First-Year Companion Guide_ and semester 2 on-line Chapter 4 prior to starting this lab. Work individually or in teams. Be familiar with the following commands:

- **show interface**
- **clear counters**

## Resources Required:

- PC with monitor, keyboard, mouse, and power cords
- Windows operating system (Windows 95, 98, NT, or 2000) installed on PC
- HyperTerminal program configured to access the router console port
- PC connected to the router console port with a roll-over cable

## Web Site Resources:

- **Routing basics** – http://www.cisco.com/univercd/cc/td/doc/cisintwk/ito_doc/routing.htm
- **General information on routers** – http://www.cisco.com/univercd/cc/td/doc/pcat/#2
- **2500 series routers** – http://www.cisco.com/warp/public/cc/cisco/mkt/access/2500/index.shtml
- **1600 series routers** – http://www.cisco.com/warp/public/cc/cisco/mkt/access/1600/index.shtml
- **Terms and acronyms** – http://www.cisco.com/univercd/cc/td/doc/cisintwk/ita/index.htm
- **IP routing protocol IOS command summary** – http://www.cisco.com/univercd/cc/td/doc/product/software/ios120/12cgcr/rbkixol.htm

## Notes:

_____

_____

_____

_____

_____

_____

_____

_____

_____

_____

_____

## Cisco Labs – Semester 2 – Router Configuration
# LAB 4.10.2.1 – SHOW INTERFACE and CLEAR COUNTERS – WORKSHEET

**Step 1 – Log on to the router.**
   **Explanation:** Connect to the router and log in. Enter the password **cisco** if prompted.

**Step 2 – Enter the show interface command (abbreviated sh int).**
   **Task:** Enter **show interface** at the command prompt.
   **Explanation:** The **show interface** command displays packet statistics that reflect router operation since the last time the counters were cleared.

   1.  Fill in the following information for all interfaces in use:

| Interface | Ethernet 0 | Ethernet 1 | Serial 0 | Serial 1 |
|---|---|---|---|---|
| Hardware address | | | | |
| Packet input | | | | |
| Packet output | | | | |
| Last clearing of counters | | | | |

**Step 3 – Enter the help command.**
   **Task:** Enter the help command by typing **?** at the router prompt.
   **Explanation**: The router will respond with all available commands for user mode.

   2.  What is the significance of entering **?** at the command prompt? _____
   _____

**Step 4 – Enter privileged EXEC mode.**
   **Task:** Enter **enable** at the router prompt. The router will ask you for the enable password. Enter **class.**
   **Explanation:** Entering the **enable** command and entering the password **class** allows you privileged mode access to the router.

   3.  What prompt is the router showing? _____

**Step 5 – Get help with the clear command.**
   **Task:** Enter **clear ?** at the router prompt.
   **Explanation:** The **clear ?** command will display subcommands for **clear**.

   4.  Is **counters** one of the subcommands that is listed? _____

   5.  What is the description of **counters**? _____

**Step 6 – Clear all interface counters.**
   **Task:** Enter **clear counters** at the router prompt. The router will ask you to confirm with **Y.**
   **Explanation:** The **clear** command will clear all interface statistics on the router.

**Cisco Labs – Semester 2 – Router Configuration**
# *LAB 4.10.2.1 – SHOW INTERFACE and CLEAR COUNTERS – WORKSHEET*

**Step 7 – Confirm that the counters have been cleared.**
   **Task:** Enter **show interfaces** at the router's command prompt.
   **Explanation:** The **show interface** command displays the statistics, which reflect router operation since the last time the counters were cleared.

6. Have the counters been set to 0? _____

**Step 8 – Generate network traffic.**
   **Task: Ping** all router interfaces in the lab network. Do this several times.
   **Explanation:** By pinging the interfaces of all routers on the labs network, you will generate network traffic. You can use the up arrow or Ctrl-P to retrieve previous commands and change the IP address to the next destination.

**Step 9 – Show interface statistics on the router.**
   **Task:** Enter **show interface** at the router prompt.
   **Explanation:** The **show interface** command displays the statistics, which reflect router operation since the last time the counters were cleared.

7. Fill in the following information in the table for all interfaces:

| Interface | Ethernet 0 | Ethernet 1 | Serial 0 | Serial 1 |
|---|---|---|---|---|
| **Hardware address** | | | | |
| **Packet input** | | | | |
| **Packet output** | | | | |
| **Last clearing of counters** | | | | |

**Step 10 – Show interface statistics terminology.**
   **Task:** Enter **show interface** at the router prompt.
   **Explanation:** The router shows information about the configured interfaces. Review the terms used for various interfaces and statistics. These can be helpful in troubleshooting.
8. Find the following information for interface Ethernet 0 with **show interface**:
   a. What is MTU? _____
   b. What is rely? _____
   c. What is load? _____
   d. What is a runt?_____
   e. What is a giant? _____

9. Find the following information for interface serial 0 with **show interface**:
   a. What is the IP address and subnet mask? _____
   b. What data link layer encapsulation is being used? _____
   c. What does "Serial0 is up, line protocol is up" mean? _____

# Cisco Labs – Semester 2 – Router Configuration
## *LAB 4.10.2.1 – SHOW INTERFACE and CLEAR COUNTERS – ANSWERS*

1. Fill in the following information in the table for all interfaces (answers will vary):

| Interface | Ethernet 0 | Ethernet 1 | Serial 0 | Serial 1 |
|---|---|---|---|---|
| Hardware address | 0000.0c3b.f3a6 | 0000.0c3b.f3a7 | HD64570 | HD64570 |
| Packet input | 27107 | 1301 | 10513 | 10446 |
| Packet output | 37514 | 10553 | 10411 | 10392 |
| Last clearing of counters | Never | Never | never | Never |

## Results of show interface Command (output generated by a Cisco 2514 router)

```
lab-b#show interface
Ethernet0 is up, line protocol is up
  Hardware is Lance, address is 0000.0c3b.f3a6 (bia 0000.0c3b.f3a6)
  Internet address is 219.17.100.1/24
  MTU 1500 bytes, BW 10000 Kbit, DLY 1000 usec, rely 255/255, load 1/255
  Encapsulation ARPA, loopback not set, keepalive set (10 sec)
  ARP type: ARPA, ARP Timeout 04:00:00
 Last input 00:00:13, output 00:00:02, output hang never
 Last clearing of "show interface" counters never
  Queueing strategy: fifo
Output queue 0/40, 0 drops; input queue 0/75, 0 drops
 5 minute input rate 0 bits/sec, 0 packets/sec
5 minute output rate 0 bits/sec, 0 packets/sec
    27107 packets input, 15017900 bytes, 0 no buffer
    Received 172 broadcasts, 0 runts, 0 giants
    3 input errors, 3 CRC, 0 frame, 0 overrun, 0 ignored, 0 abort
    0 input packets with dribble condition detected
    37514 packets output, 2657602 bytes, 0 underruns
    0 output errors, 0 collisions, 1 interface resets
    0 babbles, 0 late collision, 0 deferred
    0 lost carrier, 0 no carrier
    0 output buffer failures, 0 output buffers swapped out
Ethernet1 is up, line protocol is up
  Hardware is Lance, address is 0000.0c3b.f3a7 (bia 0000.0c3b.f3a7)
  Internet address is 205.7.5.1/24
  MTU 1500 bytes, BW 10000 Kbit, DLY 1000 usec, rely 255/255, load 1/255
  Encapsulation ARPA, loopback not set, keepalive set (10 sec)
  ARP type: ARPA, ARP Timeout 04:00:00
  Last input 00:00:59, output 00:00:05, output hang never
  Last clearing of "show interface" counters never
  Queueing strategy: fifo
  Output queue 0/40, 0 drops; input queue 0/75, 0 drops
  5 minute input rate 0 bits/sec, 0 packets/sec
```

# Cisco Labs – Semester 2 – Router Configuration
## *LAB 4.10.2.1 – SHOW INTERFACE and CLEAR COUNTERS – ANSWERS*
### Results of show interface Command – Cont. (output generated by a Cisco 2514 router)

```
   5 minute output rate 0 bits/sec, 0 packets/sec
      1301 packets input, 126197 bytes, 0 no buffer
      Received 1301 broadcasts, 0 runts, 0 giants
      0 input errors, 0 CRC, 0 frame, 0 overrun, 0 ignored, 0 abort
      0 input packets with dribble condition detected
      10553 packets output, 1038298 bytes, 0 underruns
      0 output errors, 0 collisions, 1 interface resets
      0 babbles, 0 late collision, 0 deferred
      0 lost carrier, 0 no carrier
      0 output buffer failures, 0 output buffers swapped out
Serial0 is up, line protocol is up
  Hardware is HD64570
  Internet address is 199.6.13.1/24
  MTU 1500 bytes, BW 56 Kbit, DLY 20000 usec, rely 255/255, load 1/255
  Encapsulation HDLC, loopback not set, keepalive set (10 sec)
  Last input 00:00:00, output 00:00:07, output hang never
  Last clearing of "show interface" counters never
  Queueing strategy: fifo
  Output queue 0/40, 0 drops; input queue 0/75, 0 drops
   5 minute input rate 0 bits/sec, 0 packets/sec
   5 minute output rate 0 bits/sec, 0 packets/sec
      10513 packets input, 667585 bytes, 0 no buffer
      Received 10488 broadcasts, 0 runts, 0 giants
   0 input errors, 0 CRC, 0 frame, 0 overrun, 0 ignored, 0 abort
      10411 packets output, 643047 bytes, 0 underruns
      0 output errors, 0 collisions, 2 interface resets
      0 output buffer failures, 0 output buffers swapped out
      0 carrier transitions
      DCD=up  DSR=up  DTR=up  RTS=up  CTS=up
Serial1 is up, line protocol is up
  Hardware is HD64570
  Internet address is 201.100.11.2/24
  MTU 1500 bytes, BW 1544 Kbit, DLY 20000 usec, rely 255/255, load 1/255
  Encapsulation HDLC, loopback not set, keepalive set (10 sec)
  Last input 00:00:00, output 00:00:08, output hang never
  Last clearing of "show interface" counters never
  Input queue: 0/75/0 (size/max/drops); Total output drops: 0
  Queueing strategy: weighted fair
  Output queue: 0/64/0 (size/threshold/drops)
     Conversations  0/1 (active/max active)
     Reserved Conversations 0/0 (allocated/max allocated)
   5 minute input rate 0 bits/sec, 0 packets/sec
   5 minute output rate 0 bits/sec, 0 packets/sec
      10446 packets input, 633493 bytes, 0 no buffer
```

## Cisco Labs – Semester 2 – Router Configuration
## *LAB 4.10.2.1 – SHOW INTERFACE and CLEAR COUNTERS – ANSWERS*

### Results of show interface Command – Cont. (output generated by a Cisco 2514 router)

> Received 10445 broadcasts, 0 runts, 0 giants
> 0 input errors, 0 CRC, 0 frame, 0 overrun, 0 ignored, 0 abort
> 10392 packets output, 670617 bytes, 0 underruns
> 0 output errors, 0 collisions, 2 interface resets
> 0 output buffer failures, 0 output buffers swapped out

2. What is the significance of entering **?** at the command prompt? **The ? will invoke the help facility, allowing you to get help at any time.**

3. What prompt is the router showing? ***Router name #***

4. Is **counters** one of the subcommands that is listed? **Yes**

5. What is the description of **counters**? **Clear counters on one or all interfaces.**

6. Have the counters been set to 0? **Yes. The counters may not all be set to zero due to the fact that the router is seeing traffic between the time the counters cleared and checked again.**

7. Fill in the following information in the table for all interfaces:

| Interface | Ethernet 0 | Ethernet 1 | Serial 0 | Serial 1 |
|---|---|---|---|---|
| Hardware address | 0000.0c3b.f3a6 | 0000.0c3b.f3a7 | HD64570 | HD64570 |
| Packet input | 230 | 190 | 245 | 304 |
| Packet output | 167 | 190 | 212 | 243 |
| Last clearing of counters | 00:05:48 | 00:05:48 | 00:05:48 | 00:05:48 |

### Results of show interface Command (output generated by a Cisco 2514 router)

> lab-b#show interface
> Ethernet0 is up, line protocol is up
>   Hardware is Lance, address is 0000.0c3b.f3a6 (bia 0000.0c3b.f3a6)
>   Internet address is 219.17.100.1/24
>   MTU 1500 bytes, BW 10000 Kbit, DLY 1000 usec, rely 255/255, load 1/255
>   Encapsulation ARPA, loopback not set, keepalive set (10 sec)
>   ARP type: ARPA, ARP Timeout 04:00:00
>  Last input 00:00:13, output 00:00:02, output hang never
>  Last clearing of "show interface" counters 00:05:48
>   Queueing strategy: fifo
> Output queue 0/40, 0 drops; input queue 0/75, 0 drops
>   5 minute input rate 0 bits/sec, 0 packets/sec
> 5 minute output rate 0 bits/sec, 0 packets/sec

**Cisco Labs – Semester 2 – Router Configuration**
## *LAB 4.10.2.1 – SHOW INTERFACE and CLEAR COUNTERS – ANSWERS*

**Results of show interface Command – Cont.** (output generated by a Cisco 2514 router)

```
        230 packets input, 7900 bytes, 0 no buffer
        Received 72 broadcasts, 0 runts, 0 giants
        3 input errors, 3 CRC, 0 frame, 0 overrun, 0 ignored, 0 abort
        0 input packets with dribble condition detected
        167 packets output, 7602 bytes, 0 underruns
        0 output errors, 0 collisions, 1 interface resets
        0 babbles, 0 late collision, 0 deferred
        0 lost carrier, 0 no carrier
        0 output buffer failures, 0 output buffers swapped out
Ethernet1 is up, line protocol is up
  Hardware is Lance, address is 0000.0c3b.f3a7 (bia 0000.0c3b.f3a7)
  Internet address is 205.7.5.1/24
  MTU 1500 bytes, BW 10000 Kbit, DLY 1000 usec, rely 255/255, load 1/255
  Encapsulation ARPA, loopback not set, keepalive set (10 sec)
  ARP type: ARPA, ARP Timeout 04:00:00
  Last input 00:00:59, output 00:00:05, output hang never
  Last clearing of "show interface" counters 00:05:48
  Queueing strategy: fifo
  Output queue 0/40, 0 drops; input queue 0/75, 0 drops
  5 minute input rate 0 bits/sec, 0 packets/sec
  5 minute output rate 0 bits/sec, 0 packets/sec
        190 packets input, 5197 bytes, 0 no buffer
        Received 301 broadcasts, 0 runts, 0 giants
        0 input errors, 0 CRC, 0 frame, 0 overrun, 0 ignored, 0 abort
        0 input packets with dribble condition detected
        190 packets output, 5298 bytes, 0 underruns
        0 output errors, 0 collisions, 1 interface resets
        0 babbles, 0 late collision, 0 deferred
        0 lost carrier, 0 no carrier
        0 output buffer failures, 0 output buffers swapped out
Serial0 is up, line protocol is up
  Hardware is HD64570
  Internet address is 199.6.13.1/24
  MTU 1500 bytes, BW 56 Kbit, DLY 20000 usec, rely 255/255, load 1/255
  Encapsulation HDLC, loopback not set, keepalive set (10 sec)
  Last input 00:00:00, output 00:00:07, output hang never
  Last clearing of "show interface" counters 00:05:48
  Queueing strategy: fifo
  Output queue 0/40, 0 drops; input queue 0/75, 0 drops
  5 minute input rate 0 bits/sec, 0 packets/sec
  5 minute output rate 0 bits/sec, 0 packets/sec
        245 packets input, 7585 bytes, 0 no buffer
        Received 488 broadcasts, 0 runts, 0 giants
  0 input errors, 0 CRC, 0 frame, 0 overrun, 0 ignored, 0 abort
```

**Cisco Labs – Semester 2 – Router Configuration**
## *LAB 4.10.2.1 – SHOW INTERFACE and CLEAR COUNTERS – ANSWERS*

**Results of show interface Command – Cont.** (output generated by a Cisco 2514 router)

```
     212 packets output, 3047 bytes, 0 underruns
     0 output errors, 0 collisions, 2 interface resets
     0 output buffer failures, 0 output buffers swapped out
     0 carrier transitions
     DCD=up  DSR=up  DTR=up  RTS=up  CTS=up


Serial1 is up, line protocol is up
  Hardware is HD64570
  Internet address is 201.100.11.2/24
  MTU 1500 bytes, BW 1544 Kbit, DLY 20000 usec, rely 255/255, load 1/255
  Encapsulation HDLC, loopback not set, keepalive set (10 sec)
  Last input 00:00:00, output 00:00:08, output hang never
  Last clearing of "show interface" counters 00:05:48
  Input queue: 0/75/0 (size/max/drops); Total output drops: 0
  Queueing strategy: weighted fair
  Output queue: 0/64/0 (size/threshold/drops)
    Conversations  0/1 (active/max active)
    Reserved Conversations 0/0 (allocated/max allocated)
  5 minute input rate 0 bits/sec, 0 packets/sec
  5 minute output rate 0 bits/sec, 0 packets/sec
     304 packets input, 3493 bytes, 0 no buffer
     Received 145 broadcasts, 0 runts, 0 giants
     0 input errors, 0 CRC, 0 frame, 0 overrun, 0 ignored, 0 abort
     243 packets output, 3617 bytes, 0 underruns
     0 output errors, 0 collisions, 2 interface resets
     0 output buffer failures, 0 output buffers swapped out
```

8.  Find the following information for interface Ethernet 0 with **show interface**:
    a.  What is the MTU? **Maximum Transmission Unit – Ethernet is 1500 bytes**
    b.  What is rely? **Reliability of the interface – 255/255 is 100% reliable**
    c.  What is load? **Load on the interface – 255/255 is completely saturated**
    d.  What is a runt? **An Ethernet packet that is less than the 64-byte minimum**
    e.  What is a giant? **An Ethernet packet that is greater than the 1500 byte maximum**

9.  Find the following information for interface serial0 with **show interface**:
    a.  What is the IP address and subnet mask? **199.6.13.1  255.255.255.0**
    b.  What data link layer encapsulation is being used? **HDLC (High-Level Data Link Control)**
    c.  What does "Serial0 is up, line protocol is up" mean? **"Serial0 is up" means that there is a carrier detect signal. "Line protocol is up" means that keepalive messages are being received.**

# Cisco Labs – Semester 2 – Router Configuration
## *LAB 4.11.2.1 – TROUBLESHOOTING TOOLS CHALLENGE – OVERVIEW*
### *(Estimated time: 45 minutes)*

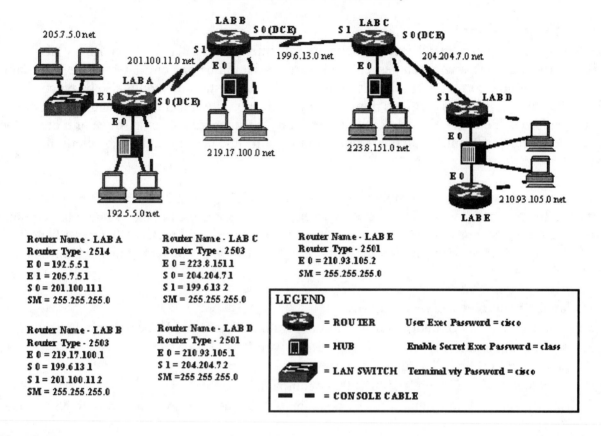

Router Name - LAB A
Router Type - 2514
E 0 = 192.5.5.1
E 1 = 205.7.5.1
S 0 = 201.100.11.1
SM = 255.255.255.0

Router Name - LAB B
Router Type - 2503
E 0 = 219.17.100.1
S 0 = 199.6.13.1
S 1 = 201.100.11.2
SM = 255.255.255.0

Router Name - LAB C
Router Type - 2503
E 0 = 223.8.151.1
S 0 = 204.204.7.1
S 1 = 199.6.13.2
SM = 255.255.255.0

Router Name - LAB D
Router Type - 2501
E 0 = 210.93.105.1
S 1 = 204.204.7.2
SM =255.255.255.0

Router Name - LAB E
Router Type - 2501
E 0 = 210.93.105.2
SM = 255.255.255.0

**LEGEND**

= ROUTER    User Exec Password = cisco

= HUB    Enable Secret Exec Password = class

= LAN SWITCH    Terminal vty Password = cisco

= CONSOLE CABLE

## Objectives:
- Identify what troubleshooting tools (IOS commands) are needed to gather basic information about your network
- Apply what you have learned in past labs to draw a logical diagram of the network

## Background:
As you know, having the topology of a network is extremely useful. It allows a network administrator to know exactly what equipment he or she has in what area (for bandwidth needs), how many devices are on the network, and the physical layout of the network. In this lab, you will figure out what a topology looks like based on the information you can gather while navigating through the network using IOS commands.

Through the use of **show** commands, you should be able to see which interfaces are up (using **show interface**), what devices the router is connected to (using **show CDP neighbors**), and how the user can get there (using **show protocols**). With the information received from the **show** commands, you should be able to remotely access the neighboring routers (using **telnet**). Through the use of troubleshooting commands (such as **ping** and **trace**), you should be able to see which devices are connected. Your final goal is to construct a logical topology drawing of the network by making use of all of these commands without referring to any diagrams ahead of time.

# Cisco Labs – Semester 2 – Router Configuration
## *LAB 4.11.2.1 – TROUBLESHOOTING TOOLS CHALLENGE – OVERVIEW*

## Tools / Preparation:

Prior to starting this lab, you will need to have the equipment for the standard five-router lab available (routers, hubs, switch, cables. etc.). The routers should be preconfigured by the instructor or lab assistant with the correct IP interface settings, etc. The workstations should also be preconfigured to have the correct IP address settings prior to starting the lab. The routers, hubs, and workstations should be labeled. You may also work with a portion of the standard lab setup (three or more of the routers) connected differently than the standard topology if time permits and try to determine the topology.

This lab assumes that you have completed the prior labs 2.2.10.1 and 2.2.10.2 and that the lab equipment (routers, hub, workstations, etc.) is assembled and connected in the standard lab topology. Work in teams of three or more. Before beginning this lab, you should review Chapters 12 and 13 in the *Cisco Networking Academy Program: First-Year Companion Guide* and semester 2 on-line Chapters 3 and 4.

## The following resources will be required:

- 5 PC workstations (minimum) with Windows operating system and HyperTerminal installed
- 5 Cisco routers (model 1600 series or 2500 series with IOS 11.2 or later)
- 4 Ethernet hubs (10Base-T with 4 to 8 ports)
- One Ethernet switch (Cisco Catalyst 1900 or comparable)
- 5 serial console cables to connect the workstation to the router console port (with RJ45 to DB9 converters)
- 3 sets of V.35 WAN serial cables (DTE male/ DCE female) to connect from router to router
- CAT5 Ethernet cables wired straight through to connect routers and workstations to hubs and switches
- AUI (DB15) to RJ45 Ethernet transceivers (the quantity depends on the number of routers with AUI ports) to convert router AUI interfaces to 10Base-T RJ45

## Web Site Resources:

- **Routing basics** – http://www.cisco.com/univercd/cc/td/doc/cisintwk/ito_doc/routing.htm
- **General information on routers** – http://www.cisco.com/univercd/cc/td/doc/pcat/#2
- **2500 series routers** – http://www.cisco.com/warp/public/cc/cisco/mkt/access/2500/index.shtml
- **1600 series routers** – http://www.cisco.com/warp/public/cc/cisco/mkt/access/1600/index.shtml
- **Terms and acronyms** – http://www.cisco.com/univercd/cc/td/doc/cisintwk/ita/index.htm
- **IP routing protocol IOS command summary** – http://www.cisco.com/univercd/cc/td/doc/product/software/ios120/12cgcr/rbkixol.htm
- **Beginning IP for new users** – http://www.cisco.com/warp/public/701/3.html
- **Internetworking design basics** – http://www.cisco/univercd/cc/td/doc/cisintwk/idg4/nd2002.htm

# Cisco Labs – Semester 2 – Router Configuration
## LAB 4.11.2.1 – TROUBLESHOOTING TOOLS CHALLENGE – WORKSHEET

**Step 1 – Gather information about the network.**
Use the standard five-router lab setup or a subset of three or more routers. Verify and document the topology of the network that you are working with or have constructed. You will be able to connect to the console of only one of the routers to find out all information about the other routers and other devices connected to you.

**A. Connect as the console to one of the routers in your network. (All information about the physical structure of the network must be obtained from only one console connection.)**

1. What command do you use to enter privileged EXEC mode?

   _____

**B. Gather information about the router you are connected to.**

2. What command do you use to gather information about the router you are on?

   _____

**C. Gather information about the devices that are connected to your router.**

3. What command do you use to gather information about neighboring devices?

   _____

**D. Gather information about devices on your network but not directly connected to you.**

4. You have gathered information about all interfaces on the router you are working with. You also have the IP address of the devices that are directly connected to the router you are working with. With the information obtained, describe how and what commands you will need to use to gather more detailed information about devices not directly connected to your router.

   _____
   _____
   _____
   _____
   _____
   _____

**Step 2 – Draw a logical topology of the network**
Using the troubleshooting tools that you have learned from the prior labs in this module, construct a network diagram based on a given topology. In your journal, draw the logical topology of this network. Include all routers, hubs, and switches. Be sure to indicate exactly where there are interfaces. For example, if there is a serial connection from router 1 to router 2, indicate that on the routers. If there is an Ethernet connection to a hub, indicate that. Label the diagram with the proper IP addresses and subnet masks and indicate which end is DCE and which is DTE for each WAN link.

5. Draw the network diagram with the information you obtained in Step 1.

**Cisco Labs – Semester 2 – Router Configuration**
## *LAB 4.11.2.1 – TROUBLESHOOTING TOOLS CHALLENGE – ANSWERS*

**A. Connect as the console to one of the routers in your network. (All information about the physical structure of the network must be obtained from only one connection.)**

1. What command do you use to enter privileged EXEC mode? <u>**enable**</u>

**B. Gather information about the router you are connected to.**

2. What command do you use to gather information about the router you are on?
<u>**The show interface command will give you information about all the router's interfaces, whether they are being used or not. This command will give you the IP address and subnet mask, along with a lot of other information that will not help you draw a diagram of the network. A better command to use would be the show protocol command. This will also give you the IP address and subnet mask of the interfaces that are internal to the router and makes it easier to sort the information to find the information you need.**</u>

**C. Gather information about the devices that are connected to you .**

3. What command do you use to gather information about neighboring devices?
<u>**The show cdp neighbors detail command. If you used the show cdp neighbors command without detail, you would not have the IP address of the neighbor's device.**</u>

**D. Gather information about devices that are on your network but not directly connected to you.**

4. You have gathered information about all interfaces on the router you are working with. You also have the IP address of the devices that are directly connected to the router you are working with. With the information obtained, describe how and what commands you will need to use to gather information about devices not directly connected to your router.
<u>**First you will need to telnet to your neighbors. After you have connected to the neighbor, you can use the show protocols command to gather addressing information about that router's interfaces and add it to your diagram. Then issue the show cdp neighbors detail command to gather information about devices connected to this router. With this information, you can determine if there are other devices connected. If so, you then telnet to all other devices until you have a complete map of the network.**</u>

5. Draw the network diagram with the information you obtained in Step 1.
<u>**Answers will vary, but the diagram should look similar to the standard five-router setup or a subset of that network, depending on which routers were used and how they were connected.**</u>

# Cisco Labs – Semester 2 – Router Configuration
## *LAB 5.2.2.1 – ROUTER SETUP COMMAND – OVERVIEW*
### *(Estimated time: 30 minutes)*

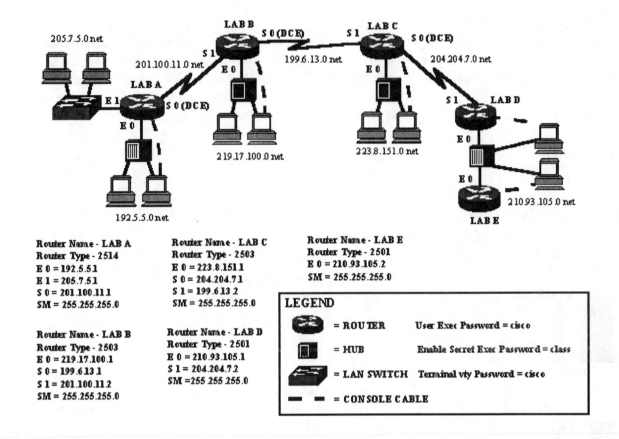

Router Name - LAB A
Router Type - 2514
E 0 = 192.5.5.1
E 1 = 205.7.5.1
S 0 = 201.100.11.1
SM = 255.255.255.0

Router Name - LAB C
Router Type - 2503
E 0 = 223.8.151.1
S 0 = 204.204.7.1
S 1 = 199.6.13.2
SM = 255.255.255.0

Router Name - LAB E
Router Type - 2501
E 0 = 210.93.105.2
SM = 255.255.255.0

Router Name - LAB B
Router Type - 2503
E 0 = 219.17.100.1
S 0 = 199.6.13.1
S 1 = 201.100.11.2
SM = 255.255.255.0

Router Name - LAB D
Router Type - 2501
E 0 = 210.93.105.1
S 1 = 204.204.7.2
SM = 255.255.255.0

**LEGEND**

= ROUTER    User Exec Password = cisco

= HUB    Enable Secret Exec Password = class

= LAN SWITCH    Terminal vty Password = cisco

= CONSOLE CABLE

## Objectives:
- Become familiar with the router setup mode
- Understand what global parameters can be configured in setup mode
- Understand what interface parameters can be configured in setup mode

## Background:
In this lab you will use the command **setup** to enter setup mode. Setup is a Cisco IOS utility (or program) that can help get some of the basic router configuration parameters established. Setup is not intended as the mode for entering complex protocol features in the router. Rather, the purpose of setup mode is to bring up a minimal configuration for any router that cannot find its configuration from some other source.

There are two ways to enter setup mode. If the router cannot find its configuration file, it will enter setup mode or the setup dialog automatically. The other way to enter setup mode is to enter the **setup** command at the command line while in privileged mode. The setup dialog prompts you for basic setup options such as which protocols you will be using and the IP address and subnet mask for each interface the router has. The setup dialog provides default values for most of the configurable options. You can either accept these or enter your own. If setup does not provide a prompted entry for specific interface information, you will have to manually enter those commands at a later time. With this lab you will run the setup utility but will not save the configuration.

# Cisco Labs – Semester 2 – Router Configuration
## *LAB 5.2.2.1 – ROUTER SETUP COMMAND – OVERVIEW*

## Tools / Preparation:

Prior to starting the lab, you will need to connect a PC workstation with HyperTerminal to a router using the router's console interface with a roll-over cable. This lab should be done at the router console station. You should review Chapter 14 in the *Cisco Networking Academy Program: First-Year Companion Guide* and review Semester 2 on-line Curriculum Chapter 5 prior to starting this lab. Work individually or in teams. Be familiar with the following command:

- **setup**

## Resources Required:

- PC with monitor, keyboard, mouse, and power cords
- Windows operating system (Windows 95, 98, NT, or 2000) installed on PC
- HyperTerminal program configured for router console access
- PC connected to the router console port with a roll-over cable

## Web Site Resources:

- **Routing basics** – http://www.cisco.com/univercd/cc/td/doc/cisintwk/ito_doc/routing.htm
- **General information on routers** – http://www.cisco.com/univercd/cc/td/doc/pcat/#2
- **2500 series routers** – http://www.cisco.com/warp/public/cc/cisco/mkt/access/2500/index.shtml
- **1600 series routers** – http://www.cisco.com/warp/public/cc/cisco/mkt/access/1600/index.shtml
- **Terms and acronyms** – http://www.cisco.com/univercd/cc/td/doc/cisintwk/ita/index.htm
- **IP routing protocol IOS command summary** –
  http://www.cisco.com/univercd/cc/td/doc/product/software/ios120/12cgcr/rbkixol.htm
- **Beginning IP for new users** – http://www.cisco.com/warp/public/701/3.html

## Notes:

_____
_____
_____
_____
_____
_____
_____
_____
_____
_____
_____
_____
_____

# Cisco Labs – Semester 2 – Router Configuration
## *LAB 5.2.2.1 – ROUTER SETUP COMMAND – WORKSHEET*

**Step 1 – Log on to the router.**
  **Explanation:** Connect to the router and log in. Enter the password **cisco** if prompted.

**Step 2 – Enter privileged mode.**
  **Task:**
     a.  Enter **enable** at the command prompt.
     b.  Enter the password **class**.

  **Explanation:** You use the **enable** command to enter privileged EXEC mode

**Step 3 – Enter the help command.**
  **Task:** Enter the help command by typing **?** at the router prompt.
  **Explanation**: The router will respond with all available commands for privileged mode.

  1.  Was **setup** one of the commands available? _____

**Step 4 – Enter setup mode.**
  **Task:** Enter **setup** at the router prompt.
  **Explanation:** Entering the **setup** command starts setup mode and executes a question-driven initial configuration routine referred to as the system configuration dialog.

**Step 5 – Continue with the setup dialog.**
  **Task:** Enter **yes** or press the Enter key to continue with the setup dialog.
  **Explanation:** The router will ask you if you want to continue with the configuration dialog.

  2.  What is the importance of the word in the square brackets? _____

**Step 6 – Show the current interface summary.**
  **Task:** Press the Enter key or type **yes**.
  **Explanation:** The router will ask "First, would you like to see the current interface summary?" You can press the Enter key to accept the default answers.

  3.  Fill in the following table with the information provided.

| Interface | IP-Address | OK | Method | Status | Protocol |
|---|---|---|---|---|---|
| | | | | | |
| | | | | | |
| | | | | | |
| | | | | | |

# Cisco Labs – Semester 2 – Router Configuration
## *LAB 5.2.2.1 – ROUTER SETUP COMMAND – WORKSHEET*

### Step 7 – Configure global parameters.

**Task:** Configure the router using the default settings for any questions the router asks.

**Explanation:** Make sure that you enter **class** as the enable secret password. Make sure you use something different (such as **cisco**) for the enable password.

### Step 8 – Configure interface parameters.

**Task:** Configure the router using the default settings for any questions the router asks.

**Explanation:** Setup mode will now configure any interfaces present on the router.

### Step 9 – Configuration command script

**Task:** Answer **no** to the question "Use this configuration?"

**Explanation:** The router will display the configuration command script. Then it will ask you if you want to save this configuration

4. If you were to answer yes to the question "Use this configuration?", where would this information be saved? _____

### Step 10 – Enter setup mode.

**Task:** Enter setup mode

**Explanation:** Repeat this lab, but this time as you enter setup mode, change the default answers. For the enable secret password, use **class**. Remember to say **no** to the question "Use this configuration?"

# Cisco Labs – Semester 2 – Router Configuration
## *LAB 5.2.2.1 – ROUTER SETUP COMMAND – ANSWERS*

1. Was **setup** one of the commands available? **Yes**

2. What is the importance of the word in the square brackets? **The square brackets indicate default answers or the current configuration.**

3. Fill in the following table.

| Interface | IP-Address | OK | Method | Status | Protocol |
|-----------|-----------|-----|--------|--------|----------|
| **Ethernet0** | **219.17.100.1** | **YES** | **NVRAM** | **Up** | **Up** |
| **Ethernet1** | **unassigned** | **YES** | **Unset** | **Admin down** | **Down** |
| **Serial0** | **199.6.13.1** | **YES** | **NVRAM** | **Up** | **Up** |
| **Serial1** | **201.100.11.2** | **YES** | **NVRAM** | **Up** | **Up** |

**Results of setup Command Interface Summary** (output generated by a Cisco 2501 router)

LAB-B#setup

    --- System Configuration Dialog ---

At any point you may enter a question mark '?' for help.
Use ctrl-c to abort configuration dialog at any prompt.
Default settings are in square brackets '[]'.

Continue with configuration dialog? [yes]:

First, would you like to see the current interface summary? [yes]:

| Interface | IP-Address | OK? | Method | Status | Protocol |
|-----------|-----------|-----|--------|--------|----------|
| Ethernet0 | 219.17.100.1 | YES | NVRAM | up | up |
| Ethernet1 | unassigned | YES | unset | administratively down | down |
| Serial0 | 199.6.13.1 | YES | NVRAM | up | up |
| Serial1 | 201.100.11.2 | YES | NVRAM | up | up |

4. If you were to answer yes to the question "Use this configuration?", where would this information be saved? **The router will save this information in NVRAM and replace the backup configuration that is already in NVRAM.**

# Cisco Labs – Semester 2 – Router Configuration
## *LAB 5.3.2.1 – ROUTER SETUP CHALLENGE – OVERVIEW*
### *(Estimated time: 60 minutes)*

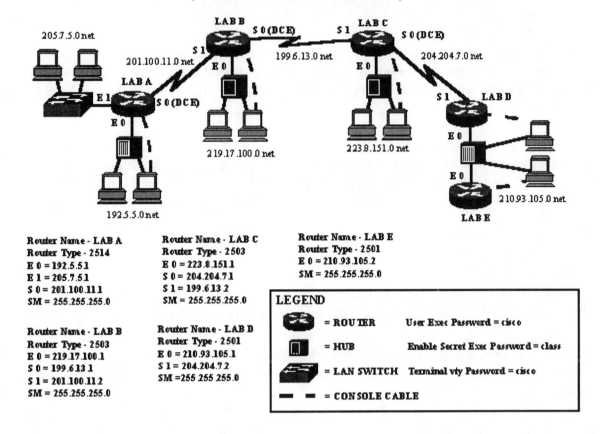

Router Name - LAB A
Router Type - 2514
E 0 = 192.5.5.1
E 1 = 205.7.5.1
S 0 = 201.100.11.1
SM = 255.255.255.0

Router Name - LAB C
Router Type - 2503
E 0 = 223.8.151.1
S 0 = 204.204.7.1
S 1 = 199.6.13.2
SM = 255.255.255.0

Router Name - LAB E
Router Type - 2501
E 0 = 210.93.105.2
SM = 255.255.255.0

Router Name - LAB B
Router Type - 2503
E 0 = 219.17.100.1
S 0 = 199.6.13.1
S 1 = 201.100.11.2
SM = 255.255.255.0

Router Name - LAB D
Router Type - 2501
E 0 = 210.93.105.1
S 1 = 204.204.7.2
SM = 255.255.255.0

**LEGEND**

= ROUTER     User Exec Password = cisco

= HUB     Enable Secret Exec Password = class

= LAN SWITCH     Terminal vty Password = cisco

= CONSOLE CABLE

## Objectives:
- Apply what you have learned in Chapter 14 in the Cisco Networking Academy First-Year Companion Guide, On-line Chapter 5, and Lab 5.2.2.1 on the **setup** utility
- Demonstrate your ability to subnet a class B IP address
- Learn to use setup mode to set basic configuration parameters for the router
- Use HyperTerminal to capture the running configuration for the routers

## Background:
When you first open a router and the operating system is loaded, you have to go through the process of initial setup. In this scenario, you have just received a shipment of new routers, and you need to set up a basic configuration. You have received a class B IP network address of 156.1.0.0, and you will need to subnet your class B address using 5 bits for your subnets. Use the standard five-router diagram above to determine which subnetwork numbers and which IP addresses you will use for the eight networks you will need to define. For this lab, set up all five routers. Be sure to configure the router you are using with a console port.

# Cisco Labs – Semester 2 – Router Configuration
## *LAB 5.3.2.1 – ROUTER SETUP CHALLENGE – OVERVIEW*

## Tools / Preparation:

Prior to starting this lab, you will need to have the equipment for the standard five-router lab available (routers, hubs, switch, cables, and so on). If the routers are configured, the lab assistant or instructor will have to erase the configuration before you begin. The routers, hubs, and workstations should be labeled.

This lab assumes that you have completed the prior lab 2.2.10.1 and that the lab equipment (routers, hub, workstations, and so on) is assembled and connected in the standard lab topology. Work in teams of three to five. Before beginning this lab, you should review Chapter 14 in the *Cisco Networking Academy Program: First-Year Companion Guide* and semester 2 on-line Chapter 5.

## Resources Required:

- 1 floppy disk
- 5 PC workstations (minimum) with Windows operating system and HyperTerminal installed
- 5 Cisco routers (model 1600 series or 2500 series with IOS 11.2 or later)
- 4 Ethernet hubs (10Base-T with four to eight ports)
- One Ethernet switch (Cisco Catalyst 1900 or comparable)
- 5 serial console cables to connect the workstation to the router console port (with RJ45 to DB9 converters)
- 3 sets of V.35 WAN serial cables (DTE male/ DCE female) to connect from router to router
- CAT5 Ethernet cables wired straight through to connect routers and workstations to hubs and switches
- AUI (DB15) to RJ45 Ethernet transceivers (the quantity depends on the number of routers with AUI ports) to convert router AUI interfaces to 10Base-T RJ45

## Web Site Resources:

- **Routing basics** – http://www.cisco.com/univercd/cc/td/doc/cisintwk/ito_doc/routing.htm
- **General information on routers** – http://www.cisco.com/univercd/cc/td/doc/pcat/#2
- **2500 series routers** – http://www.cisco.com/warp/public/cc/cisco/mkt/access/2500/index.shtml
- **1600 series routers** – http://www.cisco.com/warp/public/cc/cisco/mkt/access/1600/index.shtml
- **Terms and acronyms** – http://www.cisco.com/univercd/cc/td/doc/cisintwk/ita/index.htm
- **IP routing protocol IOS command summary** –
  http://www.cisco.com/univercd/cc/td/doc/product/software/ios120/12cgcr/rbkixol.htm

## Notes: _____

_____

_____

_____

_____

# Cisco Labs – Semester 2 – Router Configuration
## *LAB 5.3.2.1 – ROUTER SETUP CHALLENGE – WORKSHEET*

**Step 1 – Log into the router in enable mode, and issue the setup command.**
If the router has not been configured, it may enter setup automatically. If the router is configured, you will need to log into the router, enter enable mode, and issue the **setup** command.

**Step 2 – Follow the on-screen prompts, and use the following information:**
Use Lab-A to Lab-E as the host name for the routers. The enable secret password should be **class**. Use **IGRP** for your routing protocol with autonomous system number **1**. Be sure to specify the correct IP addresses and number of subnet bits for each interface. When you are asked to "Use this configuration?" answer **yes**.

1.  How many subnets can you create with a 5-bit mask and a Class B network address?
    _____

2.  How many hosts per subnet ? _____

3.  What will the subnet mask be in decimal? _____

**Step 3 – Document your configuration.**
After answering **yes** to "Use this configuration?" you will want to capture the output from the **show running-config** command of all five routers to hand in to your instructor. You do this in HyperTerminal by clicking Transfer/Capture Text. In the Capture Text window, you can specify the filename and where you want the capture text to be saved. Save your text to a floppy disk, and name the text file output from each router the same as the router name (lab-a.txt, lab-b.txt, and so on). Then click the start button to start capturing text.

From an enable mode prompt, issue the **show running-config** command. After capturing the running configuration, click Transfer/Capture text/Stop. The output from **show running-config** will be on the floppy disk. Take your floppy disk to a computer that has a printer, and print the captured text or display the text file for your instructor.

**Step 4 – Repeat for all five routers.**

4.  See the answers section for running the configuration from all five routers using the class B address with 5 bits of subnetting.

# Cisco Labs – Semester 2 – Router Configuration
## *LAB 5.3.2.1 – ROUTER SETUP CHALLENGE – ANSWERS*

1. How many subnets can you create with a 5-bit mask and a Class B network address?
   **$2^5$ (2 to the fifth power) or 32 subnets. Useable subnets would be $2^5$–2 or 30 subnets.**

2. How many hosts per subnet ? **$2^{11}$ (2 to the eleventh power) or 2048 (2046 useable)**

3. What will the subnet mask be in decimal? **255.255.248.0**

4. Captured running configurations for routers – see the next 5 pages.

## Capture Text from running-config Command – Router Lab-A

```
hostname LAB-A
enable secret 5 $1$fLVo$ZW2B3630o9KBNNpDrrVLm0
enable password cisco
line vty 0 4
password cisco
no snmp-server
!
no decnet routing
no appletalk routing
no ipx routing
ip routing
isdn switch-type none
!
 interface Ethernet0
ip address 156.1.8.1 255.255.248.0
no mop enabled
!
interface Ethernet1
ip address 156.1.16.1 255.255.248.0
no mop enabled
!
interface Serial0
ip address 156.1.24.1 255.255.248.0
no mop enabled
!
interface Serial1
no ip address
no mop enabled
!
router igrp
network 156.1.0.0
 !
end
```

**Cisco Labs – Semester 2 – Router Configuration**
## *LAB 5.3.2.1 – ROUTER SETUP CHALLENGE – ANSWERS*

## Capture Text from running-config Command – Router Lab-B

```
hostname LAB-B
enable secret 5 $1$fLVo$ZW2B3630o9KBNNpDrrVLm0
enable password cisco
line vty 0 4
password cisco
no snmp-server
!
no decnet routing
no appletalk routing
no ipx routing
ip routing
isdn switch-type none
!
interface BRI0
shutdown
no ip address
!
interface Ethernet0
ip address 156.1.32.1 255.255.248.0
no mop enabled
!
 interface Serial0
ip address 156.1.40.1 255.255.248.0
no mop enabled
!
interface Serial1
ip address 156.1.24.2 255.255.248.0
no mop enabled
!
router igrp
network 156.1.0.0
 !
end
```

# Cisco Labs – Semester 2 – Router Configuration
## *LAB 5.3.2.1 – ROUTER SETUP CHALLENGE – ANSWERS*

**Capture Text from running-config Command – Router Lab-C**

```
hostname LAB-C
enable secret 5 $1$fLVo$ZW2B3630o9KBNNpDrrVLm0
enable password cisco
line vty 0 4
password cisco
no snmp-server
!
no decnet routing
no appletalk routing
no ipx routing
ip routing
isdn switch-type none
!
 interface BRI0
shutdown
no ip address
!
interface Ethernet0
ip address 156.1.48.1 255.255.248.0
no mop enabled
!
 interface Serial0
ip address 156.1.56.1 255.255.248.0
no mop enabled
!
interface Serial1
ip address 156.1.40.2 255.255.248.0
no mop enabled
!
router igrp
network 156.1.0.0
 !
end
```

# Cisco Labs – Semester 2 – Router Configuration
## *LAB 5.3.2.1 – ROUTER SETUP CHALLENGE – ANSWERS*

**Capture Text from running-config Command – Router Lab-D**

```
hostname LAB-D
 enable secret 5 $1$fLVo$ZW2B3630o9KBNNpDrrVLm0
 enable password cisco
 line vty 0 4
 password cisco
 no snmp-server
 !
 no decnet routing
 no appletalk routing
 no ipx routing
 ip routing
 isdn switch-type none
 !
  interface Ethernet0
 ip address 156.1.64.1 255.255.248.0
 no mop enabled
 !
  interface Serial0
 shutdown
no ip address
 !
 interface Serial1
 ip address 156.1.56.2 255.255.248
 no mop enabled
 !
 router igrp
 network 156.1.0.0
  !
 end
```

**Cisco Labs – Semester 2 – Router Configuration**
## *LAB 5.3.2.1 – ROUTER SETUP CHALLENGE – ANSWERS*

## Capture Text from running-config Command – Router Lab-E

```
hostname LAB-E
 enable secret 5 $1$fLVo$ZW2B3630o9KBNNpDrrVLm0
 enable password cisco
 line vty 0 4
 password cisco
 no snmp-server
!
 no decnet routing
 no appletalk routing
 no ipx routing
 ip routing
 isdn switch-type none
!
 interface Ethernet0
ip address 156.1.64.2 255.255.248.0
 no mop enabled
!
 interface Serial0
 shutdown
no ip address
!
 interface Serial1
  shutdown
no ip address
!
 router igrp
 network 156.1.0.0
  !
 end
```

# Cisco Labs – Semester 2 – Router Configuration
## *LAB 6.3.2.1 – BASIC ROUTER CONFIGURATION – OVERVIEW*
### *(Estimated time: 45 minutes)*

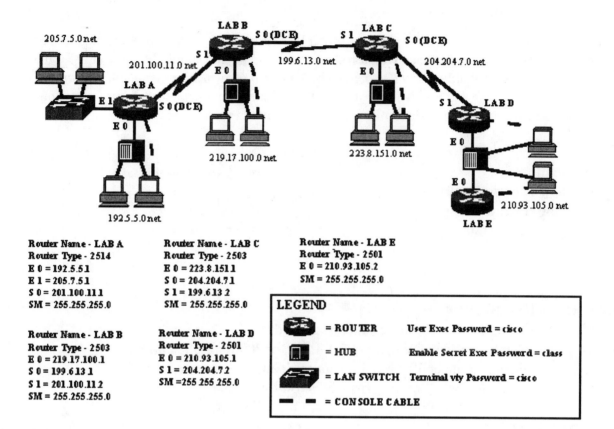

**Router Name - LAB A**
**Router Type - 2514**
E 0 = 192.5.5.1
E 1 = 205.7.5.1
S 0 = 201.100.11.1
SM = 255.255.255.0

**Router Name - LAB C**
**Router Type - 2503**
E 0 = 223.8.151.1
S 0 = 204.204.7.1
S 1 = 199.6.13.2
SM = 255.255.255.0

**Router Name - LAB E**
**Router Type - 2501**
E 0 = 210.93.105.2
SM = 255.255.255.0

**Router Name - LAB B**
**Router Type - 2503**
E 0 = 219.17.100.1
S 0 = 199.6.13.1
S 1 = 201.100.11.2
SM = 255.255.255.0

**Router Name - LAB D**
**Router Type - 2501**
E 0 = 210.93.105.1
S 1 = 204.204.7.2
SM = 255.255.255.0

**LEGEND**

= ROUTER     User Exec Password = cisco

= HUB     Enable Secret Exec Password = class

= LAN SWITCH     Terminal vty Password = cisco

= CONSOLE CABLE

## Objectives:
- Use router configuration mode to configure the routing protocol
- Configure the router's identification (name)
- Configure a message of the day (motd) banner
- Use interface configuration mode to enter a description for an interface

## Background:
In this lab you will use the router's global configuration mode and enter one-line commands that change the entire router. The router's prompt in global configuration mode is *Router-name*(**config**)#. Other configuration modes will be used for multiple command lines and detailed configurations as in configuration of interfaces. When working with the interfaces, the router prompt looks like *Router-name*(**config-if**)#. You will also configure a message-of-the-day banner using the **banner motd** command in global configuration mode and enter descriptions for the interfaces on the router in interface configuration mode.

# Cisco Labs – Semester 2 – Router Configuration
## *LAB 6.3.2.1 – BASIC ROUTER CONFIGURATION – OVERVIEW*

## Tools / Preparation:
Prior to starting the lab you will need to connect a PC workstation with HyperTerminal to a router using the router's console interface with a roll-over cable. This lab should be done at the router console station. You should review Chapter 15 in the *Cisco Networking AcademyProgram: First-Year Companion Guide* and review semester 2 on-line Curriculum Chapter 6 prior to starting this lab. Work individually or in teams. Be familiar with the following commands:

- enable
- show running-config
- show startup-config
- configure terminal
- hostname

- banner motd
- interface
- description
- reload

## Resources Required:
- PC with monitor, keyboard, mouse, and power cords
- Windows operating system (Windows 95, 98, NT, or 2000) installed on PC
- HyperTerminal program configured for a console connection
- PC connected to the router console port with a roll-over cable

## Web Site Resources:
- **Routing basics** – http://www.cisco.com/univercd/cc/td/doc/cisintwk/ito_doc/routing.htm
- **General information on routers** – http://www.cisco.com/univercd/cc/td/doc/pcat/#2
- **2500 series routers** – http://www.cisco.com/warp/public/cc/cisco/mkt/access/2500/index.shtml
- **1600 series routers** – http://www.cisco.com/warp/public/cc/cisco/mkt/access/1600/index.shtml
- **Terms and acronyms** – http://www.cisco.com/univercd/cc/td/doc/cisintwk/ita/index.htm
- **IP routing protocol IOS command summary** – http://www.cisco.com/univercd/cc/td/doc/product/software/ios120/12cgcr/rbkixol.htm

## Notes:
_____
_____
_____
_____
_____
_____
_____

# Cisco Labs – Semester 2 – Router Configuration
## *LAB 6.3.2.1 – BASIC ROUTER CONFIGURATION – WORKSHEET*

**Step 1 – Log on to the router.**
   **Explanation:** Connect to the router and log in. Enter the password **cisco** if prompted.

**Step 2 – Enter privileged mode.**
   **Task:**
   a. Enter **enable** (abbreviated **en**) at the command prompt.
   b. Enter the password **class**.
   **Explanation:** You use the **enable** command to enter privileged EXEC mode.

   1. What is the router command to view the current running configuration? _____

**Step 3 – Show the active configuration file.**
   **Task:** Enter **show running-config** (abbreviated **sh run**) at the router prompt.
   **Explanation:** The router will display information on how it is currently configured from the file that is loaded in RAM (Random Access Memory).

   2. Compare the hostname in the running-config with the router prompt. Are they the same?
   _____

**Step 4 – Show the backup configuration file.**
   **Task:** Enter **show startup-config** (abbreviated **sh start**) at the router prompt.
   **Explanation:** The router will display information on the backup configuration file stored in NVRAM (Non-Volatile RAM).

   3. Is the hostname the same as the router prompt? _____

**Step 5 – Enter global configuration mode.**
   **Task:** Enter **configure terminal** (abbreviated **config t**) at the router prompt.
   **Explanation:** To configure the router, you must enter global configuration mode. Notice how the router prompt has changed after this command.

   4. What does the router prompt look like? _____

**Step 6 – Enter the help command.**
   **Task:** Enter the help command by typing **?** at the router prompt.
   **Explanation:** The router will respond with all commands available in global configuration mode.

   5. Is **hostname** one of the command options? _____

**Step 7 – Enter the help command for hostname.**
   **Task:** Enter the help command for **hostname** by entering **hostname ?** at the router prompt.
   **Explanation:** You can get help with any command by entering the command followed by a space and a **?**.

   6. What did the router respond with? _____

# Cisco Labs – Semester 2 – Router Configuration
## *LAB 6.3.2.1 – BASIC ROUTER CONFIGURATION – WORKSHEET*

**Step 8 – Change the hostname of the router.**
    **Task:** Enter **hostname** and *your first name* at the router prompt.
    **Explanation:** This command will change the router hostname to your first name.

    7.  Did the router's prompt change to the new hostname? _____

**Step 9 – Show the active configuration file.**
    **Task:**
        a.  Enter **exit** at the router prompt to return to the privileged mode prompt.
        b.  Enter **show running-config** at the router prompt.
    **Explanation:** To check the running configuration, you first have to exit global configuration mode using **exit**. Then you will be at a privileged mode prompt and can issue the **show running-config** command. **Note:** The configuration change (hostname) you just made is in effect until the router is rebooted or reloaded.

    8.  What is the router's hostname? _____

**Step 10 – Show the backup configuration file.**
    **Task:** Enter **show startup-config** at the router prompt.
    **Explanation:** The router will display information on the backup configuration file stored in NVRAM.

    9.  Is the hostname the same as the router prompt? _____

**Step 11 – Enter global configuration mode.**
    **Task:** Enter **configure terminal** (abbreviated **config t**) at the router prompt.
    **Explanation:** To configure the router, you must enter global configuration mode. Notice how the router prompt has changed after this command.

**Step 12 – Enter a message of the day.**
    **Task:** Enter **banner motd #*This is the Message Of The Day*#** at the router prompt.
    **Explanation:** This command will create a message of the day banner that will display when someone logs into the router. Note that the message is bracketed by **#,** which tells the router the beginning and end of the message.

**Step 13 – Show information about the active configuration file.**
    **Task:**
        a.  Enter **exit** at the router prompt
        b.  Enter **show running-config** at the router prompt.
    **Explanation:** To check the running configuration, you first have to exit global configuration mode using **exit**. Then you will be at a privileged mode prompt and can issue the **show running-config** command. **Note:** The configuration change you just made is in effect until the router is rebooted or reloaded.

    10. What did the router say the message of the day is? _____

# Cisco Labs – Semester 2 – Router Configuration
## *LAB 6.3.2.1 – BASIC ROUTER CONFIGURATION – WORKSHEET*

**Step 14 – Log out of the router.**
   **Task:** Enter **exit** at the router prompt.
   **Explanation:** To exit the router, you can use either **exit** or **logout** (or **ex** for short).

**Step 15 – Log on to the router.**
   **Explanation:** Connect to the router and log in. Enter the password **cisco** if prompted.

**Step 16 – Enter privileged mode.**
   **Task:**
     a. From user EXEC mode, enter privileged EXEC mode using the **enable** command.
     b. Enter the enable password of **class**.
   **Explanation:** Enter enable mode from user EXEC mode.

**Step 17 – Show the active configuration file.**
   **Task:** Enter **show running-config** at the router prompt.
   **Explanation:** The router will display information on how it is currently configured.

11. Is there a description name for interface serial0? _____

**Step 18 – Enter global configuration mode.**
   **Task:** Enter **configure terminal** at the router prompt.
   **Explanation:** To configure the router, you must enter global configuration mode. Notice how the router prompt has changed after this command.

**Step 19 – Enter interface configuration mode.**
   **Task:** Enter **interface serial0** at the global configuration prompt.
   **Explanation:** Entering **interface serial0** at the global configuration prompt will allow you to change the configuration for serial0.

12. What does the router prompt look like in interface configuration mode? _____

**Step 20 – Enter the help command.**
   **Task:** Enter **?** at the router prompt.
   **Explanation:** The router responds with a list of available commands to configure interface serial0.

**Step 21 – Get help for the description command.**
   **Task:** Enter **description ?** at the router prompt.
   **Explanation:** You can get help with any command at any time using the **?** command.

**Step 22 – Enter a description for interface serial0.**
   **Task:** Enter **description *any text you want up to 80 characters*** at the router prompt.
   **Explanation:** This will enter a description for interface serial0.

**Cisco Labs – Semester 2 – Router Configuration**
## *LAB 6.3.2.1 – BASIC ROUTER CONFIGURATION – WORKSHEET*

**Step 23 – Exit configuration mode.**
**Task:**
    a.  Enter **exit** in interface configuration mode.
    b.  Enter **exit** in global configuration mode
**Explanation:** The first **exit** command will exit you from interface configuration mode, and the second will exit you from global configuration mode. Notice how the router prompt has changed after each **exit** command.

**Step 24 – Show the active configuration file.**
**Task:** Enter **show running-config** at the router prompt.
**Explanation:** The router will display information on how it is currently configured.

13. What is the description for interface serial0? _____

**Step 25 – Show the backup configuration file.**
**Task:** Enter **show startup-config** at the router prompt.
**Explanation:** The router will display information on the backup configuration file stored in NVRAM.

14. Is the interface serial0 description the same as in step 22? _____

**Step 26 – Reload the router.**
**Task:** Enter **reload** at the router prompt. When prompted to save changes, answer **no.**
**Explanation:** All the changes that you made to the router were in effect in the active configuration. When you reload the router, it reloads from the backup configuration file. If you wanted to keep the changes, you would have to use a command to copy the running configuration to the backup configuration file.

15. What is the command to copy the current running configuration to the backup (startup) configuration? _____

# Cisco Labs – Semester 2 – Router Configuration
## *LAB 6.3.2.1 – BASIC ROUTER CONFIGURATION – ANSWERS*

1.  What is the router command to view the current running configuration? **show running-config (abbreviated sh run).**

2.  Compare the hostname in the running-config with the router prompt. Are they the same? **Yes**

3.  Is the hostname the same as the router prompt for NVRAM? **Yes**

4.  What does the router prompt look like? **Router name(config)#**

5.  Is **hostname** one of the command options? **Yes**

6.  What did the router respond with? **WORD** *this system's network name*

7.  Did the router's prompt change to the new hostname? **Yes**

8.  What is the router's hostname? **Your first name**

9.  Is the hostname the same as the router prompt? **No (since you have not saved it yet)**

10. What did the router say the message of the day is? **This is the message of the day.**

11. Is there a description name for interface serial0? **No**

12. What does the router prompt look like in interface configuration mode? **Router name(config-if)#**

13. What is the description for interface serial0? **The description is what you typed in in Step 22.**

14. Is the interface serial0 description the same as in Step 22? **No (since you have not saved it yet)**

15. What is the command to copy the current running configuration to the backup (start) configuration? **copy running-config startup-config (abbreviated copy run start)**

# Cisco Labs – Semester 2 – Router Configuration
## *LAB 6.4.2.1 – ROUTER INTERFACE CONFIGURATION – OVERVIEW*
### *(Estimated time: 45 minutes)*

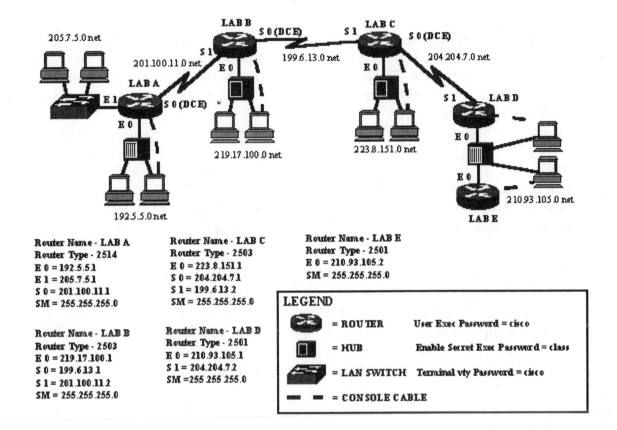

**Router Name - LAB A**
Router Type - 2514
E 0 = 192.5.5.1
E 1 = 205.7.5.1
S 0 = 201.100.11.1
SM = 255.255.255.0

**Router Name - LAB B**
Router Type - 2503
E 0 = 219.17.100.1
S 0 = 199.6.13.1
S 1 = 201.100.11.2
SM = 255.255.255.0

**Router Name - LAB C**
Router Type - 2503
E 0 = 223.8.151.1
S 0 = 204.204.7.1
S 1 = 199.6.13.2
SM = 255.255.255.0

**Router Name - LAB D**
Router Type - 2501
E 0 = 210.93.105.1
S 1 = 204.204.7.2
SM = 255.255.255.0

**Router Name - LAB E**
Router Type - 2501
E 0 = 210.93.105.2
SM = 255.255.255.0

**LEGEND**

= ROUTER      User Exec Password = cisco

= HUB         Enable Secret Exec Password = class

= LAN SWITCH  Terminal vty Password = cisco

= CONSOLE CABLE

## Objectives:
- Use interface configuration mode to configure interfaces
- Configure IP address assignments for router interfaces
- Configure subnet mask assignments for router interfaces
- Copy the running configuration to the backup configuration

## Background:
In this lab you will use the router's interface configuration mode to configure an IP address and subnet mask for each router interface. You will verify that layer 3 connectivity is OK by using the **ping** command. The **show running-config** command will help make sure the changes you have made are what was intended. You will then save the running configuration to the backup configuration.

# Cisco Labs – Semester 2 – Router Configuration
## *LAB 6.4.2.1 – ROUTER INTERFACE CONFIGURATION – OVERVIEW*

## Tools / Preparation:
Prior to starting the lab, you will need to connect a PC workstation with HyperTerminal to a router using the router's console interface with a roll-over cable. This lab should be done at the router console station. You should review Chapter 17 in the *Cisco Networking Academy Program: First-Year Companion Guide* and review semester 2 on-line curriculum Chapter 6 prior to starting this lab. Work individually or in teams. Be familiar with the following commands:

- **enable**
- **show running-config**
- **show startup-config**
- **configure terminal**

- **interface**
- **copy**
- **reload**
- **exit**

## Resources Required:
- PC with monitor, keyboard, mouse, and power cords
- Windows operating system (Windows 95, 98, NT, or 2000) installed on PC
- HyperTerminal program configured for a console connection
- PC connected to the router console port with a roll-over cable

## Web Site Resources:
- **Routing basics** – http://www.cisco.com/univercd/cc/td/doc/cisintwk/ito_doc/routing.htm
- **General information on routers** – http://www.cisco.com/univercd/cc/td/doc/pcat/#2
- **2500 series routers** – http://www.cisco.com/warp/public/cc/cisco/mkt/access/2500/index.shtml
- **1600 series routers** – http://www.cisco.com/warp/public/cc/cisco/mkt/access/1600/index.shtml
- **Terms and acronyms** – http://www.cisco.com/univercd/cc/td/doc/cisintwk/ita/index.htm
- **IP routing protocol IOS command summary** – http://www.cisco.com/univercd/cc/td/doc/product/software/ios120/12cgcr/rbkixol.htm
- **Beginning IP for new users** – http://www.cisco.com/warp/public/701/3.html

## Notes:
_____
_____
_____
_____
_____
_____
_____

# Cisco Labs – Semester 2 – Router Configuration
## *LAB 6.4.2.1 – ROUTER INTERFACE CONFIGURATION – WORKSHEET*

**Step 1 – Log on to the router.**
   **Explanation:** Connect to the router and log in. Enter the password **cisco** if prompted.

**Step 2 – Enter privileged mode.**
   **Task:**
      a.  Enter **enable** (abbreviated **en**) at the command prompt.
      b.  Enter the password **class**.
   **Explanation:** You use the **enable** command to enter privileged EXEC mode.

**Step 3 – Show the active configuration file.**
   **Task:** Enter **show running-config** (abbreviated **sh run**) at the router prompt.
   **Explanation**: The router will display information on how it is currently configured.

   1.  Fill in the following table with the information from the standard five-router lab diagram.

| Interface | IP Address | Subnet Mask |
|-----------|------------|-------------|
|           |            |             |
|           |            |             |
|           |            |             |
|           |            |             |

**Step 4 – Ping all interfaces on the router.**
   **Task:** Enter **ping** *xxx.xxx.xxx.xxx* at the router prompt, where *xxx.xxx.xxx.xxx* equals an IP address.
   **Explanation:** Using ping will test layer 3 connectivity. **Note:** If the other end of the WAN serial link (to the next router) is not configured correctly, or the other router is not powered on, you may not get a good ping result.

   2.  Did all the interfaces ping successfully? _____

**Step 5 – Enter global configuration mode.**
   **Task:** Enter **configure terminal** (abbreviated **config t**) at the router prompt.
   **Explanation:** To configure the router, you must start in global configuration mode. Notice how the router prompt has changed after this command.

   3.  What does the router prompt look like? _____

**Step 6 – Enter interface configuration mode.**
   **Task:** Enter **interface serial0** (abbreviated **int s0**) at the global configuration prompt.
   **Explanation:** Entering **interface serial0** at the global configuration prompt will allow you to change the configuration for serial0.

   4.  What does the router prompt look like? _____

## Cisco Labs – Semester 2 – Router Configuration
# *LAB 6.4.2.1 – ROUTER INTERFACE CONFIGURATION – WORKSHEET*

### Step 7 – Configure the IP address for serial0.

**Task:**
   a.   Enter **IP address** *xxx.xxx.xxx.xxx   yyy.yyy.yyy.yyy* at the router interface mode prompt. *xxx.xxxx.xxx.xxx* is the IP address, and *yyy.yyy.yyy.yyy* is the subnet mask for Serial0. Use the IP address and subnet mask from the standard five-router lab setup.
**Explanation:** This command will set the IP and subnet mask for serial0.
   b.   Enter **clockrate 56000** to set the DCE clock rate for the WAN link.
**Explanation:** The clock rate must be set on the DCE (female) connection.

### Step 8 – Exit from interface configuration mode.
**Task:** Enter **exit** at the router prompt.
**Explanation:** When you type **exit** in interface configuration mode, it will back you up to a global configuration prompt.

   5.   What does the router prompt look like? _____

### Step 9 – Exit from global configuration mode.
**Task:** Enter **exit** or press Ctrl-Z.
**Explanation:** When you type **exit** or press Ctrl-Z, the router will place you in privileged mode.

   6.   What does the router prompt look like? _____

### Step 10 – Show the active configuration file.
**Task:** Enter **show running-config** at the router prompt.
**Explanation**: The router will display information on how it is currently configured. Notice that any changes you entered will show up.

   7.   What did the router say the IP address and subnet mask were for serial0?
   _____

### Step 11 – Test layer 3 connectivity using ping.
**Task:** Enter **ping** *xxx.xxx.xxx.xxx* where *xxx.xxx.xxx.xxx* is an IP address of serial0 at the router prompt.
**Explanation:** This will test serial0 and make sure it is up and running. **Note:** If the other end of the WAN serial link (to the next router) is not configured correctly, or the other router is not powered on, you may not get a good ping result.

### Step 12 – Copy the running configuration to the backup configuration.
**Task:** Enter **copy running-config startup-config** at the router prompt.
**Explanation:** This will copy the running configuration to the backup configuration. The next time the router is turned on or reloaded, it will load from the backup configuration.

# Cisco Labs – Semester 2 – Router Configuration
## *LAB 6.4.2.1 – ROUTER INTERFACE CONFIGURATION – WORKSHEET*

**Step 13 – Repeat this lab with all interfaces identified in step 3 (clock rate is set on S0 only).**

8.  What command will tell you how many and what kind of interfaces are on your router?
    _____

**Step 14 – Reload the router's configuration.**
   **Task:** Enter **reload** at the router prompt.
   **Explanation:** This command will reload the router from the backup configuration.

**Step 15 – Show information about the active configuration file.**

   **Task:** Enter **show running-config** at the router prompt and compare the results with Step 3.
   **Explanation**: The router will display information on how it is currently configured.

**Step 16 – Exit the router.**

# LAB 6.4.2.1 – ROUTER INTERFACE CONFIGURATION – ANSWERS

1. Fill in the following table.

| Interface | IP Address | Subnet Mask |
|-----------|------------|-------------|
| Ethernet0 | 219.17.100.1 | 255.255.255.0 |
| Ethernet1 | Not Present | |
| Serial0 | 199.6.13.1 | 255.255.255.0 |
| Serial1 | 201.100.11.2 | 255.255.255.0 |

## Results of show running-config Command (output generated by a Cisco 2501 router)

```
lab-b#show running-config
Building configuration....
Current configuration:
!
!
version 11.1
service slave-log
service udp-small-servers
service tcp-small-servers
!
hostname lab-b
!
boot system igs-j-l.111-5
enable secret 5 $1$itif$vqTo8RC73KajshkzpFObr/
enable password cisco
!
interface Ethernet0
    ip address 219.17.100.1 255.255.255.0
!
interface Serial0
    ip address 199.6.13.1 255.255.255.0
    bandwidth 56
    no fair-queue
    clockrate 56000
!
interface Serial1
    ip address 201.100.11.2 255.255.255.0
    ip access-group 1 out
    !
router igrp 100
network 201.100.11.0
```

**Cisco Labs – Semester 2 – Router Configuration**
## *LAB 6.4.2.1 – ROUTER INTERFACE CONFIGURATION – ANSWERS*

**Results of show running-config Command – Continued** (output generated by a Cisco 2501)

```
network 219.17.100.0
network 199.6.13.0

ip host LAB-A 192.5.5.1 205.7.5.1  201.100.11.1
ip host LAB-B 219.17.100.1 199.6.13.1 201.100.11.2
ip host LAB-C 223.8.151.1 204.204.7.1 199.6.13.2
ip host LAB-D 210.93.105.1 204.204.7.2
ip host LAB-E 210.93.105.2
no ip classless
!
line con 0
exec-timeout 0 0
--More--
password cisco
login
line aux 0
line vty 0 4
    password cisco
    login
!
end
```

2. Did all the interfaces ping successfully? **Yes Note: If the other end of the WAN serial link (to the next router) is not configured correctly, or the other router is not powered on, you may not get a good ping result.**

3. What does the router prompt look like? ***Router_name*(config)#**

4. What does the router prompt look like? ***Router_name*(config-if)#**

5. What does the router prompt look like? ***Router_name*(config)#**

6. What does the router prompt look like? ***Router_name*#**

7. What did the router say the IP address and subnet mask were for serial0? **The IP and subnet mask for serial0 are the IP and subnet mask you typed in earlier.**

8. What command will tell you how many and what kind of interfaces are on your router? **show interfaces from a user mode prompt or show running-config from a privileged mode prompt**

# Cisco Labs – Semester 2 – Router Configuration
## *LAB 6.5.2.1 – ROUTER CONFIGURATION CHALLENGE – OVERVIEW*
### *(Estimated time: 45 minutes)*

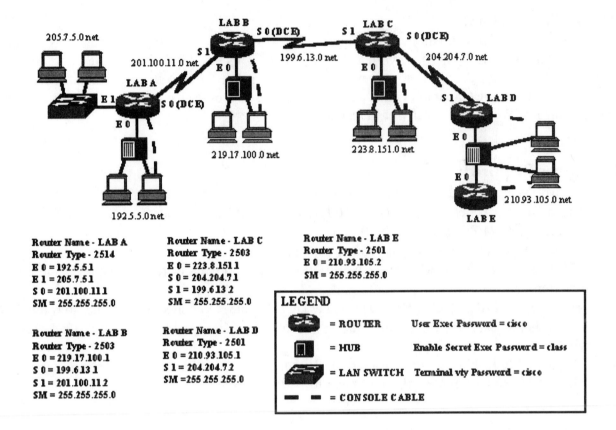

## Objectives:

- Demonstrate your ability to configure a router for a remote office
- Configure IP address assignments for router interfaces
- Configure subnet mask assignments for router interfaces
- Use **ping**, **traceroute**, and **tracert** to test connectivity between devices

## Background:

You and your group are administrators of a LAN. Due to the rapid expansion of this company, you need to link the headquarters (your group's router) to the rest of the network. You must link the networks via the serial ports, which means that your group is responsible for only your router's connections. Before starting this lab, the lab assistant or instructor should erase the running configuration and the startup configuration for Lab-A only and make sure that the rest of the routers are configured with the standard lab setup. You will also need to verify your workstation IP configuration so you can test the connectivity between workstations and routers.

**Cisco Labs – Semester 2 – Router Configuration**
## *LAB 6.4.2.1 – ROUTER CONFIGURATION CHALLENGE – OVERVIEW*

## Tools / Preparation:

Prior to starting the lab you will need to connect a PC workstation with HyperTerminal to a router using the router's console interface with a roll-over cable. This lab should be done at the router console station on Lab-A . You should review Chapter 15 in the *Cisco Networking Academy Program: First*-Year Companion Guide and review semester 2 on-line curriculum Chapter 6 prior to starting this lab. Work individually or in teams.

## Resources Required:

- 5 PC workstations (minimum) with Windows operating system and HyperTerminal installed
- 5 Cisco routers (model 1600 series or 2500 series with IOS 11.2 or later)
- 4 Ethernet hubs (10Base-T with four to eight ports)
- 1 Ethernet switch (Cisco Catalyst 1900 or comparable)
- 5 serial console cables to connect the workstation to the router console port (with RJ45 to DB9 converters)
- 3 sets of V.35 WAN serial cables (DTE male/ DCE female) to connect from router to router
- CAT5 Ethernet cables wired straight through to connect routers and workstations to hubs and switches
- AUI (DB15) to RJ45 Ethernet transceivers (the quantity depends on the number of routers with AUI ports) to convert router AUI interfaces to 10Base-T RJ45

## Web Site Resources:

- **Routing basics** – http://www.cisco.com/univercd/cc/td/doc/cisintwk/ito_doc/routing.htm
- **General information on routers** – http://www.cisco.com/univercd/cc/td/doc/pcat/#2
- **2500 series routers** – http://www.cisco.com/warp/public/cc/cisco/mkt/access/2500/index.shtml
- **1600 series routers** – http://www.cisco.com/warp/public/cc/cisco/mkt/access/1600/index.shtml
- **Terms and acronyms** – http://www.cisco.com/univercd/cc/td/doc/cisintwk/ita/index.htm
- **IP routing protocol IOS command summary** –
  http://www.cisco.com/univercd/cc/td/doc/product/software/ios120/12cgcr/rbkixol.htm

## Notes:

_____

_____

_____

_____

_____

# Cisco Labs – Semester 2 – Router Configuration
# *LAB 6.4.2.1 – ROUTER CONFIGURATION CHALLENGE – WORKSHEET*

**Step 1 – Connect the Lab-A router to the rest of the network.**

Connect to the router. The router should have no configuration prior to starting this lab. Use the standard network diagram to configure the Lab-A router. You can configure the router any way you prefer. Make sure the workstations are configured with an IP address, subnet mask, and default gateway. **Note:** If you are using the **setup** command, you will need to add additional commands, because **setup** will do only a basic configuration. If you need help, you can type **?** at any time to enter the help facility.

1. Perform the following tests to verify that you have configured Lab-A and the workstation correctly. If any of the tests fail, you must troubleshoot the problem with your router or workstation and document your results in the table below (answers will vary).

| Test | Result OK? | Problem |
|---|---|---|
| Ping Lab-B | | |
| Ping Lab-C | | |
| Ping Lab-D | | |
| Ping Lab-E | | |
| Trace route to Lab-E | | |
| Ping a workstation on Lab-B | | |
| Ping a workstation on Lab-C | | |
| Ping a workstation on Lab-D | | |
| Ping from a workstation on Lab-A to a workstation on Lab-E | | |
| Trace route from a workstation on Lab-A to a workstation on Lab-E | | |

# Cisco Labs – Semester 2 – Router Configuration
## *LAB 6.5.2.2 – CISCO CONFIGMAKER – OVERVIEW*
### *(Estimated time: 30 minutes)*

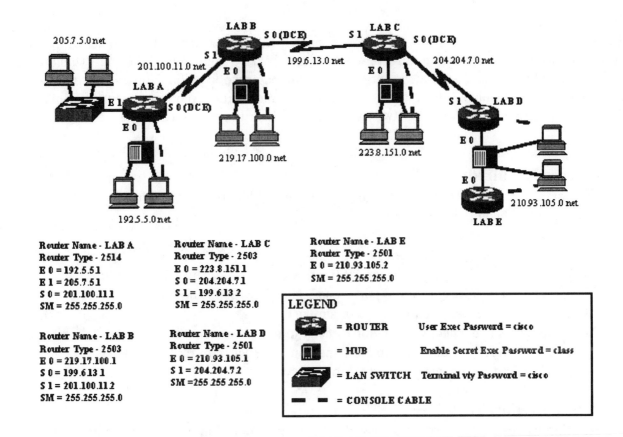

**Router Name - LAB A**
**Router Type - 2514**
E 0 = 192.5.5.1
E 1 = 205.7.5.1
S 0 = 201.100.111
SM = 255.255.255.0

**Router Name - LAB B**
**Router Type - 2503**
E 0 = 219.17.100.1
S 0 = 199.6.13.1
S 1 = 201.100.11.2
SM = 255.255.255.0

**Router Name - LAB C**
**Router Type - 2503**
E 0 = 223.8.151.1
S 0 = 204.204.7.1
S 1 = 199.6.13.2
SM = 255.255.255.0

**Router Name - LAB D**
**Router Type - 2501**
E 0 = 210.93.105.1
S 1 = 204.204.7.2
SM = 255.255.255.0

**Router Name - LAB E**
**Router Type - 2501**
E 0 = 210.93.105.2
SM = 255.255.255.0

| LEGEND | | |
|---|---|---|
| = ROUTER | User Exec Password = cisco | |
| = HUB | Enable Secret Exec Password = class | |
| = LAN SWITCH | Terminal vty Password = cisco | |
| = CONSOLE CABLE | | |

## Objectives:

- Use Cisco ConfigMaker to configure a router
- Draw a map of a network using Cisco's ConfigMaker
- Print a configuration file created by ConfigMaker

## Background:

This lab is intended to help you become familiar with Cisco ConfigMaker. Cisco ConfigMaker is an easy-to-use Windows 95/98/NT application that configures Cisco routers, switches, hubs, and other devices. Using a graphical user interface (GUI), you draw your network, and then Cisco ConfigMaker creates the Cisco IOS configuration files for the devices on your network. In addition, you can use Cisco ConfigMaker as an off-line tool. You can draw and configure your entire network without having the devices on hand until you are ready to deliver the configuration files to them. This software has many options, and you are encouraged to "play" with the configuration of the network. This lab will take you through a basic configuration to familiarize you with the software.

**Cisco Labs – Semester 2 – Router Configuration**
## *LAB 6.5.2.2 – CISCO CONFIGMAKER – OVERVIEW*

## Tools / Preparation:

Prior to starting this lab you will need to connect a PC with HyperTerminal to a router using the router's console interface with a roll-over cable. You will need to download the latest version of Cisco ConfigMaker and install the program on the computer workstation. You will need to have at least three routers available. This lab should be done at each router. Work individually or in teams. **Note:** The routers must be running IOS version 11.2 or later in order to deliver the configuration files.

## Resources Required:

- PC workstation with Windows operating system and HyperTerminal installed
- Cisco ConfigMaker (latest version)
- IOS version 11.2 or later
- 2 Cisco routers – model 1600 series or 2500 series, each with 1 serial and 1 Ethernet interface
- 1 Cisco router – model 1600 series or 2500 series with 2 serial and 1 Ethernet interface
- 2 Ethernet hubs – 10Base-T, 4 to 8 ports (use 3 hubs if switch is not available)
- 1 Ethernet switch (Cisco Catalyst 1900 or similar)
- 3 console cables to connect workstation directly to router console port
- 3 sets of V.35 WAN serial cables (male/female) to connect from router to router
- 6 CAT5 Ethernet cables wired straight through

## Web Site Resources:

- **Routing basics** – http://www.cisco.com/univercd/cc/td/doc/cisintwk/ito_doc/routing.htm
- **General information on routers** – http://www.cisco.com/univercd/cc/td/doc/pcat/#2
- **2500 series routers** – http://www.cisco.com/warp/public/cc/cisco/mkt/access/2500/index.shtml
- **1600 series routers** – http://www.cisco.com/warp/public/cc/cisco/mkt/access/1600/index.shtml
- **Terms and acronyms** – http://www.cisco.com/univercd/cc/td/doc/cisintwk/ita/index.htm
- **IP routing protocol IOS command summary** –
  http://www.cisco.com/univercd/cc/td/doc/product/software/ios120/12cgcr/rbkixol.htm
- **Cisco ConfigMaker information and download** –
  http://www.cisco.com/warp/public/cc/cisco/mkt/enm/config/index.shtml

## Notes:

_____
_____
_____
_____
_____
_____
_____

# Cisco Labs – Semester 2 – Router Configuration
## *LAB 6.5.2.2 – CISCO CONFIGMAKER – WORKSHEET*

**Step 1 – Download and install Cisco ConfigMaker.**
   **Explanation:** Check the computer workstation to make sure that the latest version of Cisco ConfigMaker is installed. If it is not installed, or you do not have the latest version, you will have to download it from **www.cisco.com** and install it (the web site URL is listed in the overview section of this lab). There is no cost for the software.

**Step 2 – Run Cisco ConfigMaker and start the tutorial.**
   **Task:** Double-click the Cisco ConfigMaker icon.
   **Explanation:** This will launch the ConfigMaker program and start the tutorial automatically if you choose. You may also run the tutorial at a later time by clicking the tutorial icon on the toolbar.

**Step 3 – Add routers to your network diagram.**
   **Task:** Under Devices, choose the Routers folder and add the routers on your lab setup.
   **Explanation:** Once you have selected the correct model number of the router that you are adding, place the router where you would like it in the network diagram area by dragging it to the network diagram area. You will be prompted for configuration information.

   1.   What other router series can you configure with ConfigMaker?
   _____

**Step 4 – Configure the router.**
   **Task:** Follow the prompts to configure the router.
   **Explanation:** First you will be asked for the name of the router. Enter **Lab-A** and click Next. Then you assign login and enable secret passwords to the router. Enter **cisco** as the password and **class** as the enable, and click Next. Now you need to tell the router what protocol you are going to use. Select **TCP/IP** and click Next and then Finish.

**Step 5 – Repeat Steps 3 and 4 to add other routers to your network diagram.**
   **Explanation:** Add at least two more routers from your lab setup to your network diagram.

**Step 6 – Add connections to the routers.**
   **Task:** In the connections window, click HDLC, and then Lab-A, and then the connecting device (Lab-B).
   **Explanation:** Once you have added the HDLC connection from Lab-A to Lab-B, the HDLC wizard opens up. Click Next. Now you will be asked what serial interface you want to use for this connection. Use Serial0 and click Next. Now you are asked for addressing information for this interface. Enter IP address and subnet mask and click Next. Now ConfigMaker will ask you to supply information about the router you are connected to (Lab-B). Select interface Serial1 for Lab-B and enter the IP address, and then click Next. Now you will have an opportunity to create a backup connection. For this lab, choose "no backup" and then click Next and then Finish. You can click the routers and rearrange them if desired.

   2.   What other connections can you configure using ConfigMaker?
   _____
   _____

# Cisco Labs – Semester 2 – Router Configuration
## *LAB 6.5.2.2 – CISCO CONFIGMAKER – WORKSHEET*

**Step 7 – Repeat Step 6 to add connections from Lab-B to Lab-C.**

**Step 8 – Check / Add to configuration.**
   **Task:** Double-click the Lab-A router in your network diagram.
   **Explanation:** This will allow you to add or change the configuration for that router. Click the IOS Configuration tab. Compare the IOS configuration for interface Serial0 with the output from the **show running-config** command listed in Lab 4.5.2.1, Router **show** Commands, Answers section.

   3.   What command was missing from ConfigMaker's IOS configuration for interface S0?

   _____

**Step 9 – Append configuration commands.**
   **Task:** From Lab-A Properties on the IOS Configuration tab, click the Add / Modify IOS commands button.
   **Explanation:** This window will let you enter additional commands for the router. As you probably noticed from Step 8, Lab-A Serial0 is the DCE and should be providing the clock rate. Any commands will be added to the bottom of the configuration list.

   4.   What commands do you need to add to the router to add clocking for interface S0?

   _____

**Step 10 – Deliver the IOS commands to the router.**
   **Task:** Highlight the router you want to load the IOS configuration into, and then click the Deliver button.
   **Explanation:** As long as you have a connection to the router where you are trying to load the IOS configuration, ConfigMaker will attempt to load the IOS config. If there is a problem or an error, ConfigMaker will tell you. You can fix the problem and then "deliver" the IOS configuration again.

**Step 11 – Print your network diagram and router configuration.**
   **Task:** Choose File/Print Network or File/Print All.
   **Explanation:** You can print a graphical diagram of the network you have drawn so far or click Print Preview to see what it will look like before printing it. Print All will print the network diagram and a listing of the configuration file for each router.

**Step 12 – Save the router configuration to a text file.**
   **Task:** Right-click the router and choose IOS Configuration. Then choose File/Save As.
   **Explanation:** You may wish to save a copy of the configuration file that ConfigMaker generates for later editing with a text editor. You can name the file; it will have a .CFG extension. You can edit it with Notepad. You can also print the config file from here or send it to a router.

   5.   A sample ConfigMaker file for router Lab-A is shown in the answers section of this lab.

# Cisco Labs – Semester 2 – Router Configuration
## *LAB 6.5.2.2 – CISCO CONFIGMAKER – ANSWERS*

1. What other router series can you configure with ConfigMaker?
   **800, 1000, 1600, 1700, 2500, 2600, 3600, and 4000 series**

2. What other connections can you configure using ConfigMaker?
   **Ethernet, HDLC, PPP, frame relay, async, ISDN, ISDN leased line, voice line, VPN**

3. What command was missing from ConfigMaker's IOS configuration?
   **Clocking signal for the DCE interface Serial0**

4. What commands do you need to add to the router to add clocking?
   **interface serial0**
   **clockrate 56000**
   **Both commands are needed on Lab-A, Lab-B, and Lab-C Serial0 interfaces.**

## Sample Configuration File for Router Lab-A Created by ConfigMaker

```
! ****************************************************************
! Lab-A.cfg - Cisco router configuration file
! Automatically created by Cisco ConfigMaker v2.4 Build 24
!   Wednesday, March 22, 2000, 09:39:30 AM
! Hostname: Lab-A
! Model: 2514
! ****************************************************************
service timestamps debug uptime
service timestamps log uptime
service password-encryption
no service tcp-small-servers
no service udp-small-servers
!
hostname Lab-A
!
enable password class
!
no ip name-server
!
ip subnet-zero
no ip domain-lookup
ip routing
!
interface Ethernet 0
 no shutdown
 description connected to Hub1
 ip address 192.5.5.1 255.255.255.0
 keepalive 10
interface Ethernet 1
 no shutdown
```

# Cisco Labs – Semester 2 – Router Configuration
## *LAB 6.5.2.2 – CISCO CONFIGMAKER – ANSWERS*

## Sample Configuration File for Router Lab-A – Continued

```
 description connected to Switch
 ip address 205.7.5.1 255.255.255.0
 keepalive 10
!
interface Serial 0
 no shutdown
 description connected to Lab-B
 ip address 201.100.11.1 255.255.255.0
 encapsulation hdlc
!
interface Serial 1
 no description
 no ip address
 shutdown
!
router rip
 version 2
 network 192.5.5.0
 network 205.7.5.0
 network 201.100.11.0
 no auto-summary
!
ip classless
no ip http server
snmp-server community public RO
no snmp-server location
no snmp-server contact
!
line console 0
 exec-timeout 0 0
 password cisco
 login
!
line vty 0 4
 password cisco
 login
!
! The following commands are not recognized by Cisco ConfigMaker
! and are therefore appended here.
!
interface s0
clockrate 56000
!
```
```
    end
```

# Cisco Labs – Semester 2 – Router Configuration
## *LAB 6.5.2.3 – ROUTER CONFIGURATION with HYPERTERMINAL – OVERVIEW*
### *(Estimated time: 30 minutes)*

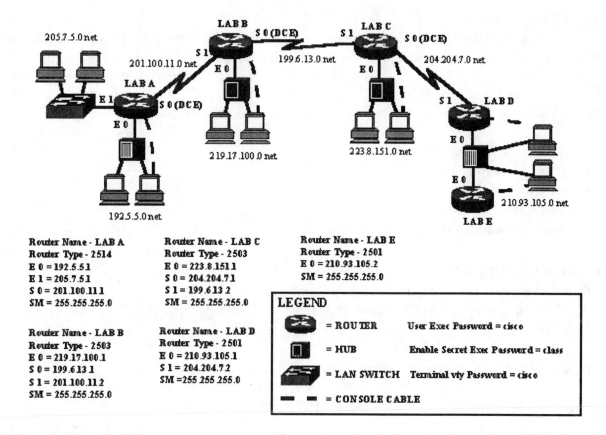

**Router Name - LAB A**
Router Type - 2514
E 0 = 192.5.5.1
E 1 = 205.7.5.1
S 0 = 201.100.11.1
SM = 255.255.255.0

**Router Name - LAB B**
Router Type - 2503
E 0 = 219.17.100.1
S 0 = 199.6.13.1
S 1 = 201.100.11.2
SM = 255.255.255.0

**Router Name - LAB C**
Router Type - 2503
E 0 = 223.8.151.1
S 0 = 204.204.7.1
S 1 = 199.6.13.2
SM = 255.255.255.0

**Router Name - LAB D**
Router Type - 2501
E 0 = 210.93.105.1
S 1 = 204.204.7.2
SM =255.255.255.0

**Router Name - LAB E**
Router Type - 2501
E 0 = 210.93.105.2
SM = 255.255.255.0

**LEGEND**

| | | |
|---|---|---|
| = ROUTER | User Exec Password = cisco |
| = HUB | Enable Secret Exec Password = class |
| = LAN SWITCH | Terminal vty Password = cisco |
| = CONSOLE CABLE | |

## Objectives:
- Capture the running configuration of a router to an ASCII text file with HyperTerminal
- Edit or modify the captured text file with a text editor such as Notepad
- Upload the text file to configure another router using HyperTerminal

## Background:
In this lab you will use the Windows terminal emulation program, HyperTerminal, to capture and upload a router configuration as an ASCII text file. This saved copy can be used as a backup for the current router, or it can be used as a basis for a new router configuration. When adding another router to a network, it is a good idea to base the new configuration on an existing one rather than reinvent the wheel.

You can use any text editor program such as Notepad or WordPad to modify the original file. You can use a word processor such as Word, but you must remember to save the file as a DOS text file. Since each router may have different interfaces, you must analyze the captured router configuration and modify it to suit the new configuration. Additionally, the IP addresses assigned to the interfaces on the new router must be different than those on the original router.

# Cisco Labs – Semester 2 – Router Configuration
## *LAB 6.5.2.3 – ROUTER CONFIGURATION with HYPERTERMINAL – OVERVIEW*

## Tools / Preparation:
Prior to starting the lab you will need to connect a PC workstation with HyperTerminal to a router using the router's console interface with a roll-over cable. This lab should be done at the router console station. You should review Chapter 13 in the *Cisco Networking Academy Program: First-Year Companion Guide* and review semester 2 on-line curriculum Chapter 6 prior to starting this lab. Work individually or in teams. Be familiar with the following commands:

- **show running-config**
- **erase startup-config**
- **reload**
- **configure terminal**
- **copy running-config startup-config**

## Resources Required:
- PC with monitor, keyboard, mouse, and power cords
- Windows operating system (Windows 95, 98, NT, or 2000) installed on PC
- HyperTerminal program configured for a console connection
- Notepad or other text editor program
- PC connected to the router console port with a roll-over cable

## Notes:
_____
_____
_____

**Cisco Labs – Semester 2 – Router Configuration**
# *LAB 6.5.2.3 – ROUTER CONFIGURATION with HYPERTERMINAL – WORKSHEET*

**Step 1 – Log on to the router.**
   **Explanation:** Connect to the router and log in. Enter the password **cisco** if prompted.

**Step 2 – Enter privileged EXEC mode.**
   **Task:**
      a.   From user EXEC mode, enter privileged EXEC mode using the **enable** command.
      b.   Enter the enable password **class**.
   **Explanation:** Enter enable mode from user EXEC mode.

**Step 3 – Enter the show running-config command (abbreviated sh run).**
   **Task:** Enter **show running-config** at the command prompt.
   **Explanation:** Using the **show running-config** command displays the active configuration file for the router that is stored in RAM.

   1.   List all of the interfaces on the router (answers will vary). _____
   _____
   _____

**Step 4 – Start capturing the configuration file.**
   **Task:** Start the process of copying the router configuration to a text file.
   **Explanation:** HyperTerminal will capture all text displayed on its screen to a text file.

   In HyperTerminal, select Transfer/Capture Text. When prompted, provide a path and name to capture the configuration to. Use the name of the router for the filename, and use .txt for the extension.

   2.   Write down the name and location of this file: _____

**Step 5– Enter the show running-config command (abbreviated sh run).**
   **Task:** Enter **show running-config** at the command prompt.
   **Explanation:** Using the **show running-config** command displays the active configuration file for the router that is stored in RAM.

   Enter the **sh run** command. Press the spacebar when the **– More –** prompt appears.

**Step 6 – Stop capturing the configuration file.**
   **Task:** Discontinue capturing the router configuration to a text file.
   **Explanation:** HyperTerminal will stop capturing any text displayed on its screen.

   In HyperTerminal, select Transfer/Capture Text. A new menu appears. Click Stop.

**Cisco Labs – Semester 2 – Router Configuration**
# *LAB 6.5.2.3 – ROUTER CONFIGURATION with HYPERTERMINAL – WORKSHEET*

**Step 7 – Clean up the captured configuration file.**
    **Task:** Remove any unnecessary information from the captured configuration.
    **Explanation:** The captured text file will have information not required for configuring a router, such as the **– More –** prompts. Note that the exclamation mark (**!**) is the comment command in a router configuration.

Click the Windows Start button, click Run, type **Notepad**, and press the Enter key. In Notepad, select File/Open. Find the file you made note of in Step 4, and click Open. Delete the lines that say
    • **sh run**
    • **Building configuration...**
    • **Current configuration:**
Delete each line that has the **– More –** prompt. Note that there will be characters that appear as black boxes on these lines. Delete any lines that appear after the word **End**. Save the clean version of the configuration by selecting File/Save. Close Notepad (select File/Close) and switch back to HyperTerminal.

**Step 8 – Erase the startup configuration.**
    **Task:** Enter the command **erase startup-config** (abbreviated **erase start**) at the router prompt.
    **Explanation:** The **erase startup-config** command deletes the configuration file from NVRAM. Caution should be used with this command since the router executes it without prompting for confirmation.

**Step 9 – Confirm that the startup configuration has been deleted.**
    **Task:** Enter **show startup-config** (abbreviated **sh start**) at the router prompt.
    **Explanation:** This step confirms that the router's startup configuration will not be available upon restarting of the router.

3.  What does the router show after this command is entered? _____

_____

**Step 10 – Restart the router.**
    **Task:** Enter **reload** at the router prompt.
    **Explanation:** The **reload** command will reboot the router.

When asked to proceed with the reload, enter **Y** and press the Enter key. Note that the router displays the message **Notice: NVRAM invalid, possibly due to write erase.** When prompted to enter the initial configuration dialog, type **N** and press Enter. When prompted to terminate autoinstall, type **Y** and press Enter. Press Enter again.

4.  What does the prompt look like?

_____

**Cisco Workbook – Semester 2 – Router Configuration**
# *LAB 6.5.2.3 – ROUTER CONFIGURATION with HYPERTERMINAL –*
# *WORKSHEET*

**Step 11 – Reconfigure the router from the text file you saved.**
 **Task:** Use the **send file** command in HyperTerminal to copy the new configuration.
 **Explanation:** The cleaned-up version of the router configuration file from Step 7 will be copied into the area of memory known as the clipboard.

 In HyperTerminal, enter the command **enable** to change to privileged EXEC mode.

 5. Why was a password not required? _____

 Enter global config mode by entering the command **configure terminal** (abbreviated **config t**). Select Transfer/Send/Text File. Select the file you saved in Step 4. Each line in the text file will be entered for you, as though you were typing them yourself.

 6. What does the router prompt change to? _____

 7. What command changes the router prompt? _____

 Press Ctrl-Z to exit global configuration mode.

**Step 12 – Save the new configuration file.**
 **Task:** Use the command **copy running-config startup-config** (abbreviated **copy run start**) to save the newly created router configuration.
 **Explanation:** The **copy running-config startup-config** command copies the active router configuration from RAM into NVRAM.

 Verify that the running configuration is correct by using the **show running-config** command (abbreviated **show run**). Enter the command **copy start run** at the router prompt.

**Step 13 – Verify the new configuration.**
 **Task:** Use the **reload** command to restart the router.
 **Explanation:** Verify that the new configuration has been saved to NVRAM by restarting the router.

 Enter the command **reload**. When prompted to confirm, press **Y** to confirm restarting the router. Once the router restarts, press the Enter key.

 8. What does the router prompt look like? _____

**Cisco Workbook – Semester 2 – Router Configuration**
## *LAB 6.5.2.3 – ROUTER CONFIGURATION with HYPERTERMINAL – ANSWERS*

1. List all interfaces on the router (answers will vary). **Ethernet 0, Serial 0, Serial 1, etc.**

2. Write down the name and location of this file. **C:\lab-a.txt or A:\lab-a.txt**

3. What does the router show after this command is entered? **Non-volatile configuration memory has not been set up**

4. What does the prompt look like? **Router>**

5. Why was a password not required? **There is no password set.**

6. What does the router prompt change to? **LAB-A#**

7. What command changes the router prompt? **Hostname LAB-A**

8. What does the router prompt look like? **LAB-A>**

# Cisco Labs – Semester 2 – Router Configuration
## *LAB 6.5.2.4 – ROUTER CONFIGURATION TFTP – OVERVIEW*
### *(Estimated time: 20 minutes)*

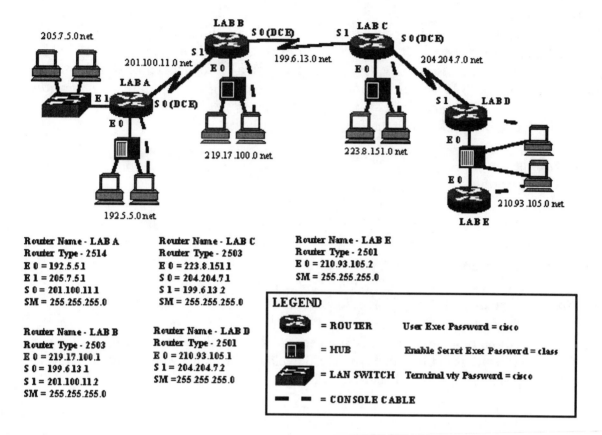

Router Name - LAB A
Router Type - 2514
E 0 = 192.5.5.1
E 1 = 205.7.5.1
S 0 = 201.100.11.1
SM = 255.255.255.0

Router Name - LAB C
Router Type - 2503
E 0 = 223.8.151.1
S 0 = 204.204.7.1
S 1 = 199.6.13.2
SM = 255.255.255.0

Router Name - LAB E
Router Type - 2501
E 0 = 210.93.105.2
SM = 255.255.255.0

Router Name - LAB B
Router Type - 2503
E 0 = 219.17.100.1
S 0 = 199.6.13.1
S 1 = 201.100.11.2
SM = 255.255.255.0

Router Name - LAB D
Router Type - 2501
E 0 = 210.93.105.1
S 1 = 204.204.7.2
SM = 255.255.255.0

**LEGEND**

= ROUTER    User Exec Password = cisco

= HUB    Enable Secret Exec Password = class

= LAN SWITCH    Terminal vty Password = cisco

= CONSOLE CABLE

## Objectives:

- Copy a router configuration file to a TFTP server
- Configure a router from a TFTP server

## Background:

In this lab you will use a TFTP (Trivial File Transfer Protocol) server to save a copy of the router's configuration file. You will also configure the router from the TFTP server. Using a TFTP server is an excellent way to keep backup copies of configuration files for routers and other network equipment, such as switches. Additionally, IOS images can be stored on a TFTP server. A TFTP server is simpler to use than a standard FTP server. TFTP does not require a user to have a password, or to navigate between directories. For this reason, it is important to have the TFTP server secure (not available to the general public). TFTP uses UDP rather than TCP like a standard FTP server does. TFTP is a very basic file transfer utility and does not require the guaranteed delivery services of TCP. The TFTP "server" can be a file server, a workstation, or even a Cisco router, and it must have the TFTP utility installed and running. You can download the Cisco TFTP server at no cost from the web site listed below.

# Cisco Labs – Semester 2 – Router Configuration
## *LAB 6.5.2.4 – ROUTER CONFIGURATION TFTP – OVERVIEW*

## Tools / Preparation:

Prior to starting the lab you will need to connect a PC workstation with HyperTerminal to a router using the router's console interface with a roll-over cable. This lab should be done at the router console station. Verify that the Cisco TFTP server is installed on a server accessible by the router. You should review Chapter 13 in the *Cisco Networking Academy Program: First-Year Companion Guide* and review semester 2 on-line curriculum Chapter 6 prior to starting this lab. Work individually or in teams. Be familiar with the following commands:

- **copy running-config**
- **erase startup-config**
- **reload**

## Resources Required:

- PC with monitor, keyboard, mouse, and power cords
- Windows operating system (Windows 95, 98, NT, or 2000) installed on PC
- HyperTerminal program configured for router console access
- PC connected to the router console port with a roll-over cable
- The TFTP installed and running on a workstation accessible from the router you are working on (Note: If the TFTP server is not installed, you can download it from the web site listed below and copy it to the workstation, which will act as the TFTP server. Click on the downloaded file to install.)

## Web Site Resources:

- **Routing basics** – http://www.cisco.com/univercd/cc/td/doc/cisintwk/ito_doc/routing.htm
- **General information on routers** – http://www.cisco.com/univercd/cc/td/doc/pcat/#2
- **2500 series routers** – http://www.cisco.com/warp/public/cc/cisco/mkt/access/2500/index.shtml
- **1600 series routers** – http://www.cisco.com/warp/public/cc/cisco/mkt/access/1600/index.shtml
- **Terms and acronyms** – http://www.cisco.com/univercd/cc/td/doc/cisintwk/ita/index.htm
- **IP routing protocol IOS command summary** – http://www.cisco.com/univercd/cc/td/doc/product/software/ios120/12cgcr/rbkixol.htm
- **Free Cisco TFTP server** (Win 9x version) – ftp://ftp.cisco.com/pub/netmgmt/utilities/tftp.zip
- **TFTP command syntax** – http://www.cisco.com/univercd/cc/td/doc/product/10_100hb/1538m_mh/cli/1538_cli.htm

## Notes:

_____

_____

_____

_____

_____

# Cisco Labs – Semester 2 – Router Configuration
## *LAB 6.5.2.4 – ROUTER CONFIGURATION TFTP – WORKSHEET*

**Step 1 – Log on to the router.**
   **Explanation:** Connect to the router and log in. Enter the password **cisco** if prompted.

**Step 2 – Enter privileged EXEC mode.**
   **Task:**  a.   From user EXEC mode, enter privileged EXEC mode using the **enable** command.
            b.   Enter the enable password **class**.
   **Explanation:** Enter the enable mode from user EXEC mode.

**Step 3 – Verify connectivity to the TFTP server.**
   **Task:** Enter **ping *xxx.xxx.xxx.xxx*** where *xxx.xxx.xxx.xxx* is the IP address of the workstation running the TFTP server.
   **Explanation:** Ensure that you can reach the TFTP server from the router. If you cannot, you will first need to check the connections and then check the configurations of the routers in the lab to ensure you can reach the TFTP server. Verify that the workstation has the TFTP server installed and that it is running.

**Step 4 – Copy the configuration file to the TFTP server.**
   **Task:** Enter the command **copy running-config tftp** (abbreviated **copy  run  tftp**).
   **Explanation**: Start the process of copying the router's running configuration to the TFTP server.

   Enter the command **copy running-config tftp** (abbreviated **copy  run  tftp**). When prompted for the remote host, enter the IP address you verified in Step 3, and press Enter. When prompted for the configuration file to write, the default is the router's name, followed by a dash and the word **confg** (such as **LAB-A-confg**). Accept this name by pressing Enter, or type in a new name and press Enter.

   1.   What is the name of the configuration file you are writing on the TFTP server? (Answers will vary.) _____

   Confirm writing the configuration file to the TFTP server by pressing Enter. You will notice exclamation marks appear on the screen, showing the progress of the TFTP file copy process.

**Step 5 – Erase the startup configuration.**
   **Task:** Enter the command **erase startup-config** (abbreviated **erase start**) at the router prompt.
   **Explanation:** The **erase startup-config** command deletes the contents of NVRAM. Caution should be used with this command since the router executes it without prompting for confirmation.

**Step 6 – Confirm that the startup configuration has been deleted.**
   **Task:** Enter **show startup-config** (abbreviated **show start**) at the router prompt.
   **Explanation:** This step confirms that the router's startup configuration will not be available upon restarting of the router.

   2.   What does the router show after this command is entered?

   _____

# Cisco Labs – Semester 2 – Router Configuration
## _LAB 6.5.2.4 – ROUTER CONFIGURATION TFTP – WORKSHEET_

**Step 7 – Restart the router.**
   **Task:** Enter **reload** at the router prompt.
   **Explanation:** The **reload** command will reboot the router.

   When asked to proceed with the reload, enter **Y** and press the Enter key. Note that the router
   displays the message **Notice: NVRAM invalid, possibly due to write erase.** When prompted to
   enter the initial configuration dialog, type **N** and press Enter. When prompted to terminate
   autoinstall, type **Y** and press Enter. Press Enter again.

   3.  What does the prompt look like? _____

**Step 8 – Enter privileged EXEC mode.**
   **Task:** From user EXEC mode, enter privileged EXEC mode using the **enable** command.
   **Explanation:** Enter enable mode from user EXEC mode. Note that since the configuration has
   been erased, no password is required.

**Step 9 – Copy the backup configuration file from the TFTP server.**
   **Task:** Enter the command **copy tftp running-config** (abbreviated **copy tftp run**).
   **Explanation:** Start the process of copying the router's running configuration to the TFTP server.

   Enter the command **copy tftp running-config**. When prompted for the remote host, press Enter to
   indicate the host configuration file. When prompted for the remote host, enter the IP address you
   verified in Step 3 and press Enter. When prompted for the configuration file to write, the default is
   the router's name, followed by a dash and the word **confg** (such as **LAB-A-confg**). Accept this name
   by pressing Enter, or type in a new name or the name you used in Step 4 and press Enter. Confirm
   copying the configuration file from the TFTP server by pressing Enter. When the process is complete,
   the router indicates the amount of RAM used for the configuration file and the total amount of RAM
   available on the router.

**Step 10 – Save the new configuration file.**
   **Task:** Use the command **copy running-config startup-config** (abbreviated **copy run start**) to
   save the newly created router configuration.
   **Explanation:** The **copy running-config startup-config** command copies the active router
   configuration from RAM into NVRAM as a backup.

   Verify that the running configuration is correct by using the **show running-config** command
   (abbreviated **show run**). Enter the command **copy start run** at the router prompt.

**Cisco Labs – Semester 2 – Router Configuration**
## *LAB 6.5.2.4 – ROUTER CONFIGURATION TFTP – ANSWERS*

1. What is the name of the configuration file you are writing on the TFTP server? (Answers will vary.) **LAB-A-confg**

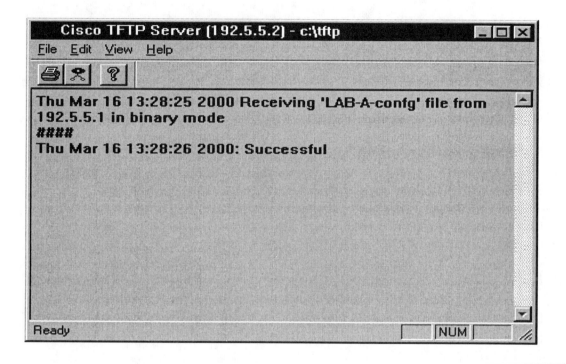

2. What does the router show after this command is entered? **Non-volatile configuration memory has not been set up.**

3. What does the prompt look like? **Router>**

# Cisco Labs – Semester 2 – Router Configuration
## LAB 6.5.2.5 – ROUTER CONFIGURATION WEB BROWSER – OVERVIEW
### (Estimated time: 15 minutes)

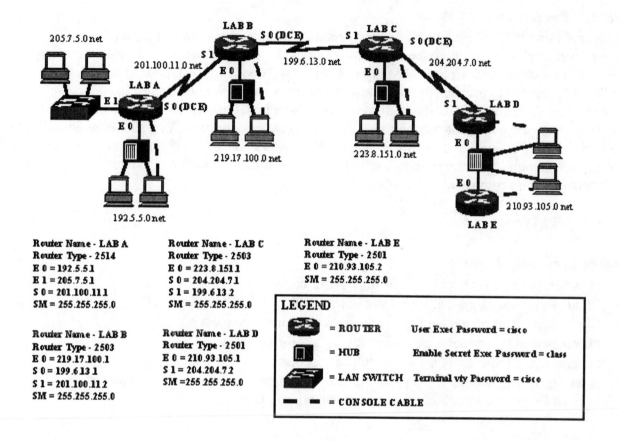

Router Name - LAB A
Router Type - 2514
E 0 = 192.5.5.1
E 1 = 205.7.5.1
S 0 = 201.100.11.1
SM = 255.255.255.0

Router Name - LAB C
Router Type - 2503
E 0 = 223.8.151.1
S 0 = 204.204.7.1
S 1 = 199.6.13.2
SM = 255.255.255.0

Router Name - LAB E
Router Type - 2501
E 0 = 210.93.105.2
SM = 255.255.255.0

Router Name - LAB B
Router Type - 2503
E 0 = 219.17.100.1
S 0 = 199.6.13.1
S 1 = 201.100.11.2
SM = 255.255.255.0

Router Name - LAB D
Router Type - 2501
E 0 = 210.93.105.1
S 1 = 204.204.7.2
SM = 255.255.255.0

**LEGEND**

= ROUTER    User Exec Password = cisco

= HUB    Enable Secret Exec Password = class

= LAN SWITCH    Terminal vty Password = cisco

= CONSOLE CABLE

## Objectives:
- Configure a router as an HTTP server to accept configuration requests via a web browser
- Learn what settings on a router can be configured via a web browser

## Background:
With Cisco IOS version 11.0, the **ip http server** command allows the router to act as a limited HTTP (HyperText Transfer Protocol) web server. There are no graphics, but rather a series of text color screens that allow the administrator to modify the configuration of and view information about the router. The browser interface to the router supports mouse control and makes it easier to do some tasks without requiring as much knowledge of the CLI (Command-Line Interface). The CLI is available once in the browser mode. It is possible to use a browser interface when accessing Cisco switches as well as routers.

A web browser is more likely to be available on a client computer than a Telnet program. It may be easier in some instances to check on the status of a router and do minor configuration from a web browser. Because it is relatively easy for someone outside your organization to find out what the IP address of your router is, you may not want to leave this function enabled at all times.

# *LAB 6.5.2.5 – ROUTER CONFIGURATION WEB BROWSER – OVERVIEW*

## Tools / Preparation:

Prior to starting the lab you will need to connect a PC workstation with HyperTerminal to a router using the router's console interface with a roll-over cable. The workstation will need a current version of a web browser (Internet Explorer or Netscape Navigator) installed. There must be Ethernet or WAN connectivity between the workstation and the router as well as a console connection. The browser function cannot be used with the console connection, but it is necessary to configure the router to allow a browser connection first using the console connection. You should review Chapter 13 in the *Cisco Networking Academy Program: First-Year Companion Guide* and review semester 2 on-line curriculum Chapter 6 prior to starting this lab. Work individually or in teams. Be familiar with the following command:

- **ip http server**

## Resources Required:

- PC with monitor, keyboard, mouse, and power cords
- Windows operating system (Windows 95, 98, NT, or 2000) installed on PC
- HyperTerminal program configured for a router console connection
- PC connected to the router console port with a roll-over cable
- PC connected to the same hub or switch as the router
- A web browser (Internet Explorer or Netscape Navigator) installed on the workstation. You must have an Ethernet connection to the router you wish to configure.

## Web Site Resources:

- **Routing basics** – http://www.cisco.com/univercd/cc/td/doc/cisintwk/ito_doc/routing.htm
- **General information on routers** – http://www.cisco.com/univercd/cc/td/doc/pcat/#2
- **2500 series routers** – http://www.cisco.com/warp/public/cc/cisco/mkt/access/2500/index.shtml
- **1600 series routers** – http://www.cisco.com/warp/public/cc/cisco/mkt/access/1600/index.shtml
- **Terms and acronyms** – http://www.cisco.com/univercd/cc/td/doc/cisintwk/ita/index.htm
- **IP routing protocol IOS command summary** – http://www.cisco.com/univercd/cc/td/doc/product/software/ios120/12cgcr/rbkixol.htm
- **Command syntax of ip http** – http://www.cisco.com/univercd/cc/td/doc/product/10_100hb/1538m_mh/cli/1538_cli.htm

**Cisco Labs – Semester 2 – Router Configuration**
## *LAB 6.5.2.5 – ROUTER CONFIGURATION WEB BROWSER – WORKSHEET*

**Step 1 – Log on to the router.**
    **Explanation:** Connect to the router and log in. Enter the password **cisco** if prompted.

**Step 2 – Enter privileged EXEC mode.**
    **Task:**  a.  From user EXEC mode, enter privileged EXEC mode using the **enable** command.
            b.  Enter the enable password **class**.
    **Explanation:** Enter enable mode from user EXEC mode.

**Step 3 – Enter global configuration mode.**
    **Task:** Enter the command **configure terminal** (abbreviated **config t**).
    **Explanation:** Global configuration mode allows you to change settings that affect the router.

**Step 4 – Enable the HTTP server function.**
    **Task:** Enter the **ip http server** command. Press Ctrl-Z to exit global config mode.
    **Explanation:** This command allows the router to act as a limited HTTP server on the default HTTP port 80.

**Step 5 – Access the router via the web browser.**
    **Task:** Activate the web browser on your workstation and enter the IP address of the router's Ethernet port into your browser address window.
    **Explanation:** By entering the IP address of your router's Ethernet interface, you will connect to the router as an HTTP client. The HTTP server that you previously activated in the router will respond to the browser requests.

1.  What is the IP address of the Ethernet port? (Answers will vary.) _____

When prompted for a user name and password, the user name field may be left blank. Enter **class** for the password.

2.  What options are available? (Note that 2500 series routers do not have the **ClickStart** option.)

|  |  |
| --- | --- |
|  |  |
|  |  |
|  |  |

**Cisco Labs – Semester 2 – Router Configuration**
## *LAB 6.5.2.5 – ROUTER CONFIGURATION WEB BROWSER – WORKSHEET*

**Step 6 – Examine the available options.**

**Task:** Click each of the options and make notes in your engineering journal.

**Explanation**: You will note the Help Resources listed on the bottom half of the router's home page.

3. Which option on the router's home page has the most suboptions? _____

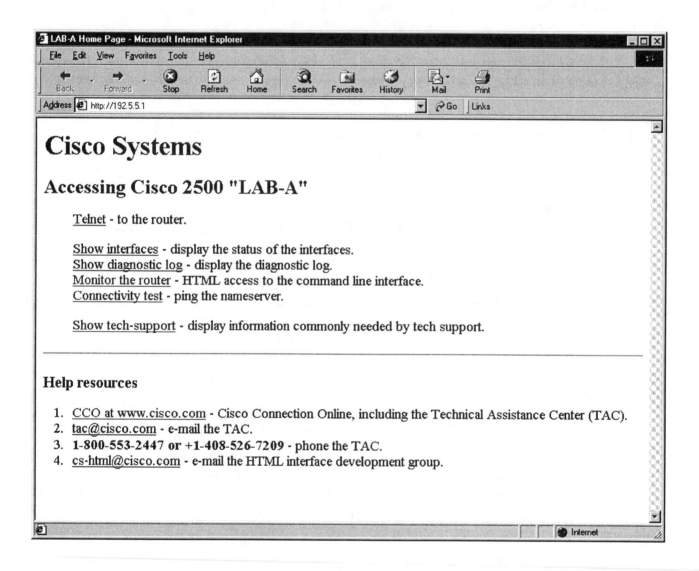

**Cisco Labs – Semester 2 – Router Configuration**
## *LAB 6.5.2.5 – ROUTER CONFIGURATION WEB BROWSER – ANSWERS*

1.  What is the IP address of the Ethernet port? **192.5.5.1**

2.  What options are available? (Note that 2500 series routers do not have the **ClickStart** option.)

| | |
|---|---|
| **Telnet** | **Show interfaces** |
| **Show diagnostic log** | **Monitor the router** |
| **Connectivity test** | **Show tech-support** |

3.  Which option on the router's home page has the most suboptions? **Monitor the router**

# Cisco Labs – Semester 2 – Router Configuration
## *LAB 7.2.2.1 – IOS IMAGE BOOT – OVERVIEW*
### *(Estimated time: 30 minutes)*

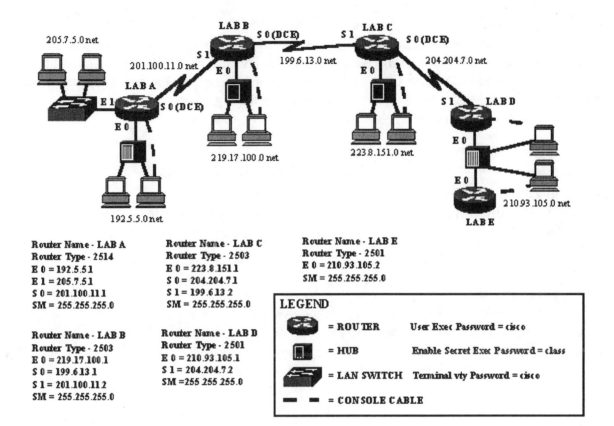

**Router Name - LAB A**
**Router Type - 2514**
E 0 = 192.5.5.1
E 1 = 205.7.5.1
S 0 = 201.100.11.1
SM = 255.255.255.0

**Router Name - LAB B**
**Router Type - 2503**
E 0 = 219.17.100.1
S 0 = 199.6.13.1
S 1 = 201.100.11.2
SM = 255.255.255.0

**Router Name - LAB C**
**Router Type - 2503**
E 0 = 223.8.151.1
S 0 = 204.204.7.1
S 1 = 199.6.13.2
SM = 255.255.255.0

**Router Name - LAB D**
**Router Type - 2501**
E 0 = 210.93.105.1
S 1 = 204.204.7.2
SM =255.255.255.0

**Router Name - LAB E**
**Router Type - 2501**
E 0 = 210.93.105.2
SM = 255.255.255.0

**LEGEND**

= ROUTER    User Exec Password = cisco

= HUB    Enable Secret Exec Password = class

= LAN SWITCH    Terminal vty Password = cisco

= CONSOLE CABLE

## Objectives:

- Display information about the Cisco IOS image (software) that is currently running
- Determine where the IOS is booting from
- Check the amount of RAM, Flash, and NVRAM memory the router has
- Check the IOS image and Flash for space used and available
- Document the parts of the IOS image filename
- Check and document the configuration register settings related to boot method
- Document a fallback boot sequence

## Background:

In this lab you will gather information on the version of IOS software that is currently running on the router. You will also check the configuration register values to see where the router is currently configured to boot from. Use the **show flash** command to gather information about the Flash memory and see what files and how much memory is free. You will also document the commands necessary to change the config register setting and the boot system commands necessary to define a fallback boot source sequence in case the IOS image in Flash is missing or corrupted.

# Cisco Labs – Semester 2 – Router Configuration
## *LAB 7.2.2.1 – IOS IMAGE BOOT – OVERVIEW*

## Tools / Preparation:

Prior to starting the lab you will need to connect a PC workstation with HyperTerminal to a router using the router's console interface with a roll-over cable. This lab should be done at the router console station. You should review Chapter 16 in the *Cisco Networking AcademyProgram: First-Year* Companion Guide and review semester 2 on-line curriculum Chapter 7 prior to starting this lab. Work individually or in teams. Be familiar with the following commands:

- **enable**
- **show running-config**
- **show startup-config**
- **show flash**

- **show version**
- **boot system**
- **config-register**
- **copy**

## Resources Required:

- PC with monitor, keyboard, mouse, and power cords
- Windows operating system (Windows 95, 98, NT, or 2000) installed on PC
- HyperTerminal program configured for router console connection
- PC connected to the router console port with a roll-over cable

## Web Site Resources:

- **Routing basics** – http://www.cisco.com/univercd/cc/td/doc/cisintwk/ito_doc/routing.htm
- **General information on routers** – http://www.cisco.com/univercd/cc/td/doc/pcat/#2
- **2500 series routers** – http://www.cisco.com/warp/public/cc/cisco/mkt/access/2500/index.shtml
- **1600 series routers** – http://www.cisco.com/warp/public/cc/cisco/mkt/access/1600/index.shtml
- **Terms and acronyms** – http://www.cisco.com/univercd/cc/td/doc/cisintwk/ita/index.htm
- **IP routing protocol IOS command summary** –
  http://www.cisco.com/univercd/cc/td/doc/product/software/ios120/12cgcr/rbkixol.htm

## Notes:

_____

_____

_____

_____

_____

_____

_____

# Cisco Labs – Semester 2 – Router Configuration
## *LAB 7.2.2.1 – IOS IMAGE BOOT – WORKSHEET*

**Step 1 – Log on to the router.**
　　**Explanation:** Connect to the router and log in. Enter the password **cisco** if prompted.

**Step 2 – Enter privileged mode.**
　　**Task:**
　　a.　Enter **enable** at the command prompt.
　　b.　Enter the password **class**.
　　**Explanation:** You use the **enable** command to enter privileged EXEC mode.

**Step 3 – Show information about the backup configuration file.**
　　**Task:** Enter **show startup-config** at the router prompt.
　　**Explanation**: The router will display information on the backup configuration file stored in NVRAM.

1.　Is there any indication of the configuration register setting? _____.

**Step 4 – Display the IOS version and other important information.**
　　**Task:** Enter the **show version** command at the router prompt.
　　**Explanation:** The router will return information about the IOS that is running in RAM..

2.　With the information that the router returns, answer the following questions:
　　a.　What is the IOS version and rev level? _____
　　b.　What is the name of the system image (IOS) file? _____
　　c.　Where was the router IOS image booted from? _____
　　d.　What type of processor (CPU) and how much RAM does this router have? _____
　　_____
　　e.　What kind of router (platform type) is this? _____
　　f.　The router backup configuration file is stored in Non-Volatile Random Access Memory (NVRAM). How much NVRAM does this router have? _____
　　_____
　　g.　The router operating system (IOS) is stored in Flash memory. How much Flash memory does this router have? _____
　　h.　What is the configuration register set to? _____ What boot type does this setting specify? _____

3.　Assuming the config-register was currently set to 0x2102, write the configuration mode commands to specify that the IOS image should be loaded from:

　　a.　Flash: _____
　　b.　ROM monitor: _____
　　c.　ROM: _____

4.　If the router were in ROM monitor mode, what command would manually boot the Cisco IOS software? _____

**Cisco Labs – Semester 2 – Router Configuration**
## *LAB 7.2.2.1 – IOS IMAGE BOOT – WORKSHEET*

**Step 5 – Show information about the Flash memory device.**
   **Task:** Enter **show flash** at the router prompt.
   **Explanation:** The router will respond with information about the Flash memory and what IOS image file(s) are stored there.

5. Document the following information.

   a.   How much Flash memory is available and used?_____

   b.   What is the file that is stored in Flash memory?_____

   c.   What is the size in bytes of the Flash memory? _____

6. What part of the IOS filename **igs-j-1.111-5** identifies the following:

   a.   Platform on which the image runs: _____

   b.   Special capabilities: _____

   c.   Where the image runs and whether it has been zip-compressed:
      _____

7. To specify a fallback boot sequence, write the configuration command to specify that the IOS image should be loaded from:

   a.   Flash: _____

   b.   A TFTP server: _____

   c.   ROM: _____ Will this be a full IOS image? _____

8. To ensure that these commands are available for the router to use the next time it is restarted, what command would you need to enter next? _____

# Cisco Labs – Semester 2 – Router Configuration
## *LAB 7.2.2.1 – IOS IMAGE BOOT – ANSWERS*

1. Is there any indication of the configuration register setting? **No (use show version)**

2. With the information that the router returns, answer the following questions (answers will vary):

   a. What is the IOS version and rev level? **Version 11.1, rev (7)AA**
   b. What is the name of the system image (IOS) file? **C1600-nsy-1.111-7.AA**
   c. Where was the router IOS image booted from? **Flash memory**
   d. What type of processor (CPU) and how much RAM does this router have? **Cisco CPA1600 (68360) processor (revision C) with 3584K/512K bytes of memory**
   e. What kind of router (platform type) is this? **Cisco 1600**
   f. The router backup configuration file is stored in Non-Volatile Random Access Memory (NVRAM). How much NVRAM does this router have? **8KB of non-volatile configuration memory**
   g. The router operating system (IOS) is stored in Flash memory. How much flash memory does this router have? **6144KB of processor board PCMCIA Flash (read-only) – approximately 6MB**
   h. What is the configuration register set to? **0x102** What boot type does this setting specify? **Examine NVRAM for boot system commands, and then boot from Flash.**

3. Assuming the config-register was currently set to 0x2102, write the configuration mode commands to specify that the IOS image should be loaded from:
   a. Flash: **config-register 0x2102**
   b. ROM monitor: **config register 0x2100**
   c. ROM: **config register 0x2101**

**Results of show version Command** (Output generated by a Cisco 1601 router)

```
lab-c>show version
Cisco Internetwork Operating System Software
IOS (tm) 1600 Software (C1600-NSY-L), Version 11.1(7)AA, EARLY DEPLOYMENT RELEASE
SOFTWARE (fc2)
Copyright (c) 1986-1996 by cisco Systems, Inc.
Compiled Thu 24-Oct-96 05:24 by kuong
Image text-base: 0x080202B8, data-base: 0x02005000

ROM: System Bootstrap, Version 11.1(10)AA, EARLY DEPLOYMENT RELEASE SOFTWARE
(fc1)
ROM: 1600 Software (C1600-BOOT-R), Version 11.1(10)AA, EARLY DEPLOYMENT RELEASE
SOFTWARE (fc1)
lab-c uptime is 1 week, 2 days, 6 hours, 54 minutes
System restarted by reload
System image file is "flash:c1600-nsy-l.111-7.AA", booted via flash

cisco CPA1600 (68360) processor (revision C) with 3584K/512K bytes of memory.
Processor board ID 04176122
Bridging software.
```

# Cisco Labs – Semester 2 – Router Configuration
## *LAB 7.2.2.1 – IOS IMAGE BOOT – ANSWERS*

## Results of show version Command – Continued

X.25 software, Version 2.0, NET2, BFE and GOSIP compliant.
Authorized for CiscoPro software set only.
1 Ethernet/IEEE 802.3 interface.
2 Serial(sync/async) network interfaces.
System/IO memory with parity disabled
8K bytes of non-volatile configuration memory.
6144K bytes of processor board PCMCIA flash (Read ONLY)
Configuration register is 0x102

4. If the router were in ROM monitor mode, what command would manually boot the Cisco IOS software? **From ROM monitor mode, manually boot the IOS with the b command.**

5. Document the following information:
    a. How much Flash memory is available and used? **1506796 bytes available; 6881812 bytes used**
    b. What is the file that is stored in Flash memory? **igs-j-1.111-5**
    c. What is the size in bytes of the Flash memory? **8192K bytes**

## Results of show flash Command (output generated by a Cisco 2514 router)

lab-b#show flash

System flash directory:
File Length  Name/status
 1  6881748 igs-j-l.111-5
[6881812 bytes used, 1506796 available, 8388608 total]
8192K bytes of processor board System flash (Read/Write)

6. What parts of the IOS filename **igs-j-1.111-5** identify the following:

    a. Platform on which the image runs: **igs (such as Cisco 1600 or 2500)**
    b. Special capabilities: **j (such as IP subset with IPX)**
    c. Where the image runs and whether it has been zip-compressed: **1.111-5 (from Flash)**

7. To specify a fallback boot sequence, write the configuration command to specify that the IOS image should be loaded from:

    a. Flash: **boot system flash *IOS-Filename***
    b. A TFTP server: **boot system TFTP *IOS-filename tftp-address***
    c. ROM: **boot system rom**          Will this be a full IOS image? **No**

8. To ensure that these commands are available for the router to use the next time it is restarted, what command do you need to enter next? **copy running-config startup-config**

# Cisco Labs – Semester 2 – Router Configuration
## *LAB 7.3.2.1 – IOS IMAGE BACKUP / RESTORE – OVERVIEW*
### *(Estimated time: 30 minutes)*

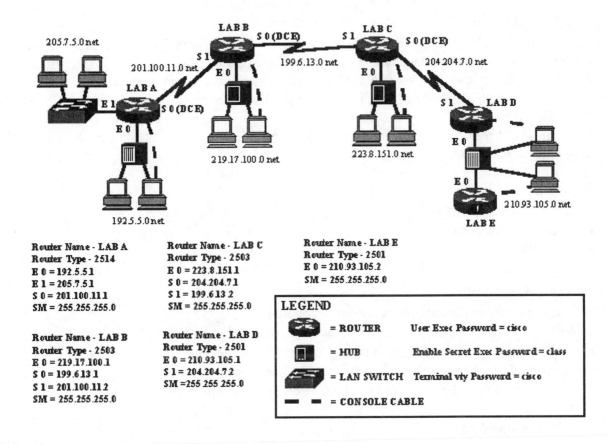

**Router Name - LAB A**
**Router Type - 2514**
E 0 = 192.5.5.1
E 1 = 205.7.5.1
S 0 = 201.100.11.1
SM = 255.255.255.0

**Router Name - LAB B**
**Router Type - 2503**
E 0 = 219.17.100.1
S 0 = 199.6.13.1
S 1 = 201.100.11.2
SM = 255.255.255.0

**Router Name - LAB C**
**Router Type - 2503**
E 0 = 223.8.151.1
S 0 = 204.204.7.1
S 1 = 199.6.13.2
SM = 255.255.255.0

**Router Name - LAB D**
**Router Type - 2501**
E 0 = 210.93.105.1
S 1 = 204.204.7.2
SM = 255.255.255.0

**Router Name - LAB E**
**Router Type - 2501**
E 0 = 210.93.105.2
SM = 255.255.255.0

**LEGEND**

= ROUTER    User Exec Password = cisco

= HUB    Enable Secret Exec Password = class

= LAN SWITCH    Terminal vty Password = cisco

= CONSOLE CABLE

## Objectives:
- Display information about the Cisco IOS software that is currently running
- Back up the IOS software image from Flash to a TFTP server
- Restore (load) a backup of IOS software image from a TFTP server to Flash

## Background:
It is a good idea to keep a backup copy of the IOS image file for each router. You will also want to always back up your current IOS before upgrading to a newer version. In this lab you will use a TFTP (Trivial File Transfer Protocol) server to act as a backup storage location for the IOS image. Production networks usually span wide areas and contain multiple routers. These geographically distributed routers need a source or backup location for software images. Using a TFTP server allows image and configuration uploads and downloads over the network.

In this lab you will check to see how much Flash memory the router has, how much of it is currently used by IOS image, and how much is free. You will then copy the current IOS image from the Flash memory of the router to the TFTP server, which can be any workstation running the Cisco TFTP software. This will create a binary backup copy of the router's IOS image on the TFTP server. Assuming the router's Flash image has been damaged, you will restore the IOS image by copying the backup image from the TFTP server back to the router's Flash.

**Cisco Labs – Semester 2 – Router Configuration**
## *LAB 7.3.2.1 – IOS IMAGE BACKUP / RESTORE – OVERVIEW*

## Tools / Preparation:

Prior to starting the lab you will need to connect a PC workstation with HyperTerminal to a router using the router's console interface with a roll-over cable. This lab should be done at the router console station. Verify that the Cisco TFTP server is installed on a server accessible by the router. If it is not, you will have to download it from the web site listed below. You should review Chapter 16 in the *Cisco Networking Academy Program: First-Year Companion Guide* and review semester 2 on-line curriculum Chapter 7 prior to starting this lab. Work individually or in teams. Be familiar with the following commands:

- enable
- show running-config
- show startup-config
- show flash

- ping
- show version
- copy
- exit

## Resources Required:

- PC with monitor, keyboard, mouse, and power cords
- Windows operating system (Windows 95, 98, NT, or 2000) installed on PC
- HyperTerminal program configured for router console connection
- PC connected to the router console port with a roll-over cable
- PC on a network that the router can send and receive to running a TFTP daemon (server)

## Web Site Resources:

- **Routing basics** – http://www.cisco.com/univercd/cc/td/doc/cisintwk/ito_doc/routing.htm
- **General information on routers** – http://www.cisco.com/univercd/cc/td/doc/pcat/#2
- **2500 series routers** – http://www.cisco.com/warp/public/cc/cisco/mkt/access/2500/index.shtml
- **1600 series routers** – http://www.cisco.com/warp/public/cc/cisco/mkt/access/1600/index.shtml
- **Terms and acronyms** – http://www.cisco.com/univercd/cc/td/doc/cisintwk/ita/index.htm
- **IP routing protocol IOS command summary** –
  http://www.cisco.com/univercd/cc/td/doc/product/software/ios120/12cgcr/rbkixol.htm
- **WinZip** (to unpack .zip files) – www.winzip.com
- **Free Cisco TFTP server (Windows 9x version)** –
  ftp://ftp.cisco.com/pub/netmgmt/utilities/tftp.zip
- **TFTP command syntax** –
  http://www.cisco.com/univercd/cc/td/doc/product/10_100hb/1538m_mh/cli/1538_cli.htm

## Notes:

_____

_____

_____

_____

# Cisco Labs – Semester 2 – Router Configuration
## *LAB 7.3.2.1 – IOS IMAGE BACKUP / RESTORE – WORKSHEET*

**Step 1 – Log on to the router.**
**Explanation:** Connect to the router and log in. Enter the password **cisco** if prompted.

**Step 2 – Enter privileged mode.**
**Task:**
a. Enter **enable** at the command prompt.
b. Enter the password **class**.
**Explanation:** You use the **enable** command to enter privileged EXEC mode.

**Step 3 – Show information about the Flash memory device.**
**Task:** Enter **show flash** at the router prompt.
**Explanation:** The router will respond with information about the Flash memory and what IOS image file(s) are stored there.

1. Document the following information from the **show flash** command.

    a. How much Flash memory is used and available? _____
    b. What is the file that is stored in Flash memory? _____
    c. What is the size in bytes of the Flash memory? _____

**Step 4 – Verify connectivity to the TFTP server.**
**Task:** Enter **ping** *xxx.xxx.xxx.xxx* where *xxx.xxx.xxx.xxx* is the IP address of the workstation running the TFTP server.
**Explanation:** Ensure that you can reach the TFTP server from the router. If you cannot, you will first need to check the connections and then check the configurations of the routers in the lab to ensure you can reach the TFTP server. Verify that the workstation has the TFTP server installed and that it is running. You can download the free Cisco TFTP server from the web site listed in the overview section of this lab.

2. What was the result of the **ping** command? _____
    _____

**Step 5 – Verify the TFTP server file location.**
**Task:** Check the TFTP server root directory location.
**Explanation:** The TFTP server root directory is where the IOS image file will be copied. This is where you should look for the file after a successful file copy. Select View/Options and note the location or browse and change the location to another directory.

3. What is the default location for the TFTP server root directory?
    _____

**Cisco Labs – Semester 2 – Router Configuration**
## *LAB 7.3.2.1 – IOS IMAGE BACKUP / RESTORE – WORKSHEET*

**Step 6 – Create an IOS software image backup.**
**Task:**
a.   Enter **copy  flash  tftp** at the router prompt.
b.   The router will ask for the IP address or hostname of the TFTP host. Enter the IP address of the TFTP server.
**Explanation:** This will copy the IOS software to a TFTP host. Before you issue this command, you need to have a TFTP host set up on a network that the router can send data to and receive data from. You also need to know the IP address of that host. You can use a host name for the TFTP server only if you have a DNS server or proper entry in the host file. **Note:** You can use HyperTerminal or Windows' copy/paste function to capture the copy process as it progresses.

4.   What was the IP address of the TFTP server? _____

5.   What did you name the file that was written to the TFTP server? _____

6.   How did the router respond when copying the file?
_____

**Step 7 – Verify the file copied to the TFTP server.**
**Task:** Check the TFTP server using Windows Explorer, the **DIR** command, or the l̲s UNIX command for the file you just wrote.

7.   What is the size in bytes of the file that was written? _____

**Step 8 – Restore the IOS software image from backup.**
**Task:**
a.   Enter **copy  tftp  flash** at the router prompt.
b.   The router will ask for the IP address or hostname of the TFTP host. Enter the IP address of the TFTP server.
**Explanation:** This will copy the IOS software from a TFTP host to router Flash.

8.   If you are copying the same filename as you backed up, the router will prompt you to overwrite the existing IOS image. Write down some of the prompts and responses you saw on the router screen. **Note:** You can use HyperTerminal or Windows' copy/paste function to capture the copy process as it progresses.

_____
_____
_____
_____
_____
_____
_____
_____
_____

# Cisco Labs – Semester 2 – Router Configuration
## *LAB 7.3.2.1 – IOS IMAGE BACKUP / RESTORE – ANSWERS*

1. Document the following information from the **show flash** command:
   a. How much Flash memory is available and used? **6881812 bytes used; 1506796 bytes available**
   b. What is the file that is stored in Flash memory? **igs-j-1.111-5**
   c. What is the size in bytes of the Flash memory? **8192KB**

**Results of show flash Command** (output generated by a Cisco 2514 router)

```
lab-a#show flash

System flash directory:
File  Length   Name/status
 1   6881748  igs-j-l.111-5
[6881812 bytes used, 1506796 available, 8388608 total]
8192K bytes of processor board System flash (Read/Write)
```

2. What was the result of the **ping** command? **The ping was successful**

**Results of the ping Command** (output generated by a Cisco 2514 router)

```
LAB-A#ping 192.5.5.2

Type escape sequence to abort.
Sending 5, 100-byte ICMP Echoes to 192.5.5.2, timeout is 2 seconds:
!!!!!
Success rate is 100 percent (5/5), round-trip min/avg/max = 1/2/4 ms
```

3. What is the default location for the TFTP server root directory?
   **C:\PROGRAM FILES\CISCO SYSTEMS\CISCO TFTP SERVER**

4. What was the IP address of the TFTP server? **192.5.5.2 (workstation IP – will vary)**

5. What did you name the file that was written to the TFTP server? **igs-j-l.111-5**

6. How did the router respond when copying the file? **Exclamation marks (!!!!!!!!!!!!!!!!!!!!!)**

7. What is the size in bytes of the file that was written? **6,721KB**

**Cisco Labs – Semester 2 – Router Configuration**
## *LAB 7.3.2.1 – IOS IMAGE BACKUP / RESTORE – ANSWERS*

### Results of the copy flash tftp Command (output generated by a Cisco 2514 router)

```
LAB-A#copy flash tftp

System flash directory:
File  Length   Name/status
  1   6881748  igs-j-l.111-5
[6881812 bytes used, 1506796 available, 8388608 total]
Address or name of remote host [255.255.255.255]? 192.5.5.2
Source file name? igs-j-l.111-5         (NOTE: the letter after the j- is a lower case L)
Destination file name [igs-j-l.111-5]?
Verifying checksum for 'igs-j-l.111-5' (file # 1)...  OK
Copy 'igs-j-l.111-5' from Flash to server
  as 'igs-j-l.111-5'? [yes/no]
!!!!!!!!!!!!!!!!!!!!!!!!!!!!!!!!!!!!!!!!!!!!!!!!!!!!!!!!!!!!!!!!!!!!!!!!!!!!!!!!!!!!!!!!!!!!!!!!!!!!!!!!!
!!!!!!!!!!!!!!!!!!!!!!!!!!!!!!!!!!!!!!!!!!!!!!!!!!!!!!!!!!!!!!!!!!!!!!!!!!!!!!!!!!!!!!!!!!!!!!!!!!!!!!!!!
!!!!!!!!!!!!!!!!!!!!!!!!
Upload to server done
Flash copy took 00:02:38 [hh:mm:ss]
```

8.  If you are copying the same file name as you backed up, the router will prompt you to overwrite the existing IOS image. Write some of the prompts and responses you saw on the router screen.

### Results of the copy tftp flash Command (output generated by a Cisco 2514 router)

```
**** NOTICE ****
Flash load helper v1.0
This process will accept the copy options and then terminate
the current system image to use the ROM based image for the copy.
Routing functionality will not be available during that time.
If you are logged in via telnet, this connection will terminate.
Users with console access can see the results of the copy operation.
          ---- ******** ----
Proceed? [confirm]
System flash directory:
File  Length   Name/status
  1   6881748  igs-j-l.111-5
[6881812 bytes used, 1506796 available, 8388608 total]
Address or name of remote host [192.5.5.2]?
Source file name? igs-j-l.111-5
Destination file name [igs-j-l.111-5]?
Accessing file 'igs-j-l.111-5' on 192.5.5.2...
Loading igs-j-l.111-5 from 192.5.5.2 (via Ethernet0): ! [OK]
```

**Cisco Labs – Semester 2 – Router Configuration**
## *LAB 7.3.2.1 – IOS IMAGE BACKUP / RESTORE – ANSWERS*

## Results of the copy tftp flash Command – Continued

Erase flash device before writing? [confirm]
Flash contains files. Are you sure you want to erase? [confirm]
Copy 'igs-j-l.111-5' from server
  as 'igs-j-l.111-5' into Flash WITH erase? [yes/no]  yes
%SYS-5-RELOAD: Reload requested
%SYS-4-CONFIG_NEWER: Configurations from version 11.1 may not be correctly under
stood.
%FLH: igs-j-l.111-5 from 192.5.5.2 to flash ...

System flash directory:
File  Length   Name/status
  1   6881748  igs-j-l.111-5
[6881812 bytes used, 1506796 available, 8388608 total]
Accessing file 'igs-j-l.111-5' on 192.5.5.2...
Loading igs-j-l.111-5 from 192.5.5.2 (via Ethernet0): ! [OK]
Erasing device... eeeeeeeeeeeeeeeeeeeeeeeeeeeeeeee ...erased
Loading igs-j-l.111-5 from 192.5.5.2 (via Ethernet0): !!!!!!!!!!!!!!!!!!!!!!!!!
!!!!!!!!!!!!!!!!!!!!!!!!!!!!!!!!!!!!!!!!!!!!!!!!!!!!!!!!!!!!!!!!!!!!!!!!!!!!!!!!!!!
!!!!!!!!!!!!!!!!!!!!!!!!!!!!!!!!!!!!!!!!!!!!!!!!!!!!!!!!!!!!!!!!!!!!!!!!!!!!!!!!!!!
   **(Note: Lots of exclamation marks here)**
!!!!!!!!!!!!!!!!!!!!!!!!!!!!!!!!!!!!!!!!!!!!!
[OK - 6881748/8388608 bytes]

Verifying checksum...  OK (0x5D14)
Flash copy took 0:03:28 [hh:mm:ss]
%FLH: Re-booting system after download
F3: 6674716+207000+264864 at 0x3000060

# Cisco Labs – Semester 2 – Router Configuration
## *LAB 8.1.3.1 – ROUTER PASSWORD RECOVERY – OVERVIEW*
### *(Estimated time: 15 minutes)*

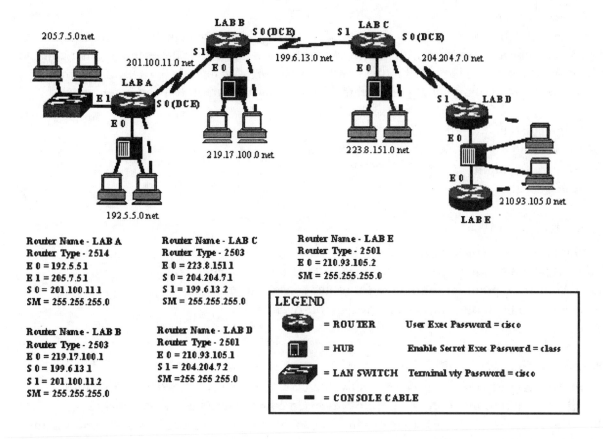

Router Name - LAB A
Router Type - 2514
E 0 = 192.5.5.1
E 1 = 205.7.5.1
S 0 = 201.100.11.1
SM = 255.255.255.0

Router Name - LAB C
Router Type - 2503
E 0 = 223.8.151.1
S 0 = 204.204.7.1
S 1 = 199.6.13.2
SM = 255.255.255.0

Router Name - LAB E
Router Type - 2501
E 0 = 210.93.105.2
SM = 255.255.255.0

Router Name - LAB B
Router Type - 2503
E 0 = 219.17.100.1
S 0 = 199.6.13.1
S 1 = 201.100.11.2
SM = 255.255.255.0

Router Name - LAB D
Router Type - 2501
E 0 = 210.93.105.1
S 1 = 204.204.7.2
SM = 255.255.255.0

**LEGEND**

= ROUTER          User Exec Password = cisco

= HUB             Enable Secret Exec Password = class

= LAN SWITCH      Terminal vty Password = cisco

= CONSOLE CABLE

## Objective:

- To learn the procedure to recover when a password is forgotten

## Background:

There will be circumstances where the password for a router needs to be reset. The password may have been forgotten, or the previous administrator may have left the company that owns the router. The technique described requires physical access to the router so that the console cable may be plugged in. Since this technique is well-known, it is vital that routers are in a secured location, with limited physical access.

The version of HyperTerminal provided with Windows 95, 98, NT, and 2000 was developed for Microsoft by Hilgraeve. This version does not issue a "break" sequence as required for the Cisco router password recovery technique. An upgrade known as HyperTerminal Private Edition (PE) is available free of charge for personal and educational use. Commercial use of the program requires registration with Hilgraeve. The program may be downloaded from the Hilgraeve web site, listed in the web site resources section below.

# Cisco Labs – Semester 2 – Router Configuration
## *LAB 8.1.3.1 – ROUTER PASSWORD RECOVERY – OVERVIEW*

## Tools / Preparation:
Prior to starting the lab you will need to connect a PC workstation with HyperTerminal PE to a router using the router's console interface with a roll-over cable. This lab will be done at the router console station. You should review Chapter 13 in the *Cisco Networking Academy Program: First-Year Companion Guide*. Work individually or in teams. Be familiar with the following commands:

- **config-register**
- **show version**
- **configure terminal**
- **enable secret**

## Resources Required:
- PC with monitor, keyboard, mouse, and power cords
- Windows operating system (Windows 95, 98, NT, or 2000) installed on PC
- HyperTerminal PE program configured for router console access
- PC connected to the router console port with a roll-over cable

## Web Site Resources:
- **Routing basics** – http://www.cisco.com/univercd/cc/td/doc/cisintwk/ito_doc/routing.htm
- **General information on routers** – http://www.cisco.com/univercd/cc/td/doc/pcat/#2
- **2500 series routers** – http://www.cisco.com/warp/public/cc/cisco/mkt/access/2500/index.shtml
- **1600 series routers** – http://www.cisco.com/warp/public/cc/cisco/mkt/access/1600/index.shtml
- **Terms and acronyms** – http://www.cisco.com/univercd/cc/td/doc/cisintwk/ita/index.htm
- **IP routing protocol IOS command summary** –
  http://www.cisco.com/univercd/cc/td/doc/product/software/ios120/12cgcr/rbkixol.htm
- **Hilgraeve HyperTerminal PE download** – http://www.hilgraeve.com
- **IOS password encryption facts** – http://www.cisco.com/warp/public/701/64.html

## Notes:
_____
_____
_____
_____
_____

# Cisco Labs – Semester 2 – Router Configuration
## *LAB 8.1.3.1 – ROUTER PASSWORD RECOVERY – WORKSHEET*

**Step 1 – Log on to the router.**
    **Explanation:** Connect to the router and log in. Enter the password **cisco** if prompted.

**Step 2 – Record the configuration register setting.**
    **Task:** Enter the command **show version** (abbreviated **show ver**).
    **Explanation:** This displays the current configuration register setting, along with other information.

1.   What is the current configuration register setting? _____

**Step 3 – Restart the router.**
    **Task:** Turn off the router for a short period of time, and then turn it back on again.
    **Explanation**: When the router is restarting, the bootup sequence can be interrupted.

**Step 4 – Interrupt the bootup sequence.**
    **Task:** Within 60 seconds of turning the router back on, press and hold the Ctrl key, and then press the Break key.
    **Explanation:** A break character is sent to the router, interrupting the bootup sequence.

**Step 5 – Change the configuration register.**
    **Task:** Enter the commands to change the configuration register.
    **Explanation:** The configuration register is changed to tell the router to ignore the configuration file in NVRAM on the next startup. The procedure varies, depending on the model of router.

    **A.  2500 series router:**
    The prompt will be > with no router name. Type **o/r 0x42** and press Enter (lowercase letter o, slash, lowercase r, space, zero, lowercase x, 4, 2). Type **I** and press Enter to reload the router. Wait until the router has rebooted. Type **N** when prompted to enter the initial configuration. Press Enter to see the **router>** prompt.

    **B.  1600 series router:**
    The prompt will be **rommon 1>**. Type **confreg** and type **Y** when asked to change the configuration. Type **N** to all questions except **ignore system config info**. When you finish responding to the questions, you will be prompted to change the configuration again. Type **N**, and then type **reset** to reload the router. Wait until the router has rebooted. Type **N** when prompted to enter the initial configuration. Press Enter to see the **router>** prompt.

**Cisco Labs – Semester 2 – Router Configuration**
# *LAB 8.1.3.1 – ROUTER PASSWORD RECOVERY – WORKSHEET*

**Step 6 – Enter privileged EXEC mode.**
    **Task:** From user EXEC mode, enter privileged EXEC mode using the **enable** command.
    **Explanation:** Enter enable mode from user EXEC mode.

    2.   Why was no password required? _____

**Step 7 – Examine the configuration the router is using.**
    **Task:** Enter the command **show running-config** (abbreviated **sh run**).
    **Explanation:** Since the configuration registers were set to ignore the configuration file in Step 5, the router has a minimal configuration.

**Step 8 – Load the router configuration file.**
    **Task:** Type the command **copy startup-config running-config** (abbreviated **copy start run**).
    **Explanation:** The configuration file is loaded from NVRAM into RAM. This will allow you to view and/or modify the router passwords.

    3.   How does your router prompt change? _____

**Step 9 – Look at passwords.**
    **Task:** Enter the command **show running-config** (abbreviated **sh run**).
    **Explanation:** Passwords that have been encrypted with the **enable secret** command show up as a series of letters, numbers, and symbols (such as $1$miYV$i9OOuSBQBde5fzgS3tn8T0). Unencrypted passwords are in plain text.

    4.   What passwords do you see? _____
    _____

**Step 10 – Change passwords.**
    **Task:** Enter the commands to change the appropriate passwords.
    **Explanation:** Passwords that are set using the **enable secret** command cannot be decrypted, even with third-party software. The only option you have is to change the password to another value.

    Go into global configuration mode by entering the command **configure terminal** (abbreviated **config t**). Enter the command **enable secret mynewpassword**. Press Ctrl-Z to exit global config mode. Type the command **show running-config** (abbreviated **sh run**).

    5.   What passwords do you see now? _____
    _____

    6.   Has the encrypted password changed from the value in Step 9? _____

# Cisco Labs – Semester 2 – Router Configuration
## *LAB 8.1.3.1 – ROUTER PASSWORD RECOVERY – WORKSHEET*

**Note:** For the purposes of this lab, you will not be saving the router configuration with the new password. You need to change the password back to the value **class**. Enter global config mode by entering the command **config t**. Enter the command **enable secret class** and then press Ctrl-Z to exit global configuration mode. Save the new configuration by entering the command **copy running-config startup-config** (abbreviated **copy start run**).

### Step 11 – Change the configuration register.

**Task:** Examine the current status of the configuration register and change it back to its original value.

**Explanation:** The configuration register is still set to ignore the startup configuration contained in NVRAM. You need to change it back to its original value.

Enter the command **show version** (abbreviated **sh ver**).

7.  What is the value of the configuration register? _____

Enter global config mode by typing the command **config t**. Enter the command **config-register 0x2102**. (**Note:** Use the original value you recorded in Step 2.) Press Ctrl-Z to exit global config mode. Enter the command **sh ver** to see the new value of the configuration register.

8.  What is the new value of the configuration register? _____

### Step 12 – Verify the new password.

**Task:**

a.  Enter the command **reload**.

b.  Enter **Y** if prompted to save the new configuration and to proceed with the reload.

**Explanation:** You need to verify that the new password you created in Step 10 works.

Enter privileged EXEC mode by entering the command **enable** (abbreviated: **en**). Enter the password **class**. If you properly set the enable password, you should see the router prompt change. View the status of the configuration register by entering the command **show version** (abbreviated **sh ver**).

9.  Has the configuration register changed back to the original value you recorded in Step 2?

_____

**Cisco Labs – Semester 2 – Router Configuration**
## *LAB 8.1.3.1 – ROUTER PASSWORD RECOVERY – ANSWERS*

1. What is the current configuration register setting? **0x2102**

2. Why was no password required? **The configuration file located in NVRAM was bypassed. The minimal configuration that the router starts up with has no passwords.**

3. How does your router prompt change? **The prompt changes from router# to LAB-A#, indicating that the running configuration has been changed.**

4. What passwords do you see?
   **enable secret 5 $1$miYV$i9OOuSBQBde5fzgS3tn8T0**
   **enable password cisco**

5. What passwords do you now see?
   **enable secret 5 $1$G6IE$1TkTp3lwYYwsQ2jV88ca9/**
   **enable password cisco**

6. Has the encrypted password changed from the value in Step 9? **Yes**

7. What is the value of the configuration register? **0x42**

8. What is the new value of the configuration register? **0x2102 (at next reload)**

9. Has the configuration register changed back to the original value you recorded in Step 2? **Yes**

# Cisco Labs – Semester 2 – Router Configuration
## *LAB 8.1.4.1 – INDIVIDUAL ROUTER CONFIGURATION – OVERVIEW*
### *(Estimated time: 30 minutes)*

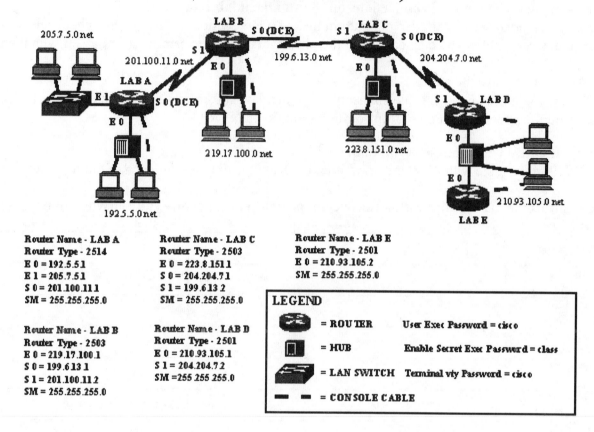

Router Name - LAB A
Router Type - 2514
E 0 = 192.5.5.1
E 1 = 205.7.5.1
S 0 = 201.100.11.1
SM = 255.255.255.0

Router Name - LAB C
Router Type - 2503
E 0 = 223.8.151.1
S 0 = 204.204.7.1
S 1 = 199.6.13.2
SM = 255.255.255.0

Router Name - LAB E
Router Type - 2501
E 0 = 210.93.105.2
SM = 255.255.255.0

Router Name - LAB B
Router Type - 2503
E 0 = 219.17.100.1
S 0 = 199.6.13.1
S 1 = 201.100.11.2
SM = 255.255.255.0

Router Name - LAB D
Router Type - 2501
E 0 = 210.93.105.1
S 1 = 204.204.7.2
SM = 255.255.255.0

**LEGEND**

= ROUTER    User Exec Password = cisco

= HUB    Enable Secret Exec Password = class

= LAN SWITCH    Terminal vty Password = cisco

= CONSOLE CABLE

## Objectives:
- Configure a router for the standard lab setup using only the lab diagram
- Configure the router using only the Command-Line Interface (CLI)
- Configure workstation IP address settings to communicate with the router via Ethernet
- Prepare for Part A of the Final Exam (Timed Router Configuration)

## Background:
In this lab you will configure one of the five lab routers from the command line by yourself without the use of any notes, only the network topology. You may use the router help facility and the router diagram above. Your goal will be to configure the router as quickly as possible without errors. You will also configure the IP settings for one of the corresponding Ethernet attached workstations.

## Tools / Preparation:
Prior to starting this lab you should have the equipment for the standard five-router lab available. The NVRAM of the router you will be configuring should be erased. At the start of this section, the instructor or lab assistant should log onto each router in enable exec mode, issue the **erase startup-config command**, and issue the **reload** command. This will force the routers to come up with a blank configuration. The IP configuration for the associated workstation should also be changed so that it is incorrect. The answer section includes examples of the detailed command sets that you will have to master. The instructor will review your configuration when you are finished.

# Cisco Labs – Semester 2 – Router Configuration
# *LAB 8.1.4.1 – INDIVIDUAL ROUTER CONFIGURATION – WORKSHEET*

**Step 1 – Review the physical connections on the standard lab setup.**
Review the standard Semester 2 lab diagram in the overview section of this lab, and check all physical devices, cables, and connections of the physical lab setup to familiarize yourself with them.

**Step 2 – Console into the router.**
Verify that you have a good console connection and that HyperTerminal is configured properly. The router should be booted with no startup configuration file in NVRAM.

**Step 3 – Identify IP address information.**
1. Fill in the table with IP interface information from the diagram for each of the five routers.

**Cisco Lab Router IP Configuration (answers from router diagram – your answers may vary)**

| Router Name | Lab-A | Lab-B | Lab-C | Lab-D | Lab-E |
|---|---|---|---|---|---|
| Model Number | | | | | |
| Interface E0 IP Address | | | | | |
| Interface E0 Subnet Mask | | | | | |
| Interface E1 IP Address | | | | | |
| Interface E1 Subnet Mask | | | | | |
| Interface S0 IP Address | | | | | |
| Interface S0 Subnet Mask | | | | | |
| Interface S0 * Clock Rate | | | | | |
| Interface S1 IP Address | | | | | |
| Interface S1 Subnet Mask | | | | | |
| Other Interface(s) | | | | | |

**\* Note: Clock rate must be set on the DCE end (S0) of the WAN link between routers.**

**Step 4 – Configure the router via the console connection.**
2. Select a router and time yourself. Configure the following information for each router: Host name, passwords, IP addresses for interfaces, routing protocol and associated network numbers, IP host lookup table. Repeat with other routers.
**Note:** Make sure you copy the running configuration to the startup configuration when you are finished, or you will lose the configuration upon next reboot.

**Step 5 – Configure the workstation IP settings using the Control Panel's Network icon.**
3. Configure the IP address, subnet mask, and default gateway to be compatible with the router.

**Step 6 – Test your configuration with ping and telnet.**
4. From the PC DOS prompt, use the **ping** and **telnet** commands to test your configuration.

# Cisco Labs – Semester 2 – Router Configuration
# *LAB 8.1.4.1 – INDIVIDUAL ROUTER CONFIGURATION – WORKSHEET*

Listed below are the outputs from the **show running-config** command for all five routers in the standard lab setup. If you have problems configuring a particular router, refer to these for help. Answers may vary, depending on the router model number and exact configuration of your lab setup.

**Router: Lab-A**

LAB-A#show run

Building configuration...
Current configuration:
version 11.1
service udp-small-servers
service tcp-small-servers
hostname LAB-A
enable secret 5 $1$xT7v$9EC3X5IBHLwq2RehHNvWc0
interface Ethernet0
 ip address 192.5.5.1 255.255.255.0
interface Ethernet1
 ip address 205.7.5.1 255.255.255.0
interface Serial0
 ip address 201.100.11.1 255.255.255.0
 clockrate 56000
interface Serial1
 no ip address
 shutdown
router rip
 network 192.5.5.0
 network 205.7.5.0
 network 201.100.11.0
ip host LAB-B 201.100.11.2 219.17.100.1 199.6.13.1
ip host LAB-C 199.6.13.2 223.8.151.1 204.204.7.1
ip host LAB-D 204.204.7.2 210.93.105.1
ip host LAB-E 210.93.105.2
ip host LAB-A 192.5.5.1 205.7.5.1 201.100.11.1
no ip classless
line con 0
 password cisco
 login
line aux 0
line vty 0 4
 password cisco
 login
!end

**Cisco Labs – Semester 2 – Router Configuration**
## *LAB 8.1.4.1 – INDIVIDUAL ROUTER CONFIGURATION – WORKSHEET*

**Router: Lab-B**

LAB-B#show run

Building configuration...
Current configuration:
version 11.1
service udp-small-servers
service tcp-small-servers
hostname LAB-B
enable secret 5 $1$xT7v$9EC3X5IBHLwq2RehHNvWc0
interface Ethernet0
 ip address 219.17.100.1 255.255.255.0
 no mop enabled
interface Serial0
 ip address 199.6.13.1 255.255.255.0
 clockrate 56000
interface Serial1
 ip address 201.100.11.2 255.255.255.0
interface BRI0
 no ip address
 shutdown
router rip
 network 219.17.100.0
 network 199.6.13.0
 network 201.100.11.0
ip host LAB-B 201.100.11.2 219.17.100.1 199.6.13.1
ip host LAB-C 199.6.13.2 223.8.151.1 204.204.7.1
ip host LAB-D 204.204.7.2 210.93.105.1
ip host LAB-E 210.93.105.2
ip host LAB-A 192.5.5.1 205.7.5.1 201.100.11.1
no ip classless
snmp-server community public RO
line con 0
 password cisco
 login
line aux 0
line vty 0 4
 password cisco
 login

**Cisco Labs – Semester 2 – Router Configuration**
## *LAB 8.1.4.1 – INDIVIDUAL ROUTER CONFIGURATION – WORKSHEET*

**Router: Lab-C**

LAB-C#show run

Building configuration...
Current configuration:
version 11.1
service udp-small-servers
service tcp-small-servers
hostname LAB-C
enable secret 5 $1$xT7v$9EC3X5IBHLwq2RehHNvWc0
interface Ethernet0
 ip address 223.8.151.1 255.255.255.0
interface Serial0
 ip address 204.204.7.1 255.255.255.0
 clockrate 56000
interface Serial1
 ip address 199.6.13.2 255.255.255.0
interface BRI0
 no ip address
 shutdown
router rip
 network 223.8.151.0
 network 199.6.13.0
 network 204.204.7.0
ip host LAB-A 192.5.5.1 205.7.5.1 201.100.11.1
ip host LAB-B 201.100.11.2 219.17.100.1 199.6.13.1
ip host LAB-C 199.6.13.2 223.8.151.1 204.204.7.1
ip host LAB-D 204.204.7.2 210.93.105.1
ip host LAB-E 210.93.105.2
no ip classless
line con 0
 password cisco
login
line aux 0
line vty 0 4
 password cisco
 login
!

**Cisco Labs – Semester 2 – Router Configuration**
## *LAB 8.1.4.1 – INDIVIDUAL ROUTER CONFIGURATION – WORKSHEET*

**Router: Lab-D**

LAB-D#show run

Building configuration...
Current configuration:
version 11.1
service udp-small-servers
service tcp-small-servers
hostname LAB-D
enable secret 5 $1$xT7v$9EC3X5IBHLwq2RehHNvWc0
interface Ethernet0
 ip address 210.93.105.1 255.255.255.0
 no ip mroute-cache
 no ip route-cache
interface Serial0
 no ip address
 no ip mroute-cache
 no ip route-cache
 shutdown
interface Serial1
 ip address 204.204.7.2 255.255.255.0
 no ip mroute-cache
 no ip route-cache
router rip
 network 204.204.7.0
 network 210.93.105.0
ip host LAB-A 102.5.5.1 205.7.5.1 201.100.11.1
ip host LAB-B 201.100.11.2 219.17.100.1 199.6.13.1
ip host LAB-C 199.6.13.2 223.8.151.1 204.204.7.1
ip host LAB-D 204.204.7.2 210.93.105.1
ip host LAB-E 210.93.105.2
no ip classless
line con 0
 password cisco
login
line aux 0
line vty 0 4
 password cisco
login

**Cisco Labs – Semester 2 – Router Configuration**
## *LAB 8.1.4.1 – INDIVIDUAL ROUTER CONFIGURATION – WORKSHEET*

**Router: Lab-E**

LAB-E#show run

Building configuration...
Current configuration:
version 11.1
service udp-small-servers
service tcp-small-servers
hostname LAB-E
enable secret 5 $1$q/QJ$EA8tfOg1/Rxn/28FSrLgJ/
interface Ethernet0
 ip address 210.93.105.2 255.255.255.0
interface Serial0
 no ip address
 shutdown
interface Serial1
 no ip address
 shutdown
router rip
 network 210.93.105.0
ip host LAB-A 192.5.5.1 205.7.5.1 201.100.11.1
ip host LAB-B 201.100.11.2 219.17.100.1 199.6.13.1
ip host LAB-C 199.6.13.2 223.8.151.1 204.204.7.1
ip host LAB-D 204.204.7.2 210.93.105.1
ip host LAB-E 210.93.105.2
no ip classless
line con 0
 password cisco
login
line aux 0
line vty 0 4
 password cisco
 login
!

# Cisco Labs – Semester 2 – Router Configuration
## *LAB 8.1.4.1 – INDIVIDUAL ROUTER CONFIGURATION – ANSWERS*

Students should be able to repetitively configure the practice lab. At the start of this section, you should log onto each router in enable exec mode, issue the **erase startup-config command**, and issue the **reload** command. This will force the routers to come up with a blank configuration and allow the students to practice the skills they will need to pass the Semester 2 final lab exam. Below are the detailed command sets that the students will have to master. All commands are provided for router Lab-A. A table of configuration settings for the other routers follows these instructions.

**Router Lab-A (2514) Basic Configuration Commands (see the next table for other routers)**

| Step Description / Explanation | Router Command Prompt | IOS Command |
|---|---|---|
| Enable privileged mode | Router> | Enable |
| Configure (the router) from terminal (keyboard) | Router# | Config T |
| **Name Router Lab-A** (the prompt will change) | Router(config)# | Hostname  LAB-A |
| Set privileged mode encrypted (secret) password to class | Lab-A(config)# | Enable  secret  class |
| Set privileged mode text password (optional) | Lab-A(config)# | Enable  password cisco |
| Disable DNS lookup | Lab-A(config)# | No ip domain-lookup |
| | | |
| **Select E0 interface** | Lab-A(config)# | Interface  Ethernet0 |
| Provide description for E0 (optional on any interface) | Lab-A(config-if)# | Description connected to LAN A |
| Set E0 IP address and subnet mask | Lab-A(config-if)# | Ip address  192.5.5.1  255.255.255.0 |
| Bring interface E0 up | Lab-A(config-if)# | No shutdown |
| | | |
| **Select E1 interface** | Lab-A(config)# | Interface  Ethernet1 |
| Set E1 IP address and subnet mask | Lab-A(config-if)# | Ip address  205.7.5.1  255.255.255.0 |
| Bring interface E0 up | Lab-A(config-if)# | No shutdown |
| | | |
| **Select S0 interface** | Lab-A(config-if)# | Interface  Serial0 |
| Set S0 IP address and subnet mask | Lab-A(config-if)# | ip address  201.100.11.1  255.255.255.0 |
| Set IGRP bandwidth metric | Lab-A(config-if)# | Bandwidth  56 |
| Set DCE clock synch at 56000 | Lab-A(config-if)# | Clock rate  56000 |
| Bring interface S0 up | Lab-A(config-if)# | no shutdown |
| | | ! |
| **Select S1 interface (not used)** | Lab-A(config-if)# | Interface  Serial1 |
| Set no IP address for S1 | Lab-A(config-if)# | No ip address |
| Administratively shut down S1 | Lab-A(config-if)# | Shutdown |
| | | |
| Exit interface config mode | Lab-A(config-if)# | Exit |

**Cisco Labs – Semester 2 – Router Configuration**
## LAB 8.1.4.1 – INDIVIDUAL ROUTER CONFIGURATION – ANSWERS

### Router Lab-A (2514) Basic Configuration Commands – Continued

| | | |
|---|---|---|
| **Start RIP routing protocol** | Lab-A(config)# | Router rip |
| Specify directly connected network for routing updates | Lab-A(config-router)# | Network 192.5.5.0 |
| Specify directly connected network for routing updates | Lab-A(config-router)# | Network 205.7.5.0 |
| Specify directly connected network for routing updates | Lab-A(config-router)# | Network 201.100.11.0 |
| | | |
| Exit router config mode | Lab-A(config-router)# | Exit |
| | | |
| **Enable browser management** | Lab-A(config)# | Ip http server |
| | | |
| **Define router host name table** | N/A | N/A |
| Specify host table entry for Lab-A (with interface IP addresses) | Lab-A(config)# | ip host Lab-A 192.5.5.1 205.7.5.1 201.100.11.1 |
| Specify host table entry for Lab-B (with interface IP addresses) | Lab-A(config)# | ip host Lab-B 219.17.100.1 199.6.13.1 201.100.11.2 |
| Specify host table entry for Lab-C (with interface IP addresses) | Lab-A(config)# | ip host Lab-C 223.8.151.1 204.204.7.1 199.6.13.2 |
| Specify host table entry for Lab-D (with interface IP addresses) | Lab-A(config)# | ip host LAB-D 210.93.105.1 204.204.7.2 |
| Specify host table entry Lab-E (with interface IP addresses) | Lab-A(config)# | ip host LAB-E 210.93.105.2 |
| | | |
| Disable classless IP routing | Lab-A(config)# | no ip classless |
| | | |
| **Configure console line** (direct attach to console port) | Lab-A(config)# | Line con 0 |
| Enable console login password checking | Lab-A(config-line)# | Login |
| Set user mode password for console connection login | Lab-A(config-line)# | Password cisco |
| **Configure telnet line** (virtual terminal or VTY) | Lab-A(config-line)# | Line vty 0 4 |
| Enable telnet login password checking | Lab-A(config-line)# | Login |
| Set user mode password for telnet connection login | Lab-A(config-line)# | Password cisco |
| | | |
| **Save the current running configuration to the startup configuration** | Lab-A# | Copy running-config startup-config |

## Cisco Labs – Semester 2 – Router Configuration
## *LAB 8.1.4.1 – INDIVIDUAL ROUTER CONFIGURATION – ANSWERS*

1. Fill in the table below with IP interface information for each of the five routers.

**Cisco Lab Router IP Configuration (answers from router diagram – your answers may vary)**

| Router Name | Lab-A | Lab-B | Lab-C | Lab-D | Lab-E |
|---|---|---|---|---|---|
| Model Number | 2514 | 2503 | 2503 | 2501 | 2501 |
| Interface E0 IP Address | 192.5.5.1 | 219.17.100.1 | 223.8.151.1 | 210.93.105.1 | 210.93.105.2 |
| Interface E0 Subnet Mask | 255.255.255.0 | 255.255.255.0 | 255.255.255.0 | 255.255.255.0 | 255.255.255.0 |
| Interface E1 IP Address | 205.7.5.1 | Not Present | Not Present | Not Present | Not Present |
| Interface E1 Subnet Mask | 255.255.255.0 | Not Present | Not Present | Not Present | Not Present |
| Interface S0 IP Address | 201.100.11.1 | 199.6.13.1 | 204.204.7.1 | Not Used | Not Used |
| Interface S0 Subnet Mask | 255.255.255.0 | 255.255.255.0 | 255.255.255.0 | Not Used | Not Used |
| Interface S0 * Clock Rate | 56000 | 56000 | 56000 | Not Used | Not Used |
| Interface S1 IP Address | Not Used | 201.100.11.2 | 196.6.13.2 | 204.204.7.2 | Not Used |
| Interface S1 Subnet Mask | Not Used | 255.255.255.0 | 255.255.255.0 | 255.255.255.0 | Not Used |
| Other Interface(s) | Console, AUX | ISDN BRI0, Console, AUX | ISDN BRI0, Console, AUX | Console, AUX | Console, AUX |

* Note: Clock rate must be set on the DCE end (S0) of the WAN link between routers.

# Cisco Labs – Semester 2 – Router Configuration
## *LAB 9.4.2.1 – SHOW ARP AND CLEAR ARP – OVERVIEW*
### *(Estimated time: 30 minutes)*

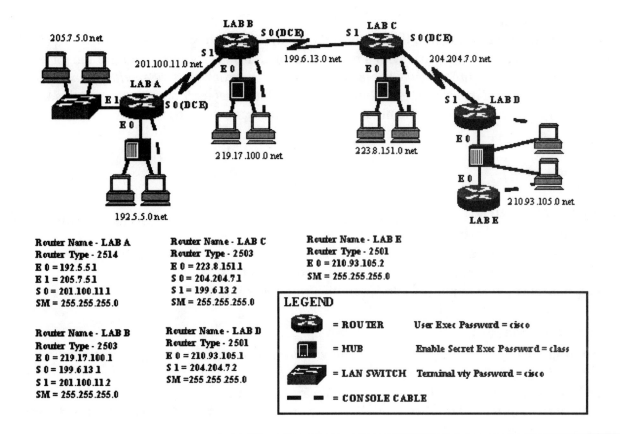

**Router Name - LAB A**
**Router Type - 2514**
E 0 = 192.5.5.1
E 1 = 205.7.5.1
S 0 = 201.100.11.1
SM = 255.255.255.0

**Router Name - LAB B**
**Router Type - 2503**
E 0 = 219.17.100.1
S 0 = 199.6.13.1
S 1 = 201.100.11.2
SM = 255.255.255.0

**Router Name - LAB C**
**Router Type - 2503**
E 0 = 223.8.151.1
S 0 = 204.204.7.1
S 1 = 199.6.13.2
SM = 255.255.255.0

**Router Name - LAB D**
**Router Type - 2501**
E 0 = 210.93.105.1
S 1 = 204.204.7.2
SM = 255.255.255.0

**Router Name - LAB E**
**Router Type - 2501**
E 0 = 210.93.105.2
SM = 255.255.255.0

**LEGEND**

= ROUTER     User Exec Password = cisco

= HUB       Enable Secret Exec Password = class

= LAN SWITCH   Terminal vty Password = cisco

= CONSOLE CABLE

## Objectives:
- Become familiar with the router's **show arp** command
- Become familiar with the router's **clear arp** command

## Background:
In this lab you will view the ARP table stored in the router and clear the router's ARP table. These two commands are very important in troubleshooting a network problem. The router keeps very detailed information about MAC addresses and associated IP addresses. From time to time this information can become corrupted and will cause packet delivery problems. When this happens, the router ARP table must be cleared and rebuilt.

# Cisco Labs – Semester 2 – Router Configuration
## *LAB 9.4.2.1 – SHOW ARP AND CLEAR ARP – OVERVIEW*

## Tools / Preparation:
Prior to starting the lab you will need to connect a PC workstation with HyperTerminal to a router using the router's console interface with a roll-over cable. This lab should be done at the router console station. You should review Chapter 6 in the *Cisco Networking AcademyProgram: First-Year Companion Guide* and review semester 2 on-line curriculum Chapter 9 prior to starting this lab. Work individually or in teams. Be familiar with the following commands:

- **enable**
- **show arp**

- **clear arp**
- **ping**

## Resources Required:
- PC with monitor, keyboard, mouse, and power cords
- Windows operating system (Windows 95, 98, NT, or 2000) installed on PC
- HyperTerminal program configured for router console access
- PC connected to the router console port with a roll-over cable

## Web Site Resources:
- **Routing basics** – http://www.cisco.com/univercd/cc/td/doc/cisintwk/ito_doc/routing.htm
- **General information on routers** – http://www.cisco.com/univercd/cc/td/doc/pcat/#2
- **2500 series routers** – http://www.cisco.com/warp/public/cc/cisco/mkt/access/2500/index.shtml
- **1600 series routers** – http://www.cisco.com/warp/public/cc/cisco/mkt/access/1600/index.shtml
- **Terms and acronyms** – http://www.cisco.com/univercd/cc/td/doc/cisintwk/ita/index.htm
- **IP routing protocol IOS command summary** –
  http://www.cisco.com/univercd/cc/td/doc/product/software/ios120/12cgcr/rbkixol.htm

## Notes:
_____
_____
_____
_____
_____
_____
_____
_____
_____
_____

# Cisco Labs – Semester 2 – Router Configuration
## *LAB 9.4.2.1 – SHOW ARP AND CLEAR ARP – WORKSHEET*

**Step 1 – Log on to the router.**
   **Explanation:** Connect to the router and log in. Enter the password **cisco** if prompted.

**Step 2 – Show the router's ARP table.**
   **Task:** Enter **show arp** at the router prompt
   **Explanation:** The router will respond with the ARP table that shows IP address to MAC address to interface number.

   1. What three important pieces of information are displayed? _____
   _____

**Step 3 – Enter privileged mode.**
   **Task:**
   a. Enter **enable** at the command prompt.
   b. Enter the password **class**.
   **Explanation:** You use the **enable** command to enter privileged EXEC mode.

**Step 4 – Enter the help command.**
   **Task:** Enter the help command by typing **?** at the router prompt.
   **Explanation:** The router responds with all commands available in privileged mode.

   2.
      a. What is the significance of entering **?** at the router prompt? _____
      b. Does the **clear** command appear as an option? _____

**Step 5 – Clear the ARP table.**
   **Task:** Enter the **clear arp** command at the router prompt.
   **Explanation:** The router will clear the ARP table.

**Step 6 – Show the ARP table.**
   **Task:** Enter the **show arp** command at the router prompt.
   **Explanation:** The router will respond with the ARP table.

   3. Are there any entries in the ARP table? _____

   4. Looking at the IP address of the ARP entries, what are the entries for? _____

# Cisco Labs – Semester 2 – Router Configuration
## *LAB 9.4.2.1 – SHOW ARP AND CLEAR ARP – WORKSHEET*

### Step 7 – Generate network traffic.
**Task:** Ping all interfaces on the network.
**Explanation:** This will generate network traffic between routers.

### Step 8 – Show the ARP table.
**Task:** Enter the **show arp** command at the router prompt.
**Explanation:** The router will respond with the ARP table.

5.  Are there any new entries in the ARP table? _____

### Step 9 – Generate network traffic.
**Task:** Open an MS-DOS command prompt (select Start/Programs/MS-DOS Command Prompt). Ping all the workstations on the lab network. **Note:** You will have to make sure that all workstations have proper IP addressing for the network they are connected to and a default gateway.
**Explanation:** This will generate network traffic from workstation to workstation.

### Step 10 – Show the ARP table.
**Task:** Enter the **show arp** command at the router prompt.
**Explanation:** The router will respond with the ARP table.

6.  Are there any new entries in the ARP table? _____

7.  Explain why there were no new entries in Step 8 but there were in Step 10.

### Step 11 – Exit the router.

# Cisco Labs – Semester 2 – Router Configuration
## *LAB 9.4.2.1 – SHOW ARP AND CLEAR ARP – ANSWERS*

1. What three important pieces of information are displayed? **IP address, MAC address, and what router interface this address pair lives out of.**

2.
   a. What is the significance of entering **?** at the router prompt? **The ? will invoke the help facility.**
   b. Does the **clear** command appear as an option? **Yes**

3. Are there any entries in the ARP table? **Yes**

4. Looking at the IP address of the ARP entries, what are the entries for? **The Ethernet interfaces on this router**

## Results of show arp Command (output generated by a Cisco 2514 router)

| lab-b#show arp | | | | | |
|---|---|---|---|---|---|
| Protocol | Address | Age (min) | Hardware Address | Type | Interface |
| Internet | 219.17..100.1 | --- | 0000.0c3b.f3a6 | ARPA | Ethernet0 |
| Internet | 205.7.5.1 | --- | 0000.0c3b.f3a7 | ARPA | Ethernet1 |

5. Are there any new entries in the ARP table? **No**

6. Are there any new entries in the ARP table? **Yes. The last entry is a workstation on the 219.117.100.0 network.**

## Results of show arp Command (answers will vary)

| lab-b#show arp | | | | | |
|---|---|---|---|---|---|
| Protocol | Address | Age (min) | Hardware Address | Type | Interface |
| Internet | 219.17.100.1 | --- | 0000.0c3b.f3a6 | ARPA | Ethernet0 |
| Internet | 219.17.100.2 | 03 | 00a0.cc26.e3e3 | ARPA | Ethernet0 |

7. Explain why there were no new entries in Step 8 but there were in Step 10. **In Step 10 you used a Windows 9x workstation to ping across the router. The router will maintain an ARP entry only for its own Ethernet networks. In Step 8, when you pinged to the other routers, there were no new entries, because you were using serial interfaces to ping from router to router, and serial interfaces do not appear in ARP cache.**

# Cisco Labs – Semester 2 – Router Configuration
## *LAB 9.5.2.1 – ARP CHALLENGE – OVERVIEW*
### *(Estimated time: 30 minutes)*

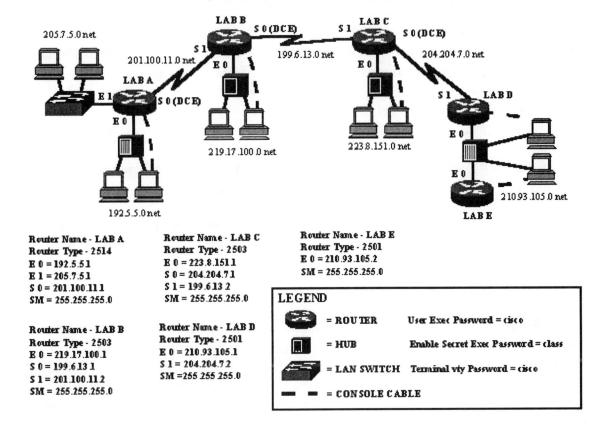

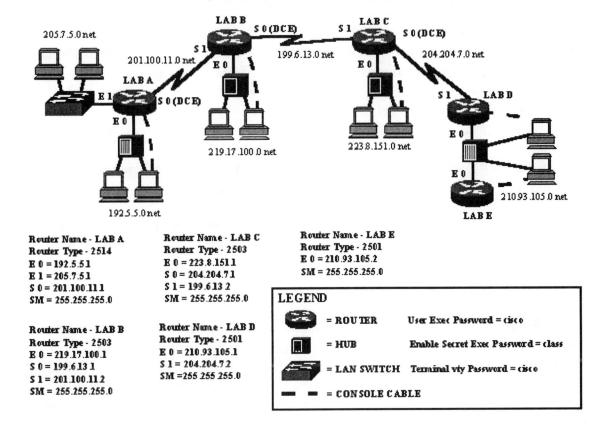

**Router Name - LAB A**
**Router Type - 2514**
E 0 = 192.5.5.1
E 1 = 205.7.5.1
S 0 = 201.100.11.1
SM = 255.255.255.0

**Router Name - LAB C**
**Router Type - 2503**
E 0 = 223.8.151.1
S 0 = 204.204.7.1
S 1 = 199.6.13.2
SM = 255.255.255.0

**Router Name - LAB E**
**Router Type - 2501**
E 0 = 210.93.105.2
SM = 255.255.255.0

**Router Name - LAB B**
**Router Type - 2503**
E 0 = 219.17.100.1
S 0 = 199.6.13.1
S 1 = 201.100.11.2
SM = 255.255.255.0

**Router Name - LAB D**
**Router Type - 2501**
E 0 = 210.93.105.1
S 1 = 204.204.7.2
SM = 255.255.255.0

**LEGEND**

= ROUTER        User Exec Password = cisco

= HUB           Enable Secret Exec Password = class

= LAN SWITCH    Terminal vty Password = cisco

= CONSOLE CABLE

## Objective:
- Practice working with ARP tables

## Background:
You and your group have been assigned to help a system administrator of a network for XYZ Company. The system administrator of this network would like to know the MAC addresses of each of the Ethernet interfaces on the routers.

## Tools / Preparation:
Prior to starting this lab you will need to have the equipment for the standard five-router lab available (routers, hubs, switch, cables, etc.). The routers should be preconfigured by the instructor or lab assistant with the correct IP interface settings, etc. The workstations should also be preconfigured to have the correct IP address settings prior to starting the lab. The routers, hubs, and workstations should be labeled.

This lab assumes that you have completed the prior lab 2.2.10.1 and that the lab equipment (routers, hub, workstations, etc.) is assembled and connected in the standard lab topology. Work in teams of three or more. Before beginning this lab, you should review Chapter 6 in the *Cisco Networking Academy Program: First-Year Companion Guide* and semester 2 on-line Chapter 9.

# Cisco Labs – Semester 2 – Router Configuration
## *LAB 9.5.2.1 – ARP CHALLENGE – OVERVIEW*

**The following resources will be required:**

- 5 PC workstations (minimum) with Windows operating system and HyperTerminal installed
- 5 Cisco routers (model 1600 series or 2500 series with IOS 11.2 or later)
- 4 Ethernet hubs (10Base-T with 4 to 8 ports)
- 1 Ethernet switch (Cisco Catalyst 1900 or comparable)
- 5 serial console cables to connect the workstation to the router console port (with RJ45 to DB9 converters)
- 3 sets of V.35 WAN serial cables (DTE male/ DCE female) to connect from router to router
- CAT5 Ethernet cables wired straight through to connect routers and workstations to hubs and switches
- AUI (DB15) to RJ45 Ethernet transceivers (the quantity depends on the number of routers with AUI ports) to convert router AUI interfaces to 10Base-T RJ45

## Web Site Resources:

- **Routing basics** – http://www.cisco.com/univercd/cc/td/doc/cisintwk/ito_doc/routing.htm
- **General information on routers** – http://www.cisco.com/univercd/cc/td/doc/pcat/#2
- **2500 series routers** – http://www.cisco.com/warp/public/cc/cisco/mkt/access/2500/index.shtml
- **1600 series routers** – http://www.cisco.com/warp/public/cc/cisco/mkt/access/1600/index.shtml
- **Terms and acronyms** – http://www.cisco.com/univercd/cc/td/doc/cisintwk/ita/index.htm
- **IP routing protocol IOS command summary** – http://www.cisco.com/univercd/cc/td/doc/product/software/ios120/12cgcr/rbkixol.htm

## Notes:

_____

_____

_____

_____

_____

_____

_____

_____

_____

_____

_____

_____

_____

# Cisco Labs – Semester 2 – Router Configuration
## *LAB 9.5.2.1 – ARP CHALLENGE – WORKSHEET*

**Step 1 – Find the MAC address for all Ethernet interfaces.**

Verify that the routers and workstations are set up according to the standard five-router lab diagram. When you are done with this, view the ARP tables and find out the MAC address of all surrounding routers. Be sure to record the ARP tables of the other group's routers. This will allow you to construct a diagram of all the routers and their IPs with MAC addresses. You might want to write down a quick step-by-step example of how you found the MAC address to one of the routers.

1. List the following MAC addresses for the routers:

   Lab-A E0 _____

   Lab-A E1 _____

   Lab-B E0 _____

   Lab-C E0 _____

   Lab-D E0 _____

   Lab-E E0 _____

**Step 2 – Generate network traffic.**

From the workstations, ping another workstation on a different router. Then, from the router, issue the **show arp** command from a privileged prompt.

2. List the MAC addresses for the workstations that are connected to the router.

   _____

# Cisco Labs – Semester 2 – Router Configuration
## *LAB 9.5.2.1 – ARP CHALLENGE – ANSWERS*

Your answers will vary because the MAC address is "burned into the NIC" and is not configurable. Here is an example of the **show arp** command. The last entry is a workstation.

### Results of show arp Command (output generated by a Cisco 2514 router)

| LAB-A#show arp | | | | | |
|---|---|---|---|---|---|
| Protocol | Address | Age(min) | Hardware Address | Type | Interface |
| Internet | 192.5.5.1 | --- | 0000.0c3b.f3a6 | ARPA | Ethernet0 |
| Internet | 205.7.5.1 | --- | 0000.0c3b.f3a7 | ARPA | Ethernet1 |
| Internet | 192.5.5.2 | 03 | 00a0.cc26.e3e3 | ARPA | Ethernet0 |

# Cisco Labs – Semester 2 – Router Configuration
## *LAB 9.6.1.1 – NETWORK TROUBLESHOOTING CHALLENGE – OVERVIEW*
### *(Estimated time: 45 minutes)*

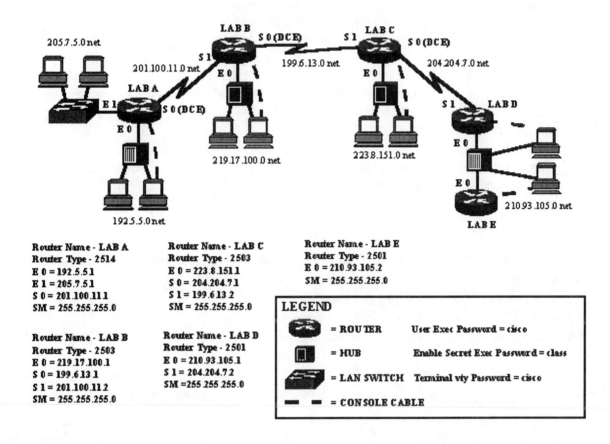

## Objectives:

- Use IOS informational and troubleshooting commands to identify network problems
- Investigate and verify physical network connections
- Demonstrate your ability to work as a team to troubleshoot network problems

## Background:

With this lab, you will use your knowledge of the router lab setup and various information such as **show version**, **show running-config**, **show interface**, and **show ip route**, as well as troubleshooting commands such as **ping**, **telnet**, and **traceroute**. You will need to group into two teams (team A and team B) with three to five members on each team. Team A will select a problem from the Problem List to introduce into the network. Team B will then have to troubleshoot the network, find the problem, and correct it.

Your goal will be to ping from a workstation on LAN A, which router Lab-A connects to, to a workstation on LAN E, which router Lab-E connects to. After you have documented the problem and your team's solution on the worksheet, Team B will introduce a problem for Team A to troubleshoot and correct. The resources you have available are the standard lab diagram shown here and the help commands at the Command-Line Interface (CLI). You may use the console connections at all five routers.

**Cisco Labs – Semester 2 – Router Configuration**
## *LAB 9.6.1.1 – NETWORK TROUBLESHOOTING CHALLENGE – OVERVIEW*

## Tools / Preparation:

Prior to starting this lab you will need to have the equipment for the standard five-router lab available (routers, hubs, switch, cables, and so on). The routers should be preconfigured by the instructor or lab assistant with the correct IP interface settings, and so on. The workstations should also be preconfigured to have the correct IP address settings prior to starting the lab. The routers, hubs, and workstations should be labeled. The team that introduces the problem into the lab setup should discuss it with the lab assistant or instructor, who can provide coaching and assistance to the team trying to find the problem.

This lab assumes that you have completed the prior lab 2.2.10.1 and that the lab equipment (routers, hub, workstations, and so on) are assembled and connected in the standard lab topology. Work in teams of three to five.

## Resources Required:

- 5 PC workstations (minimum) with Windows operating system and HyperTerminal installed
- 5 Cisco routers (model 1600 series or 2500 series with IOS 11.2 or later)
- 4 Ethernet hubs (10Base-T with 4 to 8 ports)
- 1 Ethernet switch (Cisco Catalyst 1900 or comparable)
- 5 serial console cables to connect the workstation to the router console port (with RJ45 to DB9 converters)
- 3 sets of V.35 WAN serial cables (DTE male/ DCE female) to connect from router to router
- CAT5 Ethernet cables wired straight through to connect routers and workstations to hubs and switches
- AUI (DB15) to RJ45 Ethernet transceivers (the quantity depends on the number of routers with AUI ports) to convert router AUI interfaces to 10Base-T RJ45

## Web Site Resources:

- **Routing basics** – http://www.cisco.com/univercd/cc/td/doc/cisintwk/ito_doc/routing.htm
- **General information on routers** – http://www.cisco.com/univercd/cc/td/doc/pcat/#2
- **2500 series routers** – http://www.cisco.com/warp/public/cc/cisco/mkt/access/2500/index.shtml
- **1600 series routers** – http://www.cisco.com/warp/public/cc/cisco/mkt/access/1600/index.shtml
- **Terms and acronyms** – http://www.cisco.com/univercd/cc/td/doc/cisintwk/ita/index.htm
- **IP routing protocol IOS command summary** –
  http://www.cisco.com/univercd/cc/td/doc/product/software/ios120/12cgcr/rbkixol.htm

## Notes: _____

_____
_____
_____
_____

**Cisco Labs – Semester 2 – Router Configuration**
## *LAB 9.6.1.1 – NETWORK TROUBLESHOOTING CHALLENGE – WORKSHEET*

**Step 1 – The first team introduces a problem.**
Chose two from the following ten possible problems to introduce into the network, and write down which problems you introduced and where they were introduced. Discuss these with the instructor or lab assistant so they can provide assistance if necessary.

1. Change the TCP/IP configuration on a workstation (IP address, default gateway, subnet mask).

2. Change the IP address or subnet mask of an interface on one of the routers.

3. Take down an interface on a router.

4. Remove the clocking signal on one of the DCE interfaces.

5. Add an incorrect static route to misdirect traffic.

6. Remove the RIP or IGRP routing protocol from a router.

7. Change the IP host table to remove a host or change an IP address.

8. Disconnect an Ethernet cable from a hub or router.

9. Turn off one of the routers.

10. Turn off one of the hubs.

**Step 2 – The second team troubleshoots and fixes the problem.**

1. Try to telnet from a workstation on the router Lab-A network to router Lab-E using the router's name. Always remember when troubleshooting to start with router-to-router connections and troubleshoot systematically from router Lab-A to router Lab-E. Then begin testing from workstations connected to the router Lab-A LAN to other routers. Then test from workstation to workstation. Document your results.

   _____

   _____

2. Document how and what you had to change to fix the two problems introduced.
   A. _____
   B. _____

**Cisco Labs – Semester 2 – Router Configuration**
## *LAB 9.6.1.1 – NETWORK TROUBLESHOOTING CHALLENGE – WORKSHEET*

3. Fill in the checklist to make sure you have connectivity to all nodes in the network.
   - Ping all routers' interfaces.
   - Ping all workstations.
   - Ping from one workstation to all other workstations.
   - Trace route from router Lab-A to router Lab-E.
   - Trace route from one workstation to all other workstations.
   - Telnet to all other routers.

**Step 3 – Repeat the lab with the second team introducing two of the networking problems and the first team troubleshooting the network.**

**Note: Answers will vary greatly, depending on which combination of problems are introduced. The most important thing is to write down which problems were introduced and where.**

# Cisco Labs – Semester 2 – Router Configuration
## *LAB 10.3.1.1 – SEMESTER 2 TOPOLOGY CHALLENGE – OVERVIEW*
### *(Estimated time: 30 minutes)*

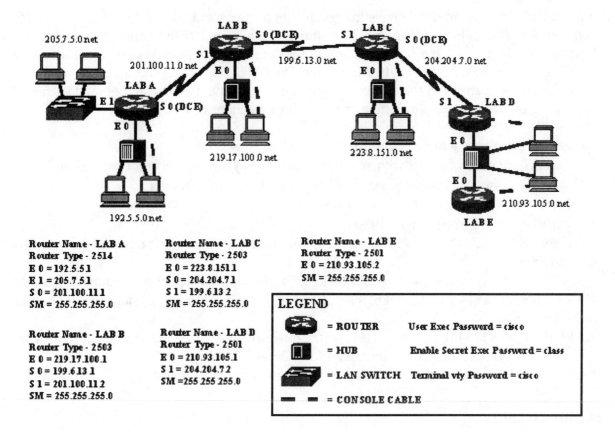

**Router Name - LAB A**
**Router Type - 2514**
E 0 = 192.5.5.1
E 1 = 205.7.5.1
S 0 = 201.100.11.1
SM = 255.255.255.0

**Router Name - LAB C**
**Router Type - 2503**
E 0 = 223.8.151.1
S 0 = 204.204.7.1
S 1 = 199.6.13.2
SM = 255.255.255.0

**Router Name - LAB E**
**Router Type - 2501**
E 0 = 210.93.105.2
SM = 255.255.255.0

**Router Name - LAB B**
**Router Type - 2503**
E 0 = 219.17.100.1
S 0 = 199.6.13.1
S 1 = 201.100.11.2
SM = 255.255.255.0

**Router Name - LAB D**
**Router Type - 2501**
E 0 = 210.93.105.1
S 1 = 204.204.7.2
SM =255.255.255.0

**LEGEND**

= ROUTER     User Exec Password = cisco

= HUB     Enable Secret Exec Password = class

= LAN SWITCH     Terminal vty Password = cisco

= CONSOLE CABLE

## Objectives:
- Design an IP addressing scheme based on a given network topology
- Use multiple Class C network addresses for LANs and WANs
- Assign IP addresses to router interfaces
- Diagram the network using ConfigMaker

## Background:
You and your group members have just received your Cisco certification. Your first job is to work with other group members in designing a topology and IP addressing scheme. It will be a five-router topology similar the standard five-router lab diagram shown above, but with a few changes. Refer to the modified five-router lab diagram shown in the worksheet. You must come up with a proper IP addressing scheme using multiple Class C addresses that are different from those of the standard lab setup. You will then use ConfigMaker to do your own diagram of the network. You may do this lab using the worksheets or work with the actual lab equipment if it is available.

# LAB 10.3.1.1 – SEMESTER 2 TOPOLOGY CHALLENGE – OVERVIEW

## Tools / Preparation:

Prior to starting this lab you should have the equipment for the standard five-router lab available (routers, hubs, switch, cables, and so on). Since this is a challenge lab, the routers may or may not be configured with IP interface settings, and so on. If they are, you will need to change the IP addresses to be different from those of the standard lab setup. The IP address configuration of the workstations will also need to be changed. If the actual lab equipment is not available to configure, design the network using the worksheets provided in this lab. Work in teams of five or more.

**The following resources will be required:**
- 5 PC workstations (minimum) with Windows operating system and HyperTerminal installed
- 5 Cisco routers (model 1600 series or 2500 series with IOS 11.2 or later)
- 4 Ethernet hubs (10Base-T with 4 to 8 ports)
- 1 Ethernet switch (Cisco Catalyst 1900 or comparable)
- 5 serial console cables to connect the workstation to the router console port (with RJ45 to DB9 converters)
- 4 sets of V.35 WAN serial cables (DTE male/ DCE female) to connect from router to router
- CAT5 Ethernet cables wired straight through to connect routers and workstations to hubs and switches
- AUI (DB15) to RJ45 Ethernet transceivers (the quantity depends on the number of routers with AUI ports) to convert router AUI interfaces to 10Base-T RJ45
- Cisco ConfigMaker software version 2.3 or later (see below for the web site)

## Web Site Resources:
- **Routing basics** – http://www.cisco.com/univercd/cc/td/doc/cisintwk/ito_doc/routing.htm
- **General information on routers** – http://www.cisco.com/univercd/cc/td/doc/pcat/#2
- **2500 series routers** – http://www.cisco.com/warp/public/cc/cisco/mkt/access/2500/index.shtml
- **1600 series routers** – http://www.cisco.com/warp/public/cc/cisco/mkt/access/1600/index.shtml
- **Terms and acronyms** – http://www.cisco.com/univercd/cc/td/doc/cisintwk/ita/index.htm
- **IP routing protocol IOS command summary** –
  http://www.cisco.com/univercd/cc/td/doc/product/software/ios120/12cgcr/rbkixol.htm
- **Cisco ConfigMaker information and download** –
  http://www.cisco.com/warp/public/cc/cisco/mkt/enm/config/index.shtml

## Notes:

_____

_____

_____

# Cisco Labs – Semester 2 – Router Configuration
## *LAB 10.3.1.1 – SEMESTER 2 TOPOLOGY CHALLENGE – WORKSHEET*

**Step 1 – Review the physical connections on the standard lab setup.**
Review the standard Semester 2 lab diagram in the overview section of this lab, and check all physical devices, cables, and connections if the physical lab setup is available.

**Step 2 – Develop an IP addressing scheme.**
With the standard five-router lab configuration shown in the overview section, there are eight networks. Five of these are Ethernet local-area networks (LANs), and three of them are serial wide-area networks (WANs). Review the modified setup of the lab diagrammed below. Using multiple Class C addresses similar to the existing standard lab, select addresses and document the IP addressing scheme by indicating where you will put each of the Class C addresses. Answer the following questions to assist your team in planning the network IP address scheme.

1. How many LANs are there? _____

2. How many WANs are there? _____

3. How many unique Class C network addresses will you need? _____

4. How many devices are there? _____

5. How many device interfaces will require IP addresses? _____

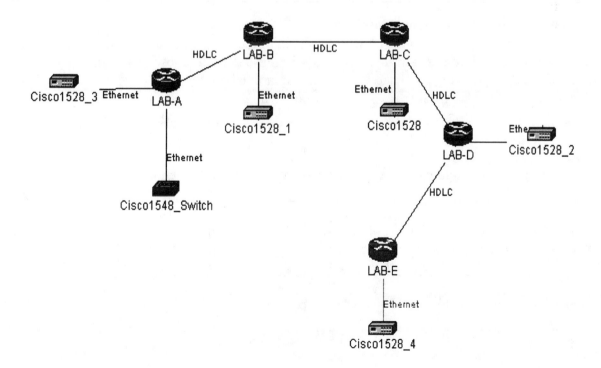

**Cisco Labs – Semester 2 – Router Configuration**
## *LAB 10.3.1.1 – SEMESTER 2 TOPOLOGY CHALLENGE –*
## *WORKSHEET*

**Step 3 – Assign IP addresses to each device interface.**
Use the table below to identify each router interface that will require an IP address. Switches do not require an IP address, but you may assign one if you want to. Hubs will not have an IP address.

| Device Name / Model | Interface | IP Address | Subnet Mask | Default Gateway |
|---|---|---|---|---|
|  |  |  |  |  |
|  |  |  |  |  |
|  |  |  |  |  |
|  |  |  |  |  |
|  |  |  |  |  |
|  |  |  |  |  |
|  |  |  |  |  |
|  |  |  |  |  |
|  |  |  |  |  |
|  |  |  |  |  |
|  |  |  |  |  |
|  |  |  |  |  |
|  |  |  |  |  |
|  |  |  |  |  |

6. Which interfaces will require clock rate to be set? _____

**Step 4 – Diagram the network using ConfigMaker.**
Use Cisco ConfigMaker to re-create the network diagram in the worksheet and add all configuration information, such as IP addresses and subnet masks. ConfigMaker will allow you to enter all interface IP addresses and help you create a finished diagram. Choose your own device names. You should be familiar with ConfigMaker if you have completed lab 6.5.2.2.

## Reflection:
What did you learn from designing a topology with such a large group of people?
_____
_____
In what router mode did you spend most of your time? _____
Could you have done it any other way? If so, how? _____
_____
_____
When doing this lab, how could a TFTP server have been useful? _____
_____

# Cisco Labs – Semester 2 – Router Configuration
## _LAB 10.3.1.1 – SEMESTER 2 TOPOLOGY CHALLENGE – ANSWERS_

1. How many LANs are there? **6**

2. How many WANs are there? **4**

3. How many unique Class C network addresses will you need? **10**

4. How many devices are there? **11 (5 routers and 6 switches)**

5. How many device interfaces will require IP addresses? **14 (8 WAN interfaces and 6 LAN)**

6. Which interfaces will require clock rate to be set? **S0 on Lab-A, Lab-B, Lab-C, and Lab-D**

**Step 4 – Diagram the network using ConfigMaker.**

**Answers will vary, but the diagram should look similar to the specified topology in this lab and have different Class C network numbers and IP addresses than the standard five-router lab topology. Device models such as switches and hubs may vary, but be sure to select router model numbers that can support the number and type of connections required.**

# Cisco Labs – Semester 2 – Router Configuration
## *LAB 10.4.1.1 – IP ADDRESSING AND SUBNETS CHALLENGE – OVERVIEW*
### *(Estimated time: 30 minutes)*

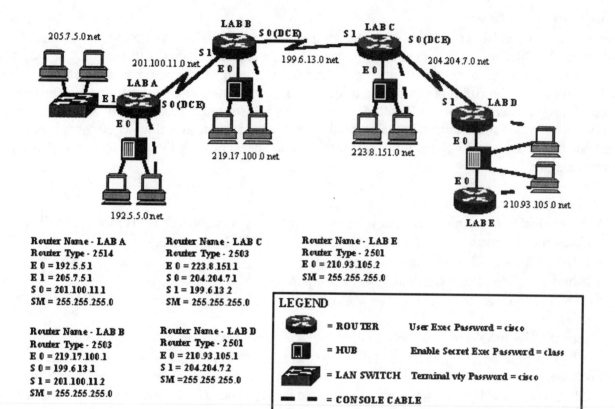

**Router Name - LAB A**
Router Type - 2514
E 0 = 192.5.5.1
E 1 = 205.7.5.1
S 0 = 201.100.11.1
SM = 255.255.255.0

**Router Name - LAB C**
Router Type - 2503
E 0 = 223.8.151.1
S 0 = 204.204.7.1
S 1 = 199.6.13.2
SM = 255.255.255.0

**Router Name - LAB E**
Router Type - 2501
E 0 = 210.93.105.2
SM = 255.255.255.0

**Router Name - LAB B**
Router Type - 2503
E 0 = 219.17.100.1
S 0 = 199.6.13.1
S 1 = 201.100.11.2
SM = 255.255.255.0

**Router Name - LAB D**
Router Type - 2501
E 0 = 210.93.105.1
S 1 = 204.204.7.2
SM = 255.255.255.0

**LEGEND**

= ROUTER    User Exec Password = cisco

= HUB    Enable Secret Exec Password = class

= LAN SWITCH    Terminal vty Password = cisco

= CONSOLE CABLE

## Objectives:
- Design and implement a five-router network topology
- Develop an IP addressing scheme based on the topology
- Use a single Class C network address with subnets for LANs and WANs
- Assign IP addresses to router interfaces and hosts
- Diagram the network using ConfigMaker

## Background:
In this lab you will work with other group members to design a five-router network topology and an IP addressing scheme. You must come up with a proper IP addressing scheme using a single Class C network address (204.204.7.0) and multiple subnets. You will then use ConfigMaker to diagram the network you have designed. You have creative freedom in designing your network.

# Cisco Labs – Semester 2 – Router Configuration
## *LAB 10.4.1.1 – IP ADDRESSING AND SUBNETS CHALLENGE – OVERVIEW*

## Tools / Preparation:

Prior to starting this lab, you should have the equipment for the standard five-router lab available (routers, hubs, switch, cables, and so on). Because this is a challenge lab, the routers may or may not be preconfigured with the correct IP interface settings, and so on. If they are, you will need to change the IP addresses to be different from those of the standard lab setup. The workstations may also be preconfigured to have the correct IP address settings prior to starting the lab. The IP addressing configuration of the workstations will also need to be changed. If the actual lab equipment is not available to configure, design the network using the worksheets provided in this lab. Work in teams of five or more.

### The following resources will be required:

- 5 PC workstations (minimum) with Windows operating system and HyperTerminal installed
- 5 Cisco routers (model 1600 series or 2500 series with IOS 11.2 or later)
- 4 Ethernet hubs (10Base-T with 4 to 8 ports)
- 1 Ethernet switch (Cisco Catalyst 1900 or comparable)
- 5 serial console cables to connect the workstation to the router console port (with RJ45 to DB9 converters)
- 4 sets of V.35 WAN serial cables (DTE male/ DCE female) to connect from router to router
- CAT5 Ethernet cables wired straight through to connect routers and workstations to hubs and switches
- AUI (DB15) to RJ45 Ethernet transceivers (the quantity depends on the number of routers with AUI ports) to convert router AUI interfaces to 10Base-T RJ45

## Web Site Resources:

- **Routing basics** – http://www.cisco.com/univercd/cc/td/doc/cisintwk/ito_doc/routing.htm
- **General information on routers** – http://www.cisco.com/univercd/cc/td/doc/pcat/#2
- **2500 series routers** – http://www.cisco.com/warp/public/cc/cisco/mkt/access/2500/index.shtml
- **1600 series routers** – http://www.cisco.com/warp/public/cc/cisco/mkt/access/1600/index.shtml
- **Terms and acronyms** – http://www.cisco.com/univercd/cc/td/doc/cisintwk/ita/index.htm
- **IP routing protocol IOS command summary** – http://www.cisco.com/univercd/cc/td/doc/product/software/ios120/12cgcr/rbkixol.htm
- **Cisco ConfigMaker information and download** – http://www.cisco.com/warp/public/cc/cisco/mkt/enm/config/index.shtml

## Notes:

_____

_____

_____

_____

**Cisco Labs – Semester 2 – Router Configuration**
# *LAB 10.4.1.1 – IP ADDRESSING AND SUBNETS CHALLENGE – WORKSHEET*

**Step 1 – Design the physical topology of the network.**
You should have at least five routers in different geographical locations. You should have at least one Ethernet LAN off of each router. Sketch out the topology as you go. Answer the following questions to assist in planning:

1. How many routers will you have? _____

2. Where will the routers be located? _____

3. How many switches will you have? _____

**Step 2 – Develop an IP addressing scheme.**
Review your topology sketch from Step 1. Using a single Class C address of 204.204.7.0, create a subnetwork design for your topology. Document your scheme by indicating where you will put each of the subnets. Answer the following questions to assist in planning:

4. How many LANs are there? _____

5. How many WANs are there? _____

6. How many unique subnets will you need? _____

7. How many hosts per subnet (LAN and WAN) will you have? _____

8. How many IP addresses (hosts and router interfaces) will be required? _____

9. What is your Class C network address? _____

10. How many bits will you borrow from the host portion of the network address? _____

11. What will your subnet mask be? _____

12. How many total useable subnets will this allow for? _____

13. How many hosts per subnet will this allow for? _____

# Cisco Labs – Semester 2 – Router Configuration
## *LAB 10.4.1.1 – IP ADDRESSING AND SUBNETS CHALLENGE – WORKSHEET*

**Step 3 – Assign IP addresses to each device interface.**

Using the following table, assign an IP address to each device interface or range of devices (hosts) that will require an IP address. Switches do not require an IP address, but you may assign one if you want to. Hubs will not have an IP address. (Answers will vary.)

| Device Name / Model | Interface | IP Address | Subnet Mask | Default Gateway |
|---|---|---|---|---|
| | | | | |
| | | | | |
| | | | | |
| | | | | |
| | | | | |
| | | | | |
| | | | | |
| | | | | |
| | | | | |
| | | | | |
| | | | | |
| | | | | |
| | | | | |
| | | | | |

14. Which interfaces will require clock rate to be set? _____

**Step 4 – Diagram the network using ConfigMaker.**

Use Cisco ConfigMaker to create a network diagram, and add all configuration information, such as IP addresses and subnet masks. ConfigMaker will allow you to enter all interface IP addresses and help you create a finished diagram. You should be familiar with ConfigMaker if you have completed lab 6.5.2.2. Use the web site listed in the overview section to download ConfigMaker if you do not have it.

**Reflection:**

_____

_____

_____

_____

_____

_____

Answers will vary widely. Students should ping and then telnet across the network to check if connections and configurations are properly implemented.

**Cisco Labs – Semester 2 – Router Configuration**
# *LAB 10.4.1.1 – IP ADDRESSING AND SUBNETS CHALLENGE – ANSWERS*

Answers are based on the standard five-router lab network topology. Your answers should be different.

1. How many routers will you have? **5**

2. Where will the routers be located? **Should be at least 4 different geographical locations**

3. How many switches will you have? **5**

4. How many LANs are there? **5**

5. How many WANs are there? **3**

6. How many unique subnets will you need? **8**

7. How many hosts per subnet (LAN and WAN) will you have? **2**

8. How many IP addresses (hosts and router interfaces) will be required? **22 (10 workstations and 12 router interfaces)**

9. What is your Class C network address? **204.204.7.0**

10. How many bits will you borrow from the host portion of the network address? **4**

11. What will your subnet mask be? **255.255.255.240**

12. How many total useable subnets will this allow for? $\mathbf{2^4 = 16 - 2 = 14}$

13. How many hosts per subnet will this allow for? $\mathbf{2^4 = 16 - 2 = 14}$

14. Which interfaces will require clock rate to be set? **S0 on Lab-A, Lab-B, and Lab-C**

# Cisco Labs – Semester 2 – Router Configuration
## *LAB 12.5.2.1 – STATIC ROUTES – OVERVIEW*
### *(Estimated time: 30 minutes)*

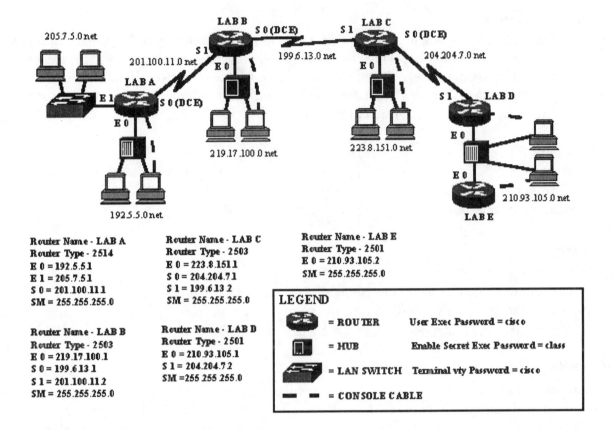

**Router Name - LAB A**
Router Type - 2514
E 0 = 192.5.5.1
E 1 = 205.7.5.1
S 0 = 201.100.11.1
SM = 255.255.255.0

**Router Name - LAB B**
Router Type - 2503
E 0 = 219.17.100.1
S 0 = 199.6.13.1
S 1 = 201.100.11.2
SM = 255.255.255.0

**Router Name - LAB C**
Router Type - 2503
E 0 = 223.8.151.1
S 0 = 204.204.7.1
S 1 = 199.6.13.2
SM = 255.255.255.0

**Router Name - LAB D**
Router Type - 2501
E 0 = 210.93.105.1
S 1 = 204.204.7.2
SM = 255.255.255.0

**Router Name - LAB E**
Router Type - 2501
E 0 = 210.93.105.2
SM = 255.255.255.0

**LEGEND**

| | | |
|---|---|---|
| = ROUTER | User Exec Password = cisco |
| = HUB | Enable Secret Exec Password = class |
| = LAN SWITCH | Terminal vty Password = cisco |
| = CONSOLE CABLE | |

## Objectives:
- Configure a static route between direct neighboring routers using the **ip route** command
- Copy the running configuration to the startup configuration

## Background:
In this lab you will configure a static route between neighboring routers. Static routes are routes that cause packets moving between a source and a destination to take a specified path. They are typically defined manually by a network administrator. Routing updates are not sent on a link if it is only defined by a static route, thereby conserving bandwidth. Another application for a static route is security since dynamic routing tends to reveal everything known about a network. Static routes are sometimes used for remote sites and for testing of a particular link or series of routers in your internetwork.

# Cisco Labs – Semester 2 – Router Configuration
## *LAB 12.5.2.1 – STATIC ROUTES – OVERVIEW*

## Tools / Preparation:

Prior to starting the lab you will need to connect a PC workstation with HyperTerminal to a router using the router's console interface with a roll-over cable. This lab should be done at the router console station. You should review Chapter 18 in the *Cisco Networking Academy Program: First-Year Companion Guide* and review semester 2 on-line curriculum Chapter 12 prior to starting this lab. Work individually or in teams. Be familiar with the following commands:

- **enable**
- **show arp**
- **show startup-config**
- **configure terminal**

- **IP route**
- **show running-config**
- **copy**
- **ping**

## Resources Required:

- PC with monitor, keyboard, mouse, and power cords
- Windows operating system (Windows 95, 98, NT, or 2000) installed on PC
- HyperTerminal program configured for router console connection
- PC connected to the router console port with a roll-over cable

## Web Site Resources:

- **Routing basics** – http://www.cisco.com/univercd/cc/td/doc/cisintwk/ito_doc/routing.htm
- **General information on routers** – http://www.cisco.com/univercd/cc/td/doc/pcat/#2
- **2500 series routers** – http://www.cisco.com/warp/public/cc/cisco/mkt/access/2500/index.shtml
- **1600 series routers** – http://www.cisco.com/warp/public/cc/cisco/mkt/access/1600/index.shtml
- **Terms and acronyms** – http://www.cisco.com/univercd/cc/td/doc/cisintwk/ita/index.htm
- **IP routing protocol IOS command summary** –
  http://www.cisco.com/univercd/cc/td/doc/product/software/ios120/12cgcr/rbkixol.htm

## Notes:

_____

_____

_____

_____

_____

_____

# Cisco Labs – Semester 2 – Router Configuration
## *LAB 12.5.2.1 – STATIC ROUTES – WORKSHEET*

**Step 1 – Log on to the router.**
> **Explanation:** Connect to the router and log in. Enter the password **cisco** if prompted.

**Step 2 – Test layer 3 (network) connectivity.**
> **Task:** Enter **ping** *xxx.xxx.xxx.xxx*.
> **Explanation:** *xxx.xxx.xxx.xxx* is the IP address of one of your neighboring routers that is directly connected to you.

1. Did the router's interface respond with a successful ping? _____

_____

**Step 3 – Enter privileged mode.**
> **Task:**
> a. Enter **enable** at the command prompt.
> b. Enter the password **class**.
> **Explanation:** You use the **enable** command to enter privileged EXEC mode.

**Step 4 – Show the backup configuration file.**
> **Task:** Enter **show startup-config** (abbreviated **show start**) at the router prompt.
> **Explanation:** The router will display information on the backup configuration file stored in NVRAM.

2. Are there any routing protocols or static routes defined? _____

**Step 5 – Enter global configuration mode.**
> **Task:** Enter **configure terminal** (abbreviated **config t**) at the router prompt.
> **Explanation:** To configure the router, you must enter global configuration mode. Notice how the router prompt has changed after this command.

3. What does the router prompt look like? _____

**Step 6 – Enter the help facility.**
> **Task:** Enter the **IP route ?** command at the router prompt.
> **Explanation:** The router will respond with the description available for **IP route**.

4. What was the router's response? _____

**Step 7 – Enter the help facility.**
> **Task:** Enter **IP route** *xxx.xxx.xxx.xxx* **?** at the router prompt.
> **Explanation:** *xxx.xxx.xxx.xxx* is the network address you want a static route for.

5. What was the router's response? _____

## Cisco Labs – Semester 2 – Router Configuration
### *LAB 12.5.2.1 – STATIC ROUTES – WORKSHEET*

**Step 8 – Enter the help facility.**
　　**Task:** Enter **ip route** *xxx.xxx.xxx.xxx* *yyy.yyy.yyy.yyy* at the router prompt.
　　**Explanation:** *xxx.xxx.xxx.xxx* is the network address of the destination network, and *yyy.yyy.yyy.yyy* is the subnet mask of the destination network.

　　6.　What was the router's response? _____

**Step 9 – Enter a static route.**
　　**Task:** Enter **IP route** *xxx.xxx.xxx.xxx* *yyy.yyy.yyy.yyy* *zzz.zzz.zzz.zzz* at the router prompt..
　　**Explanation:** *xxx.xxx.xxx.xxx* is the network address of the destination network, and *yyy.yyy.yyy.yyy* is the subnet mask of the destination network. *zzz.zzz.zzz.zzz* is the IP address of the direct neighbor interface.

**Step 10 – Exit the router's global configuration mode.**
　　**Task:** Enter **exit** at the router prompt.
　　**Explanation:** The router will exit global configuration mode.

　　7.　What does the router prompt look like? _____

**Step 11 – Show the running configuration.**
　　**Task:** Enter **show running-config** at the router prompt.
　　**Explanation:** The router will show the active configuration file.

　　8.　Was there an IP route with the static route you configured in the active configuration file?

　　_____

**Step 12 – Copy the active configuration to the backup configuration.**
　　**Task:** Enter **copy running-config startup-config** at the router prompt.
　　**Explanation:** This command will permanently write the configuration change to memory.

**Step 13 – Test the static route with the ping command.**
　　**Task:** Enter **ping** *xxx.xxx.xxx.xxx* at the router prompt.
　　**Explanation:** *xxx.xxx.xxx.xxx* is the neighboring router you set up a static route to.

　　9.　Was the neighboring router interface reachable?

**Step 14 – Exit the router.**

**Cisco Labs – Semester 2 – Router Configuration**
## *LAB 12.5.2.1 – STATIC ROUTES – ANSWERS*

1. Did the router's interface respond with a successful ping? **Yes**

2. Are there any routing protocol or static routes defined? **Yes – RIP (answers will vary)**

3. What does the router prompt look like? ***Router name*(config)#**

4. What was the router's response? **A.B.C.D** *destination_prefix*

5. What was the router's response? **A.B.C.D** *destination_prefix_mask*

6. What was the router's response?      **A.B.C.D** *forwarding router's address*
   **Ethernet  IEEE 802.3**
   **Null     *Null interface***
   **Serial   *Serial***

7. What does the router prompt look like? ***Router name*#**

8. Was there an IP route with the static route you configured in the active configuration file? **Yes**

9. Was the neighboring router interface reachable? **Yes**

# Cisco Labs – Semester 2 – Router Configuration
## *LAB 12.6.2.1 – RIP ROUTING – OVERVIEW*
### *(Estimated time: 45 minutes)*

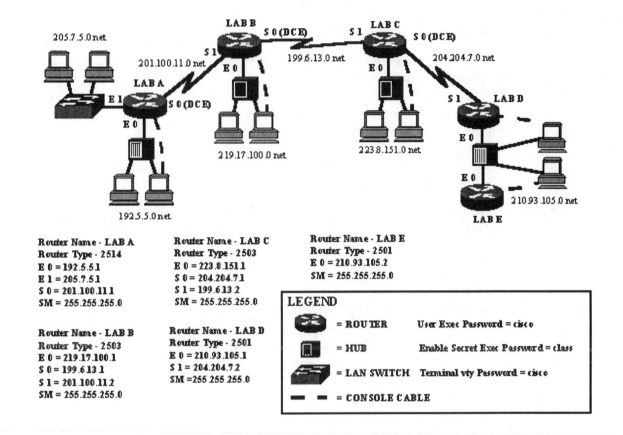

**Router Name - LAB A**
Router Type - 2514
E 0 = 192.5.5.1
E 1 = 205.7.5.1
S 0 = 201.100.11.1
SM = 255.255.255.0

**Router Name - LAB B**
Router Type - 2503
E 0 = 219.17.100.1
S 0 = 199.6.13.1
S 1 = 201.100.11.2
SM = 255.255.255.0

**Router Name - LAB C**
Router Type - 2503
E 0 = 223.8.151.1
S 0 = 204.204.7.1
S 1 = 199.6.13.2
SM = 255.255.255.0

**Router Name - LAB D**
Router Type - 2501
E 0 = 210.93.105.1
S 1 = 204.204.7.2
SM = 255.255.255.0

**Router Name - LAB E**
Router Type - 2501
E 0 = 210.93.105.2
SM = 255.255.255.0

**LEGEND**
= ROUTER   User Exec Password = cisco
= HUB   Enable Secret Exec Password = class
= LAN SWITCH   Terminal vty Password = cisco
= CONSOLE CABLE

## Objective:
- Configure RIP as your routing protocol

## Background:
In this lab you will configure RIP as the routing protocol. RIP is a distance-vector routing protocol. Hop count is used as the metric for path selection. It has a maximum allowable hop count of 15. RIP broadcasts routing updates consisting of its routing table to its neighbors every 30 seconds by default. RIP is a standard protocol that is appropriate for relatively small homogeneous networks.

# Cisco Labs – Semester 2 – Router Configuration
## *LAB 12.6.2.1 – RIP ROUTING – OVERVIEW*

## Tools / Preparation:

Prior to starting the lab, the instructor or lab assistant will have to log on to each router and delete all router RIP and static route entries from all the routers. You will need to connect a PC workstation with HyperTerminal to a router using the router's console interface with a roll-over cable. This lab should be done at the router console station. You should review Chapter 18 in the *Cisco Networking Academy Program: First-Year Companion Guide* and review semester 12 on-line curriculum Chapter 12 prior to starting this lab. Work individually or in teams. Be familiar with the following commands:

- **enable**
- **show IP route**
- **show startup-config**
- **configure terminal**
- **network**

- **show running-config**
- **copy**
- **show IP protocols**
- **router RIP**

## Resources Required:

- PC with monitor, keyboard, mouse, and power cords
- Windows operating system (Windows 95, 98, NT, or 2000) installed on PC
- HyperTerminal program configured for a router console connection
- PC connected to the router console port with a roll-over cable

## Web Site Resources:

- **Routing basics** – http://www.cisco.com/univercd/cc/td/doc/cisintwk/ito_doc/routing.htm
- **General information on routers** – http://www.cisco.com/univercd/cc/td/doc/pcat/#2
- **2500 series routers** – http://www.cisco.com/warp/public/cc/cisco/mkt/access/2500/index.shtml
- **1600 series routers** – http://www.cisco.com/warp/public/cc/cisco/mkt/access/1600/index.shtml
- **Terms and acronyms** – http://www.cisco.com/univercd/cc/td/doc/cisintwk/ita/index.htm
- **IP routing protocol IOS command summary** –
  http://www.cisco.com/univercd/cc/td/doc/product/software/ios120/12cgcr/rbkixol.htm

## Notes:

_____
_____
_____
_____
_____
_____
_____

# Cisco Labs – Semester 2 – Router Configuration
## *LAB 12.6.2.1 – RIP ROUTING – WORKSHEET*

**Step 1 – Log on to the router.**
   **Explanation:** Connect to the router and log in. Enter the password **cisco** if prompted.

**Step 2 – Test layer 3 connectivity.**
   **Task:** Enter **ping *xxx.xxx.xxx.xxx*.**
   **Explanation:** Ping all interfaces on your router and direct neighboring routers.

   1.  Did all interfaces respond with a successful ping? _____

**Step 3 – View the routing table.**
   **Task:** Enter **show IP route** at the router prompt.
   **Explanation:** The router will respond with its routing table.

   2.  Is there any routing protocol defined? _____

**Step 4 – Enter privileged mode.**
   **Task:**
       a.   Enter **enable** at the command prompt.
       b.   Enter the password **class**.
   **Explanation:** You use the **enable** command to enter privileged EXEC mode.

**Step 5 – Show information about the active configuration file.**
   **Task:** Enter **show running-config** at the router prompt.
   **Explanation:** The router will display information on the active configuration file.

   3.  Are there any static routes defined? _____

**Step 6 – Enter global configuration mode.**
   **Task:** Enter **configure terminal** at the router prompt.
   **Explanation:** To configure the router, you must enter global configuration mode. Notice how the router prompt has changed after this command

   4.  What does the router prompt look like? _____

**Step 7 – Enable RIP as your routing protocol.**
   **Task:** Enter the **router RIP** command at the router prompt.
   **Explanation:** This will enable RIP on the router.

   5.  What changed in the router prompt? _____

**Step 8 – Enable RIP routing on a particular IP network.**
   **Task:** Enter **network *xxx.xxx.xxx.xxx*** at the router prompt.
   **Explanation:** *xxx.xxx.xxx.xxx* is the network address you want to enable RIP on.

**Step 9 – Enable RIP routing on a particular IP network.**
   **Task:** Repeat Step 8 for all the networks directly connected to the router.

# Cisco Labs – Semester 2 – Router Configuration
## *LAB 12.6.2.1 – RIP ROUTING – WORKSHEET*

**Step 10 – Exit router configuration mode.**
   **Task:** Enter **exit** at the router prompt.
   **Explanation:** The router will exit router configuration mode, and you will be in global configuration mode.

**Step 11 – Exit the router's global configuration mode.**
   **Task:** Enter **exit** at the router prompt.
   **Explanation:** The router will exit global configuration mode.

**Step 12 – Show the running configuration.**
   **Task:** Enter **show running-config** at the router prompt.
   **Explanation:** The router will show the active configuration file.

6.  Is the router RIP protocol turned on and advertising the networks you defined? _____

**Step 13 – Copy the active configuration to the backup configuration.**
   **Task:** Enter **copy running-config startup-config** at the router prompt.
   **Explanation:** This command will permanently write the configuration change to memory.

7.  What does this command do? _____

_____

**Step 14 – View the IP protocols.**
   **Task:** Enter **show IP protocols** at the router prompt.
   **Explanation:** The router will display values about routing timers and network information associated with the entire router.

8.  When is the next update due? _____

**Step 15 – View the routing table.**
   **Task:** Enter **show IP route** at the router prompt.
   **Explanation:** The router will display its routing table.

9.  How many routes were discovered by RIP? _____

**Step 16 – Display the status and global parameters.**
   **Task:** Enter **show IP interface** at the router prompt.
   **Explanation:** The router displays the status and global parameters associated with an interface.

10. What information did you receive from this command? _____

_____

# Cisco Labs – Semester 2 – Router Configuration
## *LAB 12.6.2.1 – RIP ROUTING – WORKSHEET*

**Step 17 – Display RIP routing updates as they are sent and received.**
   **Task:** Enter **debug IP RIP** at the command prompt.
   **Explanation:** This command allows you to display RIP routing updates as they are sent and received.

   11. What important information did you receive from this command? _____

**Step 18 – Turn off debug for RIP.**
   **Task:** Enter **no debug IP RIP** at the router prompt.
   **Explanation:** This command will turn off the debugging for RIP.

**Step 19 – Exit the router.**

# Cisco Labs – Semester 2 – Router Configuration
## *LAB 12.6.2.1 – RIP ROUTING – ANSWERS*

1. Did all interfaces respond with a successful ping? **Yes**

2. Is there any routing protocol defined? **No, but you will get a response from directly connected networks.**

3. Are there any static routes defined? **No. There should not be.**

4. What does the router prompt look like? ***Router Name*(config)#**

5. What changed in the router prompt? ***Router Name*(config-router)#**

6. Is the router RIP protocol turned on and advertising the networks you defined? **Yes**

7. What does this command do? **This command will copy the running configuration and save it to the startup configuration so that the next time the reload command or router is turned off and back on, it will load the configuration that is running on the router now.**

8. When is the next update due? **24 seconds**

   **show IP protocol** (output generated by a Cisco 2514 router)

```
Lab-b# show ip protocol

Routing Protocol is "rip"
  Sending updates every 30 seconds, next due in 24 seconds
  Invalid after 180 seconds, hold down 180, flushed after 240
  Outgoing update filter list for all interfaces is not set
  Incoming update filter list for all interfaces is not set
  Redistributing: rip
  Default version control: send version 1, receive any version
   Interface    Send   Recv   Key-chain
   Ethernet0    1      1      2
   Serial0             1      1      2
   Serial1             1      1      2
  Routing for Networks:
   201.100.11.0
   199.6.13.0
   219.17.100.0
   205.7.5.0
  Routing Information Sources:
   Gateway      Distance      Last Update
   201.100.11.1       120          00:00:15
   199.6.13.2   120           00:00:17
  Distance: (default is 120)
```

9. How many routes were discovered by RIP? **Four (answers will vary)**

# Cisco Labs – Semester 2 – Router Configuration
## *LAB 12.6.2.1 – RIP ROUTING – ANSWERS*

**show IP protocol** (output generated by a Cisco 2514 router)

```
LAB-B#show ip route
Codes: C - connected, S - static, I - IGRP, R - RIP, M - mobile, B - BGP
    D - EIGRP, EX - EIGRP external, O - OSPF, IA - OSPF inter area
    E1 - OSPF external type 1, E2 - OSPF external type 2, E - EGP
    i - IS-IS, L1 - IS-IS level-1, L2 - IS-IS level-2, * - candidate default
    U - per-user static route

Gateway of last resort is not set

R    204.204.7.0/24 [120/1] via 199.6.13.2, 00:00:09, Serial0
R    223.8.151.0/24 [120/1] via 199.6.13.2, 00:00:09, Serial0
C    201.100.11.0/24 is directly connected, Serial1
C    219.17.100.0/24 is directly connected, Ethernet0
R    192.5.5.0/24 [120/1] via 201.100.11.1, 00:00:04, Serial1
C    199.6.13.0/24 is directly connected, Serial0
R    210.93.105.0/24 [120/2] via 199.6.13.2, 00:00:09, Serial0
```

10. What information did you receive from this command? **Status and global parameters associated with an interface**

**show IP interface** (output generated by a Cisco 2514 router)

```
show ip interface
Ethernet0 is up, line protocol is up
  Internet address is 219.17.100.1/24
  Broadcast address is 255.255.255.255
  Address determined by setup command
  MTU is 1500 bytes
  Helper address is not set
  Directed broadcast forwarding is enabled
  Multicast reserved groups joined: 224.0.0.9
  Outgoing access list is not set
  Inbound  access list is not set
  Proxy ARP is enabled
  Security level is default
  Split horizon is enabled
  ICMP redirects are always sent
  ICMP unreachables are always sent
  ICMP mask replies are never sent
  IP fast switching is enabled
  IP fast switching on the same interface is disabled
  IP multicast fast switching is enabled
  Router Discovery is disabled
  IP output packet accounting is disabled
  IP access violation accounting is disabled
  TCP/IP header compression is disabled
 Probe proxy name replies are disabled
```

**Cisco Labs – Semester 2 – Router Configuration**
## *LAB 12.6.2.1 – RIP ROUTING – ANSWERS*

**show IP interface – Continued** (output generated by a Cisco 2514 router)

Gateway Discovery is disabled
 Policy routing is disabled
Ethernet1 is up, line protocol is down
 Internet address is 205.7.5.1/24
 Broadcast address is 255.255.255.255
 Address determined by setup command
 MTU is 1500 bytes
 Helper address is not set
 Directed broadcast forwarding is enabled
 Multicast reserved groups joined: 224.0.0.9
 Outgoing access list is not set
 Inbound  access list is not set
 Proxy ARP is enabled
 Security level is default
 Split horizon is enabled
 ICMP redirects are always sent
 ICMP unreachables are always sent
 ICMP mask replies are never sent
 IP fast switching is enabled
 IP fast switching on the same interface is disabled
 IP multicast fast switching is enabled
 Router Discovery is disabled
 IP output packet accounting is disabled
 IP access violation accounting is disabled
 TCP/IP header compression is disabled
Probe proxy name replies are disabled
 Gateway Discovery is disabled
 Policy routing is disabled
Serial0 is up, line protocol is up
 Internet address is 199.6.13.1/24
 Broadcast address is 255.255.255.255
 Address determined by setup command
 MTU is 1500 bytes
 Helper address is not set
 Directed broadcast forwarding is enabled
 Multicast reserved groups joined: 224.0.0.9
 Outgoing access list is not set
 Inbound  access list is not set
 Proxy ARP is enabled
 Security level is default
 Split horizon is enabled
 ICMP redirects are always sent
 ICMP unreachables are always sent
 ICMP mask replies are never sent
 IP fast switching is enabled

**Cisco Labs – Semester 2 – Router Configuration**
## *LAB 12.6.2.1 – RIP ROUTING – ANSWERS*

**show IP interface – Continued** (output generated by a Cisco 2514 router)

```
 IP fast switching on the same interface is enabled
  IP multicast fast switching is enabled
  Router Discovery is disabled
  IP output packet accounting is disabled
  IP access violation accounting is disabled
  TCP/IP header compression is disabled
  Probe proxy name replies are disabled
  Gateway Discovery is disabled
  Policy routing is disabled
 Serial1 is up, line protocol is up
  Internet address is 201.100.11.2/24
  Broadcast address is 255.255.255.255
  Address determined by setup command
  MTU is 1500 bytes
  Helper address is not set
  Directed broadcast forwarding is enabled
  Multicast reserved groups joined: 224.0.0.9
  Outgoing access list is not set
  Inbound  access list is not set
  Proxy ARP is enabled
  Security level is default
  Split horizon is enabled
  ICMP redirects are always sent
  ICMP unreachables are always sent
  ICMP mask replies are never sent
  IP fast switching is enabled
  IP fast switching on the same interface is enabled
  IP multicast fast switching is enabled
  Router Discovery is disabled
  IP output packet accounting is disabled
  IP access violation accounting is disabled
  TCP/IP header compression is disabled
  Probe proxy name replies are disabled
  Gateway Discovery is disabled
  Policy routing is disabled
```

11. What important information did you receive from this command? **This command displays RIP updates as they are sent and received.**

# Cisco Labs – Semester 2 – Router Configuration
## *LAB 12.7.2.1 – RIP CONVERGENCE CHALLENGE – OVERVIEW*
### *(Estimated time: 60 minutes)*

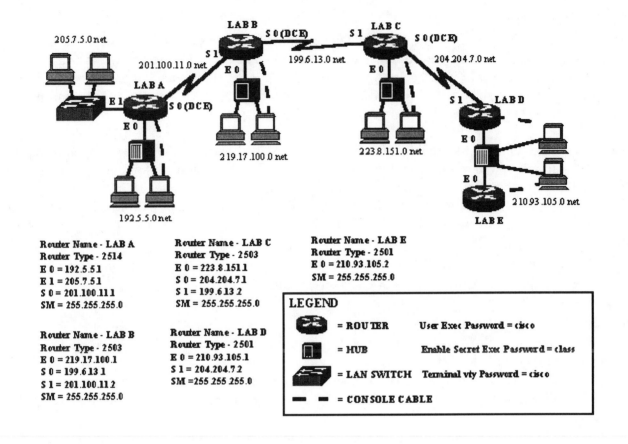

**Router Name - LAB A**
Router Type - 2514
E 0 = 192.5.5.1
E 1 = 205.7.5.1
S 0 = 201.100.11.1
SM = 255.255.255.0

**Router Name - LAB B**
Router Type - 2503
E 0 = 219.17.100.1
S 0 = 199.6.13.1
S 1 = 201.100.11.2
SM = 255.255.255.0

**Router Name - LAB C**
Router Type - 2503
E 0 = 223.8.151.1
S 0 = 204.204.7.1
S 1 = 199.6.13.2
SM = 255.255.255.0

**Router Name - LAB D**
Router Type - 2501
E 0 = 210.93.105.1
S 1 = 204.204.7.2
SM = 255.255.255.0

**Router Name - LAB E**
Router Type - 2501
E 0 = 210.93.105.2
SM = 255.255.255.0

**LEGEND**

= ROUTER   User Exec Password = cisco

= HUB   Enable Secret Exec Password = class

= LAN SWITCH   Terminal vty Password = cisco

= CONSOLE CABLE

## Objectives:
- Gain experience with and knowledge of routing protocols
- Work with and compare static routes and dynamic routes
- Understand the process of convergence

## Background:
As a system administrator, there will be times when configuring static routes can be very useful.
Static routes are useful for stub networks because there is only one way to get to that network.
Security is another reason to use static routes. If you have a network or networks that you don't want
the rest of the network to "see," you would not want RIP or other routing protocols sending periodic
updates to other routers. With simple networks (few routers), it is sometimes more efficient to use
static routes since this conserves bandwidth on WAN links. In this lab you will use static routes for
troubleshooting purposes and to see their relationship to dynamic routes and routing protocols.

# Cisco Labs – Semester 2 – Router Configuration
## *LAB 12.7.2.1 – RIP CONVERGENCE CHALLENGE – OVERVIEW*

## Tools / Preparation:
Prior to starting this lab you will need to have the equipment for the standard five-router lab available (routers, hubs, switch, cables, and so on). The routers should be preconfigured by the instructor or lab assistant with the correct IP interface settings, and so on. RIP should be enabled on all routers. The workstations should also be preconfigured to have the correct IP address settings prior to starting the lab. The routers, hubs, and workstations should be labeled.

This lab assumes that you have completed the prior lab 2.2.10.1 and that the lab equipment (routers, hub, workstations, and so on) is assembled and connected in the standard lab topology. Work in teams of three or more. Before beginning this lab, you should review Chapter 18 in the *Cisco Networking Academy Program: First-Year Companion Guide* and semester 2 on-line Chapter 12.

## Resources Required:
- 5 PC workstations (minimum) with Windows operating system and HyperTerminal installed
- 5 Cisco routers (model 1600 series or 2500 series with IOS 11.2 or later)
- 4 Ethernet hubs (10Base-T with 4 to 8 ports)
- 1 Ethernet switch (Cisco Catalyst 1900 or comparable)
- 5 serial console cables to connect the workstation to the router console port (with RJ45 to DB9 converters)
- 3 sets of V.35 WAN serial cables (DTE male/ DCE female) to connect from router to router
- CAT5 Ethernet cables wired straight through to connect routers and workstations to hubs and switches
- AUI (DB15) to RJ45 Ethernet transceivers (the quantity depends on the number of routers with AUI ports) to convert router AUI interfaces to 10Base-T RJ45

## Web Site Resources:
- **Routing basics** – http://www.cisco.com/univercd/cc/td/doc/cisintwk/ito_doc/routing.htm
- **General information on routers** – http://www.cisco.com/univercd/cc/td/doc/pcat/#2
- **2500 series routers** – http://www.cisco.com/warp/public/cc/cisco/mkt/access/2500/index.shtml
- **1600 series routers** – http://www.cisco.com/warp/public/cc/cisco/mkt/access/1600/index.shtml
- **Terms and acronyms** – http://www.cisco.com/univercd/cc/td/doc/cisintwk/ita/index.htm
- **IP routing protocol IOS command summary** –
  http://www.cisco.com/univercd/cc/td/doc/product/software/ios120/12cgcr/rbkixol.htm

## Notes: _____

_____

_____

_____

_____

_____

_____

# Cisco Labs – Semester 2 – Router Configuration
## *LAB 12.7.2.1 – RIP CONVERGENCE CHALLENGE – WORKSHEET*

### Step 1 – Show the IP route.
Verify that RIP is enabled and that there are no static routes on any of the routers. If there are static routes, remove them with the **no IP route xxx.xxx.xxx.xxx** command in global config mode.

### Step 2 – Enable debugging on Lab-D.
When you use the command **debug ip rip**, you will be able to see all routing updates the router is receiving and sending. Turn on debugging for Lab-D.

### Step 3 – Shut down the serial 1 interface on Lab-B.
Shut down the serial 1 interface on Lab-B with the **shutdown** command. Watch the debugging information on Lab-D, and issue the **show ip route** command there.

1.  Has the output from the command **show ip route** changed from when you issued the command in Step 1? _____

2.  What networks are inaccessible?
    _____

### Step 4 – Converged network.
After about 5 minutes, issue the **show ip route** command on Lab-D.

3.  Are the networks that were inaccessible in Question 2 listed in the output from the **show ip route** command? _____

### Step 5 – Enter static routes.
Bring Lab-B's serial 1 interface back up. Then enter static routes for all five routers, leaving RIP enabled. Issue the **show ip route** command. Your output from the **show ip route** command should look like the following (note that there are no R-RIP entries in the routing table):

```
Lab-D#show ip route
Codes: C - connected, S - static, I - IGRP, R - RIP, M - mobile, B - BGP
     D - EIGRP, EX - EIGRP external, O - OSPF, IA - OSPF inter area
     N1 - OSPF NSSA external type 1, N2 - OSPF NSSA external type 2
     E1 - OSPF external type 1, E2 - OSPF external type 2, E - EGP
     i - IS-IS, L1 - IS-IS level-1, L2 - IS-IS level-2, * - candidate default
     U - per-user static route, o - ODR

Gateway of last resort is not set
C    204.204.7.0/24 is directly connected, Serial1
S    223.8.151.0/24 [1/0] via 204.204.7.1
S    201.100.11.0/24 [1/0] via 204.204.7.1
S    219.17.100.0/24 [1/0] via 204.204.7.1
S    192.5.5.0/24 [1/0] via 204.204.7.1
S    199.6.13.0/24 [1/0] via 204.204.7.1
S    205.7.5.0/24 [1/0] via 204.204.7.1
C    210.93.105.0/24 is directly connected, Ethernet0
```

**Cisco Labs – Semester 2 – Router Configuration**
## *LAB 12.7.2.1 – RIP CONVERGENCE CHALLENGE – WORKSHEET*

**Step 6 – Shut down the serial 1 interface on Lab-B.**
After you shut down the serial 1 interface on Lab-B, watch the debugging information on Lab-D.

4.  Do you see any information that would let you know that Lab-B's serial 1 interface is down?
    _____

5.  Why or why not? _____
    _____
    _____

**Step 7 – Turn off debugging on Lab-D.**
Turn off debugging on Lab-D using the **undebug all** command.

6.  Now that you have a good understanding of what static routes are, what are the benefits of dynamic routes?
    _____
    _____
    _____
    _____
    _____

# Cisco Labs – Semester 2 – Router Configuration
## *LAB 12.7.2.1 – RIP CONVERGENCE CHALLENGE – ANSWERS*

1. Has the output from the command **show ip route** changed from when you issued the command in step 1? **Yes**

---

Lab-D#show ip route
Codes: C - connected, S - static, I - IGRP, R - RIP, M - mobile, B - BGP
    D - EIGRP, EX - EIGRP external, O - OSPF, IA - OSPF inter area
    N1 - OSPF NSSA external type 1, N2 - OSPF NSSA external type 2
    E1 - OSPF external type 1, E2 - OSPF external type 2, E - EGP
    i - IS-IS, L1 - IS-IS level-1, L2 - IS-IS level-2, * - candidate default
    U - per-user static route, o - ODR

Gateway of last resort is not set

C    204.204.7.0/24 is directly connected, Serial1
R    223.8.151.0/24 [120/1] via 204.204.7.1, 00:00:13, Serial1
R    201.100.11.0/24 is possibly down, routing via 204.204.7.1, Serial1
R    219.17.100.0/24 [120/2] via 204.204.7.1, 00:00:13, Serial1
R    192.5.5.0/24 is possibly down, routing via 204.204.7.1, Serial1
R    199.6.13.0/24 [120/1] via 204.204.7.1, 00:00:13, Serial1
R    205.7.5.0/24 is possibly down, routing via 204.204.7.1, Serial1

---

2. What networks are inaccessible? **201.100.11.0, 192.5.5.0, and 205.7.5.0**

3. Are the networks that were inaccessible in Question 2 listed in the output from the **show ip route** command? **No. They have been dropped from the routing table.**

---

Lab-D#sho ip route
Codes: C - connected, S - static, I - IGRP, R - RIP, M - mobile, B - BGP
    D - EIGRP, EX - EIGRP external, O - OSPF, IA - OSPF inter area
    N1 - OSPF NSSA external type 1, N2 - OSPF NSSA external type 2
    E1 - OSPF external type 1, E2 - OSPF external type 2, E - EGP
    i - IS-IS, L1 - IS-IS level-1, L2 - IS-IS level-2, * - candidate default
    U - per-user static route, o - ODR

Gateway of last resort is not set

C    204.204.7.0/24 is directly connected, Serial1
R    223.8.151.0/24 [120/1] via 204.204.7.1, 00:00:19, Serial1
R    219.17.100.0/24 [120/2] via 204.204.7.1, 00:00:19, Serial1
R    199.6.13.0/24 [120/1] via 204.204.7.1, 00:00:19, Serial1
C    210.93.105.0/24 is directly connected, Ethernet0

---

# Cisco Labs – Semester 2 – Router Configuration
## _LAB 12.7.2.1 – RIP CONVERGENCE CHALLENGE – ANSWERS_

4. Do you see any information that would let you know that Lab-B's serial 1 interface is down? **No**

5. Why or why not? **Static routes cannot be updated dynamically. Even with RIP running, it does not change the routing information of a static route, because static routes have a higher priority over a routing protocol that is dynamic.**

6. Now that you have a good understanding of what static routes are, what are the benefits of dynamic routes? **The biggest advantage of dynamic routing is its ability to select an alternate route or path when the route it was using becomes unavailable. This is known as adjustment to network topology changes.**

Points to keep in mind:

1. Manageability of dynamic routing
2. Amount of information in routing updates as opposed to static routes
3. Unmanageability of static routes
4. Lower administrative distance. Trustworthy.

In the first scenario, you created a network that was running a dynamic routing protocol, RIP. You caused a change in the network, and you watched how long it took your network to realize that change and converge. In the second scenario, you created a network that was running both a routing protocol and static routes concurrently. Again, you caused a change in the network, and you watched how long it took your network to realize the change and converge. In the first scenario, some troubleshooting commands that you issued on one of the routers to see what was happening were **show ip route** and **debug ip rip**. You saw in the routing updates and in the routing table that a route was down. Since you were running RIP, it took a while for it to finally converge. In other words, it took RIP a while to make the route invalid, put it in holddown, and then flush it out. But RIP did all that on its own. You did not have to go into each of the routers to reconfigure them so that the network change could be realized and all the routers could converge. All the routers running RIP basically converged on their own. On the other hand, in the second scenario, after you caused a change in the network and got into one of the routers to issue troubleshooting commands, you found information that was of no use to you. In the updates, you did not find any inaccessible routes. In the routing table, there were no indications of routes that were down. You did not find any information leading to a change in the network. Also with the second scenario, you had to configure each of the routers with static routes so that they could recognize the network. You basically configured the whole network on each router. In the end, after a network change occurred, you got useless information while debugging.

**Cisco Labs – Semester 2 – Router Configuration**
## *LAB 12.7.2.1 – RIP CONVERGENCE CHALLENGE – ANSWERS*

This brings up four very important points:

1. Dynamic routing is easier and more efficient to configure on a router.

2. With dynamic routing, you do not have to monitor the network incessantly to figure out if network changes occurred. If they did occur, dynamic routing will realize the change and properly converge.

3. With dynamic routing, when you issue a debug on the protocol, you find useful information on what's going on in the network. With static routes, you configure the whole network on each router, and when it comes time to run a debug, you don't receive information that you need.

4. Static routes have a lower administrative distance. The reason is because it assumes that since the administrator himself/herself configured those routes, they should be flawless and given a higher priority over a routing protocol that is dynamic. Even though static routes have a lower administrative distance, they are more of a hassle to maintain, and during a debug, they do not provide necessary information.

# Cisco CCNA Labs – Semester 2 – Router Configuration
## *LAB 12.8.2.1 – ROUTING LOOPS SETUP CHALLENGE – OVERVIEW*
### *(Estimated time: 30 minutes)*

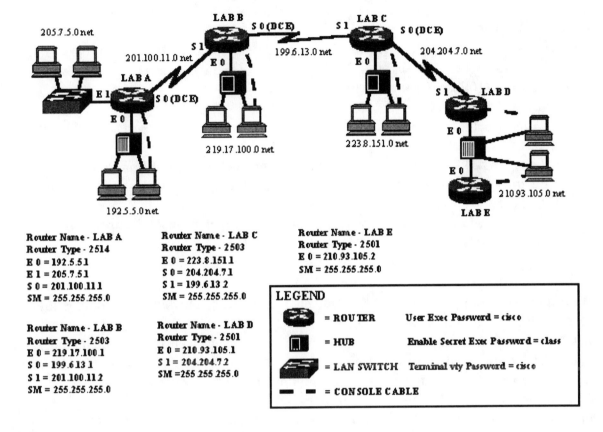

Router Name - LAB A
Router Type - 2514
E 0 = 192.5.5.1
E 1 = 205.7.5.1
S 0 = 201.100.11.1
SM = 255.255.255.0

Router Name - LAB C
Router Type - 2503
E 0 = 223.8.151.1
S 0 = 204.204.7.1
S 1 = 199.6.13.2
SM = 255.255.255.0

Router Name - LAB E
Router Type - 2501
E 0 = 210.93.105.2
SM = 255.255.255.0

Router Name - LAB B
Router Type - 2503
E 0 = 219.17.100.1
S 0 = 199.6.13.1
S 1 = 201.100.11.2
SM = 255.255.255.0

Router Name - LAB D
Router Type - 2501
E 0 = 210.93.105.1
S 1 = 204.204.7.2
SM = 255.255.255.0

**LEGEND**

= ROUTER    User Exec Password = cisco

= HUB    Enable Secret Exec Password = class

= LAN SWITCH    Terminal vty Password = cisco

= CONSOLE CABLE

## Objectives:
- Configure a WAN connection between Lab-A and Lab-E
- Demonstrate your ability to configure serial interfaces

## Background:
In this lab you will set up a WAN connection between Lab-A and Lab-E to create alternate paths in the standard router lab setup. Using a set of WAN serial cables, connect Lab-A Serial 1 to Lab-E Serial 0. Remember to set the clock rate on the DCE side of the cable (Lab-E's Serial 0 interface).

## Tools / Preparation:
Prior to starting this lab you will need to have the equipment for the standard five-router lab available (routers, hubs, switch, cables, and so on). The routers should be preconfigured by the instructor or lab assistant with the correct IP interface settings, and so on. The workstations should also be preconfigured to have the correct IP address settings prior to starting the lab. The routers, hubs, and workstations should be labeled.

This lab assumes that you have completed the prior lab 2.2.10.1 and that the lab equipment (routers, hub, workstations, and so on) is assembled and connected in the standard lab topology. Work in teams of three or more. Before beginning this lab, you should review Chapter 11 in the *Cisco Networking Academy Program: First-Year Companion Guide* and semester 2 on-line Chapter 12.

## Cisco Labs – Semester 2 – Router Configuration
# *LAB 12.8.2.1 – ROUTING LOOPS SETUP CHALLENGE – OVERVIEW*

## Resources Required:

- 5 PC workstations (minimum) with Windows operating system and HyperTerminal installed
- 5 Cisco routers (model 1600 series or 2500 series with IOS 11.2 or later)
- 4 Ethernet hubs (10Base-T with 4 to 8 ports)
- 1 Ethernet switch (Cisco Catalyst 1900 or comparable)
- 5 serial console cables to connect the workstation to the router console port (with RJ45 to DB9 converters)
- 4 sets of V.35 WAN serial cables (DTE male/ DCE female) to connect from router to router
- CAT5 Ethernet cables wired straight through to connect routers and workstations to hubs and switches
- AUI (DB15) to RJ45 Ethernet transceivers (the quantity depends on the number of routers with AUI ports) to convert router AUI interfaces to 10Base-T RJ45

## Web Site Resources:

- **Routing basics** – http://www.cisco.com/univercd/cc/td/doc/cisintwk/ito_doc/routing.htm
- **General information on routers** – http://www.cisco.com/univercd/cc/td/doc/pcat/#2
- **2500 series routers** – http://www.cisco.com/warp/public/cc/cisco/mkt/access/2500/index.shtml
- **1600 series routers** – http://www.cisco.com/warp/public/cc/cisco/mkt/access/1600/index.shtml
- **Terms and acronyms** – http://www.cisco.com/univercd/cc/td/doc/cisintwk/ita/index.htm
- **IP routing protocol IOS command summary** – http://www.cisco.com/univercd/cc/td/doc/product/software/ios120/12cgcr/rbkixol.htm

## Notes: _____

_____

_____

_____

_____

_____

_____

## Cisco Labs – Semester 2 – Router Configuration
# *LAB 12.8.2.1 – ROUTING LOOPS SETUP CHALLENGE – WORKSHEET*

**Step 1 – Verify that all physical connections are correct.**
Review the standard Semester 2 lab diagram in the overview section of this lab. You will add a fourth set of V.35 WAN serial cables (DTE male/ DCE female) to connect from router Lab-A interface S1 to router Lab-E interface S0.

**Step 2 – Configure Lab-A Serial 1 interface.**
Log on to the router and enter interface configuration mode. Configure interface Serial 1 with the following information (this is a new class C IP address):

- IP address 220.68.33.2
- Subnet mask 255.255.255.0
- Bandwidth of 56

**Step 3 – Configure IP host and RIP networks.**
After you have finished the configuration for the interface, you will need to add the 220.68.33.0 network with the **network** command to all five routers. Also add the new IP address to the host table entry for routers Lab-A and Lab-E for name resolution to all routers.

**Step 4 – Configure Lab-E Serial 0 interface.**
Repeat Steps 2 and 3 for Lab-E interface Serial 0 with the following information:

- IP address 220.68.33.1
- Subnet mask 255.255.255.0
- Clock rate 56000
- Bandwidth of 56

**Step 5 – Test your setup.**
When you have configured Lab-A's and Lab-E's interfaces, check off the items in this list:

- Ping from all routers to 220.68.22.1
- Ping from all routers to 220.68.22.2
- Ping from all workstations to 220.68.22.1
- Ping from all workstations to 220.68.22.2
- Telnet from Lab-C to 220.68.22.1
- Telnet from Lab-C to 220.68.22.2
- Telnet from a workstation to 220.68.22.1
- Telnet from a workstation to 220.68.22.2

**Step 6 – Troubleshooting**
If you were not able to finish Step 5, use your troubleshooting skills learned in previous labs to correct the problem. After you have successfully finished Step 5, save the running configuration to the startup configuration for all routers. You will be using this new configuration for lab 12.9.2.1.

# Cisco Labs – Semester 2 – Router Configuration
## *LAB 12.9.2.1 – PREVENTING ROUTING LOOPS CHALLENGE – OVERVIEW*
### *(Estimated time: 45 minutes)*

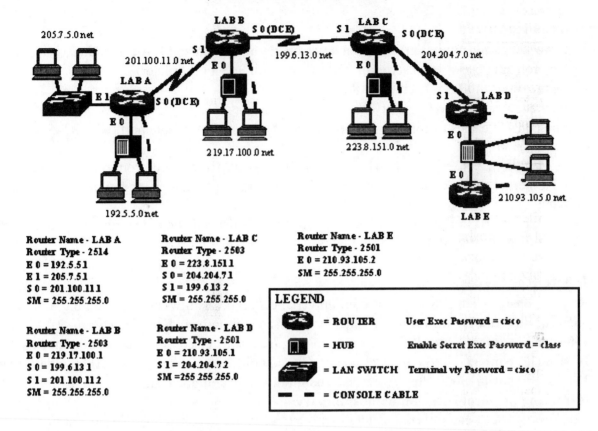

Router Name - LAB A
Router Type - 2514
E 0 = 192.5.5.1
E 1 = 205.7.5.1
S 0 = 201.100.11.1
SM = 255.255.255.0

Router Name - LAB C
Router Type - 2503
E 0 = 223.8.151.1
S 0 = 204.204.7.1
S 1 = 199.6.13.2
SM = 255.255.255.0

Router Name - LAB E
Router Type - 2501
E 0 = 210.93.105.2
SM = 255.255.255.0

Router Name - LAB B
Router Type - 2503
E 0 = 219.17.100.1
S 0 = 199.6.13.1
S 1 = 201.100.11.2
SM = 255.255.255.0

Router Name - LAB D
Router Type - 2501
E 0 = 210.93.105.1
S 1 = 204.204.7.2
SM = 255.255.255.0

**LEGEND**

= ROUTER     User Exec Password = cisco

= HUB     Enable Secret Exec Password = class

= LAN SWITCH     Terminal vty Password = cisco

= CONSOLE CABLE

## Objectives:
- Understand methods of controlling routing loops, including holddown timers, defining a maximum hop count, counting to infinity, poison reverse, and split-horizon
- Adjust the RIP maximum hop count to control routing loops

## Background:
In the previous challenge lab, you saw how long it took to converge when a link went down. In this lab, your task is to find out how to prevent and control routing loops. The use of holddown timers, defining a maximum hop count, counting to infinity, poison reverse, and split-horizon are all methods of controlling routing loops. You will use the RIP hop count metric to control routing loops in this lab. You should have finished lab 12.8.2.1 and have the fourth set of WAN cables connected from Lab-A Serial 1 to Lab-E Serial 0. To learn more about timers, look at the answers section under "Understanding Timers."

## Tools / Preparation:
Prior to starting this lab you will need to have the equipment for the standard five-router lab available. The routers and workstations should be preconfigured by the instructor or lab assistant with the correct IP settings prior to starting the lab. Before beginning this lab, you should review Chapter 11 in the *Cisco Networking Academy Program: First-Year Companion Guide* and semester 2 on-line Chapter 12.

# LAB 12.9.2.1 – PREVENTING ROUTING LOOPS CHALLENGE – OVERVIEW

## Resources Required:

- 5 PC workstations (minimum) with Windows operating system and HyperTerminal installed
- 5 Cisco routers (model 1600 series or 2500 series with IOS 11.2 or later)
- 4 Ethernet hubs (10Base-T with 4 to 8 ports)
- 1 Ethernet switch (Cisco Catalyst 1900 or comparable)
- 5 serial console cables to connect the workstation to the router console port (with RJ45 to DB9 converters)
- 4 sets of V.35 WAN serial cables (DTE male/ DCE female) to connect from router to router
- CAT5 Ethernet cables wired straight through to connect routers and workstations to hubs and switches
- AUI (DB15) to RJ45 Ethernet transceivers (the quantity depends on the number of routers with AUI ports) to convert router AUI interfaces to 10Base-T RJ45

## Web Site Resources:

- **Routing basics** – http://www.cisco.com/univercd/cc/td/doc/cisintwk/ito_doc/routing.htm
- **General information on routers** – http://www.cisco.com/univercd/cc/td/doc/pcat/#2
- **2500 series routers** – http://www.cisco.com/warp/public/cc/cisco/mkt/access/2500/index.shtml
- **1600 series routers** – http://www.cisco.com/warp/public/cc/cisco/mkt/access/1600/index.shtml
- **Terms and acronyms** – http://www.cisco.com/univercd/cc/td/doc/cisintwk/ita/index.htm
- **IP routing protocol IOS command summary** –
  http://www.cisco.com/univercd/cc/td/doc/product/software/ios120/12cgcr/rbkixol.htm

## Notes: _____

_____

_____

_____

_____

_____

_____

# Cisco Labs – Semester 2 – Router Configuration
## *LAB 12.9.2.1 – PREVENTING ROUTING LOOPS CHALLENGE – WORKSHEET*

**Step 1 – Turn on debugging.**
Working with router Lab-C, turn on debugging with the **debug ip rip** command.

**Step 2 – Shut down Lab-A's Ethernet 0 interface.**
Shut down Lab-A's Ethernet 0 interface. From Lab-C, watch the routing information, and use the **show ip route** command to see how many routing updates it takes to flush out Lab-A's Ethernet 0 network.

1. How many updates did it take to converge? _____

**Step 3 – Enable Lab-A's Ethernet 0 interface.**
On Lab-A, bring Ethernet 0 back up, and allow enough time for the network to converge.

**Step 4 – Configure default metric timers basic and split-horizon on Lab-C.**
There are other timers that can be modified to help avoid routing loops. This lab focuses on hop count. Change the RIP maximum hop count on router Lab-C to 10 (the default is 16) and adjust the routing timers and split horizon using the following commands:

```
Lab-C#conf t
Lab-C(config)#router rip
Lab-C(config-router)#default-metric  10
Lab-C(config-router)#timers  basic  30  60  150  30
Lab-C(config-router)#exit
Lab-C(config)#int s0
Lab-C(config-if)#ip split-horizon
Lab-C(config-if)#int s1
Lab-C(config-if)#ip split-horizon
Lab-C(config-if)#^Z
Lab-C#
```

**Step 5 – Shut down Lab-A's Ethernet 0 interface.**
Shut down Lab-A's Ethernet 0 interface. From Lab-C, watch the routing information, and use the **show ip route** command to see how many routing updates it takes to flush out Lab-A's Ethernet 0 network.

2. How many updates did it take to converge? _____

3. Compare Questions 1 and 2 and explain why the network converged faster after you changed the default metric timers and split horizon.

**Cisco Labs – Semester 2 – Router Configuration**
## *LAB 12.9.2.1 – PREVENTING ROUTING LOOPS CHALLENGE – ANSWERS*

1. How many updates did it take to converge? **About 12 updates**

2. How many updates did it take to converge? **Less than 5 updates**

3. Compare Questions 1 and 2 and explain why the network converged faster after you changed the default metric. **The maximum hop count is set to 10, so the router does not have to wait for the hop count to reach 16 before it considers the network unreachable. The timers were set to less than normal. Split horizon was enabled so that convergence would occur more quickly.**

**Output from show ip protocol command shows default settings for RIP routing protocol timers.**

```
LAB-C#sho ip proto
Routing Protocol is "rip"
  Sending updates every 30 seconds, next due in 9 seconds
  Invalid after 180 seconds, hold down 180, flushed after 240
  Outgoing update filter list for all interfaces is not set
  Incoming update filter list for all interfaces is not set
  Redistributing: rip
  Default version control: send version 1, receive any version
  Routing for Networks:
   223.8.151.0
   204.204.7.0
   199.6.13.0
  Routing Information Sources:
   Gateway      Distance     Last Update
  Distance: (default is 120)
```

**Understanding Timers**

**Update:** The time between routing updates sent by a router.

**Invalid:** The term *invalid* is used for routes that have not been heard from for the period of time that the invalid timer is set for. This means, for example, that if the invalid timer is set to 60, and an advertisement for a route from the router it was learned from has not been received for 61 seconds, the invalid timer expires, and the route is considered invalid.

**Holddown:** The term *holddown* refers to routes that have been marked invalid but are not yet capable of being replaced with a new route of a higher metric. This timer determines how long the route is kept under holddown. While in holddown state, the router will keep sending updates about the route and will keep forwarding packets via that route until the holddown expires.

**Cisco Labs – Semester 2 – Router Configuration**
## *LAB 12.9.2.1 – PREVENTING ROUTING LOOPS CHALLENGE – ANSWERS*

**Flush:**
The flush timer restarts every time an update is received for a route from the router that it is learned from. The flush and invalid timers restart at the same time and run concurrently. When the flush timer expires for a route, the route is removed from the routing table. For RIP, the flush timer expires before the holddown timer can expire.

### Routing Loop Prevention Techniques

**Split Horizon:**
Split horizon disables the router from sending information about a route in the routing table through the same interface that it learned about the route from. For example, if Lab-B sends information about Lab-E to Lab-A via its Ethernet 0, Lab-A will not send information about Lab-E via Ethernet 0 back to Lab-B.

**Poison Reverse:**
This is when a router informs its neighbors that routes that they were once capable of reaching via a particular interface are no longer available because the interface has gone down. Routers react to a poison reverse message by immediately placing the poisoned routes into holddown instead of waiting for the invalid timer to expire. This saves convergence time, as much as 180 seconds (default invalid timer), depending on how soon after a regular update a poison reverse update arrives.

**Defining Default Metrics:**
Default metrics are set to disable counting to infinity. Counting to infinity causes routing loops by incrementing a route that it cannot reach but believes its neighbor can. So every time a route that is not reachable by one router is sent to its neighbors, routers that have not converged yet, that route's metric increases by one. That keeps happening over and over again until the routers finally converge. Default metric sets a metric count, where a route is allowed to propagate the network a certain number of times before it is removed from the routing table.

# Cisco Labs – Semester 2 – Router Configuration
## *LAB 13.1.6.1 – TROUBLESHOOTING 5-ROUTER NETWORK – OVERVIEW*
### *(Estimated time: 30 minutes)*

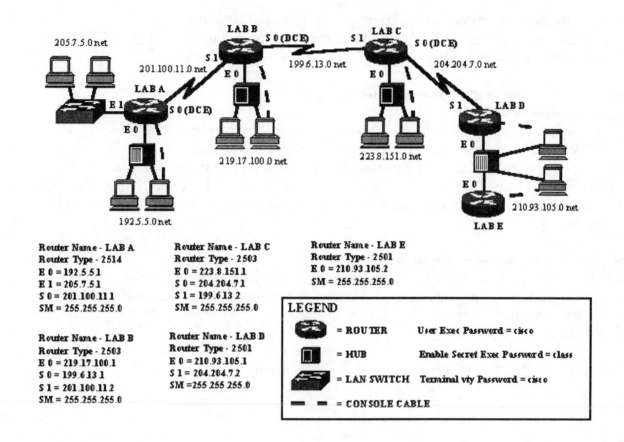

Router Name - LAB A
Router Type - 2514
E 0 = 192.5.5.1
E 1 = 205.7.5.1
S 0 = 201.100.11.1
SM = 255.255.255.0

Router Name - LAB C
Router Type - 2503
E 0 = 223.8.151.1
S 0 = 204.204.7.1
S 1 = 199.6.13.2
SM = 255.255.255.0

Router Name - LAB E
Router Type - 2501
E 0 = 210.93.105.2
SM = 255.255.255.0

Router Name - LAB B
Router Type - 2503
E 0 = 219.17.100.1
S 0 = 199.6.13.1
S 1 = 201.100.11.2
SM = 255.255.255.0

Router Name - LAB D
Router Type - 2501
E 0 = 210.93.105.1
S 1 = 204.204.7.2
SM = 255.255.255.0

**LEGEND**

= ROUTER    User Exec Password = cisco

= HUB       Enable Secret Exec Password = class

= LAN SWITCH   Terminal vty Password = cisco

= CONSOLE CABLE

## Objectives:
- Troubleshoot problems in the five-router lab network
- Document the problems found and the corrective action taken
- Prepare for Part B of the Final Exam (Router Lab Troubleshooting)

## Background:

For this lab, your instructor or lab assistant will create/introduce multiple problems in the network. You have a limited amount of time in which to find and solve the problems so that you can get your entire network up and running. The tools that you may use for the hardware are in your tool kit. The tools that you may use for the software (IOS) include **ping**, **trace ip route**, **telnet**, and **show arp**. You may use your Engineering Journal and any web-based resources (including the curriculum) that are available. As you discover the problems, you will document them along with what you did to correct them.

## Tools / Preparation:

Prior to starting this lab you should have the equipment for the standard five-router lab available. All routers and workstations should be properly configured. You will be asked to leave the room, and your instructor or lab assistant will induce from three to five problems into the lab setup.

# Cisco Labs – Semester 2 – Router Configuration
# *LAB 13.1.6.1 – TROUBLESHOOTING 5-ROUTER NETWORK – WORKSHEET*

**Step 1 – Review the physical connections on the standard lab setup.**
Review the standard Semester 2 lab diagram in the overview section of this lab, and check all physical devices, cables, and connections if the physical lab setup is available.

**Step 2 – Troubleshooting introduced network problems**
**Basic problem descriptions:**
   a.   We cannot ping a host on Lab-E's network from a host on Lab-A's network.
   b.   We cannot telnet from one router to another router's host name.
The instructor will introduce multiple problems (three to five) into the network (see the answers section) that can cause these high-level symptoms. Your team will have a fixed time period (20 to 30 minutes) to correct the problems. You may use your journals and toolkits to troubleshoot the problems.

**Step 3 – Document the problems discovered.**
Write down the problems as you encounter them, and then indicate what you did to correct them. When you are able to ping from a Lab-A workstation to a Lab-E workstation and telnet from one router to another router's host name, have the instructor or lab assistant verify that you have corrected all problems.

| Problem # | Problem Discovered | Solution | Instructor Verification |
|---|---|---|---|
| 1 | | | |
| 2 | | | |
| 3 | | | |
| 4 | | | |
| 5 | | | |

**Cisco Labs – Semester 2 – Router Configuration**
# _LAB 13.1.6.1 – TROUBLESHOOTING 5-ROUTER NETWORK –_
# _ANSWERS_

## Possible Introduced Network Problems

| # | Category | Symptom | Possible Problems | Solution |
|---|----------|---------|-------------------|----------|
| 1 | Router | Can't get from user to exec mode | Unknown enable password | Perform password recovery procedure |
| 2 | Router | Ping consistently fails on one interface | Wrong IP address or mask entered on one end of the ping | While in interface mode, properly configure IP address |
| 3 | Router | Ping test consistently fails on one interface | Interface is shut down | Use no shutdown on that interface |
| 4 | Router | Can't ping across a serial line | Clock rate not set on DCE end | Set clock rate on DCE end |
| 5 | Router | Can't ping across serial line | Clock rate is set on both DCE and DTE ends | Clock rate should only be set on DCE end |
| 6 | Router | Typing router's name doesn't substitute for its IP address; connection timed out | Bad DNS entry | Use IP host command to fix IP address |
| 7 | Router | Router won't boot into user mode | Config register has been changed | Change config register to 0x2102 |
| 8 | Router | Router has blank configuration file even when you show start | No configuration in NVRAM | Either in setup mode or line by line, create a router config |
| 9 | Router | Wrong or empty routing table | Wrong routing protocol enabled | Change routing protocol with router rip command |
| 10 | Router | Wrong or empty routing table | Wrong or missing networks when routing protocol was enabled | Issue a proper router rip and network command |
| 11 | Router | Router won't even begin boot process | Router power unplugged, or power supply has a problem | Plug in the router |
| 12 | Router | Router is running a limited IOS | No IOS image in Flash or on TFTP server | Find a source for the IOS image and copy into Flash |
| 13 | Router | Can telnet to a router but can't get past its password | You have an incorrect vty password | Go to the router in question and look up the vty password in its configuration file |
| 14 | Workstation | Can't console into router | Wrong settings on terminal emulation program | Enter correct settings for terminal emulation program |

# Cisco Labs – Semester 2 – Router Configuration
## *LAB 13.1.6.1 – TROUBLESHOOTING 5-ROUTER NETWORK – ANSWERS*

## Possible Introduced Network Problems – Continued

| 15 | Workstations | Workstation cannot link to routers, but routers and workstations seem properly configured | No power to hubs, or cable may be plugged into hub's uplink port | Supply power to the hubs or move cable |
|---|---|---|---|---|
| 16 | Workstation | Can't ping or telnet to the desired workstation | Incorrect TCP/IP settings on one of the workstations | Correct the TCP/IP settings on the workstation with the problem |
| 17 | Transceiver | No link light on Ethernet AUI connections | Transceiver is improperly seated in the sliding latch connector, or wrong cable type | Properly seat the transceiver or replace the cable with a straight-through |
| 18 | Cabling | Can't ping even though everything else seems OK | Cable unplugged, broken, or discontinuous somewhere | Isolate the bad cable and replace it |
| 19 | Cabling | Can't ping even though everything seems OK with the devices | Wrong cable used somewhere. This lab setup requires straight-through, cross-connect, and roll-over cables, and they are sometimes confused with each other | Make sure the right cable is used for every connection |
| 20 | ? | ? | Add your own errors! | |

# Notes

# Notes

# Notes

**Notes**

# Notes

# Notes